Network Security

How to Plan for It
and Achieve It

Richard H. Baker

McGraw-Hill, Inc.

New York   San Francisco   Washington, D.C.   Auckland   Bogotá
Caracas   Lisbon   London   Madrid   Mexico City   Milan
Montreal   New Delhi   San Juan   Singapore
Sydney   Tokyo   Toronto

Library of Congress Cataloging-in-Publication Data

Baker, Richard H.
    Network security : how to plan for it and achieve it / Richard H.
    Baker.
        p.   cm.
    Includes index.
    ISBN 0-07-005119-4 — ISBN 0-07-005141-0 (pbk.)
    1. Computer networks—Security measures. I. Title.
TK5105.5.B337   1995
658.4′78—dc20   94–20430
                                                             CIP

1 2 3 4 5 6 7 8 9 0   DOH/DOH   9 0 9 8 7 6 5 4

ISBN 0-07-005119-4 (h)
ISBN 0-07-005141-0 (p)

*The sponsoring editor for this book was Jerry Papke, the editing supervisor was
Joseph Bertuna, and the production supervisor was Donald F. Schmidt. It was set in
Century Schoolbook by McGraw-Hill's Professional Book Group composition unit.*

Printed and bound by R. R. Donnelley & Sons Company.

*Some of the artwork in this book is from Lotus SmartPix for Windows.
© 1991 Lotus Development Corporation.
Lotus and SmartPics are registered trademarks of Lotus Development Corporation.*

Contents

Illustrations
and Tables

Preface

Not many years ago, most computers were carefully guarded mainframes, held tightly in the hands of skilled professionals. The systems and their guardians combined to provide ironclad protection of the organization's all-important data. It was nothing like today's personal computers that anyone can get their hands on and even link into (gasp) networks!

Hindsight is not always 20-20, particularly when filtered through wishful thinking. The mainframes of yore were not the impregnable forces that the legends seem to suggest. Long before the first PC found its way into a high-rise office building, some people were complaining that computer owners were paying too little attention to security. Computerized data, particularly that in the private sector, was wide open to invasion and abuse. In those days, though, most of the interest in computer security came from two sources: those who complained about its lack and those who actively pursued sound security techniques. Most of the latter were found in the federal government. In fact, a predecessor to this book, written in 1985, relied almost entirely on government sources.

You can hear the same kinds of complaint today: Computer security is inadequate. It is still a valid complaint. The threats have changed, but the problem remains. For many users, security is on one of those lists that says, "Next week we've got to start doing something about this."

As a time standard, "next week" is even less certain than "tomorrow." Yet it could be too late. Since the warnings about computer security first were sounded, two important things have happened:

- The threats have become more serious. Once, the greatest dangers were from computerized book juggling and the occasional outside prankster. Today, both insider and outsider have grown more sophisticated. One of the greatest threats today comes from the professional thief who can use your computer to invade your telephone system. The invader then can use your phone to reach out and touch friends and family all over the world.

- Computer systems have become less secure. More to the point, the people who run computer systems are less security conscious. To be sure, networks are generally much more vulnerable than traditional central systems, particularly when you link multiple networks to span an entire enterprise. The real problem, though—and the real solution—lies in the people who run them.

All computer systems, specifically including PC network operating systems, have the means to secure themselves. If you are responsible for a system or network, you must learn what these tools are and how to use them. Then, you must take the firm steps of putting these tools to use.

This book will help you with the first part—learning how. It might also help a little with the second part—putting the knowledge to work. Though computer systems have changed greatly, the basic principles of computer security have not. In fact, much of the old government material is still valid, and you'll find it repeated throughout this book.

What's new is applying these established principles to the modern world of networking. In this book, you'll find the basic material sandwiched with specific advice on how to apply it to local area and even enterprisewide networks.

With only a few exceptions, you should also find that basic computer security is not a technologically demanding process. The real challenges are human, not technical. Old-timers will recognize a once-popular saying that the most important part of an automobile is the nut that holds the steering wheel. That's still true, even though a modern steering wheel may also contain an air bag and any number of controls and antitheft devices.

The same is true of computer technology. The technology has changed greatly, but the human component has not. If you can control your counterpart to the nut that holds the wheel, you have achieved fundamental control of your entire computing vehicle.

Richard H. Baker

1

How Can You Lock an Open Door?

Today's security challenge is to share information with the right people without also sharing it with the wrong people.

Not long ago, visitors called on the manager of a Connecticut shopping mall, introducing themselves as representatives of a New Jersey bank. They gained the manager's agreement to install an automated teller machine (ATM) near the entrance to a major department store.

The ATM dispensed some cash now and then, but it never really seemed to work right. Most who used it received receipts saying the machine could not process their transactions. Before long, someone came to take it away.

The machine had worked all too well. It was a fake ATM that had read the account numbers and access codes of every customer who tried to use it. Armed with this information, the "New Jersey bankers" went to work at ATMs in New York City, making systematic withdrawals from the Connecticut customers' bank accounts.

The scheme was audacious, but it wasn't particularly difficult. It took no great leap in technology to program the fake ATM so it would record key information about its users. By spectacular but simple means, the criminals managed to overcome even the best-laid plans of the banking industry's security experts.

A New Era for Computer Users

Few computer networks are as well secured as those that carry ATM transactions. The builders of the fake ATM were easily able to penetrate this system. What hope is there for the typical corporate network?

You can't protect everything.

- Networks are spreading too far.
- The moat-building approach no longer protects them.

Figure 1.1 Levees don't help much either.

At the outset, there's a simple answer: not much. Networking developments have far outstripped conventional security techniques based on mainframe practices. These depended largely on a moat-and-castle approach, building physical and electronic fortifications around a single, centrally located system (Fig. 1.1). If you were to try to adapt the same approach to today's and tomorrow's networks, it would be as futile as trying to build a moat around the entire world. Maybe the universe.

For better or worse, and it generally is for the better, PCs and their networks are taking over jobs once done by isolated big iron. It's easy to compare the explosive growth of networks with the Big Bang that's supposed to have started the universe. Local area networks of PCs are being linked into enterprisewide networks of networks. Practices like electronic data interchange (EDI) link customers and suppliers in single networks that treat multiple enterprises like one.

Facing frustrations

What's more, managers who are responsible for securing the new networks come up against a host of frustrations and contradictions. Among them:

- More people need more information.
- Hackers and virus carriers are becoming more sophisticated.
- Law enforcement needs to learn a lot more about computer technology.

The sonic boom of network expansion is a response to a real management need: to share more information among more people. Security forces must protect critical information while it is being ever more widely shared (Fig. 1.2).

Highly publicized threats like hackers and viruses are real. It is popular—and correct—to say they have been overemphasized. They divert attention

Challenges and conflicts

- Employees' information needs
- More sophisticated computer criminals
- Law enforcement shortcomings

Figure 1.2　New technology means new challenges.

from threats that are both more subtle and more serious. Nevertheless, they've recently developed a more sinister side. Youthful carriers of high-tech mischief have paved the way for followers with real criminal intents.

Law enforcement suffers from a distorted perspective of computer security. Instead of being part of the solution, it often creates new problems. There are plenty of first-rate people who specialize in computer-related law enforcement. There also are some who are, to put it kindly, less than first rate. The difference is usually in their understanding of computer technology. Members of the first group respond to their understanding. Those in the second group react to their fears.

Meeting the threat from inside

All three of these problems have a single theme: a belief that the greatest threat to information security comes from the outside—from competitors, youthful hackers, and virus-makers. It's this belief that sends many security and law enforcement efforts in exactly the wrong direction. That helps explain why the initial prognosis for securing far-flung networks might not be good.

You can vastly improve your chances, though, with a 180-degree course correction. Concentrate on the real threats and those you can control.

Threats from outside often are serious, of course. It would be a great mistake to underrate them or to write them off as some kind of media plot. It could be an even greater mistake, though, to let external threats distract you from the much greater vulnerability you face from inside your own organization. Both the technology and the management needs that have led to the big bang in computer networking have also vastly increased your vulnerability to fifth-column internal threats.

What Networks Need Today

Knowledge drives the modern organization. Without it, the enterprise easily could fail. The object of networking is to spread information and make it useful. This presents a new challenge in computer security. Mission-critical applications that once were tucked away in well-secured mainframes are now circulating among local, enterprise, and even interenterprise networks. People really need this information. You must protect it from unauthorized disclosure while allowing authorized disclosure. It's also important that you keep this information accurate and uncorrupted, even while it races around the network.

> **Action item**   Identify the mission-critical information in your organization. It naturally deserves first-priority attention. Mission-critical, by the way, is whatever you want it to be. Only your organization can define what is critical to its mission.

Your network's needs

Computer networks must respond to many needs. These needs often collide. The conflicts start with the fundamental incompatibility of access and security needs. You must protect your most important information. At the same time, though, it does no good to have all this well-secured information if no one can make use of it. The need for security will always conflict with the need for access.

Access and performance

To meet the organization's information needs, a network must have qualities like these:

- Interoperability
- Transparency
- Remote access
- Performance

Different kinds of networks must work smoothly together (Fig. 1.3). Not long ago, an organization would prize the rare individual who could link a roomful of computers into a local area network (LAN) and make the whole thing work. Now, the prized talent is the ability to network these networks, linking them seamlessly with other LANs, UNIX networks, Macintoshes, mainframes, and wide area networks. The ability to hook up with business partners' networks is a major plus. All these extended linkages multiply the security threats you must manage.

Not only should these networked networks function smoothly, but the information-using employee should not have to worry about where on the network that information is stored. The employee should not even have to know.

Qualities of a good network

- Networks should work together
- Their operations should be transparent to users
- They must provide remote access
- They must maintain peak performance

Figure 1.3   Needs of modern networks often conflict with security interests.

This is a great convenience for the employee. It can be just as convenient to an unauthorized user. For a security manager, it's another new challenge: You'll have to control access to unknown destinations.

Just as employees need access to distant corners of the networks, their coworkers at these distant corners need access to the rest of the network. This includes employees at branch offices, remote sites, and on the road. The problem should be obvious: Whenever you must grant widespread access to authorized parties, you also risk granting widespread access to unauthorized parties.

While doing all this, the network should be quick and responsive. That's hard enough when a message might have to travel through multiple links and networks to reach its destination. Most security measures take their own performance hits. All told, the effect is like burdening an Indianapolis car with a load of paving bricks.

Security needs

While meeting all these demands for open access, a network must also meet the organization's security needs (Fig. 1.4). The most important are:

- Confidentiality
- Reliability
- Integrity

A network should not allow anyone to see confidential information without authorization. This requires a reliable way to identify users. It also requires that you set up a system like the government's security clearances. Only cer-

Network security needs

- Protection for confidential information
- Reliable performance
- Data integrity

Figure 1.4 Networks have major security roles.

tain people should have access to certain kinds of information—your salary, to name the first and best example.

Of all the sad words of tongue and pen, some of the saddest must be, "The computer is down." To put it simply, a secure network must work right. Ideally, it will always work right. That won't happen in practice, of course, but beware of arbitrary goals that only encourage you to stop short of your best. If your goal is to make the system work right 98.6 percent of the time, you'll tend to relax and pat yourself on the back once you have achieved that statistic. In the spirit of continuous improvement, you should then be shooting for 98.7 percent. Never stop trying to do better.

An employee should always have access to accurate, timely information. That should include all the information that's needed to do the job well. Since an important element of security is to protect the system's integrity, security measures must include features like validation systems to screen out errors, both deliberate and accidental.

Increased risks from networks

Even in the moat-building era of mainframe security, it was never possible to lock up a system completely. If one human mind can create a security system, another human mind can overcome it. If you build a higher wall, don't be surprised if someone else builds a taller ladder.

Networks have countless ways to make this tough challenge even tougher. Just about anyone with a little knowledge can slip another workstation or server into a network. Often, just about anyone with a little knowledge can pick up a telephone and dial into your network. Multiple points of access multiply the risks.

Threats to network security

- Physical harm
- Natural disaster
- Mechanical failure
- Electronic signals
- External connections
- People

*Guess which is the
most serious?*

Figure 1.5 Most threats have human sources.

A network can suffer several types of vulnerability (Fig. 1.5):

- Physical threats
- Natural disasters
- Mechanical breakdowns
- Electronic signals
- External connections
- People

A network is physically vulnerable to intruders and misuse. Someone can break into your building and steal or damage both your equipment and your data. Even the unsophisticated can recover important information that supposedly was erased. They can often find important password and access information by rummaging through wastebaskets. Computer crime is often really a low-tech activity.

Successive editions of this book always seem to have been written just after notable natural disasters: an earthquake in the Los Angeles area, another in San Francisco or the bombing of the World Trade Center. Early drafts of this book were written while the Mississippi was in flood. There seems to be a pattern here. Disasters will always be happening. Even lightning and power failures can destroy a few bytes of your most critical data.

All mechanical devices will eventually fail. In a PC, the most critical mechanical device is the hard disk. When it goes—and it will—it will take a lot of valuable data with it. Electrical components like power supplies can also fail. With Murphy's law in full force and effect, it will happen at the worst possible time.

Wherever its cables run, your network sends out faint electronic signals. It doesn't take a great act of genius to intercept those signals and steal your information. Shielded cable helps; fiber optic cable helps even more. The basic principle still prevails, however: If you can install it, someone else will know how to get around it.

Your network is vulnerable at any point where it contacts other networks or systems. These include internetworking devices like bridges, routers, and modems. It also includes floppy disks and portable computers.

It's not just the incompetent or the disgruntled, either. Network administrators and department heads are major security risks because we often assume they should have access to more information than they really need to do their jobs. It is not necessary that the network manager responsible for a payroll system have access to everyone's salaries. Nor is it necessary that managers and supervisors have access to every piece of information about every one of their subordinates. Many have such wide-ranging access, though, just because someone assumes they ought to have it. Just being in charge is not an adequate reason to grant access to information.

In terms of numbers, errors and accidents represent the biggest threat to your network. Trainers often try to reassure computer novices by telling them there's little risk they will make an error that causes any harm. That reassurance is valid only as long as the trainees stick to practice files. It expires the instant they begin to work with live data.

At this moment, somewhere, someone is accidentally erasing a valuable file. Someone else is making a mistake that will permanently deny everyone access to an entire directory full of information.

> **Action item** Go through this list of vulnerabilities again. Make a preliminary assessment of how and where each might affect your organization and its networks.

The Major Security Threats Today

One of the biggest obstacles to effective computer security today is an epidemic of misplaced emphasis. Corporations spend a lot of time and money buying and installing elaborate security systems to protect themselves from well-publicized outsiders like youthful invaders and virus carriers. They do next to nothing to train employees to make regular backups or to avoid that stereotype of computer insecurity: the password on a sticky note attached to the monitor. By one estimate—really a guess, but a reasonable one—system administrators who accidentally destroy data by punching the wrong key outnumber crazed hackers by at least 10 to 1.

Your competitors are probably no better off. They may be the folks who installed a vast underground flood-control system against the type of storm that is statistically likely to hit the area only once every century. Meanwhile, an executive takes off to Boston with an unprotected copy of the next year's business plan in a portable computer stashed in an overhead compartment.

Gaining some perspective

An important step toward establishing effective network security is to get the right perspective. Learn to concentrate on the most serious threats: not those that get the most publicity, but those that are most likely to damage your organization. Security experts say these are probably the most serious threats you face today (Fig. 1.6):

- Toll fraud
- Theft of portable computers
- Viruses
- Unhappy employees

This list covers only deliberate acts. It doesn't account for the most common threats of all: accidents and ignorance.

The threat of toll fraud

The youthful invaders who gave hackers a bad name have never been as numerous or as destructive as their publicity has suggested. Until now. The original hackers were spurred mainly by misdirected experimentation. There's a later arriving breed, though, whose incentive is simple theft. These electronic B&E artists use the methods of the original hackers to invade a system and steal valuable information.

The biggest threats

- Toll fraud
- Theft of portable computers
- Viruses
- Unhappy employees

Figure 1.6   New threats expand the list.

The fake ATM was one form of this. A more common offense is to use computers to invade telephone systems to make thousands of dollars worth of unauthorized calls. Once toll thieves have found their way inside your system, they often resell their knowledge to others.

Telecommunications Advisors, Inc., a consulting firm based in Portland, Oregon, says toll fraud has spread fast among vulnerable and unprepared American businesses. They now shell out about $4 billion a year to pay for stolen toll-call services.

Don't take estimates like that too seriously. There are few reliable statistics on any form of computer crime because there are few reliable means to report them. The statistics are often understated because victims tend to keep their experiences to themselves. Others may be overstated because those who sell deterrents often present worst-case scenarios.

The threat is real, even if you can't always measure it. Someone gets free calls at your expense, and these calls are hard to trace. That's why you may receive a telephone bill someday with assessments for all the calls someone made to set up a drug deal.

One measure of how widespread toll fraud has become: You now can buy insurance against it. Most of the major casualty carriers offer coverage. Financial institutions have been the main buyers, and the coverage can be expensive: up to $50,000 a year for $1 million in coverage.

If you're a toll fraud victim, you pay. Long-distance carriers originally denied responsibility. They maintained that it's your equipment that was invaded, not their services. They also pointed out that their traffic volume is much too high to monitor individual calls or customers. More recently, the carriers have begun to show a greater sense of shared responsibility. Some long-distance carriers do sell toll fraud support as an additional service. AT&T, MCI, and Sprint all offer services that detect and report unusual activity and insure customers against losses.

Unusual activity is usually the first sign of a toll fraud problem. The carriers' services are based on monitoring variations from a customer's normal calling patterns. Toll fraud monitoring products are available from other sources too, including Complementary Solutions (Atlanta) and Xiox Corporation (Burlingame, California).

No doubt other resources have become available since this was written. Nevertheless, security advisers point out that it's up to telephone customers to protect themselves—and that too few do it.

Action item Set up a system to monitor your telephone activity and spot departures from normal patterns. Do it now. The earlier you spot these clues, the earlier you can catch and correct a problem.

Action item Start a project to work with local high schools, trade schools, and community colleges to include ethical standards in their computer training course. Help young enthusiasts find constructive outlets for their energy and curiosity, before they start exploring pathways to crime.

Portable computers and their contents

Portable computers have become smaller, lighter, and less expensive with each new product release. This has made them more popular, easier to afford, easier to use, and easier to steal.

It's not that the computers themselves are particularly valuable. They are inexpensive enough through conventional channels, and, as stolen goods, they are offered at deeply discounted prices. What's really valuable is the information on these computers' hard disks. A typical thief can grab a compact, 5-pound object whose hard disk is loaded with sensitive information. Often, a portable will also have the means to dial directly into the company's mainframe or client-server database.

Many managers unwittingly encourage this kind of theft with careless treatment of their portables. According to one poll published early in 1993, only 1 percent of the respondents said they even recognized portable computers as a possible security risk. Some have learned at the school of experience, paying the usual steep tuition rates. With the benefits of this higher education, they have adopted steps like these:

- Including laptop security in their policies and training programs.
- Designing checkout systems that leave a record whenever someone takes a portable from the office.
- Encrypting the data on portables.
- Requiring that laptop users save data only on their floppy disks. This can be an inexpensive and effective step under a couple of conditions: the users protect the floppies, and management backs up the requirement with periodic audits of the portables' hard disks.

Action item   Assess your company's use of portable computers and consider policies for protecting valuable data (Fig. 1.7). The most important first step is simply to recognize that the threat exists. Then let others know about it.

Viruses and the profit motive

The subject of viruses requires a similar shift in focus. They too were over-publicized in the beginning, causing some damage and a lot of distraction. Just as toll fraud has followed the trail blazed by hackers, new strains of viruses have gone beyond malicious mischief. They also have found a profit motive.

Most viruses spread at random. Their creators are simply interested in seeing what kinds of problems they can cause. They have no specific targets. Some new kinds of viruses, however, are more discriminating. They are aimed at specific targets and are designed to cause specific damage. They may be the work of malicious employees. Or thieves might inject a virus intended to write themselves some unauthorized checks. These developments

Protecting portables

- Checkout systems
- Encrypted data
- Security policies

Figure 1.7 Include portables in your security program.

put viruses in a much different perspective. They are no longer just for computerized thrill-seeking. They are becoming specific vehicles for crime.

A new type of "cruise virus" or "attack software" enters a company's network in one of the usual ways, from an infected disk or a contaminated download, for example. Instead of causing random destruction, this virus circulates through the network until it finds its intended target. Then, instead of trashing disks or writing political slogans on-screen, the virus carries out a planned attack. It may broadcast confidential information or private communication, or it may sabotage the target system.

An attack virus differs from other types in that it is designed to inflict specific damage on a specific target. It does have many things in common with other kinds of viruses, though. The most important is that all viruses attack a network's weakest link. It is the computer network equivalent of a legendary automotive failure point: the nut that holds the wheel.

Attention-seeking viruses

Computerworld writer James Daly put it this way: "Like rattlesnakes, computer viruses exist and should be avoided. But they're not lurking behind every rock."

Like human invaders, viruses have created some whiplash publicity. On one hand, they've been overpublicized. Many computer security managers matched the media attention with preventive measures of their own. This often diverted their attention from more serious problems like careless and retribution-minded employees. Then, about the time people started to realize that viruses had been overpublicized, the viruses started to live up to their reputations.

The 1992 Michelangelo virus was a case in point. It was first a much-publicized threat, then a much-publicized fizzle. The publicity that first created unreasonable fear may now have created unreasonable complacency. Not only are today's viruses more serious and sophisticated, but their targets are more tempting and vulnerable. In giving employees better access to information, client-server networks also open themselves to questionable outsiders. More systems and networks have access to the company's most valuable data. These data are also in scattered locations, making it harder to secure.

Immunizing the network

An overreaction to viruses can distort your perspective, but awareness is still your best defense. Take a preventive approach. It's no coincidence that the methods of preventing computer viruses sound a lot like the methods of preventing the AIDS virus:

- Install a reliable antivirus protection package.
- Scan all disks before you use them.
- Back up all critical data and applications. Scan the backups regularly to make sure they aren't infected.
- Remember the consumer protection adage: If something seems too good to be true, it probably is. In particular, that applies to free or bargain-priced application.
- Write-protect original application disks before you use them.

Being aware also means being alert to the symptoms of a virus. They include:

- Unexpected changes in an application file's characteristics, such as its size or time stamp
- Programs that are slow to load or respond
- Programs that repeatedly or unexpectedly try to write to write-protected disks
- Application files that disappear or are suddenly modified
- Unexplained decreases in a computer's available memory
- Unusual increases in reports of bad disk sectors or clusters

Unhappy people

Vengeful ex-employees who spray bullets around their former workplaces can say two things with confidence:

- Their deeds will be highly publicized.
- They will not soon need to look for other employment. They will be otherwise engaged for years to come.

Almost all these high-profile revenge seekers are quickly caught and prosecuted, and their cases will fill news holes and air time for days to come. Not so the disgruntled workers who choose a PC instead of an Uzi. They work in such secrecy that their victims sometimes do not even know they've been victimized. And they can be very hard to catch.

The employee need not even have much of a grudge. Take the case of a Tampa, Florida, television station that literally, though unwittingly, bet the station itself on a newly hired employee. The employee arrived with a personal computer and the continued ability to tap the system at the newspaper where he had formerly worked. The newspaper found it was regularly losing scoops to the TV station. An investigation produced evidence that the new employee was using his uncanceled computer access rights to keep tabs on what his former employer was up to. The reporter and a supervisor were fired and prosecuted.

There's more, and it illustrates why overzealous prosecutors are sometimes more harm than help. They used state property-forfeiture laws to confiscate the reporter's personal computer. Then they went after a much bigger prize: the TV station itself. The entire station had been used as the instrument of a crime, they argued. The station owners finally agreed to pay a settlement that amounted to ransom.

Meanwhile, what of the newspaper that suffered the invasion? It learned the hard way that when an employee leaves—whatever the circumstances—management should immediately cancel that person's user identification and password.

The junk mail caper

Then there was the employee who left a California software company after a pay dispute. The ex-employee soon turned up as the head of a new company, selling a product remarkably like his former employer's. What's more, he was trying to sell it to the software company's own customers.

A customer list is a valuable commodity, and the ex-employee had managed to get his hands on it. When customers asked questions, the software company installed monitors on its system and discovered the ex-employee's activity. By then, the company had lost about 50 customers to the upstart.

Ounces of prevention

Two developments increase your vulnerability to this kind of invasion:

- The economy, which has vastly increased the number and severity of layoffs and staff cutbacks.

- The repetitive, high-stress nature of many modern jobs. This appears to have been a major factor in the U.S. Postal Service cases.

To avoid attacks by ex-employees, remove their means of access. Do it immediately if not sooner. Remind departing employees of any obligations they may still have to refrain from using your confidential information. Few employers do this well, says Charles Cresson Wood, a security consultant based in Sausalito, California.

Then, take care of your remaining work force. The best thing you can do to protect yourself from unhappy employees is to avoid making them unhappy. You can't always do this, of course, but you can do your best to create an atmosphere of teamwork and mutual respect. There are still too many supervisors out there who think it's more important to prevail over their employees than to prevail over their competitors. They're the cause of a lot of deep-seated resentment that could express itself in computer crime.

This work force should also be well informed. The World War II slogan "Loose lips sink ships" still applies. Make sure your orientation and training programs educate employees in their responsibilities. They should learn to recognize the tricks used on employees to get them to give away their passwords or access codes.

> **Action item**   Sponsor a security awareness week, with seminars, slogans, surveys, and plenty of motivation. Follow it up with posters, newsletter articles, and refresher training.

The Computer As a Burglary Tool

American businesses are victims of many kinds of crime. Most of it is in the white-collar class. A small but growing part is computer related. The computer is an important element of modern white-collar crime for two reasons:

- It gives people new ways to commit traditional kinds of crime.
- It stores a new kind of loot: not just goods, but information.

People commit computer crimes. The computer is just one kind of burglary tool. It's true that in creating new kinds of occupations, computers have also created new kinds of criminals. Nevertheless, it's still people who commit computer crimes. Embezzlers who once juggled the books now juggle spreadsheets instead.

The growing value of computer-stored information has many security experts worried. Their predictions seem to be coming true: As more people recognize the value of information, more people try to steal it. It's also a safe kind of theft. Why hold up a bank when in a few milliseconds you can conduct a rigged fund transfer from hundreds of miles away?

That doesn't mean computer crime is entirely nonviolent. There was a period when hackers were regularly breaking into hospital computers and altering patient records. Some patients' treatments were altered in response to the inaccurate information. Most of the culprits backed off when they learned their activities could easily have fatal consequences.

A History of Computer Crime

Computers play four major criminal roles:

- *As the object of a crime.* Criminals have stolen valuable information. They also have destroyed programs and data and, at times, entire computers.
- *As the scene of a crime.* An example is altering the contents of a computer record.
- *As the instrument of a crime.* Here, someone uses a computer to commit fraud, embezzlement, or some similar offense.
- *As a decoy.* Here, someone uses the computer to intimidate or deceive. Someone might advertise a fake computer dating service to gain information about those who respond.

Computer crime has been around for as long as there have been computers. SRI International, a leading security consulting organization, says unofficial reports date back to the 1940s. The first officially reported incident was in 1958. The first federal prosecution for a computer crime, specifically identified as such, was in 1966. This case involved the use of a computer to alter the records of a Minneapolis bank.

For many years, there were only a few reported computer crimes. An SRI study found only 669 recorded incidents of computer abuse from 1958 through 1979. Only a few of these produced hard proof of criminal activity. One research report published in 1970 concluded that the level of computer crime was so low it wasn't worthy of further serious study.

Even then, though, some agencies were beginning to worry. The federal government became concerned about the growing number of computerized secrets it had to protect. Law enforcement began to take a serious interest, too. The techniques of fighting computer crime were added to the standard FBI training course in 1976.

That was also the year of the first congressional hearings on computer crime. The next year, the first anti-computer crime bill was introduced in the Senate. After 10 years and many more bills, the Computer Fraud and Abuse Act of 1966 was adopted. It represented the first major congressional effort to attack crime by computer. Nearly all states now have computer crime statutes on the books.

Criminals polish their skills

The telephone system has long been a target of computer crime. These activities have become increasingly sophisticated. In 1970, John Draper adopted the nickname Captain Crunch, after the similarly named cereal. He began publicizing the peculiar quality of a toy whistle distributed in the cereal boxes. Blown into a telephone, the whistle duplicated the access frequency for a WATS line. The whistler could use it to make free long-distance calls. It seems almost quaint in this era of sophisticated toll fraud.

The 1970s were also the decade when Kevin Mitnik became the unofficial prototype of the hacker who breaks and enters by computer. Mitnik was reported to have altered the credit reports of people who had offended him and to have disconnected celebrities' telephones. When he managed to penetrate the North American Defense Command system, he inspired the movie *War Games.*

Hackers get a bad name

It was people like Mitnik who gave hackers a bad name. Originally, the term *hacker* referred to any young, independent computer genius. Their feats were much more likely to be constructive than destructive. Two self-described hackers, Steve Jobs and Steve Wozniak, accomplished the now-legendary feat of inventing the Apple computer in a garage.

In time, though, *hacker* came to refer mainly to young, independent computer geniuses who committed illegal acts. This change in connotation brought on the natural protests that such a designation casts an unfair stigma on a vast majority of young enthusiasts who apply their genius more constructively. The protesters have a point, but they miss one too. There are plenty of people around who will disparage the young and independent for nothing more than their youth and independence. No doubt you can still find some folks who criticize Jobs and Wozniak for working outside established corporate or government channels.

A prank gets out of control

You can describe much of the activity attributed to hackers as misplaced curiosity. Often it is badly misplaced. The young people who invade others' computer systems often do it just for the challenge. That was the case with Robert Morris, ironically the son of the National Security Agency's chief computer scientist. In 1988, he created a *worm,* a close cousin to a virus, and injected it into the vast Internet communication network. Morris had designed the worm to reproduce itself slowly. Instead, it immediately went out of control, cloning itself all over the country. Damage estimates have ranged from $40 million to $90 million.

The Legion of Doom organizes

About the same time, computer crime became more or less organized. A group calling itself the Legion of Doom adopted the practice of raiding companies for internal technical documents, then posting these on public bulletin boards. Investigators believe one of these documents, containing data on a 911 emergency number system, caused 1990s massive crash of the AT&T computer system. Again, notably, the telephone system was the victim.

Law enforcement agencies respond

As computer crime has changed, so has the law enforcement response. In the early days, when computer crime was rare, there were many who thought it required no special response. Existing laws were enough to do the job. The crime was the important element. The use of a computer was incidental.

That approach didn't satisfy everyone. In 1982, SRI International prepared a report for the Justice Department that had this to say:

> Unfortunately, the business community is neither adequately prepared to deal with nor sufficiently motivated to report this new kind of crime to authorities. Although reliable statistics are as yet unavailable to prove this, computer security studies for the business community and interviews with certified public accounts have indicated that few crimes of this type are ever reported to law enforcement authorities for prosecution.
>
> On the one hand, many business interests complain that even when they do report this crime, prosecutors frequently refuse to accept the cases for a variety of reasons, including their lack of understanding of the technology and their already heavy caseloads. On the other hand, prosecutors and investigators say that the victims' records and documentation of crimes associated with computers in the business community are inadequate for effective prosecution.

There was little change in that picture for several years. By 1989, there had been established the National Center for Computer Crime Data (NCCCD), and its report for that year showed some development: The number of cases referred to prosecutors had tripled over the previous year, the center reported. Even so, only an estimated 6 percent of all serious computer incidents were being reported.

At about the same time, William Cook, head of a Justice Department task force on computer fraud and abuse, reported the continuing sentiments of many in law enforcement. "Many companies do not want to publicly acknowledge that they have suffered a computer crime," he said. "Instead, they want to cover it up."

Law enforcement agencies fumble investigations

The 1990 AT&T crash and its catastrophic disruption of telephone communication got both parties' instant attention. Business saw how vulnerable it could be, and law enforcement was quick to react. Unfortunately, it was the wrong reaction.

The actions of a few people have given hackers a bad name. Law enforcement has had exactly the same experience. The Arizona-based investigation, *Operation Sun Devil,* is now remembered mainly for the number of innocent people it harmed. Investigators traced the crash to a file of 911 numbers, believed to have been stolen by Legion of Doom members from the Bellsouth regional telephone company. When they found another file of Bellsouth 911 numbers in an online electronic magazine, they arrested Craig Neidorff, its 19-year-old editor, and charged him with illegally publishing the documents. Neidorff's computers and documents were confiscated. The charges were later dropped when it was learned that anyone with $30 could buy the same information from Bellsouth itself.

A few months later, Secret Service agents raided the Austin, Texas, home of Steve Jackson, who published role-playing computer games. Again, they confiscated equipment and software, including a document described as a "handbook of computer crime." It turned out that it was only another role-playing book Jackson had been developing, and he was never charged with a crime. The seizure of his equipment, though, nearly drove him into bankruptcy.

Much of the harm in these cases came from property-seizure laws that trivialize the distinction between guilt and innocence. It also reflected some longer-standing problems. Agents misunderstood the technology and were too quick to equate computer bulletin boards with illegal activity. Notably, too, Neidorff and Jackson were both young and independent.

Things get better

Since then, the cops and robbers have both gotten better at what they do. In 1992, five young men were charged with breaking into the computer systems at telephone companies, credit bureaus, corporations, and universities. The investigation marked the first use of court-ordered wiretaps to obtain digital evidence. Later that year, Kevin Poulsen was charged with invading military computers and stealing the orders for an Air Force exercise. He was charged under a federal espionage statute.

These cases show how far computer criminals have come since the days of Captain Crunch. It also appears that law enforcement has made a lot of progress itself since the days of Operation Sun Devil. Intelligent reactions based on solid knowledge are beginning to replace mistaken reactions based on fear and ignorance. That improves the chances of catching real criminals and reduces the risk of harming the innocent.

A New Approach

Basic security techniques have not changed much over the years. The tactics that protected the earliest vacuum tube computers can also protect today's servers and workstations. Change has come from another source: The demands of information security in a networked era are much different from those of the past. They demand that you take a new approach to computer security. The cornerstones of that approach are to recognize that:

- Networks are real and here to stay. Often, the competitive health of your organization depends on them.

- You cannot physically secure every element of the network. Don't even try.

The basic responses are:

- Instead of protecting locations, protect information. Concentrate very hard on protecting your organization's most important information.

- Emphasize people, not technology. This has always been important, but it is even more important in the networking age.

   Action item   *"It's people, stupid."* Make a note of that, and post it someplace where you'll see it often. If you don't like that wording, choose something of your own that conveys the same message.

2

Building a
Security Plan

*At a time when networks are making central security
planning almost impossible, planning is more
important than ever.*

When the First Boston Corp. restructured its computer security organizations, one of the first jobs to be eliminated was that of the executive in charge of data security. That was a drastic step, but in many respects First Boston was just acknowledging two well-established trends:

- The decentralizing effects of networks
- The need to cut out layers of management and create a flatter, more responsive organization

As networks decentralize computing systems, it no longer makes much sense to try to maintain a centralized security system.

Modern Security Management

As networks have expanded, they have dramatically changed the nature of network security. The traditional security officer was a gatekeeper. Now, says one consultant, "there are many gates, and someone has to be in charge of the gatekeepers." Security is no longer a single function. It is the responsibility of each department. The modern security manager is not a security czar, imposing and enforcing rules of access. The job now is to teach, motivate, and support people who have taken charge of their own computing resources. These are not "users," in any sense of the word, and they certainly are not the enemy. They and their departments are clients, and the purpose of computer security is to support them in doing their jobs (Fig. 2.1).

Users must take responsibility.

- You can't lock all the gates yourself
- So you have to train more gatekeepers

Figure 2.1 Security demands cooperation, not conflict.

Many companies have spotted this trend. After all, it's been hard to miss. Some firms, like First Boston, have decided they no longer need high-level security chiefs with executive-level salaries and perks. They can hand over the job to lower-level managers.

The value of old skills

That's an extreme point of view, and many have criticized these firms for going too far. The critics have a point. Networks have brought great changes to security management, but they have not yet done away with the need for security managers. Even if the security manager's job has greatly changed, the jobholder has at least two vital assets:

- Security knowledge and expertise
- An influential position in top management

Instead of simply eliminating the position and the jobholder, it would be better to redirect the security executive's attention, from central control to organizational support (Fig. 2.2).

A mistake here could be particularly serious if you base your security arrangements on an easy-to-make assumption: Since security is no longer centered on large systems, security knowledge based on mainframes is obsolete—along with the experts in that kind of technology. That's a natural assumption, and it's almost right. You can't secure a network by adopting mainframe techniques. But you can secure a network by *adapting* mainframe techniques. The basic techniques of computer security are well established. The challenge is to apply them in a new, decentralized environment.

Adding new skills

Traditional computer knowledge is still valuable. The networked organization does require, though, that you supplement this basic knowledge to adapt to

Security is changing.

- Less need for central control
- More need for enterprisewide support

Figure 2.2   Security management requires new skills.

networked conditions. That means you must gain a sound basic understanding of network technology. It also means you must master what many technical professionals still feel is a demanding, unfamiliar new skill: managing people.

Experienced security professionals can make the switch, but they can't do it alone. Making the networked enterprise secure requires the cooperation of many people: security professionals, network managers, department heads, and other employees.

As you develop a network security plan, you'll find yourself working less with technology and more with people.

Steps Toward Network Security

The basic goals of a network security system are pretty much like the security goals for any kind of computer system (Fig. 2.3):

- To protect information from accidental destruction or modification
- To protect information from deliberate destruction or modification
- Make sure the data is available to authorized users, when they need it and in a form they can use

The self-contradictions are obvious. Furthermore, you'll probably encounter that familiar management bugaboo, resistance to change. New methods will challenge the people who have vested interests in old methods. That means you can never rely on technology alone to implement a network security plan.

Neither can you issue a new set of security policies and expect that everyone will immediately begin to observe them. Many employees say they'll welcome the new program—and they'll mean it. But at the first sign of difficulty, they'll revert to familiar, more comfortable ways of doing things. These old ways often run contrary to effective security practice. The classic example is

Goals of network security

- Protect data from accidents
- Protect data from deliberate acts
- Make data available whenever it is needed

Figure 2.3   Availability is the important new challenge.

the password on a sticky note attached to a monitor. The near-classic example is the password on a sticky note attached to the bottom of a keyboard.

Recruiting allies

To secure a networked system, you'll need nearly as much diplomatic sense as technical know-how. For example, you'll have to influence people in client departments—people over whom you have no particular authority. You will find yourself in many situations where you must build alliances in support of a working security plan.

One of the most effective alliances you can form is with Human Resources (HR). There are many ways HR can assist you, including (Fig. 2.4):

A plan for a security plan

- Line up support
  - User departments
  - Top management
- Make a preliminary assessment
- Form a project team

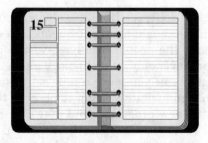

Figure 2.4   Get started in a security plan.

- Helping you identify the key managers in each client department

- Devising professional surveys and other means to learn about employees' current attitudes toward security

- Helping to set up and conduct interviews with department managers and employees

- Planning and delivering training programs to support the security program

> **Action item**   Contact Human Resources. Suggest ways HR can help design and implement a security plan. Listen to their suggestions, too.

Making a preliminary assessment

Lining up these contacts is an important first step. With their help, the next step is to make a preliminary assessment of your network security needs. This is a draft report that doesn't need to be very fancy. Your main objective is to determine just where the organization's security might need improvement. On the basis of this assessment, you can present a case to top management, pointing to specific problems and offering legitimate solutions.

Department heads and key employees can be helpful here. Most want to do their jobs well. Many feel a formal security program would interfere with that. If you consult these people in the initial assessment, you will involve them almost from the beginning. You'll get a variety of responses, of course, when you approach department representatives. Most, though, will welcome the chance to present their ideas and concerns, at a time when this will do the most good. Many employees also have useful ideas about security problems in their areas of responsibility and may even have some suggestions for solving them.

Areas to examine in the preliminary assessment (Fig. 2.5):

- Enterprise-wide systems that carry sensitive information but may be lacking in security. Electronic mail systems are a common example.

- Applications and networks that see heavy use in day-to-day operations. These busy services are the most likely to carry information that should be protected.

- Danger spots where data might be altered or lost during transmission. For example, a large transmission of engineering drawings may overload the capacity of a local area network.

- Network components that need physical protection. These can include servers and wiring hubs.

- Existing security policies and practices. Assess how well they respond to identified needs and how well they are observed.

- Prevailing employee attitudes about security. 152,314

Possible sources of danger

- Unprotected sensitive information
- Heavy use
- Possible alteration
- Unsecured hubs
- Company policies
- Employee attitudes

Figure 2.5   Look here for your most vulnerable spots.

Sometimes, knowing what employees think can give you significant clues to the major challenges you face. You can ask questions like these to determine employees' sentiments and their levels of security awareness:

- What do you understand about computer security?
- How do you feel about present security practices? Are they effective? Do they interfere with your doing your job?
- What do you do in your job to protect sensitive information?

Selling Security to Management

Few things in corporate life succeed without the approval—even the commitment—of top management. Security is no exception. Though the need may seem self-evident to you, one of your major tasks will be to present your case to your firm's senior officials and ask for their support. It's the modern equivalent to asking for someone's hand in marriage. Take it just as seriously.

The presentation

Work up the most professional presentation you can. If you have presentation software, video production facilities, or other assets, make use of them. Use the preliminary assessment as your guide. Cover these points:

- The places you have found where information is vulnerable to theft, loss, or damage
- The likely impact of losing this information

- Actions that can be taken to reduce the risk
- The costs and benefits of taking action

Remember, executives everywhere are interested in specific, bottom-line results. Make it clear exactly what dangers you hope to avoid. Your proposal to management should also include:

- A list of priorities for action. Identify the information resources that most seriously need protection.
- A proposed plan of action for dealing with the most serious threats.
- A timetable for action and milestones at which to measure progress.
- Any additional actions, such as publishing new policies, that will be necessary.

> **Action item** Prepare a list of additional reading and research on information security. Present the list at the end of your presentation. The more senior managers know about the subject, the more enthusiastically they will support your efforts.

The project team

As you prepare your presentation to management, you should also begin to assemble a project team to create and implement the security plan. Everyone involved should be represented, including:

- Senior management
- Network administrators
- Representatives of client departments

Make sure every possible interest has a voice in the plan. For example, in a manufacturing firm, it would be wise to include managers and employees from the shop floor, plus representatives from the engineering staff, maintenance, marketing, finance, personnel, legal, and, yes, information systems.

A diverse membership makes sure that everyone has a chance to present needs and ideas. This helps client departments feel that security is something *we* are doing, not something *they* are doing. Involvement is also a solid sign of interest. It helps make sure that the completed security plan will bring about necessary changes in attitudes and ways of doing things.

In a larger organization, you may have to set up special task forces to deal with security needs in particular parts of the information system. One group, for example, could focus on local area networks, another on wider area communication, and a third on electronic data interchange (EDI) transactions with outside firms.

> **Action item** Begin to prepare a list of potential task force members, the parts of the organization they represent, and the contributions they might make to a security plan.

What a plan should contain

- Identify the risks
- Identify solutions
  - Physical
  - Procedural
  - Technical

Figure 2.6 Find your problems—and solve them.

Elements of a Security Plan

Your completed security plan should have two major sections (Fig. 2.6):

- A risk assessment
- Strategies to deal with the identified risks

These strategies fall into several categories:

- Procedural tactics like revised security policies
- Physical protection, to prevent direct access to important resources
- Technical security, which includes both hardware and software techniques

Some authorities may divide the categories a little differently. Furthermore, some techniques don't fit neatly into any arbitrary classification scheme. For example, a password system relies on technical methods, but its administration is a procedural task.

Assessing the risk

The project team's first major assignment will be to prepare a *risk assessment*. Expanding on the work you did for the preliminary assessment, identify the threats to your system and estimate how serious each could be. This formal assessment will become the foundation of your security plan. Properly done, it will guide you in setting priorities and implementing security measures.

Don't jump to conclusions about where the threats may lie. Viruses are a legitimate threat, but they may not be the most serious. Invasion from outside could be serious but does not actually happen very often.

If your assessment is typical, most of the major threats will come instead from inside the organization. Furthermore, most will not be deliberate. In most organizations, errors and accidents are the biggest threats. Deliberate actions by dishonest or unhappy employees are next. Outside invasions and viruses bring up the end of the list. Even then, the outsider is more likely to be an ex-employee than a total stranger.

A good way to assess your risks is to examine the kind of data you handle. Ask questions like these:

- What kind of data do you maintain?
- For what purposes does the organization use it?
- What would the organization lose if the data were lost or stolen?

If your budget is limited—and whose isn't—it makes sense to concentrate your effort on the threats that are most serious to your organization. Once you have countered the most serious threats, additional spending will be less cost-effective.

There's also a tradeoff between security and the ease with which people can get their jobs done. Some security professionals take exception to the idea that legitimate employees can be hampered by having to penetrate a security blanket. They fall back on familiar self-justifications like "It's for your own good," or "If you aren't doing something wrong, you have nothing to worry about." Neither is a particularly valid judgment. If a security measure interferes with someone's job performance, there had better be a very good reason.

Selecting the strategies

The best security strategy is—no surprise—the most effective way to attack the most serious identified risks. There are enough varied approaches available that you can't use them all. In fact, you shouldn't try. There is such a thing as too much security: costly measures aimed at unlikely dangers, adding to cost and diminishing the organization's efficiency.

Be particularly careful not to be blinded by technology. There are plenty of high-tech security measures out there. They look exciting, and often they can give you a feeling of power. These measures are also very effective when properly used.

The key is *properly used*. No security measure is a good security measure unless it effectively responds to a specific, significant risk. A case in point would be a sophisticated access-control system designed to block hackers. It would be sadly out of place in an organization that has never had a hacker invasion, but it has suffered thousands of dollars in losses from data entry errors.

For most organizations, you'll get better security for fewer dollars with procedural security measures like these (Fig. 2.7):

- *Secure policies and procedures.* Don't go overboard. The thicker your policy manual, the harder it is to understand and enforce. You should establish a

Procedural options

- Policies
- Training
- Audits

Figure 2.7 Establish a basic set of policies, but don't try to build a law library.

basic set of policies, though, to back up your other measures. Possible subjects for policies include the proper use of passwords, guidelines for administering access to the system, antivirus procedures, and provisions for auditing, backups, and audit trails.

- *Training.* This is a security tactic that's frequently overlooked. People often endanger data because they don't know how to do things right. A good training program can be an effective weapon against a major cause of loss and errors.

- *Audit trails.* The system should maintain a record of everyone who logs on and off the system. You don't just want to identify authorized users of your network. It can be just as important to identify the unauthorized—including their unsuccessful attempts. When something goes wrong, this audit record can be a valuable clue to what happened.

Physical security is less important in a networked environment for the simple reason that it's less effective. You no longer have a single, central data resource you can physically protect.

Though you can't secure a network by physical means alone, a network has many components where physical security can help prevent theft and manipulation. These include cables, connection points, and servers.

Technical security options include (Fig. 2.8):

- *Identification.* This is the foundation of many other security techniques. If you know who is trying to get the use of your network, you will have a much better idea how to respond. The most common form of access control is a unique combination of user identification and password.

Technical options

- Identification
- Access control
- Ensuring data integrity
- Encryption

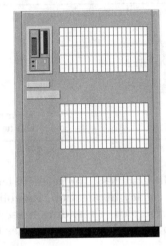

Figure 2.8 Technical measures support other tactics.

- *Passwords.* No security system is perfect, and passwords offer no exception. Nevertheless, there's a good reason passwords are so fundamental to most security plans. Every authorized user should be assigned a unique password, and it should be matched with an equally unique user ID. Provide by policy that no employee can share either form of identification with anyone else.

- *Data integrity.* The best database management systems have multiple ways to check new entries and flag possible errors. These integrity checks are effective responses to the common threat of data entry errors.

- *Encryption.* Coding a message helps thwart network eavesdroppers. Encryption can be clumsy and time-consuming, though. It's most useful when you send critical information over long distances or outside the organization.

The Legacy of Mainframe Security

One of the big problems for organizations that switch from host systems to client-server networks is what to do with *legacy applications*. These are applications that were written for large systems. They are still valuable to the business, but their clumsiness often betrays their age.

There is a legacy of mainframe security practices as well. Most of the security techniques now in use originated in the mainframe era. They have relied on the ability to protect a central data resource.

There is no central resource in today's enterprise networks. That means you can't simply lift the legacy of mainframe security and apply it to far-flung

TABLE 2.1   Implementing Basic Security Principles

	Procedural	Physical	Technical
Identification and authentication	Password administration		
Access control	...	...	Password access control
Auditing	Logging Access		
Object reuse	...	...	Full erasure of storage media
Secure communication	...	Securing servers and network hubs	

networks. Nevertheless, the security legacy is as valuable in its way as a mission-critical legacy application. Established security systems are based on a few basic principles. Extending a security plan to the network is mainly a matter of applying these old principles to the new environment:

- Identification and authentication
- Discretionary access control
- Auditing
- Object reuse
- Secure communication

You can implement these principles with a combination of procedural, physical, and technical controls. Table 2.1 shows a suggested approach.

Knock, knock. Who's there?

Identification and authentication describe a basic password system. It relies on passwords and user identification codes to make sure you know who is using your network—or is trying to use it.

Access control

Once an authorized user has been identified, an access-control system regulates the applications and files to which the person has access. It can also determine which activities, like reading or editing a file, this individual is allowed to conduct. You'll often find this kind of access control in a client-server database manager.

Recording access

An auditing system keeps a log of everyone who uses the network, or even tries to do so. You can also keep track of when and how long the person had access and which files he or she used or modified. You can often spot suspicious patterns of activity in these records.

There's one potential drawback, though: An auditing system may generate so much information the suspicious patterns are hidden in an overwhelming mass of data. If you install an auditing system, plan on fine-tuning it to regulate the amount of detail it reports.

Cleaning the erasers

Erasing a disk doesn't always erase the data, as Oliver North learned the hard way. Electronic mail messages he thought he had erased reappeared as evidence in court. Object reuse is designed to recycle storage media and other resources without unwittingly circulating sensitive information that still might be within reach of a determined search. It completely clears sensitive data both from computer memory and storage media.

Secure communication

Some see communication security as an addendum to mainframe security, but it is critical to a network. This area of security includes restrictions on dial-in access and encryption of sensitive information sent over private or public networks.

The Baseline Alternative

A full-scale security plan is a complex document that can take a large toll on your time and energy. Not everyone writes a complete new plan from scratch. Not everyone has to.

SRI International, a major security consulting firm, polled many security managers several years ago and found that few of them were conducting their operations according to textbook examples of risk assessment and security planning. They were unwilling or unable to follow this detailed process of evaluation for every possible security risk and precaution. Many felt the evaluation process itself was not cost-effective. Some didn't even think it was necessary. Most organizations pay more attention to security now than they did when this survey was taken. Even so, many organizations want to minimize the effort and expense they devote to a security program.

SRI can tell you that your computer security problems are not nearly as unique as you might think. Whatever your problem, you probably share it with many other people. Many security problems are common to all computer users. Others are shared by members of the same industry or even groups of industries. Few if any are totally unique to you.

On that basis, SRI has developed what it calls a *baseline system* of security planning. It starts with the premise that many controls are so universal and have such proven value that you should not routinely have to justify their use. These are, in effect, the default precautions. They are risks you should attack and the controls you should use to attack them. Implement these controls unless you have a good reason to do something else.

Three levels of security

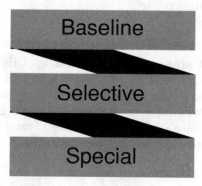

Figure 2.9 Use these levels as a framework for planning.

The only time you need to go through the full process of analysis and justification is if you decide not to follow the prevailing standard. For example,
should you decide a particular risk is too small, and its solution too expensive, to be used in your organization, you should be prepared to defend that
judgment. Be equally prepared should you believe your unique situation dic-
tates a higher than normal degree of security.

The baseline system is based on three levels of security (Fig. 2.9):

- At the first level, *baseline controls,* the need is so universal nearly everyone will use them.

- At the second level are *selective controls.* These are used less universally
  than the baseline techniques, but they still are familiar, standardized, and
  well accepted. Someone who proposes one of these controls should demonstrate that the risk is worth the effort, but the selection of the strategy
  itself is more or less automatic.

- At the third level are *special controls.* Here, both the risks and the responses are truly unique to your situation. Anyone who makes a proposal at this
  level should be prepared to strongly justify both the need and the response.

Table 2.2 illustrates how the baseline system works. It starts with a list of
standard security techniques that represent the baseline elements for a typical computer network. You should plan to adopt these measures unless you
have a specific reason not to do so. Also listed are the type of security measure into which each measure falls: physical, procedural, technical, or disaster control. Some measures include elements of more than one type.

Table 2.3 is a list of selective network security controls. These are standard
tactics you can use when conditions indicate. The table includes some conditions under which you would normally consider them.

TABLE 2.2   Baseline Controls

Item	Class
Administer computer access control.	Procedural Technical
Back up data files and programs.	Procedural Technical
Comply with laws and regulations.	Procedural
Allow for contingency recovery-equipment replacement.	Disaster control
Control access to data files.	Technical Procedural
Create a disaster recovery plan.	Disaster control
Encrypt the password file.	Technical
Establish computer security management committees.	Procedural
Establish passwords for network access.	Procedural Physical Technical
Isolate sensitive production jobs.	Procedural Technical
Log user trouble calls.	Technical Procedural
Maintain a terminal log-in protocol.	Technical
Minimize the number of copies of sensitive data files and reports.	Procedural
Minimize traffic and access to work areas.	Physical
Place employee identification on work products.	Procedural
Protect electrical equipment	Disaster control Physical
Provide for electric power shutdown and recovery.	Physical Disaster control
Provide physical security of remote network nodes.	Physical
Record network activity records.	Procedural
Restrict computer terminal access and use.	Physical
Restrict the display of sensitive information.	Technical
Secure sensitive areas during unattended periods.	Procedural Technical
Validate data input.	Technical

Seeking the base baseline

In some ways, a baseline approach recalls the frustrated editor who described his newspaper's indecisive editorial as "two-fisted." "On one hand," he explained, "and on the other…"

On one hand, the baseline tactics are supposed to be so universal and well established there is seldom any question that you should include them in any

TABLE 2.3   Selective Controls

Item	Use when:	Class
Appoint a computer security officer.	You have enough computer resources to justify the position.	Procedural Physical
Control access to loading docks.	You want to maintain strict control over all access.	Physical
Encrypt data.	You need the highest degree of protection.	Technical
Generate passwords automatically.	There are many people with access to the network.	Technical
Limit transaction privileges from network notes.	You want to control a system that permits access by way of multiple nodes or terminals.	Technical
Monitor computer use.	You want to ensure that only employees have access.	Procedural
Provide alternative power supply.	You need a high degree of reliability.	Disaster control
Provide for dynamic password. changes by users.	There may be frequent interruptions in network node use.	Technical
Provide for identification and trustworthiness of couriers.	You use couriers to carry sensitive information.	Physical Procedural
Provide terminal identifiers.	You need a high level of security at individual access points.	Technical
Require universal use of security badges.	You must manage a large staff or many visitors.	Physical Procedural
Separate critical network components.	Large, complex systems need disaster protection.	Disaster control
Separate test and production systems.	You have a large system of linked networks.	Technical
Sign agreements with remote users.	You want to control remote access.	Procedural

security program. On the other hand, there is no single, standardized list of universal, well-established baseline controls. This is particularly true in networking, where diversity tends to frustrate standardization.

That means you will have to establish your own list of baseline tactics. That may sound suspiciously like building your own security plan from scratch. That's not necessarily the case. There is a growing body of well-accepted security techniques available. You can select from them to build your own baseline foundation.

Other types of controls may become generally accepted through a process of increasing exception taking. If enough people find reasons to depart from standard lists, the exceptions will themselves become the standards. There also is disagreement among various organizations, perhaps even within your organization, about which goals and methods should be included in a baseline system. It's also quite likely you will decide to use variations on standard techniques, tailoring them to your own needs.

Building your own baseline

Appendix A is a list of well-accepted computer security controls. Start by picking those that fit your situation. Add the ideas you pick up from other publications and in your professional contacts. Stay alert for new developments in the field. With a little information and good judgment, you probably can establish a valid baseline system for your own use.

There are two conditions to using this approach:

- Don't fall into the trap of *mindless checklisting,* picking items from App. A or any other list just because someone else thinks they are good ideas. This must be an easy snare to fall into; so many people have done it. A tactic is right for you only if it suits your own needs and situation.

- Evaluate these individual controls as part of an overall *security system.* These controls don't work in isolation. Judge them for how well they will work together to meet your specific needs.

Building a Baseline

The process of building a security baseline has seven basic steps (Fig. 2.10):

- Determine the *scope of the review.*
- Identify *existing controls.*
- List *additional control objectives.*
- See what *other companies* are doing.
- Build a *preliminary list* of baseline controls.

Baseline security steps

- Scope
- Existing controls
- Additional goals
- Industry practice
- Preliminary list
- Refinements
- Proposal

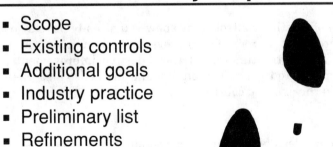

Figure 2.10 Follow these steps to identify your baseline measures.

- Identify and address the *remaining risks* that require nonbaseline treatment.
- Prepare a *management proposal*.

Spotting the scope

Start by identifying, at least in broad strokes, the people and facilities that will be involved in the security plan. Include:

- Facilities
- People
- Equipment
- Application programs
- Production processes
- Data sources and files
- Storage and processing areas
- Documentation
- Support functions such as auditing, safety, and human resources
- Client departments

This will naturally be a list of potential risks and vulnerable areas. It isn't necessary at this stage, though, to identify specific potential threats.

Existing controls

Identify and document all existing security controls. List them according to their objectives. Include descriptions of any variations.

Seeking improvement

The inventory of existing controls may show you already have a good security program. There must be room for improvement, though, or you wouldn't be reading this. This is the time to list those desired improvements, including additional controls and variations on existing methods. List these by objective, as you did the existing controls.

What others are doing

A good source of ideas is to visit other computer centers and see what they are doing. The more a center is like yours, of course, the more fruitful the visit can be. You may be able to arrange reciprocal idea swapping with other computer security professionals, letting them check out your program in exchange for a look at theirs. All should agree in writing to keep their findings in confidence. On your visits, try to identify:

- The most effective controls
- How controls were chosen and justified
- How cost-effective controls have been
- The organization's success with controls
- Controls that were rejected or have not proven effective

Getting it together

You should now have a collection of information on:

- Your security needs
- Existing controls
- Unmet needs
- Experience in other firms

Now, put these together into a preliminary list of baseline controls. Make a list of:

- The controls
- Their objectives
- Acceptable variations
- Whether they are currently in place

Make a similar list of selective controls to be implemented when conditions indicate a need.

Looking for gaps in coverage

Conduct a risk analysis, looking specifically for problems that would not be covered adequately by the baseline or selective controls. Since there should be few of these, this analysis need not be as exhaustive as one that seeks to identify every vulnerable spot. Places to look include:

- Areas where new technology has been introduced
- Areas where there are special circumstances
- Areas of disagreement over the application of baseline or selective controls

Once you have identified these controls, you can plan for special controls to deal with them.

Reporting to management

Make your recommendations to management in the three main categories of a baseline system:

- *Baseline controls,* which should require no special justification
- *Selective controls,* to be applied when you can establish a need
- *Special controls,* for exceptional cases in which both the need and the method require specific justification

Set priorities for implementing these controls, according to this scheme:

- Immediate need
- Needed soon
- Future need

3

Security Is a People Problem

Computers don't commit computer crimes. People do.
An effective security system must begin with the human
element.

Some computer professionals still get nervous when you talk about having to deal with people. Most have accepted it by now, but some are much more comfortable with their technology than with the people who use it. If you're in that group, don't get too comfortable. First, last, and always, computer security is mainly a people problem. The fact that some criminals use computers is as incidental as the fact that some bank robbers wear masks. The best technology will be of little use if you overlook the human component of computer security.

Not only do people commit computer crimes, but people are the key to preventing them. You can't launch an effective security program without the positive involvement of the entire organization. Otherwise, your program will become just a stack of unread policy manuals and a collection of technical barriers that frustrated employees try their best to overcome.

Employees Get Involved

Employees have been involved in the computing process since they first had personal computers to use. That much is obvious. What's not as obvious is that their level of involvement has continued to grow. At the basic level, PC users grappled with the fundamentals of application programs. They learned enough about WordPerfect or Lotus 1-2-3 to make their computers useful tools in getting their jobs done. Lots of employees will continue to work at that level. Other employees take advantage of the large and thriving computer training industry, whose course offerings reflect the widespread need to gain basic competence in standard PC software packages.

Still other employees are going further—a lot further. Many PC applications have become virtually application development packages in their own rights. You don't even have to know how to program, though it helps. These desktop-level development tools come in two basic forms:

- *Descendants of spreadsheet macros.* Spreadsheets, word processors, and a world of other PC applications now come with their own built-in programming languages. Originally, these macro languages were intended to create program swatches that speed up and customize the parent program. Today, they are almost full-fledged programming languages in their own right.

- *Forms-based products that make use of Windows and other graphic interfaces.* You draw a form on the screen; the program generates the code to manage the form. Applications in this class often are client-server, front-end products that connect with corporate databases.

The forms-based application builders aren't always as easy to learn as their promoters would have you believe. Nevertheless, some of the persistent learners who once made their way through basic software classes have now learned to use these features to build useful applications themselves.

Groupware Gets It Together

E-mail used to be a convenience. Now, it is maturing into a technology that could become the core of enterprise networking. One reason for this is the *mail-enabled application,* or *groupware.* This is a network-oriented product that empowers employees. It does so by linking them to other people and to multiple sources of data.

Groupware's definition involves a state of mind instead of technical specifications. It's not a comfortable idea for the systematic mind. There's no single technology at which you can point and say, "That's it." Authorities are divided on a formal definition. Some say groupware and mail-enabled applications are the same thing; others classify groupware as a type of mail-enabled software.

Much of the current interest in groupware is based on supporting interactions between people. These people may be members of single departments, members of work teams, or even people from far-flung parts of an organization who work on related parts of a project. They can even be members of different organizations, such as an auto manufacturer that has learned to control quality by working in close partnership with its part suppliers.

Groupware has particularly strong implications for the people who make up the enterprise. Terry Winograd, Stanford professor and director at Action Technologies, predicts that "groupware is going to make people more directly conscious of the interactions among people—the responsibilities, the commitments, the communications—and personalize something people usually think of as depersonalizing."

The special role of Notes

Lotus Notes holds a special role in the development of groupware. It's been by far the best-noticed and most successful example of its type. The key to that success is that Notes relies on open platforms and the client-server model. This makes it easier for both users and third-party developers to build links with other applications. Significantly, the impetus behind Notes extends outward from users, by way of their PCs, instead of downward by way of large-system hosts.

From workgroup to workflow

Beyond the idea of mail-enabled and workgroup applications is *workflow management*. This is a new term, but it is really just an extension of earlier e-mail developments.

Workflow systems automate business procedures, taking advantage of computers, networks, databases, and messaging systems. With workflow software, employees can create and move data between individuals, departments, and even organizations. They can do it transparently, of course, without regard to geographic location or the respective computer systems.

Workflow management is a logical extension of groupware. Basic e-mail systems provide a way to transmit messages. Groupware uses this ability to perform an ever-growing range of useful tasks. Workflow software manages the process. More to the point, it lets employees manage this process. Workflow software lets employees automate routine parts of their work. It not only gives them more control over information but it also gives them more control over their time.

Workflow software comes in several varieties. The most common include applications that manage document flow or automate tasks and processes. Some do both. Image processing systems, for example, support document flow by automating paper-based systems and procedures.

Helping yourself

Another small but growing phenomenon is the ability to generate your own help files and other online documents. A few adventurous employees have discovered the potential of the compiler that's used to turn text files into Windows help documents. It's an inexpensive and relatively easy way to create reference and training material and other on-screen documents. Its price and ease of use are both within the range of an experienced PC user.

All of these developments have security implications. They not only increase the amount of user involvement in computing, but they also increase the level of that involvement. Whatever their level of expertise, the people with PCs on their desks are not just "end users" who exist on the outskirts of something. They are full participants in the computing process. You can't ignore them where security is concerned. You must always keep them in mind, and not just as potential criminals—though that will be true of a few. Your coworkers' more important role, if you can achieve it, is as full participants in the security program.

The Problems With People

A host of polls and articles indicate that managers worry a lot about security. Each time a new threat appears and gets heavy publicity, managers worry even more.

Unfortunately for the security of their systems, the concern isn't always translated into effective action. Law enforcement officials universally complain that they get too little cooperation from the victims of computer crime. Statistical analysis shows that only a few business losses via computers lead to criminal prosecution.

There are several reasons for the business community's apparent failure to act. Not all of them reflect badly on management, but some of them do:

- Managers mistakenly think of security as *only a technical problem.* Even the most sophisticated security system can be overridden by a determined human being. Security starts in the office and on the shop floor, not in the data processing department.

- Many victims of computer crime are *afraid of bad publicity.* They don't report their losses to authorities. This can be a valid concern if the fact that the company was victimized would undermine its customers' respect. For example, customers would tend to be wary of a bank whose system had been proven vulnerable.

- Managers do not fully recognize that *security is a management responsibility.* It involves every part of the organization. You will not have good security without a firm organizational commitment to it.

The threat from inside

Your first security concern must be with the people who work for your company. Long-distance hackers and virus spreaders have gained publicity and demonstrated many weak spots, but the real threat comes from people within your own organization (Fig. 3.1). In fact, the greatest threat comes from people who:

- Are part of your organization
- Have legitimate access to the computer

Look at it this way: What kind of information do you maintain that would really interest a youthful hacker? A youngster looking for computerized

Who threatens your data?

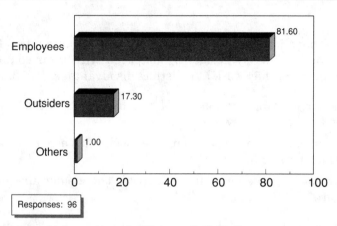

Figure 3.1   How do chief executives view the security threat?

excitement isn't likely to find it in your endless transaction records or in the monthly sales figures from Seattle. The vast majority of all computerized information is that kind of stuff. You are most vulnerable to hackers when your data gives a youngster a chance to make a mark. You also are vulnerable to a small group of outsiders who might find your data worth trying to steal. You are even more vulnerable to insiders who really do take an interest in your data.

Some employees may be greedy, and others may hold grudges. Either way, they can capitalize on their computer access to cause you untold grief, stealing information or fouling up important files.

Insiders take billions

Banks have found their institutions particularly vulnerable to computer crime. Historically, for every Bonnie and Clyde, there have been dozens of innocent-looking clerks who quietly juggle the figures. They used to do it in a stack of large account books. The damage this old-timer could do was limited by the time it took to find and manually alter all the necessary figures.

Modern history has inserted the computer into this picture. Millions of dollars can be sucked up in a matter of minutes, and it can be hard to detect. For example, the *salami technique,* in which a criminal siphons odd fractions of interest payments into a personal account, is almost invisible because every customer gets a correct payment. It's proven popular among embezzlers, probably for that very reason.

Security managers who have encountered these techniques don't share the view that networked personal computers pose only a minor threat. They believe that as more people are given the means to commit fraud and other crimes, more will take advantage of the opportunities.

Crime of opportunity

The youths who have invaded government and business computers have hit their targets more or less by accident. Compared with their counterparts inside the organization, they work at a distinct disadvantage (Fig. 3.2):

- To the outsider, finding the password is a highly educated guess. The insider often knows the password.
- The outsider is on a fishing expedition. The insider has a good idea of what to look for and where to find it.
- The outsider has to probe for your weak spots. The insider already knows where they are.

In this light, some experts feel, the growing numbers of PCs hooked up to corporate networks don't really offer much danger that wasn't there in the first place. If yours is one of the many organizations moving from a large system to a client-server network, the effectiveness of your security program may depend on what kind of security you had going in.

In the view of Alvin Begun, a University of California systems analyst, "If you don't have adequate mainframe security, chances are you won't have it with personal computers either. On the other hand, if you do have adequate security safeguards in a timesharing environment, personal computers probably won't be able to crack them." By that reasoning, the personal computer

Insiders have an edge.

- They know the system
- They know what to look for
- They know your weak spots

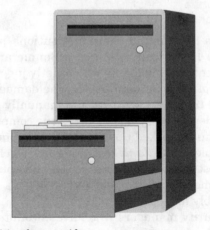

Figure 3.2 Insiders have many more opportunities than outsiders.

won't have much effect on either the motive or—under a good security system—the method and opportunity.

Managing the People Problem

Security has always been a people problem, and it always will be. This is an issue that technical-minded people often overlook, but if you do that, you're in trouble. Significantly, that people-first view comes from a sales executive who deals in technical security products. Many other security experts say the same.

The people problem presents two distinct challenges for managers of all functions:

- You must *manage the change* that inevitably comes about when you implement a security program.

- You must also try to *avoid discontent,* which can turn an otherwise loyal employee into an electronic saboteur.

Learning to manage change

When you implement security measures, you are asking employees to change the ways they previously had been doing their jobs. Wherever there is change, managing that change presents a separate issue on top of any others you may have.

One way to deal with change is through training and awareness programs. Explain why you are implementing a security program, and explain what you will expect of the employees. Security measures can make a job more difficult. Make sure the employee doing the job understands why the change is necessary.

You also will probably have to educate employees more fully on the accepted ethical standards of computer use. Bring employees up to date on their responsibilities. Help them understand why security is not a threat but a benefit. You can explain, for example, that the steps taken to prevent errors and unauthorized access will mean less chance of erroneous data they will have to correct later.

This training is a continuing process. Some organizations have gone through pretty elaborate security awareness programs. Then the subject is dropped. These companies forget that there's employee turnover, and new employees need to hear the same things other employees heard the previous year. Additionally, it's not a bad idea to reinforce your message and continually let employees know this wasn't just a hot issue that has waned in importance.

Setting an example

In addition to this assignment, you may find yourself with a larger organizational role, identified as the person who's going to coordinate a security program and get it all off the ground. In either role, there will be committee meetings and various requests that a manager identify his or her employees and the kinds of processing they're doing.

This may not be the way you wanted to do things, but it's up to you to set an example for other employees and departments. You must always be supportive and cooperative and set that example. You must do this even in times of great stress, and there will assuredly be times of great stress. If you succeed, other employees will learn to support the security program and cooperate in it. Your example is also important in client departments. The nontechnical manager needs to elicit staff cooperation and must set an example for department members. That assumes, of course, that people at some higher level of management are aware that security is an issue. If security is not an issue, then it's your responsibility to make it one. You don't necessarily have to solve every problem, but it's every employee's responsibility to recognize exposures and do what he or she can to address them.

Maintaining good human relations

Many forms of computer abuse are not hard to accomplish. Consider the hypothetical employee who gains computer competence and one day says, "Gee, I didn't realize I could do that." This employee is not necessarily someone with strong technical skills, just someone with basic personal computer skills who stumbles upon a way to defeat the system.

If this employee feels satisfied and loyal, he or she won't do anything with that newly discovered knowledge. The knowledge still may be tucked into the back of the employee's mind. Several months later, the same employee could develop a grievance. If the matter is not settled to the employee's satisfaction, the nest egg of computer knowledge may seem like a way to put things right. Security experts widely agree that this type of employee—not a mischief-minded student from outside—is by far your greatest security threat. Poor management at the basic human level creates the climate in which this threat will flourish.

Keeping the lines open

There are some things, of course, you should not tell your employees. Keep tight control over passwords, and don't discuss technical details that might help someone overcome the security system. Beyond that, however, most experts recommend that you be honest and open with your employees—about security and about everything else.

If you give as much loyalty as you expect, you can expect as much loyalty as you give. That alone could do more than any high-tech device to keep your computers secure.

Dealing With Resistance to Change

When you are implementing a new security program, particularly one that requires a change in habits and methods, you are bringing change to the organization. "Change is an unnatural act, particularly in successful companies; powerful forces are at work to avoid it at all costs." So said Michael Porter in a *Harvard Business Review* article.

Resistance to change has itself proven highly resistant to change. Some of this resistance comes from employees who feel comfortable with their old methods. They don't want to change, particularly if that change threatens their jobs. Sometimes their resistance takes the form of outright sabotage.

Some of the resistance will come from the IS staff. For people who work with advanced technology, some can be surprisingly resistant to new ideas. The stubborn old IS hand has become an industry stereotype. More typically, IS staff members are willing to accept change but have not been trained and prepared to deal with it. This problem can feed on itself since veteran programmers understandably dislike the idea of becoming novices again.

Where security is concerned, though, the main resistance will probably come from the client departments. Cheryl Currid, the consultant and columnist, describes "users who still lurk in the hallways of corporate America. They are technology-resistant, clutching yellow writing tablets, calculators, and calendars. Their old, tried-and-true methods still work, and they don't want anyone fixing them." Not only do these people resist change, they also seem to have a host of inventive ways to make things go wrong.

Training PC users

Overt resistance is only part of the problem. Passive resistance can be just as troublesome. PC operators regularly frustrate security professionals with their less-than-careful habits. In particular, those who have come to regard PCs as personal tools may not understand that in a networked environment, they may become responsible for corporate data that needs more protection.

Many security experts and PC managers say education is a critical part of their security policies. Training is a high priority, concentrating on such subjects as how to recognize hazards and observing security procedures. One bank's security training program includes sessions in such subjects as managing change.

The idea behind this: Installing a new network is a major change in the way an organization does business. A system is most vulnerable at times of change. It's a time when errors are frequent: A new program disk may contain a virus, or access controls may not yet be in place or may not work properly. The training is intended to help managers monitor and educate their employees more closely during this period.

Says one PC manager, "Users need to understand that even transferring a file from a floppy disk to their hard drive is a significant change in their system." That means there is a potential hazard they should learn to recognize.

Why people resist

Most often, resistance stems from fear. When people resist change, there's a good chance it's because they are afraid of what might happen to them. Other

Coping with resistance

- Tap employees' self-interest
  - "What's in it for me?"
- Build involvement
  - Form teams
  - Encourage participation

Figure 3.3   To overcome resistance, give employees a stake in the change.

employees are paralyzed by procedure. They match up lists by hand, rekey information from hard-copy reports, and keep documentation that no one ever reads. It's the "we've always done it this way" syndrome.

You can turn resistance in a more constructive direction (Fig. 3.3). Try to replace "what's going to happen to me?" with "what's in it for me?" Show reluctant employees how they can benefit from the changes in their way of working. Most employees want to be able to do their jobs better; only a cynical few do not. Show them how the new technology can improve their value to the organization. This is an opportunity for them to become more productive and better-appreciated employees.

One way to make this kind of demonstration is to create a *shining star* (Fig. 3.4). Work with a few sharp, willing people to create a model of success. Use it to show the more reluctant how much the new system can benefit them.

Create a shining star

- Build a model of success
- Use it as an example
  - Show reluctant employees what it can do for them

Figure 3.4   Work with a few good volunteers to create an example of success.

Dealing with the reluctant

New systems and methods are supposed to produce happy results. Too often, people react with fear, denial, and anger. They won't accept change just because it looks good to you. It must also look good to them.

> **Action item**   Look for ways to reach people in their WIIFMs: Answer the burning question, "What's in it for me?" The best way to do that is to show them. Use the shining-star approach to show reluctant employees exactly what is in it for them when they accept the coming changes.

Allow sufficient time

People accept change at varying rates. Based on these rates, you can classify them into several groups:

- *Experimenters.* You'll have a few of these, but probably only a few. These are the people who are willing to try anything new, just because it's new. They tend to be fickle, though, dropping yesterday's trend as soon as tomorrow's appears.

- *Early adopters.* They also are willing to try new ideas, but they aren't interested in newness just for its own sake. They want to see if the new methods can help them do something better.

- *Practical minded.* This is usually your largest group. Its members are willing to accept new ideas, but first they must be convinced the new ideas are really good ideas. They will accept new technology only when the early adopters have demonstrated that it truly is an improvement.

- *Late adopters.* They don't really want to change, but they'll grudgingly accept it if they must.

- *Resisters.* These are the people who actively dig in to fight off the new way of doing things. Sometimes, they disguise their opposition with rational-sounding, highly intellectual arguments.

Early adopters: the key

The key to a shining-star method is to identify the early adopters. The experimenters will identify themselves. If you aren't careful, they'll trample you in the rush to see what's new. The early adopters don't always make themselves obvious, and that can be the source of a serious mistake.

Consider this scenario: You announce plans to tighten security over the company's e-mail system. You emphasize a big benefit for employees: increased privacy for their electronic messages. The experimenters will quickly take up the cause. Their enthusiasm makes them look like prime candidates to become shining stars. You need go no further, you might think, than to use these bright, eager people to lead the way. You don't even bother to discuss your plans with anyone else in the department. But the enthusiasm, the shine and the light, soon burn out, and your champions are off to play with some other new toy.

In contrast, once a few early adopters get their teeth into the project, they will become its most substantial long-term boosters. They will put the new technology to work, test it, and suggest worthwhile improvements. The trick is to find them. There's no sure-fire method, but there is one technique that can be a big help. It comes from the example of a newspaper which upgraded its editorial computer system. Management needed someone to teach and sell the new system; the choice was a bright, eager young staff member who had expressed a strong, early interest in the new system.

This champion proved to be an experimenter, and soon his active imagination turned to something else. Meanwhile, a couple of other staff members got together one evening to express their mutual disappointment. They were both interested in computers, eager to learn the new system, and eager to put it to use. Both agreed they would enjoy helping other staff members get comfortable with it. But no one had come around even to talk about the new technology, much less to solicit their involvement.

These two were unseen early adopters. Both were quiet people, not prone to great bursts of enthusiasm. They could have been great assets to their organization, but no one else knew it.

The key to finding people like this is to keep on talking. Don't stop when you think you've found your shining star. You could be disappointed. Discuss the change with everyone in the department. You easily could find a couple of serious-minded early adopters in the group. As a bonus, you can help reduce resistance in another way: by helping everyone to feel actively involved.

Step by step

With a few early adopters on your side, you can create a shining star that will keep its luster. Then, you can approach your large group of cautious but practical-minded employees. Let the early adopters demonstrate the WIIFMs. Once they see there really is something in it for them, your pragmatists will come on board. So, perhaps, will some of the late adopters who, even reluctantly, will conclude that the change is a good idea.

At this stage, three of your four major groups are ready to accept the change and put it to work. That leaves only one other group: your most troublesome. These are the active resisters who have vowed not to change, regardless of the consequences.

You might have to resort to those consequences. Discipline and discharge are not pleasant subjects, but neither is active resistance to the organization's chosen course of action. Those who refuse to adapt may have to go elsewhere.

Charting Cultural Change

In addition to the practical challenges of implementing a better security system, you will also have to resolve several cultural, philosophical, and ethical issues. One of the biggest is to convince people that there is a security problem. One of the next biggest is to convince people that helping to overcome the security problem is their responsibility.

One reason: People often fail to see the security implications of their own work. A typical question: "What could I possibly do that would interest an industrial spy?"

You have to teach them how intelligence organizations work by putting together small pieces of seemingly insignificant information. They have to understand that simply what they're doing, and how they're doing it, could be of interest to the wrong people.

Educating PC users

The main reason personal computer users often seem so uninterested in security is that they don't see what is so important about the information with which they work. They don't see themselves, either, as points of entry to expanding corporate networks. You must educate these people in their responsibilities. Then, you must constantly reeducate them. Remind them of the potential liabilities of lax security. Help them see the implications should someone gain improper access to their seemingly insignificant data.

An example you can use: Someone gains access to a hospital's medical records and discovers that a celebrity patient suffers from AIDS. This could cause:

- Loss of privacy to the patient
- Loss of business for the hospital
- Greater income for lawyers handling all the liability suits that could result

Even when the impact would not be nearly as severe, a security slip could have serious results. Your entire organization could be at risk, and everyone should understand that.

Matters of ethics

You must also deal with ethical questions, particularly those concerning privacy. For example, you could install a monitoring system that charts every keystroke. You could use this knowledge to identify questionable use patterns, one of the best and earliest signs of a security problem. At the same time, you would give employees reason for some real concern about their privacy. Furthermore, you would play into the hands of the "stressmeister" who tries to manage infinitely small slices of time. Instead of judging a day's work, this character judges a second's. People like this use technology to support an ultra-short-term outlook, and they can do a lot of damage to both the organization and its people.

Longer-term judgments put less stress on employees. They usually are much more fair and realistic. Keep that in mind when you monitor any kind of employee activity. Looking at the big picture—traffic patterns, origins, and destinations, for example—is as effective as charting keystrokes. It's probably more so.

Fighting the Vengeful Ex-employee

Whatever else the economy has done in the last few years, it has created a lot of ex-employees. Retribution-minded former employees are among the most serious security threats. They know their way around your organization. And they are highly motivated to make use of that knowledge.

When someone's job disappears, the computer system can look like a very good place to get some revenge. The best way to prevent that problem is to prepare for it in the first place. This is particularly important when major staff reductions are being planned. A large new class of bitter ex-employees is about to be created. Your best chance of dealing with them is to be ready well in advance. Unfortunately, security people are often among the last to know.

Being prepared

That familiar saying "Be prepared" is particularly important in an era of both system and personnel downsizing. Stay alert for signs of trouble. When you see them, start preparing for the consequences. For example, viruses usually appear only occasionally and at random. An unusual number of virus attacks may be a sign of an unhappy employee. Alert management to the possibility. Then step up your antivirus screenings.

Preparation requires advanced knowledge. That isn't easy when a staff cutback is in the works. Management usually withholds the news until the last possible moment. Security people then must grapple with the resulting chaos. The chaos will be present whether or not you know it is coming, but at least you can be ready for it.

If you should see signs of a coming job loss, contact Human Resources quickly. Try to verify your information. Make it clear that a major staff reduction will involve security concerns for which you should prepare.

Treating workers with respect

There's one old management tradition that fortunately is disappearing. It is a tendency to treat employees with suspicion and resentment. Most employers these days are more willing to recognize employees as partners in the enterprise.

If there is a major layoff, it is particularly important to treat departing employees with respect. Make sure they understand that the layoff is a reflection of the company's problems. It does not reflect any shortcomings of theirs. Blame the economy. You're probably right, and pointing that out can deflect a lot of anger away from the company. More important, let the departed employees keep as much dignity as they can muster under the circumstances.

An outplacement program can also help maintain security. Providing counselors to help people find new jobs is an important sign of respect. It also helps create a positive atmosphere by concentrating the ex-employees' attention on the future and recovery. This is a valuable alternative to leaving people to dwell on the pain of the past.

Cutting off access

Fair treatment helps keep good employees from becoming something else, but it can't do everything. For some, even your best efforts cannot possibly be enough. In addition to the stereotype bad actor—a rare breed—there is the good employee who feels ill-rewarded. It can be particularly frustrating to know that you did a good job but you are still out of work. The employee who feels betrayed is a strong candidate to try to get revenge.

That's why it is important that you immediately cancel all forms of computer access departing employees have held. Employers often fail to do this, leaving an easy opening for the disgruntled. At the first possible moment:

- Cancel the employee's password and user ID.
- Remind the employee of any agreements that remain in effect about protecting proprietary information.
- Collect all company property that is in the employee's possession. Include keys, access cards, credentials, and manuals.

Try to keep a close watch on the ex-employee's friends and coworkers who are still on the job. They will sometimes act as inside confederates. They may even try on their own to avenge what they see as an injustice to a friend.

Selling Security to Management

Managers who work directly with the computer systems usually are well aware of their security needs. They have this in common with most computer criminals: They know the system and are its weak spots. The problem is to persuade senior managers who don't have this kind of first-hand knowledge. Security consciousness is a state of mind, and your task is to instill the right attitude among the people whose moral and financial support you need.

A sales campaign

The previous chapter dealt with preparing a proposed security plan for management. You can't just lay the plan on a conference table and expect it to sell itself. You must market security to a tough audience that wants to see results for its money (Fig. 3.5).

Your initial goal is to make management more security conscious. Plan your attack around these basic points:

- Emphasize the *degree of risk* the company faces from poor security.
- Present your case in terms of the kinds of *business risks* management already understands.

Selling to management

- Emphasize the risk
- Show the consequences
- Assign responsibility

Figure 3.5 Talk to management in its own language.

- Make the people who have *custody* of computerized information responsible for its security.
- Conduct a formal *risk analysis*.

The degree of risk

Business computers exist in a constantly changing environment, and these changes bring new security risks. Look at the things that probably have happened within your own organization:

- Increasing numbers of people have personal computers on their desks.
- More computing is done by end users and less by specialists in the data processing department.
- Networks and other forms of computer communication make your data more widely available to more people than ever before.
- Several applications may share a common database.
- Employees are becoming more at ease with the use of computers.

Your language

Your job is to point out these increasing risks to managers who may not yet fully understand the problem, even if they agree it is serious. Don't undermine your efforts to bring about this understanding by burying managers in computer jargon. Even those who do understand it may find the technical argument for security inadequate. State your case, then, in language they do understand and respect.

For example, instead of simply stating that inadequate security could invite data manipulation, emphasize the consequences of such an act:

- A *reduced bottom line* due to improperly used assets or misstated operating results
- Management decisions based on *incomplete or inaccurate information*
- Business operations *interrupted* by lost data or processing capacity
- *Confidential data* open to access by competitors, investors, or employees
- Possible *legal difficulties* involving privacy, corrupt practices, and other laws

Assigning responsibility

Make it clear to management that it is important not only to control access to the company's data but to make sure it remains accurate, complete, and reliable. The best people to handle this task are the individuals and groups that have direct custody of the data.

One reason management may hesitate to accept your security program is a doubt that it will be effective. In the view from the head office, the computer system may look like such a large, interconnected entity that it seems almost impossible to police its proper use. The answer to that concern is to cut the system down to size. Develop and propose a plan that makes individual custodians responsible for protecting the limited amounts of data that are under their control.

Each custodian should have the authority to read, alter, and use the data. Each also should have the power to insist that other users abide by necessary security controls. The custodians, of course, will be responsible for installing and maintaining these controls. If the proper means are not available, the custodian should have the authority to request the necessary financing or other support.

Analyzing the risk

Suppose an assessment of security risk reveals that PC users who have access to a network system have the ability to steal, modify, and destroy valuable information. Consequently, the analysis of this risk should assess the probability of the occurrence of such an event and the likely losses should it occur. The likely loss, weighted by the chance the event will occur, then can be compared with the cost of effective security measures in a basic cost-benefit analysis.

A risk assessment will make such an analysis for every possible risk. The completed assessment should present a detailed picture of the risks you face and the measures that can deal with them effectively. These are the black-and-white figures any manager can understand.

Management's support

You can't mount an effective security program unless you have top management behind you, with financial support, moral support, and any other kind of support you need. Unless you are fortunate, though, the executive suite could easily be a pocket of ignorance where data security is concerned. It's not that they're deliberately ignorant. Instead, they're waiting for you to demonstrate the need for security in the hard numbers that are an executive's universal language.

4

Assessing Your Risks

Don't rely on publicity or other people's experiences to determine your security needs. The right security plan for you starts with assessing your own risks.

On one hand, the dangers from hackers and viruses have been greatly overstated. On the other, some other threats to your system have been greatly understated. You can't effectively act against any kinds of threats until you know what they are. That's the purpose of a risk assessment.

A good risk assessment can give you a sense of balance between overreacting to highly publicized threats and underreacting to those that are less well known. To accurately assess your risks, you must consider four major elements:

- Who might be trying to enter or damage your network
- What they are looking for
- Where they might find it
- What you can do to keep them from getting it

Risk assessment can be a highly formalized process, but it basically works like this: Put yourself in the place of the person who threatens your system. Try to imagine what he or she might try and what you can do about it.

You've probably already figured out that security has its costs. The cost only starts with the direct expenses of staff, equipment, and training. It also includes things like lost productivity and hard-to-use systems. You can't secure everything. The main purpose of a risk assessment is to help you identify the points at which the danger is greatest and the security investment most likely to produce results.

Five types of computer criminals

- Amateur
- Apprentice
- Visitor
- Advanced amateur
- Professional

Each can come from either inside or outside the organization.

Figure 4.1 It's not the amateurs but the professionals who can cause the greatest loss.

The Many Faces of Intruders

There are five types of computer intruders:

- The amateur
- The apprentice
- The visitor
- The advanced amateur
- The professional

Each has different levels of skill, and each has his or her own objectives. Furthermore, any of these five types can come from inside or outside your organization (Fig. 4.1).

Inside or outside

Insiders are by far your greatest security threats. The definition of an insider, though, can sometimes be a little uncertain. For example, members of a department may think of each other as insiders, but people who work in a different department in the organization may see them as outsiders. For security purposes, an insider is someone who is familiar with the organization's workings, has friends inside the group, and has access to systems and resources. Someone who has any or all of these traits is a much greater security threat than someone who has none of them.

To make the insider more dangerous, he or she is harder to identify than an outsider. You often can spot an outsider when he or she tries to cross a barrier between the organization and the outside world. The insider has no such barrier to cross.

Guarding against the novice

The novice is usually a lone beginner. This person probably doesn't have much experience with computers, much less any detailed knowledge of how to crack them from outside. The novice works alone and has little or no contact with others of the kind.

The typical novice invader is an insider who mounts a clumsy attack on a system he or she uses. It's not hard to detect the activity, but it can be hard to identify the novice as a threat. The legitimate beginning user has just about the same habit pattern. For example, it's easy to write a program that sends a system into an endless loop. When it happens, it's hard to tell whether the author was malicious or just ignorant.

Novices are usually just experimenters who rarely commit crimes. That and their lack of sophistication usually make them easy to deter. You can also find novices' work in a few familiar locations:

- Password files
- User configuration files
- System configuration files

In these places, the novices will usually leave clear trails of evidence. They will leave copies of their files in the invaded directories or will brag too much on bulletin boards. Sometimes they will encrypt records of their activities using easy-to-use but weak encryption tools.

The first and best way to guard against novice invasions is user education. Novices can take advantage of lapses in password administration; about 80 percent of all entries happen this way. Keep after password holders to choose and protect their passwords properly.

Serving an apprenticeship

Those invaders who progress beyond the early phases usually do it by way of bulletin boards. They start exchanging messages with others of their kind. Not only does this expand their knowledge, but they become part of a network. Its more advanced members are eager to pass on their knowledge to the beginners, who now begin to service an apprenticeship.

One of the big differences between beginners and apprentices is that apprentices know how to cover their tracks better. They learn how to get in and out of a system without attracting attention. They may not know how a security system works, but they have learned how to get around it quietly.

A common mode of attack by an apprentice is to invade password files to find valid log-on schemes. The administrator of one system admits that he foolishly included live passwords in messages sent to the password holders. Someone found the way into those message files and found a lode of valid passwords.

This invader was readily caught. Administrators of an invaded system watched his activity and traced his telephone calls. The young apprentice said he had found an initial password to the system on a bulletin board. Using it, he gained access to the system. Then, he followed a mentor's instructions on how to download the entire password file.

Apprentices often invade password systems, and they know something about other security measures as well. That means they are harder to catch than amateurs. Passwords are still the key to their access, though, so user education and careful password administration is still the best protection.

Just visiting

The visitor is probably the most benign form of invader—if there is such a thing. These trespassers usually just want to look around. They seldom try to compromise your system unless an obvious opportunity presents itself. This is also one of the easiest forms of invasion to deter. If a visitor encounters any kind of obstacle, he or she will probably back off and look for easier access in someone else's system. The only exception—and it's rare—is when the visitor finds something particularly interesting and is willing to expend some extra effort to get a look at it.

You can tell you've been visited when you see signs of improper access, but there is no serious loss and the most basic security measures appear to have been effective. Your main objective should be to discourage casual snooping. Erect barriers at the main points of entry, and add extra protection to your most sensitive resources.

The semi pro

Unlike the curious visitor, the serious crackers are capable, hard to detect, and often intent on doing some real damage. For many in this class, the goal is to see how much harm they can do.

A cracker is usually proficient at capitalizing on operating system bugs to gain access. This person will not bother to try to compromise your password file. He'll just find a way around it. Once inside, though, one of his first activities may be to extract some valid passwords—not a difficult task for an expert.

If you are worried about this type of invasion—and if your system contains anything at all of value, you should be—it's time to look for the strongest, most effective forms of security you can devise. Tighten up password management, and make sure users change them frequently—once a month is not too often. Consider password-checking software that periodically asks anyone logged onto the system to reenter his or her password.

There's also much to be said for a Chinese wall type of defense. Set it up to filter out all network connections that have not passed rigorous access-control tests. Set up a logging system outside the wall to monitor unsuccessful as well as successful tests to get past it.

The professional

You might think there could be nothing worse than an amateur who gets into your system intent on causing damage, but there is: the well-trained, professional computer spy. These professionals are very good at entering your system and are just as good at getting out again without your knowledge. They can alter and evade logging systems just as easily as they can compromise any other part of the system. They have access to technology that can easily defeat even such telephone security devices as call-back modems.

Once inside the system, the pros have specific objectives. They want to obtain a certain kind of information or compromise a particular person or activity. They don't explore. They go straight to the target, and straight back out, in a minimum amount of time.

The best defense against someone this skilled is literally to pull the plug. If you are really serious about preventing this kind of invasion, you will not leave networks with sensitive data connected in any way to the telephone system. Be just as strict in controlling physical access. Encrypt every message that travels across the network.

Check out the people, too. Anyone who might gain access to hardware, software, or information should be thoroughly cleared.

Another analysis

There's more than one way to group computer criminals. Another source classified them this way:

- People who have physical access to the system and the ability to perform physical acts of theft or damage
- People who have access to and know how to operate the system
- Programmers and other computer professionals who have access to the system
- People who have access and also have computer engineering knowledge

There is an obvious common denominator: access to the system. It stands to reason that even the most talented computer criminal needs access of some kind to your computer. Except for physical access, that access need not be direct. Unprotected telephone lines make up the interstate highway system of computer abuse.

> **Action item**   Start the job of identifying potential abusers by identifying those who have access to the computer. Among those who have access, you then can look for those who have the ability to make improper use of the computer once they get into it.

Occupational hazards

Because the potential for computer abuse depends on access and knowledge, it naturally varies among occupations. Table 4.1 lists several computer-related occupations according to the levels of risk they present. This list clearly reflects a mainframe environment; in a PC network there are fewer distinctions between IS and "user" specialties, and the only truly low-risk occupa-

TABLE 4.1   Occupations and Their Risk Levels

Level of risk	Occupation
Greatest	EDP auditor
	Security officer
Great	Computer operator
	Data entry and update clerk
	Operations manager
	Systems programmer
Moderate	System engineer
	Programming manager
Limited	Application programmer
	Communication engineer-operator
	Database administrator
	Facilities engineer
	Peripheral equipment operator
	Tape librarian
	User programmer
	User transaction and data entry operator
Low	Terminal engineer
	User tape librarian

tions are those that have no access at all to a computer. On the other hand, application and departmental programmers are assigned relatively low scores in relation to their ability because it's assumed normal security precautions would control their access to the system.

One thing this analysis does not consider, though, is a combination of skills. An individual who has more than one type of ability has more than one way to damage your system. The same is true when two or more individuals with differing skills get together to attack your system.

Studies of computer crime indicate the typical computer criminal may also have characteristics like these:

- Computer criminals tend to be young. In one study of a group of computer abusers, the ages ranged from 18 to 46 with a median of 25. It's not quite clear why. The sponsors of this study suggest it's because the younger employees are recent graduates of colleges and universities where "attacking campus computer systems is not only condoned but often encouraged." That may be an example of world-class conclusion jumping. More plausible: The younger workers have not yet acquired fully developed senses of professional responsibility. This suggests that an effort on your part to help newcomers develop such an attitude could pay off in better security.

- Computer criminals are among your best and brightest employees. These highly motivated people often find themselves overqualified for the routine type of work they often are called upon to do. This may help explain the rate of abuse among young workers since they often bring great expectations to entry-level jobs. Maintaining a good level of motivation and professional challenge, then, can also help avoid security problems.

TABLE 4.2   **Relationships Between Occupations and Victims**

Occupations	Victims
Teller	Large bank
Accountant	Computer service
Company owner	Small manufacturing company
Timesharing user	Timesharing system
Business programmer	Small bank
Systems programmer	State government agency
Computer operation and systems manager	Financial institutions
President of a firm	Electronics supply company
Business manager	Large manufacturer
Sales manager	Large retail service organization

- Computer criminals often are in positions of trust. Most computer criminals do their damage during their normal working routines, using systems with which they are intimately familiar. Your security plan should closely monitor the activities of these people through close supervision and effective auditing.

- Computer criminals often have help. In about half of all computer crime cases, the criminal has had to conspire with some other party. Sometimes the crime requires more skill and access than any individual holds. Other cases have involved an employee working on the "inside" in partnership with an outside party.

Table 4.2 lists the criminals and their victims in several typical computer abuse cases.

Attitude problems

Computer abusers also have certain attitudes in common. One problem, for example, stems from a psychological condition called *differential association*. This is the willingness to accept small deviations from normally accepted standards. These small variations can be harmless by themselves, but they can escalate into major crimes. For example, one organization was victimized by programmers from a competing firm who started by playing games on the bureau's computer, moved up to checking the bureau's customer lists, and eventually stole a complete program.

Then there's the *Robin Hood syndrome*. Among computer criminals interviewed by researchers, most expressed the moral view that it is wrong to harm an individual but all right to victimize a large organization. One early embezzler, for example, was careful never to take more from any one account than federal deposit insurance would cover.

Game playing is another common characteristic. Many computer abusers are attracted by the challenge of trying to beat your security system. They also tend to believe that there's nothing wrong with using an idle computer for nonofficial purposes. Taken to an extreme, this idea leads to an elitist syndrome: The criminals believe their expertise uniquely entitles them to play with the computer.

Who's mad over what?

It often takes two people to commit a computer crime, but the two don't have to work closely together. Investigators have found that there are some classes of people who make unlikely collaborators because they do not work well together. Resentment can easily lead to retaliation. Table 4.3 lists some of the grievances people in occupations listed across the top have against people in occupations listed down the side. It's hardly a mutual admiration society. These problems could erupt into computerized retaliation. If you consider the table for a while, you also should be able to see areas where people in some specialties depend on those in other jobs—prime candidates for collaboration in computer crime.

One word of caution: The fact that one or more people have the characteristics listed in this section does not mean they should be regarded as prime suspects in a computer crime case. Use these factors instead as points to consider in your analysis and in the resulting security plan. These are the points where human characteristics make you vulnerable and where you should consider controls to reduce your weaknesses.

Types of Computer Crime

Computer criminals have proved remarkably inventive over the years, but most of their crimes fall into well-identified patterns. You can best protect yourself if you know what you're fighting.

One reason your system has so many apparent weak spots is that computer criminals have developed a wide variety of ways to find and exploit them. A computer criminal need not enter your system or manipulate your data in order to steal from it. Some of the most successful simply sit on the outside looking in.

Scavenging

This was exactly the technique applied by one customer of a Texas timesharing service used by several oil companies. The customer would request that, when its jobs were run, the data would be recorded on a temporary storage tape. An operator began to notice, though, through signal lights on the console, that the customer would "read" the storage tape before any new data were entered on it. The suspicious operator reported the discovery, and an investigation found the customer was scavenging information its competitors had recorded earlier on the same tape.

Unlike some kinds of computer crime, scavenging often doesn't require spe-

TABLE 4.3 Potential Causes of Conflict

	Operators	Programmers	Media librarians	Data entry clerks	Source data preparers	Users	Vendors
Operators	...	Job failures; failure to report errors	Unrecorded removals and submissions	...	...	Job failures; failure to report errors	Misuse of equipment; failure to report errors
Programmers	Poor program design; misleading or missing instructions	...	Misleading or absent instructions	Poor input formats; poor instructions	Poor input formats; poor instructions	Lack of problem understanding; poor documentation	Programs; improper use of media
Media librarians	Slow or incorrect media selection	Loss of media; incorrect labeling	...	...	...	Loss of media	Poor handling of media
Data entry clerks	Data errors	Data errors not anticipated in program design; program entry errors	Loss of media	...	...	Data entry errors cause erroneous output	Misuse of equipment
Source data preparers	Data errors	Data errors and out-of-range data	...	Poor legibility on data entry forms	Poor instructions; inconvenient work schedule demands	Data errors	
Users	Inconvenient run schedule demands; poor job instructions	Unclear or missing problem specifications; inconvenient change demands; equipment failures	Missing or unclear instructions	Inconvenient work schedule demands			
Vendors	Inconvenient maintenance schedules; equipment failures	Equipment failures	...	Inconvenient equipment maintenance schedule; equipment failures			

TABLE 4.4   Detecting Scavenging Crimes

Potential offenders	Detection method	Evidence
System users	Trace discovered proprietary information to its source.	Output media
Others with computer access	Test the operating system for residual data after executing a job.	Similar information produced in unusual ways on the same form

cialized knowledge. A pair of Florida newspaper reporters, checking the opportunities for computer crime, found critical information on printouts in a trash can. In Wisconsin, another reporting team found the password for a state government computer system posted on a bulletin board. Notes and printouts can help a scavenger, who need not even enter your system to take advantage of it.

You can also use the paper trail in reverse. Should you believe confidential information has been taken from your system, you can try to trace the problem to its source. In one such case, the suspect information was itself found on a printout. From numbers on the paper an FBI agent was able to trace it, first, to the company that had made it and, then, to the computer center where it had been used. From there, the numbers led directly to the particular job and programmer involved. Table 4.4 illustrates some more ordinary defenses.

Leakage

Here we have the kind of intelligence gathering practiced by the James Bonds of society. It makes use of subtle clues and bits of information absorbed from a surveillance of computer operations. Picking up stray signals from network cables and nodes is a high-tech version of this crime. Other inventive criminals have devised techniques like these:

- Someone rigged a report that contained large blocks of numbers so the sensitive information was slipped into the blocks.

- Someone else manipulated a printout so lines of a certain length contained sensitive information.

- Yet another leak absorber figured out how to read the back-and-forth swings of a mainframe tape drive.

- Someone else recorded a printer at work, then played it back at a slow speed.

Most of the other forms of computer crime, particularly scavenging, logic bombs, and Trojan horses, can be sources of data leaks. Keeping records of computer use and maintaining backup versions of older data can help you trace the source of leaked material. Also on your side: In many of the leakage

TABLE 4.5   Detecting Crimes From Data Leakage

Potential offenders	Detection methods	Evidence
Programmers	Discovery of stolen information	Storage media
Employees	Tracking storage media back to the computer facility	Output forms
Former employees		Type fonts
Contract workers		
Vendor employees		Evidence of scavenging scavenging or a Trojan horse attack

methods, the thief must be physically present to record the leaked data. Table 4.5 summarizes how to detect data leakage crimes.

Piggybacking and impersonation

This is another type of crime that doesn't necessarily require an expert. It involves getting past your security system—either physically or electronically—by using a legitimate user's authorization.

It can be as simple as this: One of your operators arrives at a security entrance to find a frustrated-looking person standing there with arms full of tapes, printouts, or other official-looking material and in need of assistance to open the door. The unthinking employee agrees to help, and the impostor slips into the computer room.

Good security education is the main safeguard against this kind of invasion. Employees should be warned not to let people they don't know or who don't carry clear authorization into a secured area. Posting guards at these entrances might help. Some companies have installed turnstile entrances that let only one person through at a time.

Piggybackers usually are more inventive than expert. One young impostor posed as a magazine writer and was given a full public relations-style tour of a telephone company's computer facilities. He learned enough about the security system to steal more than $1 million worth of equipment.

A more sophisticated form of piggybacking is the use of a second terminal to impersonate the terminal of an authorized user. This is most useful in systems that depend on automatic verification of the user's identity. The thief will hook another terminal into the same line as the authorized user's. Waiting until the user is away, the thief will use the added terminal to enter the system. When the terminals are hooked up in this fashion, the automatic verification system can't distinguish between the real terminal and an impostor's.

Then there's the impostor who pulled off an electronic version of the old "bank examiner" scam. He used this method to take thousands of dollars through automated bank teller machines.

ATMs normally use customer identification cards with coded magnetic

TABLE 4.6 Detecting Impersonation Acts

Potential offenders	Detection methods	Evidence
Employees	Access observations	Logs, journals, and equipment-use meters
Former employees	Interviewing witnesses	
Vendor employees		
Contractors	Examining journals and logs	Other physical evidence
Outsiders	Programs to analyze the characteristics of online access	

stripes. The customer inserts the card and then enters a personal identification code. The machine will respond only if the personal code identifies the authorized user of the card.

The thief would steal the access cards, then phone the customers, pretending to be a bank security official. He had found the customer's card, but he also wanted to catch the thief. For this he needed the customer's personal identification code. Gullible customers would give out the numbers—and later would find large sums missing from their accounts.

Yet another version is to learn the system by which passwords and access codes are determined. If your code depends on some physical characteristic of the authorized user or is based on something only the right people are supposed to know, unauthorized users easily can learn and imitate these characteristics.

A detailed log is one of your best protections against impersonators. You can automatically record access attempts, and a guard can log physical comings and goings. The log can tell you who may have had access to the computer and at what times. If there is a pattern of unauthorized access, it usually will show up in the log. Table 4.6 summarizes how to detect impersonation acts.

Wiretapping

With all kinds of network cabling strewn about the modern enterprise, wiretapping would seem to be a major security threat. No threat is minor, but the danger of wiretapping may not be as great as it would seem. SRI International suggests that wiretapping is limited because it requires that the thief make a major capital investment. Other forms of entry are much easier and cheaper.

Still, the rapid spread of networking can leave you increasingly vulnerable. Industrial espionage professionals might be willing to go to the expense. In addition, intercepting electronic signals from computer equipment can be a form of wiretapping without the wire.

The best defense is to encrypt your data before you transmit it. Table 4.7 summarizes ways to detect wiretapping in your system.

TABLE 4.7   Detecting Wiretapping

Potential offenders	Detection methods	Evidence
Communication technicians and engineers	Voice wiretapping methods	Voice wiretapping evidence
Communication employees		

Data diddling

Another class of criminal works by getting inside your system and manipulating data for fun or profit. Some forms of data manipulation can be among the simplest, safest, and most common ways to commit a crime by computer.

An example: A time clerk was responsible for filling out the work-hours records of about 300 railroad employees. He noticed that each data entry included both the employee's name and number, but when the computer processed the payroll, it referred only to the number. In a typical database management application, the program used the number as a key. It used the number to look up the employee's name, address, and other information. Meanwhile, office employees hardly ever used the numbers in their noncomputerized work. All the manual processing of payroll records was done by name.

It would be gratifying to report that this employee notified the railroad of an opportunity for fraud in the payroll system, but he didn't. Instead, he took advantage of the system to give himself some "overtime." He would prepare overtime entries for the computer, using the names of employees who frequently worked extra hours, but putting his own employee number on the form. The computer then would issue him a check for the extra time. It was several years before an auditor thought to ask about the unusually high figures on the clerk's W-2 forms.

Here was a crime that cost the company thousands of dollars, committed by a clerk who actually had little inside knowledge of the computer. He just took advantage of a loophole in the administrative system.

One way to avoid this problem is to replace the numerical keys with entries that combine the names and numbers—perhaps adding the first three letters of the employee's name to the existing numbers. Other defensive techniques can include:

- Comparing the totals of newly entered items with the proper figures for those items.

- Using check digits embedded in other numbers. There are several ways to do this. One of the simplest would be to add the digits in an employee's number and add the last number of the sum. For example, employee number 123456 adds up to 21. Put it into the computer as 1234561.

- Programming the computer to kick back entries that are outside a speci-

TABLE 4.8 Detecting Data Diddling

Potential offenders	Detection methods	Evidence
Transaction participants	Data comparison	Data documents reflecting source data and transactions
Data preparers	Document validation	
Source data suppliers	Manual controls	Disks, tapes, and other media
Nonparticipants with access	Validation and verification with exception reporting	
	Reports analysis	Manuals, logs, journals, and exception reports
	Computer output	Incorrect output
	Integrity tests	

fied range. You could ask it to reject a date that is not a payday, for example, or a figure that is well above the employee's normal pay. The questioned amount may indicate fraud. It also may come legitimately from unusual amounts of overtime. In either case, the computer would let you check to find out.

- Comparing the data in the computer with its source material or with a separate entry of the same data used as a control.

Table 4.8 summarizes this activity and the defenses you can use.

The salami technique

This practice gets its name because the criminal takes only a thin slice at a time from any one source. The key is to take too little to be missed from any one source but to carve those small slices from a lot of sources. In a bank, for example, the criminal might deduct 10 or 15 cents from each of 100 accounts. No alarms are set off within the system because no one element suffers a significant loss. What's more, if the money is transferred to the thief's own account within the system, there is no large withdrawal to be accounted for. When the thief removes the accumulated money from this account, it all seems quite legitimate. The assets could be small items from an inventory instead of pennies from a bank account.

A variation on this technique is called the *round-down system*. To use this method, the thief must have access to a computer system in which large numbers of financial accounts are processed. The process also must involve multiplication, as it does when interest payments are calculated. Another requirement is that the resulting figures be expressed in fractions of less than 1 cent and use a "running remainder." SRI offers the following example.

A savings account in a bank may have a balance of \$15.86. Applying the 2.6 percent interest results in adding \$0.41236 (15.86×0.026) to the balance, for a new balance of \$16.27236. However, because the balance is to be retained only to the nearest cent, it is rounded down to $16.27, leaving $0.00236. What is to be done with this remainder? The interest calculation for the next account in the program sequence might be: $425.34 × 0.026 = $11.05884. This would result in a new balance of $436.39884 that must be rounded up to $436.40, leaving a deficit or negative remainder of $0.00116.

The net effect of rounding in both these accounts, rounding down to the calculated cent in the first and adding 1 cent in the second, leaves both accounts accurate to the nearest cent and a remainder of $0.0012 ($0.00236 − $0.00116). This remainder is then carried to the next account calculation, and so on. As the calculations continue, if the running remainder goes above 1 cent, positive or negative, the last account is adjusted to return the remainder to an amount less than 1 cent. This results in a few accounts receiving 1 cent more or less than the correct rounded values, but the totals for all accounts remain in balance.

This is where the creative programmer can engage in some treachery to accumulate a large stack of small change, yet still show a balanced set of books to the auditor. He merely changes the rules slightly. Instead of assigning an accumulated penny to the next account in line, he can slip it into his own account.

Its almost impossible to detect this practice except by a close check of the culprit's personal account, and many are careful not to maintain these accounts under their real names. Among the ways to watch for this technique:

- Be alert to sudden changes in an employee's financial habits.
- Monitor work habits, too, because this technique requires a great deal of maintenance time.
- Keep employee accounts under strict scrutiny, particularly if the employees have the skill and access to employ this scheme.

This scheme requires a combination of favorable conditions, including the right kind of access and knowledge and particular types of customer and employee accounts. Try to remove at least one of these conditions; more if you can. Ask your auditors about any doubts you might have. Even when they can't find hard proof, they can point in the right direction. Table 4.9 summarizes the detection of salami techniques.

TABLE 4.9 Detecting Salami Techniques

Potential offenders	Detection methods	Evidence
Financial system programmers	Detailed data analysis	Many small financial losses
Employees	Program comparison	Unsupported account buildups
Former employees		
Contract programmers	Transaction audits	
Vendor employees	Observing suspects' financial habits	Changed or unusual financial practices

The superzap

This technique applies a legitimate tool in an illegitimate way. In fact, it takes its name from a utility program used in IBM mainframes.

In any protected computer system, you'll occasionally need something that will override the built-in security measures—SRI calls it a "break glass in case of emergency" or "master key" procedure. The computer may stop, malfunction, or need attention that your normal procedures and access methods don't allow. You sometimes need a universal access program to bypass the security system and get at the heart of the problem.

A program such as this is a necessary tool but a dangerous one. Its use should be restricted to systems programmers and maintenance people who absolutely must have it. However, many companies store copies of the program in libraries where they are open to anyone who knows where they are and how to use them.

In one case, the managers of a New Jersey bank discovered that the system they normally used to correct errors in account balances wasn't working properly. This system had been overlooked during an equipment changeover, and it had become obsolete and prone to errors. As a result, the computer operations manager began using a superzap program to override the faulty system and make the corrections.

In the process, the manager discovered how easy it was to make changes in the system, without the usual controls and audit records. He put this knowledge to work, switching money into the accounts of three friends. Unlike clever users of the salami technique, the manager took enough from one customer's account that the customer noticed the shortage. A quick response by bank officials led them to the manager and his friends.

That's about the only way you'll discover a fraud of this kind. An experienced programmer with the means to override most security controls can make changes that won't be detected in the normal course of operations. Most application programs aren't written to detect the kind of changes such a person would make. The only person likely to notice a problem is a user like the bank customer who is able to compare the current data with past reports. Even then, it's easy to conclude that the discrepancy was a data entry error.

One way to protect yourself is to maintain "father" and "grandfather" copies of each file that is processed with the operating program. You then can check the new version against the previous ones for any differences that shouldn't be there.

Also, maintain records of who uses the computer and when. If there is a discrepancy, check the use records, particularly for the times just before and after the application program is run. That's the most likely time for a superzap. Table 4.10 is a guide to dealing with superzapping crimes.

Asynchronous attacks

Of necessity, a host or server must be prepared to handle several jobs at one time. To keep one user's data from mixing with another's, these systems are

TABLE 4.10   Dealing with Superzapping Crimes

Potential offenders	Detection methods	Evidence
Programmers with access to superzap programs, and the means to use them	Comparing files with historical copies	Discrepancies in output reports
Computer operation staff members with applications knowledge	Discrepancies noted by recipients of output reports	Undocumented transactions
	Examining computer-use journals	Computer-use or file request journals

designed to handle one request at a time. The asynchronous attacker overrides the separation mechanism to gain access to someone else's operation.

In one simple example, many long programs have periodic checkpoints at which a user can stop and resume work later. These checkpoints require that the program store its data and flag the point at which to resume. An attacker can make use of this stored data to enter the system and cross over into another application.

Most crimes of this type are much more complex. That helps, at least, to narrow down the list of people who can commit them. The main method of detection is to check out any unexpected deviations from the expected output. Table 4.11 summarizes the detection of these attacks.

TABLE 4.11   Detecting Asynchronous Attacks

Potential offenders	Detection methods	Evidence
Sophisticated system programmers	System testing of suspected attack methods	Output that varies from normal expectations
Advanced computer operators	Repeat execution of a job under normal and safe circumstances	Logs that reflect characteristics of computer operation

Simulation and modeling

Acts in this category almost seem like television drama: A master criminal sets up an electronic simulation of a real program, then substitutes his or her version for the real thing.

It's been done in real life. An accountant set up a duplicate of his company's accounting and general ledger system on his own computer. He would use this computerized clone to enter various kinds of data to examine the "what-if" effects of his embezzlement activities. By running his own system in reverse, he was able to determine the changes he must make to the real books to cover up his acts.

In another case, an insurance company used a spreadsheet type of model to determine the effects of various levels of sales. Someone used the system to create 64,000 fake policies and introduce them into the company's working system.

This kind of activity requires someone with a knowledge of simulation and modeling techniques, but this person is not necessarily the criminal. SRI reports several cases in which programmers were led into these schemes with no idea that their work was being used illegally.

A better clue might be the large amount of time a scheme like this requires. Again, logs of computer use can be valuable. Also check the customer logs of available online services and look into suspects' recent business dealings. You are still vulnerable, though, to modeling techniques done at home on personal computers. Table 4.12 illustrates the detection of simulation and modeling techniques.

TABLE 4.12   Detecting Simulation and Modeling

Potential offenders	Detection methods	Evidence
Application programmers	Investigate suspects' computer use	Programs and documentation
Simulation and modeling experts		Input and reports
Managers in position to engage in large, complex embezzlements		Use logs and journals

The Trojan horse

Some criminals enter your system to steal. Others are there to cause damage, sometimes just to prove they can do it. Techniques like the Trojan horse can be used for theft as well, but usually they are like viruses: tools of damage and destruction.

The Trojan horse is an ancestor of the virus and is often mistaken for one. The two do have much in common, including the fact that both are sneaky. This invader slips instructions into an operating program so the computer will appear to be running properly, even while it plants—and reaps—the seeds of its own destruction. A clever programmer can easily hide instructions like these in the thousands of lines that make up a major program. Even if you find them, you still won't know who put them there.

There still are some ways, though, to combat this technique. Keep a backup copy of the original program listing. If you suspect you've been the victim of a Trojan horse, compare the backup with the version now running in the computer. This could be a time-consuming process that requires expert help. It's also important that you keep the backup copy up to date with any changes you make in the working program.

If your search turns up a Trojan horse, you may not know who is responsible, but your search for a culprit has been narrowed. Your suspect is someone who is expert enough to have altered the program and has had the necessary access.

Another test is to run the same data through another version of the pro-

TABLE 4.13   How to Corral the Trojan Horse

Potential offenders	Detection methods	Evidence
Programmers who have knowledge of, and access to, the suspected part of the program	Compare program code.	Unexpected results of program execution
Employees	Test the suspect program.	Foreign code in the suspect program
Contract workers		
Vendor employees		
	Trace the possible gain from the act.	

gram and compare the results. This will work best if you have some initial idea of the kinds of manipulation for which you are looking. Although a difference in the data can indicate that you have a Trojan somewhere, you still must locate both the alterations and the responsible party. Table 4.13 outlines the detection of Trojan horse crimes.

Trapdoors

A large program will often have built-in breaks, where you can check the output at intermediate stages of the operation. These trapdoors were intended as debugging tools, but they are open to misuse. The Internet virus was placed through just such an unprotected trapdoor.

A thief could use such an opening to insert a routine that could override normal security controls, in much the same manner as superzapping. Because trapdoors are mainly intended for use during program development, most are removed before the application goes into regular service. Some are left in, though, for the sake of later program maintenance. A thief might already be involved at this stage, leaving places in the program for later entry and manipulation.

There also are times that poor program logic leaves an inadvertent trapdoor. Or the computer's circuits may provide an unseen opportunity. An undocumented combination of commands could allow the system to be compromised.

That's exactly how one programmer made use of a trapdoor. The trapdoor allowed the programmer to transfer control of the program into a region normally used to store data. This meant the computer would respond to instructions formed by the data that was entered. All the programmer had to do was to enter a string of data that was translated into program commands.

In another incident, several automotive engineers in Detroit discovered a trapdoor in a system in Florida. Through it, they managed to find the password assigned to the president of the Florida company. With this they obtained free use of several programs that were supposed to have been protected as trade secrets.

TABLE 4.14 Detecting Trapdoor Crimes

Potential offenders	Detection methods	Evidence
Systems programmers	Exhaustive testing.	Output reports that indicate a departure from specifications
Advanced application programmers	Compare specifications with performance.	
	Conduct specific tests as indicated by the evidence.	

Both of these violations were discovered purely by accident, and no one knows how many other users might have taken advantage of the openings. There is no direct technical way to discover a trapdoor, and only expert programmers can find one at all.

The best way to guard against trapdoors is to try to prevent them. Monitor your program listings, and have them checked by outside experts, to make sure there are no remaining traps. Then proceed on the assumption that you have found and closed all but one. Table 4.14 summarizes the detection of trapdoor crimes.

Logic bombs

A logic bomb is the offspring of a Trojan horse by way of a Hollywood screenplay. Most viruses set off logic bombs when they are activated.

In one case, the instructions were secretly inserted into an operating system: At 3 p.m. on a designated date, all 300 terminals on the network would display the culprit's confession of a crime. The program then would crash. The perpetrator arranged, of course, to be many miles away at that date and hour.

In another case, a programmer arranged for automatic retaliation should he ever lose his job. If his name was removed from the payroll, everyone else's name would be removed from the payroll, too.

Because a logic bomb is closely related to viruses and Trojan horses, your lines of defense are much the same. Most worms and viruses also use both Trojans and logic bombs. That means Table 4.13 applies to logic bombs as well as Trojan horses.

Of course, there's one sure way to detect a logic bomb: when it goes off, you'll almost surely know it.

Where Are Your Weak Spots?

Along with knowing who might attack your system, you should also determine where they are most likely to strike. The two are closely related, of course. The nature of the criminal often determines the nature of the crime. You will often find, though, that your weak spots fall into one of two distinct groups:

- Weakness in *system functions*
- Weaknesses in controlling *physical access*

Functional weaknesses

An analysis of computer abuse cases for the Justice Department produced a list of eight functions where data processing systems tend to be most vulnerable. They are:

- Poor controls over data handling
- Weak physical controls—sometimes none at all
- Inadequate procedural controls
- Weak ethical standards
- Poor programming practices
- Operating system weaknesses
- Lack of user identification
- Inadequate control over storage media

To this list, you could easily add a ninth item:

- Inadequate controls over people

As nearly everyone knows by now, the computer revolution has failed to produce the paperless office. In fact, computers generate much more paper than any of the manual processes that preceded them. All this paper leaves a trail, and authorities like SRI International say this is by far your single most vulnerable spot. Hacker legend to the contrary, your data assets are safest inside the computer. They are most vulnerable before they are entered or after they have been retrieved. This is when the information is more accessible, even to people with little computer knowledge.

> **Action item** Find ways to extend your security program beyond the boundaries of the computer. Protect valuable data wherever it is used, including paper and floppy disks as well as in the computer's memory.

Weak physical controls invite crime. Effective controls can convince the most dedicated criminal to try an easier mark. Of course, every security system has its limits. There are at least a few cases on record in which computer criminals have used firearms; few security systems can adequately stop that kind of force. These cases remain the exceptions, though. As a general rule, the stronger your physical controls, the more likely you are to turn back a would-be invader.

The knowledgeable computer criminal will often use a familiar means of access: the keyboard. This individual is in position to do a lot of damage. Countermeasures against this type of activity include separating staff duties, establishing dual control over sensitive functions, setting up a system of staff accountability, and maintaining a security information program and carefully written operating instructions. Backup systems and disaster plans can help limit the losses.

Poorly written programs often include unprotected trapdoors and other points of entry that criminals can exploit. In other cases, criminals have used the programs themselves as entry tools. This usually happens because the program lacks one of several vital controls: labels that indicate ownership, formal development methods that include testing and quality control, separation of the responsibility for parts of sensitive programs, programmer accountability, and safe storage of programs and documentation. Regular audits should compare operating programs with the master copies.

Operating systems have been a particular problem, dating back to the era of timesharing services. The networked PC has made this an even greater problem. DOS has no access controls of any consequence. Popular network operating systems aren't as weak as some of their critics suggest, but they don't always completely meet the need. Criminals take advantage of design weaknesses and bugs in the operating systems to get past the access controls. In fact, they'll often search for bugs or for shortcuts put in by the programmers.

Another possible weak spot is the system's ability to determine whether users are who they say they are. Weakness here could leave you vulnerable to impersonation. This is the hacker's field: getting past access-control systems by pretending to be an authorized user. The main cause of weakness here has been failing to protect password lists or leaving the system open to educated guesswork.

An early computer crime survey, which concentrated on mainframes, reported several cases in which the criminals gained access to magnetic tapes. Again, the PC and local area network have increased the risk. A lot of critical information circulates—properly or otherwise—on unprotected floppy disks.

Computer security ultimately depends on people, and the human factor is always a high-risk area. Lately, computer security professionals have spent a lot of time talking about *psychological subversion*. This is the art of persuading people to part with confidential information such as their passwords.

Vulnerable locations

The functions that are vulnerable to computer abuse are related, of course, to the physical locations where you will find the weak spots. The most vulnerable locations include:

- Data and report preparation areas
- On-line systems
- Media storage locations

Since preinput and postoutput processes are highly vulnerable, so are the locations where these activities take place. In a data center, these areas include data conversion, job setup, output control and distribution, and transportation. In a networked environment, your concern must extend to any location where similar activities take place.

Online systems are vulnerable because they are connected to that common means of improper access: the telephone. Enterprise networking will increase your problems in this area. Not only are networks being extended to greater numbers of sites and activities, but more and more networks are accessible by telephone.

In a mainframe system, data storage areas are isolated pockets of vulnerability. With a network in operation, you can have acres of vulnerability instead. This is another example—a widespread one—of how a functional vulnerability is related to a physical one. If floppy disks are everywhere, so is the problem of securing them.

There are also some physical locations where the degree of vulnerability makes little difference. For example, there is no great distinction between areas where computers are present or absent. Computers are everywhere these days, but that isn't the real reason. Even in the days of a single mainframe and a few terminals, there was as much computer crime committed in business offices as in data centers.

Another physical location that is less vulnerable than you might think is a central data center. These usually are so well protected physically that criminals invade by other means.

Other Sources of Danger

Computer criminals get most of the publicity, but they aren't the only sources of danger. Don't focus so hard on computer crime that you lose sight of other sources of danger. These can range from simple accidents and errors to natural disasters.

Preventing accidents

In spite of their many labor-saving advantages, computers still involve a lot of people, many of whom do precise, detailed types of work. Mistakes will happen in this kind of atmosphere, and they do. Most data processing managers know this, and it presents two kinds of problems.

First, it can be hard to tell the difference between an accidental loss and an intentional one. In fact, some abusers have closed what little gap there is, finding errors in their favor and taking advantage of them instead of reporting or correcting the mistakes.

The real problem here, though, is that when something goes wrong, you tend first to suspect that it's a hardware problem or a bug in the program. This is a convenient reaction since it often lets you blame a vendor, an outside programmer, or an inanimate piece of equipment. Only after you have eliminated these possible outside causes do you take a look inside your own operation and open yourself to the possibility that the loss was intentional.

Many computer abusers thrive on their superiors' unwillingness to face facts.

The second problem is that, in contrast to its lag in facing many security issues, the computer industry almost from the beginning has been working to prevent and correct errors. Most programs try to anticipate the mistakes their human users will make and have error-trapping routines to keep the error from causing any damage.

It's natural to believe, then, that the many precautions you have established against errors will also protect you against intentional acts that have the same effect. They won't.

Remember, your opponent probably is a knowledgeable person who knows these error-trapping techniques at least as well as you do. That means they can be evaded early, easily, and often. The security controls you implement must be specifically suited to their purpose: protecting your system from intentional acts.

Coping with natural forces

Among your major areas of vulnerability is the proverbial act of God. Fires, hurricanes, and earthquakes routinely play havoc with computer operations. It's important to recognize and deal with the kinds of risk to which your area is vulnerable.

At the same time, it's important to watch out for the intentional act that appears to be a natural disaster. Just as some criminals will take advantage of an error or disguise their activities to look like a mistake, others will create or capitalize on what seem to be natural disasters.

For example, in the 1960s, magnetic fields were identified as major sources of danger to data stored on tapes and disks. Sure enough, in 1962 a disgruntled employee in a New York office tried to sabotage a tape reel by holding a magnet next to it. There was no significant damage, but only because the magnet was not large enough or close enough. One way the employee might have succeeded would have been to use a bulk tape eraser which does have the power to do that job. Keep these in secure storage.

Radio and x-ray signals could have similar effects, but again they must be strong and close. This alone may help alert you to the difference between deliberate and accidental damage.

If an apparent natural force is strong and close enough to do real damage but only to an isolated area, it's time to start looking for human, not natural, causes. Table 4.15 lists some dangers due to natural forces.

Simplifying Risk Analysis

In sum, you face a host of perils and a spider web of vulnerable networks. The main purpose of risk analysis is to zero in on the most serious threats to the most vulnerable areas. There is a simplified risk analysis framework that can help you do that. This analysis, based on a design by Don Erwin of Dow Chemical Canada, sets up a matrix on which you can pinpoint your most seri-

TABLE 4.15   Dangers Due to Natural Forces

	Extreme temperature	
Hot weather	Cold weather	Fire

	Gas	
Military action	Commercial vapors	Humid air
Steam	Wind	Tornado
Explosion	Smoke	Dust

	Liquids	
Water	Rain	Flood
Ice	Snow	Sleet
Hail	Chemical solvents	Fuels

	Projectiles	
Bullets	Shrapnel	Powered missiles
Thrown objects	Meteorites	Vehicles

	Earth movements	
Sinkholes	Slides	Flows
Liquefaction	Shaking	Waves
Cracking	Separation	Shearing

	Electromagnetic	
Electric surge	Electric blackout	Static electricity
Microwaves	Magnetism	Laser beams
Atomic radiation	Cosmic waves	

ous needs. Then, you can use the same matrix to identify the security controls that can best meet your identified needs. This is a simple approach, but it's also a fast one—Erwin says you can complete the process in about half an hour. The results can reveal priorities for immediate action. They can also serve as a foundation for a more comprehensive assessment.

The first step is as simple as filling in the empty boxes in Table 4.16. Each column represents a major class of risk. The two rows distinguish between accidental and deliberate acts. Each block represents a potential opening in your security system. Assemble your security team and ask members to mark the boxes that represent their most serious security needs. Suggest typical

TABLE 4.16   Risk Analysis Matrix

	Integrity: Protecting information from modification or destruction	Sensitivity: Protecting confidential information from disclosure	Availability: Making critical information available when needed
Accidents, errors, and natural events			
Deliberate acts			

TABLE 4.17   Suggested Responses

	Integrity: Protecting information from modification or destruction	Sensitivity: Protecting confidential information from disclosure	Availability: Making critical information available when needed
Accidents, errors, and natural events	Desk checking Checks and balances	Form classification Access control Segregation Physical security	Backup System design Duplication
Deliberate acts	Passwords Log-in procedures Audits	Passwords Log-in procedures Waste disposal Storage processes Site security	Off-site storage Disaster plan Physical security Emergency procedures Security specifications

types of risks that might fit into each box; encourage the group to evaluate them and suggest others.

The matrix in Table 4.17 is a near duplicate of the first. Here, the group should fill in possible measures that can meet the identified security needs. The table suggests some responses to various needs, but the team members should look at their own situations and suggest the controls that would work best in their particular circumstances.

Once you have assessed the needs and responses, there is an important third step: Assign responsibility to team members to put the controls into effect.

5

Controlling
Physical Access

The most basic form of computer security is to restrict access to the computer. This includes—but is not limited to—physical protection.

Once upon a time, a computer control access system called *Knapsack* was thought to be the equal—at least—of the best security control systems available, but about 50 times faster. Its inventors were so sure Knapsack could not be beaten that they proudly offered a $1,000 prize to anyone who could crack its code.

It took 2 years and a supercomputer, but Ernest F. Brickell of the Sandia National Laboratories in Albuquerque, New Mexico, finally claimed the prize. The money hardly paid for Brickell's time, but he demonstrated one important point: You can make access difficult, but you cannot make it impossible.

A hard-to-crack access code like Knapsack can give you a strong measure of protection. It dramatically shortens the list of people who have the means, motive, and opportunity to get past it. Just don't make the mistake of assuming that any method is absolutely unbreakable. Brickell said a key to his success was the discovery that the Knapsack code was a relatively simple mathematical formula disguised as a difficult one. He admits he would not know how to break an access code that actually used the more difficult formula— but someone else might.

Kinds of Computer Security

Classifying computer security is easy. It must be—many people have done it.

Different people recognize different classification systems. This book follows the lead of authorities in classifying security measures into physical, procedural, and technical groups. Others prefer to divide them into physical, hardware, and software classes.

Also, any attempt at pigeonholing requires the cooperation of the pigeons.

They often refuse to nest comfortably in the spaces to which you assign them.

With all that in mind, this book will discuss security measures in these three classifications:

- Physical controls, which restrict access to the computer
- Procedural controls, which govern use of the computer system
- Technical controls, which are built into the system itself

This division has been chosen over several alternatives for these two reasons:

- It is used in much of the available source material.
- It divides about three chapters worth of material into three conveniently sized chapters.

The second reason is more important.

These control methods are related to the threat assessment and types of computer crime discussed in Chapter 4. The threat assessment identifies weak spots. The categories of security techniques present tactics you can apply to your identified areas of vulnerability.

None of these categories is neat or self-contained. You may well find a technique discussed under one heading that seems to belong under another. For example, a password, strictly speaking, is a software control that many might prefer to treat as a technical measure. Managing a password system is a procedural concern. Ultimately, the password is used for access control.

The distinctions among types of security are useful mainly for discussion purposes. None of these techniques will be the one and only answer to your security problems. Look at them as components in an overall security strategy. The exact mix will depend on what you are trying to protect and the environment in which you are trying to protect it. If you have properly assessed the threats you face, you will have a basis on which to decide which mix of techniques should be used.

The proper focus of a security program is not on whether a control method falls within any particular class but whether it effectively responds to an identified threat. You'll often find that the right response is a combination of physical, administrative, and technical measures.

What the Right Protection Can Do

If you select the right combination of protective measures, you should be able to:

- Ward off threats to the welfare of your company.
- Establish different degrees of access, depending on the needs and responsibilities of each user.

- Hold users clearly responsible for their own computer use.
- Maintain a clear separation between users, programs, data files, and other resources.
- Identify attempts to misuse the computer or evade its protective measures.

The central purpose of any security program is to protect your resources and assets while allowing maximum use and flexibility to authorized users. You can choose from a variety of physical, procedural, and technical controls. With proper selections you can put your computer users into a type of maze. At each intersection, the system evaluates the users and the types of access, if any, for which they are authorized. If the evaluation is positive, the user is sent in the proper direction. Otherwise, the unauthorized entrant is repelled or misdirected.

In such a maze technique, the user usually first encounters a set of physical barriers. These can identify the user and admit only those who are authorized. Next, a set second level of access controls will read the user's identification and determine what level or types of access this person should have. Technical controls then can ensure that the access is limited to proper programs and files.

Back up the built-in security system with written policy and procedure statements. Explain the types of assets you feel it is important to protect. Spell out each employee's responsibility for protecting specific kinds of information. Explain the operating requirements for using the computer. This kind of information will help prevent accidental security violations. More important, it helps make the employees aware of your security requirements, why they exist, and how to work within them.

New Challenges for Traditional Methods

When most people think of computer security, they think first of physical security. Many physical security techniques are traditional security methods: locks, guards, badges, and other means to limit access to your computer and its valuable contents.

Good physical security, though, will go beyond the traditional techniques and back them up with technology to match the computer you are trying to protect. Electronic keys or video cameras, for example, can back up or even replace a human security guard.

The physical techniques you implement also can help in other areas: protecting against disaster, for example, or against errors and crashes.

What physical security can do...

Physical security measures can serve three main purposes (Fig. 5.1):

- *Control access to your equipment and data.* Locked doors, passwords, and similar techniques restrict access, keep authorized people from entering security-sensitive areas, and impede their access to valuable information.

Physical security roles

- Control access
- Protect the site
- Guard against damage

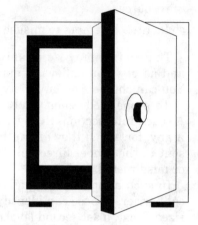

Figure 5.1 Physical security can lock up things that are easy to lock up.

- *Protect the computer site, particularly its structures and surroundings.* The basic idea is to extend circles of protection outward from the central computer location.

- *Protect against hazards that can damage the computer or its contents.* These hazards include unintentional access by untrained and unauthorized people.

...And what it can't

Today's networked computer system is no longer locked up in a central location where it is easy to protect. You still might have such a location for a central processing unit, and it's a good idea to install network servers behind locked doors. Other elements of the system can be scattered around a building, a plant site, the nation, or even the world. You can no longer concentrate your efforts on preventing physical access to a single operating site (Fig. 5.2).

Your job is also made more difficult as computers change in size and function. It's likely, for example, that major elements of your computer system will soon become indistinguishable from major elements of your telephone system. This makes the computer system more vulnerable to abuse and misuse, and it is a particular challenge to the physical elements of your security program.

New ways of storing data also present new physical security challenges. The floppy diskette is a major example: It started with a diameter of 8 inches, then shrunk to about 5, and later versions are now little over 3. It becomes easier all the time to slip several hundred pages of valuable information into a shirt pocket or the hidden corner of a briefcase. CD disks are also pocket-sized media, with the ability to hold vast amounts of information.

Physical security weaknesses

- Scattered networks
- Telephone access
- Data storage

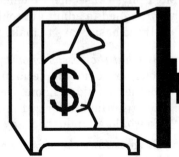

Figure 5.2 Protecting networks is not a strong point.

Even when you're dealing with larger items, physical security can be difficult. It's not all that hard for someone to steal a tape from an unprotected library or to walk out with pages of valuable documentation on how to alter or manipulate your programs. The ever-present office photocopier and the copy command of a PC operating system probably rank very close to each other as threats to your security.

A physical security system must protect data as well as equipment. In fact, protecting the data easily could be the more important objective of the two. Sometimes information escapes in low-tech ways. Discarded printouts, used printer ribbons, and passwords left visible on monitor screens are common sources of loss.

Another major danger: Some people become such familiar figures around a computer facility they are allowed to move around at will, even in places to which they should not have access. If you were an outsider looking for ways to steal or sabotage your data, you probably would look for exactly such a person to do the job for you.

Recognizing the limits

The spread of networks has added new limits to traditional physical security methods. They can do part of the job, but there is no way they can do all of it. That's always been true, but it is even more important now. Good physical security will continue to be necessary, but consider it in combination with other types of techniques. Make it part of an overall computer security system.

Computer security is a complex field. It requires a hard look at what physical security methods can—and cannot—accomplish in the new Information Age.

Types of Physical Security

Most physical security techniques are built around this central feature: They are designed to admit authorized persons and reject those who are not. There are three basic ways to make this distinction:

- *By what the person knows.* This can be a password, a more complex access code, or some simple identifier. One simple but effective question: Your mother's maiden name. Don't assume, though, that this can automatically identify the authorized individual. A relative also would know the name. So would an industrial spy who has looked it up.

- *By something the person has.* This could be a security badge or an electronic key card.

- *By who the person is.* Some security systems identify an individual by a fingerprint, a voice characteristic, or a written signature. Others will read the shape of a hand or even the pattern of blood vessels in the eyeball.

As usual, all have their limits. The first two depend heavily on the individual's willingness not to reveal the key knowledge or share the access badge. The third group involves costly hardware that probably can be justified only for the highest security needs.

Major security methods

The most common physical security measures usually are tailored to the type of protection you need. They are best at protecting equipment and data, the computer site, or disaster relief and recovery. They also are used in combination with procedural and technical controls. Among the techniques used to protect equipment and data are:

- *Physical access controls.* Includes numerical access controls, security badges, magnetic card readers, and biological detection methods

- *Procedural controls.* Includes guards and sign-in logs

- *Technical controls.* Includes passwords, locking devices, and surveillance by closed-circuit television

Techniques to provide site security include:

- *Fire-control systems.* Includes alarms, extinguishers, fire-resistant construction, and smoke and heat detectors

- *Water-damage controls.* Includes waterproof equipment covers, water-tight ceilings, and under-floor drains

- *Secure heating, ventilation, and air conditioning.* This includes proper maintenance and housekeeping, adequate design and construction, and the availability of backup

Chapter 14 will cover disaster recovery in detail. The major physical security methods for the purpose revolve mainly around the use of backup sites. Both the disaster area and the backup site would also probably require some form of access control.

Types of identification badges

Physical access to a computer room or building is normally controlled by some kind of personal identification. The most common is the security badge. This ordinary item, though, comes in many variations. Several kinds of badges have been developed (Fig. 5.3). Some are familiar; others use advanced electronic techniques:

- The photo ID badge is by far the most common. It's also vulnerable to counterfeiting, theft, and loss. Laminated cards discourage some substitution of pictures and other tampering, but they don't prevent it entirely.

- An optical coded badge uses a geometric pattern of spots laminated into the badge. They can be seen only under infrared light and are hard to counterfeit.

- An electric coded badge carries its own printed circuit. The guard can test the circuit by slipping the card into a standard card edge connector. However, it's almost as simple to decode and counterfeit the circuit.

- A magnetic coded badge uses a pattern of magnetic spots. It is moderately difficult to counterfeit or alter this type of badge. The coding is vulnerable to exposure to magnetic fields. Magnetic coated stripes now are commonly used on credit cards. In fact, the American National Standards Institute has established a pair of alternative standards for them. Unfortunately, tampering and duplicating are easy.

Types of badges

- Photo ID
- Optical coding
- Electrical coding
- Magnetic coding

Figure 5.3 Badges range from high to low tech.

- Passive electronic coding uses a built-in circuit that absorbs certain radio frequencies generated by the badge reader. The badge need only be placed near the testing device to get a reading of which frequencies are absorbed. As happens so often, though, ease of use also means ease of abuse.

- An active electronic badge supplies power to the badge by magnetic induction and reads an encoded serial number. The unit will automatically read the badge of any employee who passes. It also can keep a log of who was there.

Biometric techniques

Designers have been working on some new approaches to access control, including ways to identify voice patterns, fingerprints, signatures and eyeballs. All are still experimental and are too limited, expensive, or time-consuming for most applications. Consider, too, the personal privacy problems of registering someone's fingerprints or eyeball vein patterns in a system which itself might be vulnerable to improper access.

Still, some of these approaches offer hope for the future, and perhaps for the present as well. Of particular interest are biometric techniques. These offer a way to determine who a person is, as opposed to whether someone knows a password or has a badge.

The first biometric techniques were placed in defense installations and other locations where national security was at stake. At that time the method was considered too expensive and experimental for more widespread application, but when a method shows promise, conditions like these seldom endure for long. In fact, some of the more well-established and less expensive biometric systems have been installed in lower-security locations.

Biometric devices measure the physical traits that make each person unique. The fingerprint is an early and familiar example: The ridges and whorls that appear on our fingers are like no other in the world. The newest biometric devices replace ink with an electronic reader that can scan your thumb as you press it against a button. The sensor translates its readings into digital signals that can be compressed and stored electronically. When the system reads your fingerprint, it compares these signals against the electronic profiles of authorized users it already has on file.

Other biometric devices work on much the same basis but read different characteristics:

- *A retina scanner.* This device adds new meaning to looking deeply into your eyes. The back of your eyeball contains tiny blood vessels. They are arranged in patterns that are as unique as your fingerprints. The scanner reads the size, location, and arrangement of these blood vessels.

- *Signature dynamics.* A forger can imitate the appearance of your signature but cannot replicate the subtle changes in motion and pressure that you use while signing your name. This technique reads those signals and compares them with an advanced version of your personal signature.

- *Keystroke dynamics.* This method brings the same technique to the computer keyboard. The sensor records the subtle, unique differences in pressure as you type a standard phrase.

- *Hand geometry.* This measures the length of your fingers, the thickness of your palm, and the shape of your hand. It even calibrates how thin-skinned you are.

- *Voice recognition.* This has been developed to the point that it doesn't just measure sound. It tracks the actual physiology that produces speech.

- *Neural network technology.* This is a high-tech version of the mug shot. It tracks the patterns of nerves in your face.

- *The DNA fingerprint.* This takes a genetic portrait and compares it with those on record.

Addressing Site Security

The well-developed state of data communication and related technology means you can no longer rely just on physically securing the computer site itself. That doesn't mean, though, that site security is no longer important. It's still an important component of the overall security package.

In fact, the increasing use of communication can have one security advantage: It becomes more feasible to locate your major computer facilities at some distance from other operations. That means you will have fewer people in the vicinity and fewer problems trying to control traffic. It also means a fire or other emergency in the main building will not as readily endanger the computer center.

Site security checklist

In planning your site security, consider these points (Fig. 5.4):

- The location
- The site's characteristics

Site security factors

- Location
- Characteristics
- Fire protection
- Utility support

Figure 5.4 Don't list the site in directories, either.

- Fire protection systems
- Supporting systems, such as power and air conditioning

One of the simplest beginnings to a site security program is to remove any signs that point to the data center. Those who are authorized to use the center should know where it is. Those who aren't authorized don't need to know.

In that light, the only people who would find the signs really useful would be illicit users, who would be told exactly where to go to begin their dirty work. If you must have direction signs for some reason, post them outside the main flow of traffic. Make the unauthorized user seek some other way of locating the room—like asking directions from a security guard.

While you're getting rid of signs, don't forget any listings that might be found in building directories.

Conditions to consider

If you have the luxury of picking a site, look for a place that is not susceptible to damage from natural forces, like wind, floods, or earthquakes. Try not to install your sensitive electronic gear in the path of blowing sand.

Build to suit the location. There's hardly anywhere on earth that a basement location is suitable for a computer. If the equipment isn't quickly drowned by a storm or bursting water pipe, it could slowly rust to death. Remember this bit of news from the insurance industry: More computer damage claims are due to water damage than any other source.

Fire in any kind of electronic equipment will do a lot of expensive damage before it can put out much heat. That means you'll need highly sensitive fire detection devices in the computer center. Standard sprinkler systems usually are set to go off when the temperature at the ceiling reaches about 165°F. Your fire detector should be set much lower, 130° tops, lower if you can do it.

Don't install a system that will douse your equipment with water. A soaked computer is just as useless as a burned one. Most authorities recommend Halon equipment, although it's expensive and has been criticized as unreliable. Put water sprinklers in noncomputer rooms, particularly those where paper is stored.

If possible, combine the fire detection system with alarms that will warn of power or air-conditioning failures. Wire the system to shut down operating equipment before the Halon is discharged.

The secure floor plan

The layout of your building will have a big effect on its security. Most authorities recommend two entrances at most: one for employees, the other a loading dock for supplies and equipment.

From each entrance to the computer area itself, there should be a single route, easy to monitor and used by no one else. One company found that questionable access to its computer fell sharply when it moved a terminal that had been stationed at a major intersection of office traffic. Try to make each person pass through successive layers of security. Unfortunately, the barriers that restrict unauthorized people will restrict your regular workers much more often. You'll have to strike a balance between access for workers and restrictions on others.

Backup systems for your power and air-conditioning can keep the computer running when everything else goes down. Again there's a tradeoff, though, because backups are expensive. Whatever support equipment you install, establish a strict preventive maintenance program to improve its reliability.

Planning and evaluating physical security

As with every aspect of security planning, the first step is to assess your needs. Then develop a security plan designed specifically to meet them. That plan will be a mix of the right kinds of tactics.

Analyze your needs, and find out where you are vulnerable. Then examine the available tactics, and decide which best fit your situation. An ideal physical security system would minimize the number of false alarms and maximize the number of true alarms. It would be hard to deceive, evade, or counterfeit. It would be inexpensive to buy and operate. It also doesn't exist.

Every security system is a compromise between good features and problems. The test is whether you can enjoy most of the advantages and avoid most of the drawbacks in your own circumstances. You must analyze your needs and tailor your solution to meet them.

The answers to these questions can help you determine whether you have established an adequate physical security program for your needs:

- Is your physical security program part of a larger overall plan for the total security of your computer system?

- Have your systems and methods kept up with changes in technology, particularly the advent of personal computers?

- Have employees been made fully aware of both their rights to computer access and the restrictions under which they must work?

- Have you included adequate security provisions in the design and construction of new facilities?

- Have you provided ways to limit fire and water damage?

- Is a single person clearly in charge of monitoring security and access controls?

Badges and Identification Tokens

The possession of a token, such as a key or a machine-readable card, is one of the basic ways to verify a person's identity. Strictly speaking, though, a machine that identifies a token of this kind does not reliably identify the person who carries that token. With that in mind, recent research has concentrated on ways to identify a person by his or her physical characteristics.

That research is still incomplete, and there are drawbacks to most of these methods.

If a badge or token provides machine-readable data, it may be used to establish identity. Possession usually verifies the user's identity (assuming that it has not fallen into other hands). Or the user may enter a name or identification code using a keyboard, numeric keypad, or combination dial. You could then use the token to verify the claimed identity.

Computer terminals can be fitted with key locks or badge readers for use in this manner. Alternatively, the token-actuated device could be distinct from the terminal and could control the terminal's operation by some means such as controlling the power or communications lines. This might be more vulnerable, though, than incorporating the mechanism as an integral part of the terminal, using tamper-resistant construction.

A penetrator who succeeds in obtaining a token can use it as readily as the authorized user. That means it is a good idea to include some type of password scheme to identify the carrier as well as the token.

Types of identification tokens

A variety of machine-readable cards has been developed for access control. These can conveniently be described by the methods used to encode information on the card. Here are the various types now in use:

- *Photo ID badge.* The most common credential is a color coded badge with a photograph that can be checked visually by a guard. The common practice is to require that a laminated photo ID badge be used for access to controlled areas.

- *Optical coded badge.* This type of badge contains a geometric array of spots printed on an insert that is laminated into the badge. Photo detectors in the badge reader check the relative optical transmission of the spots. To make this badge resist tampering, the spots can be concealed so they can be detected only by infrared light.

- *Electric circuit coded badge.* This is a plastic laminated badge that contains a printed circuit pattern that selectively closes electrical circuits when inserted into the reader. For this type of badge, the reader is simply a card edge connector of the type normally used for a printed circuit board. The badge can be decoded with a simple electrical continuity tester, so it is easy to counterfeit.

- *Magnetic coded badge.* This badge contains a sheet of flexible magnetic material on which an array of spots has been permanently magnetized. The code is determined by the polarity of the magnetized spots. The badge reader contains magnetic sensors that are checked electrically or magnetic reed switches that are activated mechanically. The spots can be accidentally erased if the badge is placed in a strong magnetic field, but in practice this has not been a serious problem. It is possible to build equipment that would recode or duplicate the pattern of magnetic spots and duplicate the badge. It is more difficult, though, to falsify this type of badge than to fabricate an electric circuit coded badge.

- *Magnetic stripe coded badge.* Magnetic stripe coding is widely used in credit card systems, and many vendors make equipment that is compatible with American National Standard Institute standards for this technique. With this type of a badge, a stripe of magnetic material is located along one edge of the badge and is encoded with identifying data. A magnetic head reads the data. Forgery is relatively easy since data from the magnetic strips can be decoded and applied to duplicate badges. All it takes is a common tape recorder.

- *Passive electronic coded badge.* The passive electronic coded badge is one into which electrically tuned circuits are laminated. The reader generates a radio frequency field and checks the frequencies at which significant energy is absorbed. These frequencies correspond to identifying information encoded into the badge. An important advantage of this technique is that the badge need not be inserted into a reader mechanism; all you need do is bring it near an antenna. On the other hand, the badges can be counterfeited with common radio frequency test instruments, and you are limited to only a few thousand unique code combinations.

- *Capacitance coded badge.* This is a badge into which a small array of conducting plates has been laminated. Selected plates are connected, and the code is read from the badge by a reader that measures the capacitance of the plates and distinguishes which are or are not connected.

- *Metallic strip coded badge.* The metallic strip coded badge uses rows of copper strips that are laminated into the badge. The presence or absence of the strips in certain rows determines the code pattern, which is read by an eddy current sensor. This technique was developed to be used with a controlled access by individual number system. The badges are durable and can be read reliably. Each badge can be encoded with about 40 data bits.

- *Active electronic badge.* This system consists of a portable, electrically coded badge and a stationary reading unit. The unit supplies power to the badge by magnetic induction. It then receives and decodes a credential number transmitted from the badge. When the interrogation unit is placed at strategic locations, such as halls or doorways leading into controlled areas, it can automatically monitor, identify, and log every badge that enters or leaves the area. The employee needs to do nothing at all since the badge is read automatically as he or she passes by a radio frequency field generated by the interrogation unit.

Updating systems

The longer a security safeguard is in place, the more opportunity there is for would-be penetrators to become familiar with it and to devise a penetration scheme, such as duplicating a key or making a counterfeit card. Therefore, the coding should be updated at intervals, such as replacing lock cylinders or reissuing cards with new codes. In the case of a card reader that reads and transmits a code, you can carry out the change by issuing new cards and updating the master control list. Rekeying the locks may be less convenient.

If a particular terminal is to be used by more than one authorized person, there should be some way to distinguish which person is using the terminal. This will enable the central facility to enforce the proper authorization for the particular user. If you use a lock and key, there will be no way for the computer to determine whose key is being used. The use of cards with unique codes for each user lets the computer determine which user is seeking access (or at least whose card is being used).

A variety of machine-readable cards has been developed for access-control purposes. With some cards, the coding can be altered rather readily in the field; with others, the coding is either permanently built in or requires special equipment for alteration. Many types of cards can include printed material and photographs and can serve as identification badges as well.

Design objectives

Several badge sizes are in common use. The selection is usually a compromise between a small, easily handled badge and a larger badge with more room for a photograph, color code indicators, and printed information. Most commercially available coded credential systems use the standard credit card size, 54 by 86 millimeters ($2\frac{1}{8}$ by $3\frac{3}{8}$ inches). This size is at best marginally acceptable for a picture badge. A slightly larger common badge size is 60 by 83 millimeters ($2\frac{3}{8}$ by $3\frac{1}{4}$ inches). This is not much larger than the standard credit card, but it provides significantly more usable badge area when the badge is worn in a vertical position.

If none of the standard sizes is satisfactory, you may have to require that each employee wear a larger photo badge and carry a separate card to be used in electronic readers.

Preparing badges

Ideally, badges should be assembled and laminated at the facility site. If not, you face delays, administrative overhead, and reduced security. Coded badges must be enrolled in the memory of the control processor after they are fabricated. For simple systems, enrollment is done on a keyboard at the control console. Provide for backup copies of the control processor's memory; otherwise, all badges must manually be reenrolled after a power failure or equipment malfunction. This could be a serious problem for large installations.

A badge should be able to withstand daily use for 5 years with normal care. Some PVC plastic materials deteriorate rapidly when exposed to sunlight and become brittle when the temperature drops below freezing. Most common credit card materials have these problems, but some PVC formulations are available that eliminate most of them. Polyester-based badges are more durable, but take care in the selection process to make sure you can laminate them reliably and permanently.

Resisting decoding and counterfeiting

A badge exchange system reduces the possibility that a badge will be counterfeited, lost, or stolen. Duplicate badges are held at each controlled entry point. When an employee requests entry, a guard matches the individual to the photograph on the corresponding exchange badge held at the control point. If the individual passes the check, the guard exchanges the badges and grants the employee access. The employee's badge is held at the control point until the employee leaves the area, when the badges again are exchanged.

The exchange badge worn within the controlled area is never allowed to leave the area. However, this system would not prevent someone from using face makeup to match the image on a stolen badge.

Any type of coded badge can be decoded and duplicated if you devote enough money and talent to the task. Of the major encoding techniques, electric circuit and magnetic stripe codes are the easiest to duplicate. The others are much harder.

In general, it is not necessary to decode a badge to duplicate it. In some systems, though, the code data is cryptographically encoded or contains other internal checks. Counterfeiting a new badge then would require both decoding and understanding the internal check algorithm; this type of counterfeiting is much more difficult.

Resistance to decoding and counterfeiting is not as important if the badge is used in conjunction with a separate identity verification system based on a personal attribute. In this type of system, the badge number simply indexes a reference file where personal identification data are stored in a central computer. Access is allowed only if the personnel identity algorithm is satisfied. In this case counterfeiting a badge will not, in itself, guarantee access.

Badge readers are vulnerable points at which to attack an entry-control system. The readers should be equipped with tamper sensors. Further, protect communication lines between the badge reader and any central console or computer by line supervision, encryption, or both.

Verifying Personal Attributes

There are inherent drawbacks in identification systems that depend on something a person knows or has. For that reason, much attention has been given to authentication methods based on something about a person.

Among the personal attributes that can be measured are hand geometry, fingerprints, signatures, and speech. This is an actively developing field, and it is premature to say that any particular technique is superior in security and economy at this time. For any given application, though, one of these techniques may have a natural advantage over the others.

The rapid growth in remote computer use and the increasing sensitivity of computer applications have combined to intensify the need for authentication methods that can positively establish the identity of users at remote terminals. At the same time, advances in instrumentation technology together with improved methods of signal processing and pattern recognition, have opened up new possibilities for automated identity verification based on unique aspects of personal attributes.

All of these methods have shown their imperfections. Critics of DNA tracking, for example, worry that its use requires too much knowledge about an individual's ancestry. They fear it could invade privacy or become a vehicle for discrimination.

There are problems with other techniques, as well. Like medical science, voice recognition technology has yet to find a solution to the common cold. A hand geometry system can be fooled by a manicure. A nervous user may not provide the "right" responses to a handwriting or keyboard test. In most cases the system does an effective job of keeping unauthorized users out. The problem is, it also does an effective job of keeping authorized users out.

For example, Security Pacific Bank, which operates in about 600 widespread locations, implemented a voice recognition system to identify managers who call in requesting confidential business data. The bank had previously relied on passwords but did not feel these were secure enough. At the same time, though, the bank dropped an experimental program that tried to use the same system to identify key customers. The customers did not always call from the same telephones, and differences in tone quality caused the system to reject them.

Problems of measurement

One of the chief problems in using personal attributes for identity verification is the difficulty of performing precise, repeatable measurements of the human body. This is true whether the attribute is a relatively static quality, such as the fingerprint or finger length, or whether the attribute is dynamic, such as handwriting or speech. Because body surfaces are soft and curved, it is hard to establish accurate reference points and good registration for taking measurements or matching patterns.

This lack of precise repeatability must be taken into account when testing and evaluating identity verification systems. In testing such systems, be prepared to vary all factors that are considered to have an influence on the attribute being used.

Two kinds of variation

The inability to precisely repeat the measurement for a given individual is called *intrapersonal variability*. The variation from one individual to another is designated *interpersonal variability*.

To allow for the statistical variations that result from intrapersonal variability, the system must have a certain amount of tolerance. If the tolerance is too great, though, you lose the ability to distinguish between individuals.

An identity verification device can have an adjustable threshold you can use to tighten or loosen the tolerance. Tightening it improves the ability to discriminate between individuals, reducing the chance you will accept an impostor but at the same time increasing the chance of incorrectly rejecting an authorized user.

Method of operation

Devices to identify personal attributes generally operate this way: The user enters his or her claimed identity, by entering a name, identification number, or other identifier. Or the user may insert a token such as a magnetic stripe card that bears identification information in machine-readable form.

The device then prepares to verify the claimed identity. This will be done by comparing a reference profile of the attribute associated with the claimed identity with a measurement of the attribute as derived from the individual who seeks access. Depending on the device and the application, the reference profile may be obtained from a central file, from a local file in the device, or from a machine-readable token supplied by the individual.

An alternate method is to measure the attribute and send the measured profile to a central location for comparison with the reference profile. It may not be necessary to send the entire volume of measured data to the central location. Instead, a local processor can derive a set of parameters to represent the measured profile, and these features can be used for the comparison.

Or you can use a sequential decision scheme that transmits information until a decision is reached at a specified level of statistical confidence. This makes the entry process shorter for the normal authorized user and longer for the impostor.

The measured profile then is compared with the reference profile, and a measure of similarity is obtained. This generally results in an output signal that has a value between some minimum and maximum. The resulting value is compared with a preset threshold that results in a binary decision to accept or reject the individual or to request more data.

Two classes of error

An identity verification device can make either of two types of error:

- A type 1 error falsely rejects an authorized user.
- A type 2 error falsely admits an impostor.

In operation, an identity verification device carries out a series of measurements, processes this data, and compares the results with a reference profile. If the results match within a specified tolerance, the identity is considered to be verified. Because of the intrapersonal variation, the match will not usually be exact.

Figure 5.5 shows an analysis of such a process. The data from a series of measurements are plotted, matching a range of possible scores with the degree of match or mismatch. Ideally, all the scores for correct individuals would all be grouped at the right edge of the graph, indicating the highest scores, while those for impostors would all be grouped at the left edge.

Ideal screening process

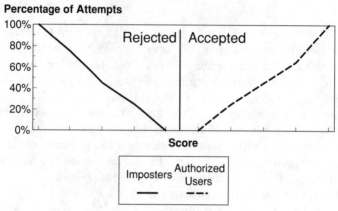

Figure 5.5 In an ideal world, decisions are always right.

Real-world authorization

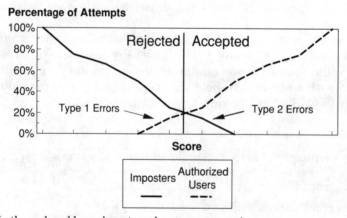

Figure 5.6 In the real world, you have to make some compromises.

In practice, the device does not operate in that ideal fashion; instead, it might produce the results shown in Fig. 5.6. Here, the scores are spread out considerably, and the scores of some overlap the scores of a few unauthorized users. There is no score you could safely use as a threshold that would reliably separate authorized users from impostors. In practice, you must compromise. You might set the score at the point in Fig. 5.6 where the two curves cross. This is known as the *equal error point,* at which the type 1 and type 2 error rates are equal.

Or you can adjust the threshold to favor one type of error over the other. Move the threshold to the right, to a higher score, and you can improve the probability that you will reject an impostor. A lower score would do a better job of admitting all authorized individuals.

Part of this statistical problem arises from a physical one: Even when you are able to measure them accurately, a person's physical characteristics are subject to change. It's been found, for example, that tomorrow you can be as much as 5 pounds heavier or lighter than you are today. You lose a fraction of an inch in height during a working day as your spinal disks compress.

You must build enough tolerance into this system to allow for these variations and avoid the error of rejecting an employee with an important job to be done. This same tolerance makes it harder to identify impostors.

Using multiple attributes

It also is possible to improve an error rate by testing more than one attribute, as shown in Table 5.1. With two tests, you have two possible rules for making a decision:

- Rule 1 accepts the person if either device does so. It greatly reduces the chance of false rejection at the expense of an increased chance of accepting an impostor.

- Rule 2 accepts the person only if both devices agree it should be done. This greatly decreases the chances of accepting an impostor but with an increased chance of false rejection. Of course, if each device has a variable threshold, these may be varied to achieve an acceptable balance.

This type of analysis is based on using two personal attributes. It is possible, of course, to combine the use of different methods of verifying identification. A system might use one device based on an attribute and another based on passwords or an identification token.

For example, the ATM system uses a combination of a magnetic stripe card and a personal identification number (PIN), which is a type of password.

TABLE 5.1   Using Multiple Checks to Change the Probabilities

| | Assumed Values | | Error Probability |
	Device A (%)	Device B (%)	(%)
Type I error rate	3	4	
Type II error rate	1	2	
Rule 1: Access Granted If Accepted by Either Device.			
Authorized user rejected	3	4	0.12
Imposter accepted	1	2	3
Rule 2: Access Granted Only If Accepted By Both Devices			
Authorized user rejected	3	4	7
Imposter accepted	1	2	0.02

When identity verification based on personal attributes becomes established, a person could be asked to verify his or her identity both via an attribute and through one of the other methods.

Multiple trials

The possibility of a type 1 error has prompted many users to allow more than one trial to pass an access test. In one way, this process gives an impostor an extra chance or two to crack the system. Used properly, multiple trials can improve either a type 1 or type 2 error rate, but they cannot improve both at the same time.

There are some important conditions here. First, if a verification process is good to begin with, multiple trials can substantially improve its effectiveness in distinguishing between impostors and authorized users. However, repeated trials cannot improve performance that is poor at the outset. Also, the trials must be statistically independent. The outcome of any one trial should not influence the results of any repeat.

If you allow two trials to gain access, several decision strategies are available, as Table 5.2 illustrates. By allowing two trials, it is possible either to greatly benefit the correct users or to greatly enhance the rejection of impostors, but as usual, the improvement in one area comes at the expense of the other.

TABLE 5.2   Multiple Trials: Improving the Chances for Authorized Users and Imposters Alike

	Assumed Values		
	First trial (%)	Second trial (%)	Error probability (%)
Type I error rate	2	2	
Type II error rate	1	1	
Rule 1: Access Granted If Accepted by Either Device.			
Authorized user rejected	2	2	0.04
Imposter accepted	1	1	2
Rule 2: Access Granted Only If Accepted by Both Devices.			
Authorized user rejected	2	2	4
Imposter accepted	1	1	0.001

Rule 2 always requires two trials, increasing the time needed to carry out the verification process. With rule 1, the process can be completed if the user passes the first trial. The likelihood of being rejected is small to start with, so only an occasional second trial will be needed.

Allowing more than two trials

If you increase the number of trials, a greater variety of decision rules becomes available. Table 5.3 shows that it now becomes possible to improve

TABLE 5.3   **Effects of a Third Try**

	Assumed Values	
	Each trial (%)	Error probability (%)
Type I error rate	2	
Type II error rate	1	
Rule 1: Access Granted If a Single Trial Succeeds.		
Authorized user rejected	2 2 2	0.00008
Imposter accepted	1 1 1	3
Rule 2: Access Granted If Two Trials Succeed.		
Authorized user rejected		0.12
Imposter accepted		0.03
Rule 3: Access Granted Only If All Three Trials Succeed.		
Authorized user rejected	2 2 2	6
Imposter accepted	1 1 1	0.001

Note: Rule 2 calculations involve multiple outcomes and are too complex to be shown here.

the performance in both categories simultaneously. For example, with three trials the rule can be written to accept a person who passes one trial, two, or all three. Under rule 2, which requires at least two successful trials, the performance is greatly improved for both categories. In reality, the improvement would probably be less dramatic than the table indicates, but it still could be significant.

Examples of personal attributes

Several methods have been developed to verify identity on the basis of personal attributes. No one technique has been identified as completely superior in all respects. They vary in accuracy, the length of time required, acceptance by users, cost, and other factors. Some of the equipment used still is in the early development stages, and that can affect performance.

Fingerprints.   Verifying identity by manual fingerprint comparisons is a well-known technique. Fingerprints are compared mainly on the basis of *minutiae,* the ridge endings and bifurcations that can be identified by an examiner. A fingerprint can contain up to 150 minutiae—40 to 60 is typical. These can be described in an *X-Y* coordinate system in which the coordinates of the minutiae are indicated along with certain feature information such as the angle at which the ridges lie at that point and the type of feature.

Fingerprint impressions are invariably distorted. A skilled examiner can make allowances for these distortions and given a sufficient number of features can make a positive decision on whether two prints match. However, the distortions still are a source of variation.

More recently, research and development efforts have addressed the automation of fingerprint matching. Equipment has been produced that permits an image of the fingerprint to be obtained without using ink, after which the image is compressed or details extracted from it into a reference file. Two basic methods have been used. In the first, a direct comparison is made between the "live" print and a file print. This approach has the disadvantage of requiring a file of actual print images, with a mechanism for rapidly selecting and positioning them. It has the advantage of being relatively simple.

The second viewpoint relies on signal processing, such as on a digitized image, to extract information about the location and direction of the minutiae. It then compares this information with a list of characteristics from a reference file. A typical system requires a few hundred bytes of data for a print. Digital processing is used both to extract candidate records from the file and in the matching process.

It is feasible to scan a finger and carry out a comparison in about 1 second. To this you must add the time to key in a claimed identity or to insert a card that bears this formation and the time to position the finger on the measuring device. In addition, if a match is not obtained the first time, it may be necessary to reposition the figure or to switch to an alternate finger. The number of retries can add significantly to the time, particularly if this happens very often.

An extensive test of an early automated fingerprint system produced a type 1 error rate of 6.5 percent, a type 2 error rate of 2.3 percent, and an average verification time, including retries when necessary, of 8.9 seconds. Later technology should be capable of much better performance, but it has not been as thoroughly tested.

Hand geometry.   The shape of a person's hand has been found to have enough interpersonal variability to distinguish one individual from another at a useful level of accuracy. The basic technique is to measure the length of the fingers, but it is a subtle process. The measurement starts at a point determined by the rounding at the end of the finger and ends at a point determined by the translucency of the web between the fingers.

In one form of this device, the user carries a magnetic stripe card on which an ID number and his or her finger length data have been recorded. The data on the card is scrambled to deter the unsophisticated. To use the device, the user places the card in a slot, then positions the hand on the measuring device with each finger resting in a slight groove. The device then measures the finger lengths to obtain four 3-digit numbers that are compared with the data deciphered from the card. The process takes less than a second, and the pass-fail output signal can be used for any purpose. The identification data also can be stored in a central computer that makes the comparison. In this case, the user would enter an identification code at the device, and it would be transferred to the computer along with the readings from the hand. Used on a remote terminal, such a device could be used to establish the individual's identity as a proper user of that terminal. Be sure, though, to protect the data that is transmitted during the identification process.

The reliability of this process depends on the degree of repeatability for a given individual and the degree to which people's finger lengths tend to cluster around normal values. Most people produce results that are quite consistent, but a few individuals exhibit somewhat more variability. Typically, most errors occur among a relatively small group of individuals.

When you file the information in a computer, you also can provide for varied tolerance rates, based on the individual's characteristics. Recognize, though, that a clever penetrator will try to find out whose identification records call for the greatest tolerance. This means that any assessment of your computer security should be based on the most relaxed tolerances you allow.

Signature dynamics.   There recently have been several significant efforts to derive electrical signals from the process of writing a signature. These then could be analyzed by computer to establish the writer's identity. These efforts have demonstrated that the physical motions of writing a signature can be used with very reasonable error rates. The writing of a signature is a conditioned reflex, done with little conscious attention. Consequently, while it is possible to forge a person's signature, it is hard to duplicate the dynamic motions associated with writing it. Forging a signature requires conscious control, which results in different signature characteristics.

There are various ways to obtain signals that represent the dynamics of a signature. Qualities include positions, forces, and acceleration. The means to measure these could be designed into the writing instrument, the writing surface, or a combination. The instruments may be applied to one, two, or three axes of motion.

Time-varying position information can be derived by using an instrumented writing surface that can read out the coordinates of the stylus at selected times during the act of writing. It is important to measure the time as well as the positions. You also can measure force, such as the pressure applied to the writing surface or the drag forces along the surfaces.

Writing also is a jerky process, with rapid changes in velocity and acceleration. These can be measured with transducers mounted in the stylus.

One automatic signature verification system showed a type 1 error rate of 1.9 percent, a type 2 error rate of 5.6 percent, and an average verification time of 13.5 seconds. This was a relatively simple system that measured a single force on the writing surface. A more extensive system, that measures both pressure and acceleration, showed a type 1 error rate of 1.7 percent, and a type 2 rate of 0.02 percent. In a test of deliberate forgery attempts, the type 2 error rate was 0.4 percent.

Speaker verification.   If all aspects of human speech are considered, the result is sufficiently complex and exhibits sufficient variation from one person to another to make it an attribute with potential for distinguishing among members of a large group. The computer is an effective tool for analyzing the many subtle distinctions between one person's speech and another's.

Speech may be viewed as a series of transitions separated by regions of varying duration in which the sounds are relatively steady. These regions are due mainly to vowels. The transitions have a noisier quality, coming from the various consonants. During the "steady" regions, the sound is influenced by the structure of the individual's vocal tract, throat, mouth, and nasal passages. This results in resonances and a harmonic structure that is partly controllable and partly inherent to the individual.

In analyzing a person's speech for identity verification by a computer, the "steady" regions have most often been employed. While the steady regions contain most of the speech energy, most of the information about what is being said is contained in the transitions, and the way in which individuals use their tongue, lips, and teeth is lost. This drastically reduces the size of the database at any given level of reliability.

A person to be enrolled first creates a reference file in the computer by repeating a "training set" of selected utterances a number of times. The resulting signal is digitized and sent to the computer. Various kinds of processing via special hardware may be done before or after the digitizing. The computer builds a reference file for each of the utterances in the training set. Thereafter, when the person wishes to verify his or her identity, the computer requests that he or she repeat these utterances, and it matches the new data against those in the reference file.

To prevent an impostor from simply recording a valid user's voice and playing it back to gain access, a specific strategy must be used. For example, when the person enrolls, the training set is made up of words from each of four categories, such as adjectives, nouns, verbs, and adverbs. Then, when the person wishes to verify his or her identity, he or she is asked to repeat phrases made up of words selected at random from these categories.

A sample phrase might be, "Young Ben swam far." The words each have one syllable and have a prominent vowel sound. The computer can readily isolate the appropriate regions for making its comparisons. If another try is required, another random phrase is generated. Use of recordings is thus effectively thwarted for all but the most sophisticated penetrator.

The matching of features from speech by computer is done by processing algorithms that rely on a database to characterize the desired response to an input. If a successful intrusion effort should be discovered, it would be possible, if a record has been kept of the original speech input, to analyze the successful deception, determine how it had been able to succeed, and refine the algorithms further to prevent a recurrence.

It also is possible to track a person's voice to adapt to slow changes, such as might occur with aging or with growing familiarity with the system. Recognition by voice generally will present problems when a person has a health problem affecting the voice, such as a cold or laryngitis.

Tests of one type of automatic speaker verification produced a type 1 error rate of 1.1 percent, a type 2 rate of 3.3 percent, and an average verification time of 6.2 seconds.

Physical security techniques

Table 5.4 is a list of physical security techniques, whether they are baseline or selective, and the types of systems for which they are advised.

TABLE 5.4   Physical Security Techniques

Item	Type	Use
Areas where smoking and eating are prohibited	Baseline	PC Large system
Computer security officer (for organizations with enough computer resources to justify this position)	Selective	PC Large system Network
Courier identification and background checks when couriers are used to deliver output	Selective	PC Large system Network
Delivery access control when you require the strongest physical access restraints	Selective	PC Large system Network
Electric equipment protection	Baseline	Large system Network
Electric power shutdown and recovery	Baseline	PC Large system Network
Inspection of incoming and outgoing materials when traffic is high and force of law is advisable	Selective	PC Large system
Isolation of sensitive production jobs	Baseline	Network
Low building profile	Baseline	Large system
Minimal traffic and access to work areas	Baseline	PC Large system Network
Passwords for access from workstations and terminals	Baseline	Network
Physical access barriers	Baseline	PC Large system
Physical security perimeter	Baseline	Large system
Placement of equipment and supplies	Baseline	PC Large system
Programming library access control	Baseline	PC Large system
Protection of data used in system testing	Baseline	Large system PC
Remote terminal physical security	Baseline	Large system Network
Security for sensitive areas during attended periods	Baseline	PC Large system
Tape management that avoids external labels when tape use is high	Selective	Large system
Universal use of badges when staff or visitor traffic is high	Selective	Large system PC Network
Use restrictions on terminals and workstations	Baseline	Network
Validation of authorized versions of production programs	Baseline	PC Large system

6

Building
Security Procedures

*Computer crimes are committed by people, not
machines. Strong policies and procedures attack this
human element and reinforce other security measures.*

It may have been the largest bank robbery in Vermont's history: The thief
made off with about $400,000. Yet no weapons were used, no one was hurt,
and the thief never even entered the state. It was all done by a long-distance
computer connection, which drew the money out of customers' accounts.

In spite of the high-tech nature of the crime, Bruce Brickman of TMS
Consulting Services, a New Jersey firm that specializes in bank security, laid
blame for this loss not on the computer system but on the people who ran it.
Banks are often more concerned with speed and production quotas than they
are about security, he charged. The victimized bank did not need more technically sophisticated security systems, he said. What it did need was "people
who can check and determine the validity of the transfer."

The type of security this consultant recommended was procedural. That's
no accident. If security is primarily a human problem, procedural security is
the type that aims most directly at that need. It governs the actions of people,
not systems.

The Role of Procedural Security

The best physical and technical methods are of little value if your employees
do not use them properly. More important, you can use procedural methods to
build computer security into the way your employees conduct your overall
business operations. At the same time, you can minimize the degree to which
security measures interfere with full, productive use of your computers.

Management and supervisory controls

At its heart, procedural security is a set of management and supervisory controls. It includes rules for the use of computers and data and ways to detect unauthorized use.

- Data input
- Data processing
- Program development
- Output
- Communication
- Storage

Figure 6.1 illustrates the types of procedural security installed by a survey group of network managers. Since procedural security covers the entire range of computer operations, it becomes an integral part of your business. You'll consider it when hiring employees. Many operating controls will be based on security considerations. Auditing and supervisory techniques will be designed with security in mind.

With this overall emphasis by management, you can establish a secure computer system and back it up with adequate checks and balances, as an everyday management activity.

It should be clear by now that any one security technique is a mixture of strengths and weaknesses. You can't fully protect a computer by any one method or any one of the three major approaches. Procedural methods are

Security procedures in use

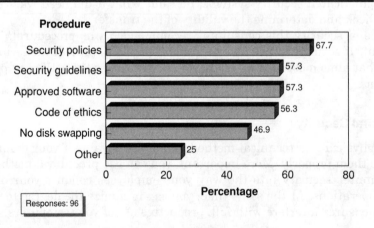

Figure 6.1   These are the most popular kinds of procedural security.

valuable primarily because they strongly back up the other two and help keep other controls in proper working order.

Do you worry enough?

Surveys have uncovered what might qualify as a latent complaint by data processing (DP) managers. Top management is concerned about security, and the DP people agree. They wonder, though, whether their superiors are as fully concerned as they ought to be.

Several of the surveys mentioned in Chap. 2 came to essentially the same conclusion: Top management thinks it gives adequate support to computer security, but its actual support often falls seriously short of the need as systems professionals see it. The general level of management awareness has improved since those surveys were taken, but security isn't always a high priority, particularly when it competes with productivity.

This lack of attention increases your vulnerability. If you don't insist on secure procedures, you are open to loss from such things as sloppy operating procedures, open access to computers, unprotected data storage, and insecure communications.

You depend on your computers. You have no choice but to actively oversee their secure operation. Computer security should occupy a central part in your list of business objectives.

Whatever other security methods you choose, their effectiveness will depend on how well you provide continuous control over your data, equipment, and employees. Procedural controls, then, will include such considerations as your organizational structure, the quality of supervision, and your ability to detect and correct abuses.

Setting Your Objectives

Any good plan starts with a list of the goals to be met. This is particularly important with procedural security since it covers such a broad range and should be integrated with so many other aspects of your operation. The major objectives of a procedural plan should include those shown in Fig. 6.2.

Establishing a need to know

The rapid changes that computers have brought to the business world have strained traditional lines of supervision and control. Established lines of authority are crossed easily and often.

Computers and the need to secure them require that your organization be structured to avoid these problems. Your new structure should divide individual jobs and duties on the basis of the particular employee's need to know. Traditional organization patterns still can be applied here. It's common, for example, to have one person conduct a financial transaction and to appoint separate supervisors and auditors to monitor it. Whenever possible, separate

Setting security goals

- Put security where it's needed
- Establish a need to know
- Match access to the need
- Provide easy access for those who need it

Figure 6.2 Goals also help resolve conflicts between control and ease of access.

job duties to provide a system of checks and balances. The person who does the work should not be the same employee who checks it for accuracy.

It's not always easy. A small company must use more generalists and fewer specialists. So must a firm that has adopted the increasingly popular horizontal form of organization. The personal computer puts the entire range of computing functions on a single employee's desk. These cases call for closer supervision of the employees and more frequent reviews of their work. You also can restrict the access over personal terminals and computers to information in the central storage unit.

Tailoring your access controls

A second objective, related to the first, is to tailor your controls to ensure that your data is available only to the limited number of people you authorize to use it. This is largely a matter of managing your use of physical access controls, tailoring them to your specific needs. After you have structured your job assignments on the basis of checks, balances, and a need to know, you must set up a control structure that will maintain the necessary limits and separation.

One way to accomplish this is with a multilevel password system, as presented in Chap. 8, that will restrict an authorized employee only to the data and programs that are necessary to the job assignment. The design of your access controls should depend on:

- Who must use the system? Which employees will be granted access?
- For what purpose is the access needed?
- When is it needed? You might be able to limit access to specified times.
- From where will the employee require access? Will this be a local or remote terminal or a personal computer?
- How is the information to be acquired and used?

Journalists should recognize these as the traditional five elements of a basic news story. Here, they've been applied to another use where they work just as well.

Promoting use along with protection

It's possible to take security to extremes. Many security measures interfere with easy, productive use of the computer. Some of this is necessary, but it's possible to go so far that the information is almost impossible to use because it's so well protected. At that extreme, the security feature defeats itself. Honest users will go to great lengths to defeat it, just so they can get their work done.

Look at the incentives you give your employees. They're probably under strong pressure to produce, to "make the numbers" in both quantity and quality. The security shortcut often can help boost their output. Supervisors, their own reputations enhanced by productive employees, overlook or even encourage these security lapses. Employees are allowed or even encouraged to share passwords or use other means to bypass access restrictions. Necessary security tasks like making backup copies are postponed or avoided.

Security that totally blocks authorized use is an extreme; careless evasions are a common problem. Both should be avoided. It requires a reasonable balance between security and efficiency. Your procedures must not be so difficult or time-consuming that there is a strong incentive to evade them. At the same time, security should be made as important as production. Keep employees and supervisors informed about their particular security responsibilities. Your evaluations of individuals and departments should include their proper use of required security procedures.

Tell your department heads—and understand it yourself: Increased production is of no value if it is offset by a major loss due to lax security.

Providing an integrated program

You need to combine a variety of approaches into an overall program. Procedural methods can serve as vital links in doing this. Good procedures will reinforce other security measures, making them more effective and helping them to work in combination.

It can work the other way, too. If your procedures are not strictly observed, your other controls can be seriously undermined. Employees who swap passwords or supervisors who fail to properly monitor operations can leave you as vulnerable to abuse as if you had no security program at all. Security should be part of the overall management picture. Observing a security procedure should be just as important as any other job requirement. Let your people know they will be judged accordingly.

Putting security where it's needed

Well-tailored procedural controls also let you aim your security programs directly at the operations that are in most need of attention. These places might deserve your particular attention:

- *Payroll.* This is often the first place a computer criminal will look. Follow that example, and emphasize payroll in your security plans. Dishonest employees have programmed computers to inflate their paychecks, to be paid for work not done, to continue to pay employees who have left the company, and even to pay nonexistent employees. Even without this kind of dishonesty, a payroll system is vulnerable to calculating errors.

- *Accounts receivable.* Money also is handled here, making this another vulnerable area. A dishonest employee in this department can send out fake invoices for sales that never were made—many companies pay these invoices without checking their own records. The employee then can pocket the proceeds. Other sources of possible trouble are an employee's failure to properly credit a receivable or to follow up a customer's complaint of being overcharged. That complaint could mean an error—or a padded bill with a dishonest employee claiming the excess.

- *Accounts payable.* A big source of risk here is to be on the receiving end of a fake invoice and to pay the bill without checking. Payments can be made without proper authorization or support. Employees could buy or sell important assets without recording them.

- *Inventory.* This is a prime area for computerization and thus a prime candidate for fraud and error. One computer manufacturer recently discovered that thousands of dollars worth of parts had disappeared with no trace or record. The computer showed them in a warehouse. The warehouse was empty. It's not certain whether the items were stolen or whether the fault was in the computerized inventory system. Either way, poor procedures probably contributed to the loss.

Many of these activities are traditional business crimes performed in years past without the aid of computers. Computerization has made them easier, particularly since businesses that install computers often do away with manual audits and controls. But, these controls are even more important in the information age. Proper security of your computerized business assets should be a major business objective.

The Keys to Security Procedures

Most procedural security measures are based on two established principles—the keys to effective security procedures:

- Make each employee personally accountable.
- Make sure that it takes more than one person to commit a fraudulent act.

If a sensitive transaction is being made, you should be able to identify the person responsible and hold that employee personally responsible for the results. You can log the use of passwords and connect the holders with the transactions for which the passwords were used. Audit trails also identify individuals with transactions. You also can use such traditional methods as checking control totals against the actual results.

Some bank checks require two signatures, and safe deposit boxes need two keys. Don't leave an opportunity for a single criminal working alone. Make the improper user face the risk and difficulty of bringing at least one other person into the scheme.

Good procedures made better

Even good procedures sometimes can be made better. If you keep these points in mind, you can put a keen edge on your program:

- Some files are more sensitive than others. They deserve protection according to their value as an information asset and the amount of damage an unauthorized user could do.

- A user doesn't have to know all the procedural controls that are applied to a particular task. Many controls, like logging the employees activity or verifying a data input, can be done without visible on-screen activity. These controls should become visible only when someone tries to evade them.

- Maintain audit trails to show who conducted what transaction. This is a proven way to assign responsibility for correct, proper methods.

- Keep in touch with your security force. Management holds the primary means to control computer misuse, but when unusual activity or some other sign makes you suspect you have a problem, let Security know immediately.

A procedural security checklist

A good procedural security program should include:

- A written policy that spells out employees' responsibilities, provides a means to detect violations, and has enough management control to make sure it is properly implemented.

- Management controls to make sure the policies are observed. Make sure they keep up with the development of your computer systems.

- Control over processes, computer use, and access to programs and data.

- Regular tests of your security system, to make sure it is adequate and employees are observing the proper procedures.

- A standard procedure to deal with anyone caught misusing the system. This can range from minor disciplinary action to criminal charges if necessary. Be ready to take this action even if it might mean bad publicity for the company.

- Constant communication. Management officials and members of the technical staff should stay in touch to discuss security needs and problems.

■ Security provisions in any purchase agreement for new computers or software.

Controls Built Into the Organization

The organizational controls in your security policy should define exactly who is authorized to what and under which conditions (Fig. 6.3). Computerization usually reduces the number of checks and balances you have over the operations of the business. That means your level of security must increase. Maintain individual accountability, and assign check-and-balance functions to different people. Set up supervisory and review systems to monitor each employee's use of your computer resources.

Work department by department. Establish controls over both the uploading and downloading of sensitive data. Establish procedures to be used when entering the system. Encrypt the most sensitive data, and keep track of which individuals have access to the code. Make sure the system identifies everyone who uses it, including the time and the programs and files used.

All these measures are designed to maintain the integrity of your data and to assign accountability to each user. A department can determine that all work is properly processed, without improper alterations.

Be particularly sure that only authorized employees are allowed access to central database files and then only to the files necessary for that employee's job. Protect the file contents with read-only restrictions.

The people who use the data should not be the same people who are authorized to make major changes in it. If you can't do that, substitute more active supervision and monitoring.

Organizational controls

- Personnel
- Programming
- Operating

Once in place, make sure they continue to work.

Figure 6.3 Organizational controls promote accountability.

Personnel controls

An important class of controls deals with the people who make up your company, starting when they are hired and extending until—and even after—they leave. You may not think of it in this way, but your hiring procedures are part of a computer security program. Check out the references and records of everyone you hire. Many employers don't—an open invitation to crime and industrial sabotage.

Nondisclosure agreements are becoming a standard job requirement for people who work with computers. IBM, for example, obtains signed agreements not to reveal its trade secrets even after the employee has left the company. When employees have moved to competing companies, IBM has gone to court several times to enforce its agreements.

Other precautions against abuses by your employees include mandatory vacations that keep each employee away from the computer for at least 2 weeks at a time. An employee who is trying to cover some fraudulent use of the computer usually will have to cover the tracks more often than that. Regular and mandatory job rotations also can make it difficult to engage in long-term abuse.

The departing employee presents a particular problem. Whether the employee resigned or was fired, there may be some resentment that could return in the form of a sabotaged computer. The passwords of departing employees should be canceled immediately. Give a particularly close check to their recent activity records. Increased access time or the use of unusual files or programs may indicate that the ex-employee has been up to something.

Your employees' privacy is an important concern, too. Any file that contains individual information about an employee—payroll and personnel records are the prime examples—should be treated as highly sensitive. Except when it is necessary, to process the payroll or to evaluate the employee, for example, this information should be available only in the form of broad statistical data from which no individual can be identified. A clear policy statement on employee rights informs the employees of where he or she stands and reassures him or her that personal information will be protected. It also discourages searching for data on other employees.

Programming controls

Controls in this class direct the way in which programs and procedures are written. The employees involved here are programmers, analysts, and other highly skilled people.

One way to implement programming controls is to establish a set of standards for writing programs that trap errors and otherwise help maintain the integrity of their data. A program should resist use in any way that can threaten sensitive data. It should not allow uncontrolled access to important data files or financial transactions.

You can enforce these standards through a continuing review process. Make sure any program or procedure that is developed is strictly for legitimate company purposes. Otherwise, you could find yourself harboring a well-programmed routine that would quietly strip your computerized resources, putting false records in their place, without anyone's knowledge. You also should conduct regular reviews of your program structures, software development techniques, access controls, and authorization techniques.

Operating controls

These controls consist of the rules to be observed when entering, changing, or using data. The procedures should be set up to check entries against normal value ranges, trapping errors, and deliberate incorrect entries. The employees should be held strictly accountable for the data they enter and use. This aspect of the security system also includes the means to detect and correct errors and to hold the appropriate employees accountable for them.

Staying in control

The preceding list of controls is not a list of alternatives from which you can make selections. These are baseline standards. You should implement all the procedural controls except those that clearly don't apply to your situation. Many of these controls also require periodic reviews to make sure they still are in place and working as they should. It's your job to make sure that the monitoring and control functions continue to help maintain your security goals.

Security Training

The department heads at one recent training session were a bit surprised to be served fortune cookies along with their seminars. When the first cookie was opened, the reason was obvious. The message inside read, "Ill fortune will befall one who shares password." Other cookies contained messages (minus the pidgin Chinese) like these:

- Choose a password no one else can easily guess.
- Change your password at least once a month.
- Information on customers is to be treated in strictest confidence.
- You are responsible for anything done under your password.
- Log off before you leave your terminal.

Procedures

The fortune cookies were a gimmick, although probably an effective one, designed to remind these experienced people of their data security responsibilities. It was devised by Carolyn Crowson, security manager for Seattle First National Bank, as part of an overall information and education program to make all employees more security conscious—and to keep them that way.

As Crowson points out, educating employees to think of data security as important should be one of your major priorities. The procedures you put into place must be executed by people. The people must be trained to observe these procedures. They'll also require regular reminders of their duties and responsibilities.

What training should accomplish

A good security training program should meet these objectives (Fig. 6.4):

- New employees should learn the company's computer security policies and procedures.

- More experienced employees should develop a greater understanding of why the procedures are in effect and how they are implemented. Better understanding usually brings better compliance.

- Managers should gain more knowledge of security policies and techniques.

- Managers also should be able to make effective decisions, directing effective security measures at the specific threats they face.

Many ways to go

Formal training is only one way to educate employees about their roles in the security program. There are many ways to provide both formal training and regular refreshers. Again, look for the methods that work best in your organization. Some possibilities include:

- Data security articles in company publications.

- Management letters distributed to department heads and other managers at various levels.

Training objectives

- Know policies
- Understand methods and purposes
- Make effective management decisions

Figure 6.4 A good security training program will meet several objectives.

- Staff-written security articles for trade journals in your field. Also look into computer industry publications. Their editors are almost always interested in articles on your in-the-field experiences, particularly if you've been able to solve a problem of some kind.

- A password awareness program to teach the importance of password security. It could include a bumper sticker type of message on a computer terminal, reminding the user of one password protection rule. You also could provide more detailed explanations in brochures or bulletin board notices.

Using existing programs

Computer security can easily be added to many existing training and orientation programs. Normally, all you need to do is to write a data security module to be inserted into the appropriate programs. These modules could be tailored for use in various types of training:

- Employee orientation, management training, technical training, and project management programs are all good places to add material on data security.

- Security training courses are obvious candidates for data security material. At Seattle First National Bank, for example, a robbery training course required by law has been fleshed out to include material on data security. Crowson says that program has had a direct impact in detecting and preventing attempted fraud in wire-transfer transactions.

- An orientation session for new employees can include an awareness program to emphasize the importance of computer security.

Developing material

Some employees will need more specialized training. For example, auditors, programmers, project managers and similar employees will need detailed training in security. These should cover the company's main areas of vulnerability, emphasizing the available solutions to these problems.

Take advantage of any in-house resources you have, or can develop, for preparing and presenting training sessions. Look in particular for people who can prepare strong visual presentations, using such media as videotapes. Don't try to make a standard presentation cover everything. Consider the nature of your audience, and prepare a program directly related to these employees' needs and responsibilities. Test your initial presentations on pilot audiences to get their reactions. Use that experience to polish your act.

Remember, training is expensive. It requires good materials, and it takes people away from their jobs. Make sure you prepare a sound program that will effectively help employees do their parts on the computer security system.

Subjects to cover

Depending on the needs of the audience, a computer security training program should include these topics:

- The company's physical security system, including the procedures employees should follow when passing security checkpoints
- Procedural security measures, again emphasizing the proper actions you expect employees to take
- Security controls built into the system and how to use them properly
- The legal and social needs for security, including privacy, trade secrets, and liability problems

A choice of format

Don't limit yourself to the traditional training process of an instructor who lectures a room full of students. Consider all forms of communication, and use those that best get the message across. Among the possibilities:

- Workshops and seminars
- Videotape and other visual presentations
- Written materials, including books, reports, and specialized publications

Procedural Backups for Physical Controls

Most physical controls require procedural support. You cannot use the physical controls to full effect unless you back them up with equally effective procedures.

Restricted file access

Any file whose compromise or modification would be a serious loss should be protected by a password system, the Justice report recommends. That should include restricting the type of access allowed: Read only, add only, modify, change the access controls, change the file name, or some combination of these.

There are commercial file-access-control systems available for some makes of systems, and similar controls are built into the operating systems of some other brands. The system should include a journal of access activity, including an exception report that would note such things as unauthorized attempts to reach specific files. Like most other kinds of control, this system relies on effective administration in such areas as assigning passwords and access rights.

This is one area where human nature works in your favor. Employees who know their activities are controlled and monitored are less likely to attempt unauthorized activity. You can use the journals and activity reports to investigate unusual events.

On the other hand, access-control systems tend to slow down the system's performance. They are inconvenient at best for authorized users who must cope with the controls.

Controlling the controls

Establish a formal procedure to be used when anyone wants to have a new kind of access to the system or wants to change the existing control methods. Prepare a standard request form to be submitted to a computer security coordinator. Give the successful requester a written permit that specifies the conditions of the access and the user's other privileges. Have the user sign a document indicating that he or she understands the conditions.

These are examples of procedural controls, but they also are instruments of access control. The written conditions and signed documents help establish an understanding among the users of the types of access you are willing to grant to them. They impress the users with the limits of their authority and help discourage violations. This procedure also defines the duties of your access coordinator and the users' responsibilities.

A major drawback is that this system can create a mountain of paperwork, and its procedural requirements may be excessive for a small, informal organization. People are most tempted to evade a system when it frustrates them in the performance of what they feel are their most important duties.

Controlling the use of terminals

One of the best ways to keep unauthorized users out of your computer is to keep them away from the PCs or terminals in the first place. The simplest way: Just keep the door locked. For that matter, how many people use the system locks that have virtually become standard equipment on personal computers? Do you know where your key is? If that doesn't seem sufficient to protect your sensitive information, consider locks that can be used to shut off the terminals themselves. There also are locking devices to keep terminals and PCs from being removed.

Even a physical security technique like a lock is aimed ultimately at the human side of computer security. Locks have a strong psychological effect. Coupled with other well-enforced security techniques, they help make employees more security conscious.

At the same time, each new technique imposes a new burden on authorized users. Locking and unlocking can be a pain, particularly if different users need access to a device. You could unlock the terminal at the beginning of the day and lock it at the end, but that would require that the unit be watched all day.

Log-on procedures

You can limit unauthorized access by setting up a standard procedure for logging onto the system. In effect, the user who knows the procedure has a kind of extended password. This is no time to be user-friendly. The system should expect the user to complete a full identification sequence before it makes any response that isn't absolutely necessary. It should do nothing, either, to correct an improper entry. Until the user has completed the entire sequence successfully, the system should not identify itself or display a prompt that's any more helpful than, say, the C> of a standard PC operating system. After the user has properly completed the sequence, the computer can issue an effusive welcome to the system. Until then it should display a stolid blank screen.

At a minimum, the expected sequence should include the assigned password plus some other kind of personal identification such as the user's name or account number. Better yet, also expect the user to enter a correct, unprompted code for the file or program to be used. Make sure the screen display does not show the password as it is entered. Try to avoid any command that would send a password to a printer. Then, in case it should happen anyway, provide for immediate repeated overprints that will quickly make it illegible.

Give the user a chance to correct mistakes, but three consecutive wrong entries should disconnect the telephone line. Hang up, too, if there is an excessive delay before the user enters the password or other information.

Include a record-keeping system that keeps track of log-ins and produces exception reports of improper or unsuccessful attempts.

Another tactic suggested in the Justice report is not to cut off all unauthorized access. Instead, provide something innocuous for the unauthorized user to play with while an alarm alerts you to the invasion.

Another good idea is to display after a successful log-in the time and date of the user's last access. This could alert the user to unauthorized use of the password.

These controls can help exclude unauthorized users and make authorized people more security conscious. Like many other access controls, they impose an often inconvenient procedure, particularly if an authorized user must make several attempts to travel the full access route.

Other tactics

Other ideas suggested in the federal reports:

- Store passwords in code within the computer.
- Prepare a signed agreement that details the user's rights and responsibilities.
- Bill all computer use to the user's department. This gives the department head a chance to check for unauthorized access.
- Maintain logs and documentation of all program changes.
- Restrict access to utilities that could bypass the security system.
- Control access to system documentation.
- Keep detailed records of access to particularly sensitive files.
- Maintain a log of any commands that would modify programs or data.
- Establish special passwords, modified daily, for the most critical data and users.
- Require secondary passwords for access to particularly sensitive material.

- Automatically disconnect unneeded access lines during off hours.
- Modify your hardware and software so it will not recognize systemlike prompts from a terminal. This can keep an invader from gaining access by making the system believe the messages are coming from the computer instead of the terminal.
- Determine normal use patterns for authorized individuals and departments. Note and check out any significant exceptions.

What a Good Program Requires

An ideal procedural program should have these characteristics:

- It should be nondiscretionary. Employees should have no practical choice but to observe the prescribed procedures.
- It should be automatic. The controls should be a built-in part of normal working procedures.
- It should not be a serious problem to authorized employees who do their jobs properly.
- It should sound a warning when the system is used improperly.
- It should be self-monitoring, depending as little as possible on constant supervision. Human monitoring is an important part of the process, but the system should not be designed so an error could slip past at some moment when the supervisor is not available.
- It should leave room for innovations and new developments.

It's not easy, or even always possible, to meet all these demanding criteria. But come as close as you can.

Assumptions to avoid

Don't assume that traditional management controls will automatically work in a computerized setting. This is a quick invitation to false security. Don't make the follow-up mistake, either, of assuming that controls developed primarily in a mainframe setting will automatically work for PCs and networks. You can adapt traditional techniques, but you usually cannot lift them intact.

There's another assumption to avoid, too: that the program you have in place will continue to be good enough. As computers and security techniques advance, the program that seems adequate may actually be seriously deficient. Keep abreast of new needs and techniques, and make sure your program does the same.

Strong points

Procedural controls have these positive qualities you can consider in your planning:

- They usually are inexpensive. You often can use employees and resources you already have.
- Properly implemented, they improve the working relationship between people and machines.
- Good security can become part of your overall business objectives.
- Employees can be given a clear picture of their expected duties and responsibilities.
- Management has the means to exercise review and control.
- You can exercise direct supervision over data integrity and the security of your information assets.

Cautions

There are some weak spots, too. Watch out for these:

- Pressures for increased production often take priority over observing security procedures.
- A policy always is easier to write than to observe.
- Your level of protection easily can slip behind fast-moving developments in the computer field.
- Regular reviews easily can become irregular.
- Knowledgeable people often can bypass your established procedures.

Procedural Security Techniques

Table 6.1 is a list of procedural security techniques, whether they are baseline or selective, and the types of systems for which they are advised.

TABLE 6.1　Procedural Security Techniques

Item	Type	Use
Assets accountability management	Baseline	PC Large system
Assigning data use accountability to users	Baseline	PC Large system Network
Completion of external input data (when external sources provide incomplete information)	Selective	PC Large system Network
Compliance with laws and regulations	Baseline	PC Large system Network
Computer security management committees	Baseline	PC Large system
Computer system activity records	Baseline	Large system Network
Computer use access-control administration	Baseline	Large system Network
Confirming receipt of documents	Baseline	PC Large system
Cooperation of computer security officers	Baseline	PC Large system
Correction and maintenance of production system	Baseline	Large system
Courier trustworthiness and identification (when couriers are used to deliver output)	Selective	PC Large system
Data classification (when some data is more sensitive than others)	Selective	PC Large system
Data file and program backup	Baseline	PC Large system Network
Destruction of discarded documents	Baseline	PC Large system
EDP auditors participating in setting requirements and specifications	Baseline	Large system PC
EDP auditing (when internal-audit resources are used)	Selective	Large system Network
Employee identification on work products	Baseline	PC Large system
Financial loss contingency and recovery funding	Baseline	PC Large system
Human subjects review	Selective	PC Large system
Independent computer use by auditors (for advanced auditing)	Selective	PC Large system

TABLE 6.1   Procedural Security Techniques (*Continued*)

Item	Type	Use
Inspection of personnel data input and output (when personal data is exchanged with outside organizations)	Selective	PC Large system
Isolation of sensitive production jobs	Baseline	Network
Keeping security reports confidential	Baseline	PC Large system
Limited use of system utility programs (when general-purpose utilities are in use)	Selective	Large system PC
Logging user trouble calls	Baseline	PC Large system Network
Magnetic tape erasure	Baseline	Large system
Minimizing copies of sensitive reports	Baseline	PC Large system Network
Monitoring computer use (when access is to be limited)	Selective	PC Network Large system
Participation of users at critical development times	Baseline	Large system Network PC
Passwords for system access	Baseline	PC Large system
Proprietary notice printed on sensitive documents	Baseline	PC Large system Network
Remote user agreement (when workstations or terminals are outside your immediate control)	Selective	Network
Secrecy of data file and program names (when the system handles a large variety of transactions)	Selective	Network Large system
Security for sensitive areas during attended periods	Baseline	PC Large system Network
Separation and accountability of EDP functions	Baseline	Large system
Suppression of incomplete or obsolete data	Baseline	PC Large system
Universal use of badges (in cases of heavy traffic by staff members or visitors)	Selective	Large system Network PC
Validating authorized versions of production programs	Baseline	Large system

7

Hardware and Software Security

Contrary to rumor, networks and PCs do have the means to protect themselves. Don't expect security to be automatic, though, and don't expect technical security to make up for lapses in other areas.

Both in its hardware and its software, the computer has the ability to protect itself. That's true even of PCs and networks, despite what large-system partisans sometimes claim. Nevertheless, there are two important points to remember:

- No form of security is automatic. Whatever the size of your system, you must work to make it secure. Networks require more work than centralized systems.

- No form of security can do it all. Even the most advanced and comprehensive forms of large-system security can do only part of the job.

Consider the case of a man who stumbled on an access code that let him make mass withdrawals from a network of Massachusetts automatic teller machines. The man rounded up two accomplices, and they spent the night cruising from ATM to ATM making cash withdrawals. With bundles of cash sewn into their clothes, they headed for the airport and a flight to safety.

Like many high-tech crimes, this one had a low-tech ending. The men attracted the suspicion of a security guard, not because they looked like bank robbers but because they looked like airplane hijackers. They carried no luggage and paid cash for their tickets—key elements of a hijacker profile.

This case illustrates an important point to remember when planning a security program: ATMs have some of the most elaborate built-in security systems ever devised. Yet there was at least one flaw, and someone was almost able to exploit it. This theft was solved through human intervention, not technical wizardry.

Cases like this just reinforce the point that no form of computer protection is perfect. Each has weaknesses that reduce its effectiveness. In the case of technical security, the big weakness is that you cannot ignore the human component. Careless people can mess up your plans. Those who cause trouble on purpose can do even more. Remember, any technical device that one person can invent, another can overcome.

Use technical security as a part of your overall program. Make it your goal to build a system of security measures that complement each other and offset each other's shortcomings. In spite of its shortcomings, as illustrated in the ATM case, the technical security built into a computer system—or that you can build in yourself—is an important part of the total security package. Just don't let yourself become excessively impressed by a computer's power to protect itself. You can find yourself presuming that it never really needs your help. That can be a dangerous attitude. Technical security needs a lot of backup from physical and procedural techniques.

The Role of Technical Security

The increased use of networks and personal computers has directed new attention to technical types of protection. The nature of a network makes it necessary. Physical protection is obviously much more difficult than it was with old centralized systems. There is also the vastly increased number of users. Once, only a few people knew how to use computers. Now, those who don't know how are usually seen as targets for retraining. These numbers make it infinitely more difficult to manage a system of procedural controls. Meanwhile, computer systems and the networks that link them are constantly getting better. Thus, technical protection is becoming both easier and more important. It is now possible to design technical measures that will protect you against most types of crime and abuse. Technical security can also be cost-effective. Often, the protection requires more ingenuity than it does money.

A matter of definition

Built-in security is a combination of controls within your hardware, software and communication systems. As you can see from Table 7.1, their purposes are similar to those of physical and procedural methods. The three types of security interact and support each other (Fig. 7.1). The major types of technical security also overlap and work together:

- Hardware controls are used to make sure the operating system functions properly and to control access to the programs and data.

- Software controls are used primarily to identify users and control their access. They also let you monitor use of the system.

- Communication controls are applied to networks, modems, and other communication system components to control access and the flow of data over the system.

TABLE 7.1   Keeping Up With Technical Developments

Development	Potential problems	Technical responses
Computer processors have become faster and more complex.	Passwords may be bypassed before the system can react.	High-speed identification method
More people have computer knowledge and experience.	Unauthorized employees can gain access to sensitive information.	Multiple levels of access controls.
More people have detailed technical knowledge.	Programs can be modified to bypass normal controls.	Input-output protection to isolate users.
PCs and enterprise networks have decentralized computer operations.	More opportunities for improper access.	Isolate users and regulate their access.
Information has been made more widely available in client-server database systems.	More opportunity to manipulate and misuse data.	Allow access only to authorized files

Types of technical security

- Hardware controls
  - Ensure proper operation
- Software controls
  - Govern access
- Communication controls
  - Manage data flow

Figure 7.1   Technical controls reinforce each other.

All work together to help improve your security. Sometimes they are combined, such as when security controls are built into the "firmware" of read-only memory.

Technical security goals

Most technical security methods are aimed at one or more of these objectives (Fig. 7.2):

- Maintaining the integrity of your computer system and its contents. The computer should do its job correctly and consistently. Your data must be reliable, and your programs must process it without error. These qualities can be important in such functions as payroll, inventory, and finances. Poor integrity can leave you open to fraud, theft, and embezzlement.

- Keeping sensitive information in confidence. This is largely a matter of access control. The information in your database files often is essential to

Technical security goals

- Maintain system integrity
- Protect sensitive information
- Make system available

Figure 7.2   Technical methods assure reliability.

the operation of your business. It may include critical financial details or trade secrets which, if revealed or corrupted, can have a catastrophic effect on your business. You also must be careful to protect the privacy of personal data on your employees and customers.

- Making the computer's services available whenever they are needed. You certainly know the perils and frustrations of a computer that goes down. Good technical controls can help you minimize that problem, protecting the system from sabotage, accidents, misuse, and even poor design.

Overcoming obstacles

Technical security measures have something in common with their physical and procedural counterparts. No matter how badly they are needed, there always seems to be some reason they cannot be applied immediately and to their full effect. Usually that reason is that they get in the way of normal business operations.

Employees, and even managers, aren't always willing to support the security effort, particularly when it interferes with the ease or productivity of their work. Often, programmers and technicians can easily create all the technical security measures you want. Your real problem is to resolve the many conflicts that arise between your need for security and the other goals of your business.

For instance, access control requires, at a minimum, a daily delay while the user enters a password and the computer responds. Then consider the costs and delays you face should someone lose a password. Encryption can protect data, but at the expense of delays, difficulties, and slower performance. You aren't always able to exercise the close supervision good security often requires. Then there is the common problem of a budget that simply doesn't have enough money for all the security measures you would like to have in place. It's hard to accept these problems, particularly when you depend on your computer for quick decisions.

The only way to resolve these conflicts is to set priorities. Determine how important security is to you, compared with other goals, such as efficiency and productivity.

The priority you give to security will depend in part on how much value you place on the competing functions. Compare this with the value of the information you are trying to protect. You may find that security deserves a higher priority than you'd thought. You also may find that it deserves a lower priority.

Where to Use Technical Security

Technical security often is work in tandem with physical and procedural methods, complementing each other. For example, the physical requirement for a password can be backed up by procedures that protect its security and require its use and by built-in features to prevent evasion and misuse.

Technical security methods may do many of the same jobs as other techniques, but they do them in different ways (Fig. 7.3). Some of the major applications of technical security techniques include:

- Separating the material to which a user is allowed access from other resources inside the system
- Protecting one user's data from other users
- Controlling access from remote locations
- Defining and enforcing levels of access control
- Monitoring the system for improper use

Technical security applications

- Isolating sensitive information
- Isolating users' data
- Controlling remote access
- Enforcing access control
- Monitoring the system

Figure 7.3 Technical methods accomplish familiar jobs in different ways.

Maintaining separation

Some of the most sensitive information your organization maintains is in its personnel file. This data must be kept in confidence, both to protect the employees' privacy and to avoid the disruption and jealousy that could infect your organization should someone know the details of everyone else's personal and economic life.

You can use technical methods to help protect information like this. The information should be compartmentalized within the computer's active memory and its storage facilities. Place the data in small, segregated files. Then use hardware and software techniques, along with the procedural and access-control methods, to restrict a user's access only to those chunks of information that individual needs to do the job. Access to particularly sensitive files, like the personnel records, should be on the basis of a strict need to know. Then have the system provide only the data that needs to be known.

You can include these restrictions in programs, which allow the holder of a certain password or other identification code access to material in a specified file. You also can use technology to control access to particular computers, peripherals, or stored media. The available methods can include controls on access to information within the computer memory, or you can block unauthorized users from operating certain procedures.

Isolating users

If there's one file more sensitive than your personnel records, it is your collection of payroll data. If there's one file that is harder to protect, payroll is it. The problem: You must maintain security at the same time your payroll clerks work with this file—all of it—every pay period.

Again, separation is the basic technique. An employee's ability to alter payroll data should be restricted to prevent such common criminal techniques as crediting extra time or even creating phony employees. The separation techniques will also be effective in protecting you from accidental access as well as deliberate acts.

Another level of separation is needed, too. You must include blocks that keep the data called up by a payroll employee from becoming available to someone else who logs onto the system at the same time. Once the payroll operation has been finished, the data should be cleanly purged from memory.

The network setting is one place where this could be important. Take a sales force operating out of several branch offices, all connected to your central computer by a communications network. Each sales office maintains its own file of customer records. Where is this system vulnerable? Let's say a competitor should become interested in finding out who your best Chicago area customers might be. It would take only a little computer and communications expertise to tap into your network and get a look at the customer files. The competitor may find an unprotected terminal or learn the dial-up access procedure for your computer. While he's at it, he can get Denver and Atlanta, too.

This means your entire communication system must be secured. One way is to encrypt the customer file data (do your password files, too). Or you could use a call-back routine to identify either the individual or, more likely, the authorized terminal. You might also use the physical security techniques of patrols or cameras around the terminals and other access points.

Setting levels of sensitivity

Many of the elements of a security system tend to define each other. How you separate employees according to their needs for various data also largely defines how you will separate the data into "compartments" for access by the authorized employee.

Many access-control software programs work by compartmentalizing the files according to levels of sensitivity, much like the military system of top secret, confidential, and so on. An individual is "cleared" for access to information at a certain level, and that access right is connected in the computer with the user's access code. To reach a file at a certain level, you must give a password that reflects your access to material on that level.

Leaving an audit trail

A good security system will not stop at access control alone. It also should keep a record of its work. Anyone who tries to gain access—successfully or not, legitimately or not—should leave a distinct trail of electronic footprints. The system should tell you who was there, when, and what they did. Pay particular attention to the use of your most sensitive files. If you see any reason to suspect a problem, check it out right away.

Some Typical Applications

Since they work together, the functions and applications of technical security are a lot like the functions and applications of other kinds of security. All are intended to do much the same thing: keep unauthorized users away from your computer. Your technical measures should back up your physical and procedural techniques, and all three should reinforce each other as part of an overall security program. Consider the following examples.

Backing up passwords

Passwords aren't always as effective as people think they are. A password is effective only as part of a larger security program, and then only if it is well managed. It makes sense, too, to back up the physical and procedural aspects of a password system with technical controls. In fact, a password system relies so heavily on all three types of protection, it's hard to classify in any one group.

A fundamental technical control for passwords is a routine that will keep the password from being displayed on a screen or printer. At the next level of sophistication, the system should encrypt the files that contain password assignments. A system that can generate random passwords for assignment to their users is another example of technical support.

Restricting remote access

As the hacker community has demonstrated, the telephone lines coming into our computers are major sources of damage and disruption. The networks that connect remote terminals and computers are highly vulnerable to security problems. Technical controls can't block all unauthorized access by themselves, but like everything else, they can contribute to the cause.

An automatic dial-back system is one technical feature that can help close a major opening to crime and misuse. There also are devices to determine without the call back that a remote device hooked to the computer is actually one of yours. If the terminal is not one you've authorized for access, the system might be able to locate it and close down its access. Controls like these identify the hardware, not the user, and they still leave you vulnerable to an unauthorized person misusing an authorized terminal, or even an authorized user on an authorized terminal doing some act that shouldn't be done. However, that only illustrates what now should be a familiar point: Don't depend on one technique alone—or even one type of technique alone. Use them in combination to back each other up.

A Security Shopper's Guide

Because technical security is largely a hardware-software solution, establishing this part of your security program will largely be a matter of obtaining the right kind of hardware and software. Of course, writing a check isn't all there is to it. Good security requires that your purchases be evaluated and that you fit them into your overall security scheme. They will do no real good if they don't suit your individual needs. You also must expect to take some steps on your own.

There is a wide variety of security products on the market, enough to cover most of your technical security needs. This list is neither complete nor necessarily representative, but it does indicate some of the types of products now on the market:

- Comprehensive mainframe security packages designed to work with the system's existing operating system. This is the type of system purchased by banks and other large, highly security conscious organizations.

- Product validation software that maintains a database of system and application program characteristics. Before a program is run, the software checks the program against these characteristics to ensure that the program has not been modified by a virus or some other cause.

- Software that establishes password control over a PC hard disk.

- Features include varied levels of protection for individual subdirectories and a feature that prevents booting from a floppy disk that has not first been flagged by the security system. Other PC systems offer multiple levels of network security and a limited-use trial function for dealers and service personnel.

- A multifeatured protection system that authenticates messages, encrypts information, and organizes the information access in network systems.

- A software program designed for personal computers as well as larger units. At any chosen point in the program, you can call for a security check. The user must use a hand-held decoder to continue.

- Fiber optic communication cables, which generally are more secure than conventional electronic links.

- Communication by infrared light beams. These can be made so small they are almost impossible to locate and intercept.

Standardized rating system

There is a wealth of software and equipment on the market to help you improve your system's security. To help evaluate the options, you can use a standard rating system for computer system security developed by the federal government. Called the Trusted Computer System Evaluation Criteria, it was developed with help from the Institute of Electrical and Electronics Engineers and the Association for Computing Machinery. One part of the rating system is a list of six fundamental requirements a secure system should meet. A second major part is a rating system that ranks systems and components according to the level of security they provide.

The basic requirements

According to the evaluation criteria, a secure system should meet these requirements:

- It must implement an explicitly defined security policy. This policy should fully describe how you wish to grant access to information.

- All information should be classified according to its security level.

- Every individual who is authorized to use the system should be positively identified and granted access only to designated processes.

- Any action that might affect security must be recorded.

- The hardware and software components of the system should be designed so each can be evaluated independently.

- The system must provide as much protection to your security mechanisms as it does to the information it is supposed to guard.

Systems classified for security

Based on how well a system meets these requirements, the evaluation guide will place it in one of four classes, according to the level of protection it offers. The classes are:

- *Class A,* the most secure. These systems must have a secure, verified design based on a formal model of an established security policy. The hardware and software must work together to ensure that the policy is constantly enforced. The main requirement for this class is a verification system to guarantee that the security functions will work as intended.

- *Class B* systems also implement a formal security policy, and they maintain separate levels of sensitivity. Systems in this class control all access by users, and they maintain extensive audit trails. Some systems in this class have reference monitors to direct proper access to sensitive material. Some also contain formal mathematical models for the security policy.

- *Class C* systems provide access on a need-to-know basis, either by the individual or by members of designated groups. Each authorized group or user is recognized by a unique identification code. A subdivision of this class adds features that keep authorized users from scavenging data from memory or storage, identifies each user and establishes an audit trail.

- *Class D* is made up of systems that fail to qualify for any of the more secure classes. Users of these systems rely primarily on procedural and physical controls.

Security by default

An important feature to look for in any security system offer is security by default, not as the exceptional condition. Security by default is the basis of the baseline system of security planning. A system of security by default initially covers everything in the system. Then, if you decide it is not necessary to secure a particular asset, you can exclude it from the security coverage.

Under a system of security by exception, you must decide, item by item, which files and activities the system should protect. This requires a long decision-making process with the ever-present possibility that you might forget to cover something important.

An exception system might be the right choice for a small user who wants to protect only a few sensitive files. For larger systems, a default system is much easier to manage. It also ensures that if you make a mistake in a coverage decision, you err on the side of safety.

Security by default also protects newly created files from the moment they enter the system. This eliminates the chance someone will neglect to secure an important new file.

Considering Encryption

Not long ago, the federal government gave an unintended endorsement to the effectiveness of encrypted data. The government produced a proposal that would give federal investigators a "back door" through which to examine anyone's encrypted data.

Specifically, the National Institute of Standards and Technology proposed that suppliers who furnish communication equipment to the federal government use encryption based on the Clipper Chip. The chip is an encryption processor developed for the National Security Agency. Built into each chip is an 80-bit split-key encryption key you could use to lock and unlock data transmissions.

Unlike the leading encryption system now in use, the basic algorithm of the Clipper Chip system was to be kept secret. There was one notable exception: Government agencies would maintain a key escrow database that would let authorized investigators gain access to encrypted material. The government's logic was that it should have access to computerized material on much the same basis that it is now entitled to administer wiretaps. Investigators want to be able to examine the data transmitted by drug dealers, terrorists, and similarly delightful people. The prevailing reaction has been a loud protest that the Clipper Chip would provide an avenue for "big-brother" intrusions by federal officials.

The government has a valid point, but it doesn't go far enough. In their zeal to go after the bad guys, officials have failed to adequately consider the legitimate interests of thousands of honest people who want to encrypt their data. The protesters have a valid point, but they have gone too far. They have been understandably reluctant to turn the keys to their security over to the government, but fears of big-brother snooping are probably overblown.

Lost in the debate has been another valid point: There is an effective and highly trusted encryption system already in use. It is based on the well-known Data Encryption Standard (DES). Even if the Clipper Chip never becomes more than a federal purchasing specification, some fear it might drive the makers of encryption products to abandon DES in favor of the less-trusted system. With that argument, the protesters are in accord with the government over one key point: DES is a tough nut to crack.

A long history

Encryption is an ages-old way to protect information. The computer has brought it to new levels of complexity and sophistication. Even so, few computer users actually use their devices to encrypt their data. The computer's contribution to this particular art has not been to make it easy or inexpensive.

The basic encryption process encodes text material, converting it into scrambled data that must be decoded to be understood. When encrypting, an algorithm converts the message or document into an unreadable jumble of characters and symbols.

Encryption is used most often for sensitive data that is transmitted over networks or public communication systems such as phone lines, satellites, microwaves, coaxial cables, and fiber optic cables. An encryption routine is provided in the program, or an encryption device is installed in the line somewhere between the computer and the modem. When the encrypted material reaches its destination, a user with a decryption key can convert it back to its readable form.

The key, essentially a string of digital information, allows users to encode or decode a message. Key management has been the most complex and costly part of encryption, but newer electronic methods are simplifying the process.

The leading encryption systems set up a mathematical challenge. DES uses a 56-bit key, designed so it can be deciphered only by trying every one of an unmanageable number of computations. This can be done, but it requires the right combination of time, equipment, and expertise.

Security experts consider a code like DES suitable only for short-term protection. For longer-term protection or if you need the best possible security, they recommend coding schemes that require multiple passes through the codes written into a DES chip.

Coming back

For many years, encryption was much discussed but little used. In the past, it was often regarded—correctly—as cumbersome and expensive. More recently, two forces have combined to make it a much more attractive security option:

- Technical advancements have made encryption easier to use.

- The spread of local and enterprise networks has made encryption more attractive as it travels across vulnerable hardware.

Encryption, in its many types and uses, is becoming recognized as one of the best ways to address network vulnerability. For example, after suffering repeated attacks from worms and viruses, the Internet system decided to offer encryption services for the first time in the nationwide research network's history. Internet uses software-based encryption, which is slower but significantly less expensive than the hardware encryption schemes commonly used in such applications as electronic fund transfer (EFT). The cost difference is dramatic. Internet charges its users $25 for a key. Citicorp, which uses hardware encryption for its electronic mail system, has paid $1,500 per network node for a hardware system.

Uses of encryption

Encryption addresses two distinct security needs. The most obvious is to keep information secret. Trade secrets and other confidential information might require this protection. The Chevron Corporation encrypts information on drilling sites. There is also a matter of legal liability. An employer may be held legally responsible for even the accidental or unauthorized disclosure of information from employees' personal records.

A less-known but equally important use is to keep data from being altered. Users of EFT and electronic data interchange (EDI) are usually worried more about alteration than theft. A bank, for example, wants to keep outside parties from altering the figures in its data transmissions.

The Data Encryption Standard

The best-known algorithm is DES (for Data Encryption Standard), which was developed in the early 1970s for government use. It has since gained widespread use in the private sector as well.

In 1988, the National Security Agency (NSA) stopped using DES for classified security needs and began steering private users toward its own new algorithms like those now incorporated in Clipper Chip. In fact, throughout the process there have been suggestions that DES may not be entirely secure. And while the government questions its effectiveness, there have been rumors in the private sector that DES has its own trapdoor. No one has been able to find it, though, and DES remains popular.

DES users know it well, and it is the basis of many products, even within the government. The National Institute of Standards and Technology (formerly the National Bureau of Standards) has continued to reaffirm DES for nonclassified use. Officials who chose DES for the Internet encryption scheme said they did not seriously consider anything else. Other users have pointed out that most purloined commercial information must be used immediately if it is to have any value. Even if an unauthorized user could decrypt a DES message, the process would be too time-consuming.

The public key

One reason encryption has seen limited use in the past is its cost and complexity. Consider the difficulty of distributing the keys and ensuring they are not compromised. These are easily stolen, and street prices for stolen commercial keys have been as little as $150. For that reason, the first thing you might do with an encryption system is to give away a key to the code.

That is the basis of one of the best-recognized encryption systems available: the public key system, in which you provide a key to outside users who feed data into your system. You can receive information from anyone to whom you give the key to the system.

Of course, you must then keep people from using the same key to decode information you don't want them to have. For that purpose, here's a second key. You use the public key to encode the information; your own private key to decode it. Naturally, you give out only the public key.

The public key system, introduced in 1976 at Stanford University, has enjoyed widespread recognition and use. It has had a major impact on the art of encrypting data. Encryption, in turn, is picking up new attention, particularly as a way to maintain security over communication networks.

The public key is, of course, a natural alternative to a single-key system, in which there is only one key for both encoding and decoding. Naturally, you have to keep the key itself under tight security. The public key system offers several advantages over the single keys. For one thing, you don't have to worry about protecting the public key. You also can do such things as placing electronic signatures within the system to identify users and trace their activities. On the other hand, there is no particular advantage over single-key systems if everyone who feeds data into the encrypted files also is authorized to retrieve and use that material.

In particular, either system must be backed up by some form of access control to identify authorized users of your decoding key. The system must be able to distinguish an authorized user from someone who has stolen the code or has managed to crack it. The system should also control access to multiple levels of security.

Other systems

The RSA Digital Signature is an authentication tool that verifies the originator and the integrity of the transmitted data. In this case, the messages may not be hidden, but the recipient will know if they've been tampered with. A variation on this type of security product is used to protect networked software. One user, the Labor Department's Bureau of Labor Statistics (BLS), has 1,200 networked PCs. BLS isn't seriously concerned with protecting information, an official points out, but it uses encryption against viruses that might alter its statistical data.

Things to consider

Not all your information—and perhaps not even much of it—may need the full protection of encryption systems like DES or public key systems. These can be expensive to obtain and time-consuming to use. Don't subject yourself to this continuing expense unless the data you are trying to protect is worth it.

There is at least one less costly alternative: Data compression programs are a simple form of encoding data so it requires less storage space. In the process, it also puts your material under a simple encoding scheme that must be decoded to use the material. Many PC software packages include similar encryption schemes. They are not as hard to crack as the more sophisticated systems, but they could be useful when a cost-benefit comparison doesn't justify the more advanced methods.

An encryption system has two main weaknesses. The first is that only the most complex codes are unbreakable—and perhaps not even these. Less sophisticated codes yield to less sophisticated code cracking.

The more likely source of loss is that the code itself will be compromised. Your most sensitive information deserves a strong protection system. A strong system, in turn, demands that you protect the access code itself. This is a human factor, and you must take adequate steps to control it. An encryption system also requires the help of a good access-control system.

Encryption also can produce a false sense of security. Be careful not to assume that it's the answer to all your problems or that once installed, it will continue to provide security without regular checkups and maintenance.

Qualities of a good system

If you do decide encryption is for you, your system should have these qualities:

- It should work transparently. It should inhibit normal and efficient operations as little as possible, and the process should not be overtly visible to the users.

- It should be automatic. Data saved on disks, tapes, and other offline media should be encoded as it is recorded, and this information should be deciphered only as it is retrieved by authorized users.

- It should allow individual users to place private data under individual codes, independent of the automatic process.

- If used in an extensive communication network, it should provide for managed distribution of the keys.

Problems With Technical Security

No type of protection is perfect, and technical security is no exception. In fact, technical security has one particular soft spot: the human factor. It's easy to rely so much on technology that you expect too much from it and neglect other forms of security.

In particular, warns one security consultant, many managers who build security into their systems feel they have achieved "the best security money can buy." They fail to realize that technical systems are only parts of a security plan, which in an era of expanding networks, must extend far beyond the system itself if it is to be successful. They don't bother to go through the entire process of assessing their risks, developing a plan that will meet those risks, and selecting security methods that will implement the plan.

No system, no matter how good, can offer full protection by itself. Don't lull yourself into thinking that you don't have any weak spots. They are inevitable. And someone whose attitude is far from complacent may be looking for them.

A Technical Security Checklist

Any evaluation of your technical security plan, planned or existing, should include these points:

- Determine the degree of technical protection you now enjoy—or lack—with particular attention to networks and communication lines.

- Look into special access-control software, checking it for useful application to your specific needs.

- Design the system to detect and trace unauthorized access attempts.

- Make sure you don't rely too heavily on passwords. Back them up with other types of controls.

- Establish a firm security policy, and make sure all your controls are useful for implementing that policy.

- Set standards for including security considerations in the design, development, and modification of software.

- Consider encryption for sensitive data.

- Make sure you protect your security provisions as well as you protect other elements of the system.

- Check out the security features of any new equipment or programs you buy.

Strong points

Consider technical security measures when you can make use of these features:

- Built-in security measures often can automate security routines that otherwise would be slow and clumsy.

- Technical security measures are an integral part of the system. They aren't just added on to it.

- Technical measures can overlap and reinforce other types of security measures and the technical measures built into other parts of the system.

- Their operation usually is automatic; they require no special effort by the operator.

Problems to avoid

At the same time, beware of these drawbacks:

- Technical security measures can easily be overemphasized, at the expense of other types of security. You need a proper mix of security techniques, arranged to reinforce each other.

- Installing technical measures can give you a false sense of security.

- Technical security measures can interfere with efficient use of the computer, particularly if they are poorly designed.

- Built-in devices are vulnerable to tampering by knowledgeable users.

- If so, their work probably will be well hidden, and you may not learn about it until serious damage has been done.

- A technical security device can protect only the part of the system in which it is installed. Other elements—particularly communication lines, remote terminals and networked PCs—may remain unprotected.

Technical Security Techniques

Table 7.2 is a list of technical security techniques, whether they are baseline or selective, and the types of systems for which they are advised.

TABLE 7.2   Technical Security Techniques

Item	Type	Use
Computer program change logs	Baseline	PC Large system
Password file encryption	Baseline	Network Large system
Computer use access-control administration	Baseline	Large system Network
Log trouble calls from users	Baseline	PC Large system Network
Data file access control	Baseline	Large system Network
Data file and program backup	Baseline	PC Large system
Exception reporting	Baseline	PC Network Large system
Validate data input	Baseline	PC Large system Network
Erase magnetic tapes (lets users participate at critical points in development)	Baseline	Large system PC
Passwords for workstation access	Baseline	Network Large system
Restrictions on displaying privileged information	Baseline	Large system Network
Protecting data used in system testing	Baseline	Large system PC
Auditors participate in setting requirements and specifications	Baseline	PC Large system
Assign responsibility for application program controls	Baseline	PC Large system
Suppress incomplete or obsolete data	Baseline	PC Large system
Technical review of operating system changes	Baseline	Large system
Telephone access universal selection	Baseline	Network
Workstation log-in protocol	Baseline	Network Large system

TABLE 7.2   Technical Security Techniques (*Continued*)

Item	Type	Use
Vendor-supplied program integrity	Baseline	PC Large system
Automated computer operations (in large production systems)	Selective	Large system
Completion of external data inputs (when external sources provide incomplete information)	Selective	PC Large system
Program quality assurance (when quality assurances are available)	Selective	PC Large system
Cryptographic protection (when you need the greatest protection of data, particularly when traveling over a network)	Selective	Large system Network
Data classification (when sensitivity is variable)	Selective	PC Large system
Dynamic password change control by user (when there might be frequent interruptions in terminal use)	Selective	Network
Limit transaction privileges from workstations (in systems that permit access from multiple workstations)	Selective	Network
Limited use of system utility programs (when general-purpose utility programs are in service)	Selective	Large system PC
Monitor computer use (when use should be limited to employees or other authorized parties)	Selective	PC Large system Network
Automatic password generation (consider when there are many remote workstation users)	Selective	Network
Secrecy of file names (when the system handles widespread transactions)	Selective	Large system Network
Separation of personal identification data (when processing personal information)	Selective	PC Large system Network
Separate test and production systems (in larger networks)	Selective	Network Large system
Use personal identifiers to govern database searches (for control when processing sensitive data)	Selective	PC Large system
Workstation identifiers (when high workstation security is needed)	Selective	Network

8

The Perils
of Passwords

*When you think of security, a password should be one
of the first things that comes to mind, not the last.*

A computer instructor had a serious lesson not long ago for executives at a Virginia consulting firm. As a classroom experiment, trainer John Simons demonstrated a simple, easy way to break into a Novell network. Later, the company was almost grateful as it acknowledged the lesson it had learned and wanted to pass on. "For full security, you really need to have your file server locked up," a company representative said. "Password protection is not enough; system managers (also) need to have physical security in place."

If necessity is the mother of invention, the instructor's strategy is a black sheep offspring. It all started with a mistake. Someone had inadvertently set a supervisor's password, and no one knew what it was. The instructor had to find a way around the password system to regain control of the network. It wasn't difficult, Simons told a *Network World* writer. "This is so very simple you can probably train a dog to do it."

The basic process is probably well known to anyone who's familiar with Netware administration. Simons dismounted a SYS volume at the server, renamed it, and brought the volume back up. That fooled the network into thinking it was a new installation, and it asked for a new supervisor password. The trainer was only too happy to enter it and get back to work.

Nearly everyone who's commented on this issue has presented it as a lesson in relying too much on one form of security. The Novell representative said the work-around would not have been possible if the company had done three things:

- Install a password at the workstation as well as on the server.

- Lock the keyboard.

- Place the server in a secure room.

These physical steps would have been elements of a total system, strengthening the password requirement and preventing such easy evasion.

The Key Role of Passwords

Passwords play a key role in network security. They are at the heart of the identification and authentication process. That process is designed to ensure both that you are an authorized user and that you really are who you say you are. No other element of the security system will be effective unless you can first identify and authenticate those who try to use it.

When large-system specialists criticize PCs for falling short in security, the lack of a password system usually tops the list of examples. PC operating systems are designed for one-person use, and large numbers are still used that way. Some critics have called DOS vendors shortsighted for failing to require passwords, but that viewpoint ignores the millions of nonnetworked PCs for passwords would truly be an unnecessary encumbrance to their users.

On the other hand, Netware and other network operating systems do offer passwords and other forms of protection that *can be made* nearly as effective as those on larger systems. The key phrase is *can be made*. Like the folks at the Virginia consulting firm, you have to actively promote security; you can't just sit back and assume you're protected.

A Long History

With PCs as the leading current exception, the password has a long and useful history. It extends, at least, from the "Open Sesame" of Ali Baba to the personal identification number (PIN) of an automatic teller machine. The password is a simple, yet flexible, form of security. The proper password can identify an authorized user and make sure only a person with proper clearance gains access to your system. More than that, you can use an identification based on the password at the next security phase: to selectively grant or deny access to selected portions of your computerized assets. For example, even if a certain list of passwords admits their holders to your system, you can set up a second access barrier that lets only the holders of certain passwords gain access to the payroll system.

The password's popularity leads to another problem, though. Because password protection is so familiar, there is a tendency to overrate its effectiveness. Many managers install password systems and think they have done about all that is necessary to protect their computers. That is a dangerous assumption. Even this most basic protective strategy, used alone, often is not enough. The password is an essential, front-line protective mechanism, but it can do the job only if you remember two important points:

- A password is not a single, all-purpose security tool. Think of it instead as the screwdriver of computer security. It is an important item in a security tool kit, but it can't do everything. A password is most effective when it is used as part of a larger security plan.

- An effective password system is only as good as its administration. You must work to maintain the effectiveness of your system. Otherwise, it could fail. It could do so without warning, leaving you with a false sense of security.

The PIN used to gain access to an ATM machine is a familiar type of password. The PIN is typically a 4- to 6-digit number assigned by the bank or selected by the card holder. It is usually used in conjunction with a magnetically coded card that the ATM can read to verify the correct password and account number.

A data encryption key is another form of password. This key controls the encryption process that is performed on data to make it unintelligible without a decoding key. Just as with a password, you can't read the data without it.

What's Wrong With Passwords

An early group of hackers made Milwaukee famous by adopting its telephone area code as their name. They went about their work with ridiculous ease. Their first step was to dial the local telephone number that connected them with a public packet-switched data network. There are several of these networks, which makes reaching another computer nearly as easy as reaching another telephone.

Once they had hooked into the system, the network software asked them which remote computer they were trying to reach. They didn't know, and actually they didn't care. Each system hooked to the phone network has its own identity code. The young raiders simply punched in a few likely sounding numbers to see what they would get. What they got were places like the Los Alamos National Laboratory, a nuclear research center, and the Sloan-Kettering Cancer Center in New York City.

The not-so-secret password

The Sloan-Kettering computer was used to plan and monitor patients' treatments, and it was protected by a password system. Among the available passwords was one the computer's manufacturer had installed to allow access by maintenance technicians. As Groucho Marx used to say, "It's a common word, one you hear every day." The Milwaukee youths knew it well.

The standard maintenance passwords used by computer manufacturers are a common item of exchange on the fringes of the computer hobby. When the mainframes are installed, the new owners are advised to change these widely known passwords, but the owners often didn't bother. Among other things, they wanted to provide easy assess for the maintenance workers.

Sloan-Kettering's computer service director told the *New York Times* that the hospital's computer did respond to one of the common maintenance passwords. The unit had been programmed, though, so the password would provide access only to a few elementary functions that were necessary for service work. The system was supposed to block access through the maintenance password to critical information and functions.

It didn't. Once they had gained access with the maintenance, the young invaders found themselves in the same type of computer they had used in high school data processing courses. Using their knowledge of this system, they overrode the access-limiting program to roam at will through the hospital's data. They managed to shut down the computer twice. Both incidents were late at night, and no patients were harmed. Still, hospital officials said they spent "a month of workhours" trying to track down the source of their problems.

This incident was among the first of its kind, but it was by no means unique. The world is full of such raiders, all with the potential to do serious damage to programs and privacy. Many have more sinister motives than testing the limits of a teenager's world. For example, when a *Newsweek* reporter infiltrated a hacker network for a story, his subjects retaliated by penetrating the records of a credit bureau and devastating his credit rating. The people who do such things have shattered three comfortable old assumptions about computer security:

- The assumption that, except for computers that protect defense secrets or large amounts of money, few people ever would want to gain access to your computer

- The assumption that a password offers adequate protection and that it's not necessary to change even widely used passwords and access codes

- The assumption that few people have the technical knowledge to gain access to your computer or to manipulate the information inside it

Wanting in

The fact is, many people might want to get into your computer—and know how to do it. Computerized theft and fraud now are recognized as major white-collar crimes. Stealing data is a standard technique of industrial espionage. Even young hackers who have no evil intentions can cause catastrophic damage.

The password system is one way to protect yourself, but it's far from foolproof. A password is like any other kind of secret: hard to maintain and becoming harder as more and more people know about it. More seriously, many passwords have lost their effectiveness through the unthinking carelessness of their owners. The computer owner who fails to change a widely known maintenance password doesn't just risk trouble. It's an open invitation.

Much of the complacency has its origins in the high-priest atmosphere in which data processing professionals worked before personal computers came into widespread use. Until then, computer knowledge was a special kind of expertise, held only by knowledgeable insiders who were given expensive toys to play with. No mere mortals need apply. The expansion of computer literacy has given thousands of people the means to use computers and manipulate programs and data.

Most of the world's newly computer literate people use their knowledge properly and privately, but many do not. It's no wonder, then, that after the Milwaukee case received wide publicity, the makers of computer security products reported that customer inquiries nearly tripled. There was a comparable surge in sales of antivirus programs after those forms of computer mischief gained headlines. As the marketing data of one such service put it, when events like these are publicized, "the chiefs go to the data processing managers and ask, 'are we exposed?'" When they found out the answer is yes, the phone starts ringing.

Building a Limited Access Route

The traditional computer password demonstrates a basic principle of computer security: Most problems are caused by people, not machines.

On a technical level, the password has its limits. You can put one into effect with a simple IF/THEN/ELSE routine: IF the user offers the right password, THEN the computer will acknowledge it; ELSE the computer will not respond. Even more sophisticated password systems often are written as add-ons to the basic control systems of the computers they protect. In the PC world, they appear in application programs and even screen savers. Nothing this simple will stand up against a determined raider.

The simplicity exists because of the human factor. On one hand, any password system you devise must be designed to be used by ordinary people. The more complex you make the system, the better security it will provide. At the same time, though, the harder it is for your own people to use it.

This may be important, for example, if your system must be used by a roomful of inexperienced clerks or if you are selling a service to paying customers. Neither group will respond well to a system that forces them through a complex series of access codes. You'll be asking for even more trouble if you take the otherwise sensible precaution of periodically changing the passwords.

Some computer experts are coming to believe that user-friendliness is overrated. This may be true particularly if you achieve it at the expense of security. Even so, there is an obvious tradeoff to be made: your interest in security against the interests of legitimate users. There are limits to the amount of unfriendliness you can build into the system, and these translate into limits on how secure you can make the system.

The human factor also shows up in the type of carelessness that the Milwaukee incident uncovered. People assume that a password provides automatic protection and once you have installed one there's nothing more you need to protect your security. We've recently had some painful lessons in how wrong that assumption can be. The system will not wait like Ali Baba's treasure cave until the proper party comes along with the magic words to open the door. Others will try to open it, too, and some will succeed.

TABLE 8.1   The Strengths and Weakness of Passwords

Strong points	Weak spots
A password can stop most people simply because they don't know it.	A password system is only as strong as its administration.
Password protection is a common, accepted practice that most employees understand and respect.	Password protection is vulnerable to ordinary human carelessness.
It takes specialized skill to overcome password technology.	An effective system requires constant attention and maintenance.

The basic schemes

In spite of its limits, the password still stands as the entry-level computer security technique. Specific password schemes differ according to several factors:

- Selection technique
- Lifetime of the system
- Physical characteristics
- Information content

Table 8.1 summarizes the uses, advantages, and drawbacks of various password schemes.

The password holds its popular position for a good reason. Lack of a password can stop many casual raiders. That's a valuable asset if you recognize its limits and use it as part of a larger security program.

Secure the security measure

One additional part of that program must be to maintain a high level of security over the passwords themselves. Release them only to employees who have both the need and the clearance to use them. Change the passwords regularly to guard against leaks.

Two newspaper reporters in Madison, Wisconsin, conducted a test of how easy it was to break into the state government computer center there. As most of these tests seem to have gone, they found it easy. An official of the computer center later complained that someone out to embarrass the department must have slipped the reporters the password. Not so, said the state attorney general, who had monitored the test. The reporters used a password they had found posted on a bulletin board in the state capitol.

After prosecuting a major case of credit card fraud, an assistant U.S. attorney in the Washington, D.C., area said he was alarmed at the ease with which the suspect had gained access to the personal records of credit card holders. In one instance, he was able to obtain the passwords for a major department store's credit records by posing as a credit bureau employee.

Prosecutors accepted a plea bargain in which the suspect pleaded guilty to one of an original list of 13 charges of fraud. In all, said the prosecutor, the suspect had used information obtained from personal credit records to charge more than $50,000 to other peoples' accounts. Like many other computer criminals, this suspect had exploited a big weak point in any protective system: simple human carelessness.

You must guard against human failings, then, if the password is to be an effective security device. With proper precautions to maintain its secrecy, a password can help you deny access to anyone who lacks the knowledge to evade it. It's a good initial barrier of the type that helps keep honest people honest.

It won't do you much good, though, if you don't give it the care it deserves. If you post it in public view or give it out to too many people, it can become no good at all. In fact, it can be worse than no good. The invader who steals or evades a password often can do so without a trace. You can suffer a serious loss and never know it until the intruder has disappeared.

Administering a Password System

In a technical sense, passwords work very well. They can control admission not only to the system but to selected parts of it. The success of a password depends less on its technology than on the procedural aspects of its administration.

Normally, each user should have his or her own password. Occasionally, a group of people will share the same password, but the most secure method is to let each user select a password known only to the user and stored in the system. It's a good idea to clear personally selected passwords through a computer security administrator to make sure the chosen terms are appropriate and not easy for someone else to guess.

An alternative is to let the computer generate passwords at random and assign them to the users. Or the security administrator could invent the access codes and make the assignments. Another variation is to assign a user an initial password that he or she should immediately change.

If you use a group password, you'll have to change it every time someone leaves the group, particularly if that person also is leaving the company. Passwords should be changed regularly in any event; the more privileged the user, the more often the password should be changed. Change passwords, too, when you find any sign that the system has been entered or compromised.

Watch out for security leaks in the process of assigning the passwords. Have a trusted employee deliver each password in a sealed envelope directly to the assigned user. A sealed carbon paper envelope of the kind often used for customer statements could be ideal for this purpose. Get a receipt, acknowledging that the user has received the password and accepts responsibility for using it properly. Keep password records only in a well-protected master file within the computer system. Never save paper copies. Inevitably, someone will lose or forget an assigned password. In that case, assign a new one.

How to create passwords

One method of password administration is a system in which the computer automatically generates passwords, using a random letter-number generator. Deliver them to the users in sealed envelopes.

This system has some built-in safeguards. If a user expects a new envelope but receives none, that's a signal something is wrong. The best response usually is to cancel the missing password. Do the same if the envelope shows signs of tampering.

There is no guarantee that computer-generated passwords will be foolproof. One researcher examined several seemingly attractive systems of generating passwords. He found that most of these use a simple number theory analysis with which many programmers and mathematicians are familiar. Table 8.2 summarizes the advantages and drawbacks of computer-generated passwords.

The leading alternative to computer generation is a system in which users can select their own passwords. This method requires that you install some way to keep anyone but the password holder from changing his or her password. It might be a program element the user could activate, or you could restrict changes to designated times. Users could create passwords, for example, when they first establish their online identities or periodically when new passwords are required. This can be a useful precaution when users tend to leave their running workstations unattended once in a while. Without it, anyone who strolls past a vacant, running workstation can quickly alter the password and gain future access.

The password changing program also should require that the user enter the new password twice. If the two versions don't match, allow for one or two retries, but don't give an unauthorized user a chance to keep on trying until he or she finally gets it right.

User-selected passwords are far from secure. People tend to pick words and numbers that have some personal meaning, such as birthdays, children's names, and street addresses. The movie *War Games* depicted one common failing: a password visibly connected with its creator. A young man who invaded a Defense Department computer correctly guessed that the password would be the name of the programmer's deceased son.

On the other hand, there is one way in which a personally selected password can be more secure than one assigned by some other authority: It is

TABLE 8.2   Assessing Automatic Generation

Strong points	Weak spots
The system provides for regular, automatic password changes.	Even when delivered in sealed envelopes, there are ways new passwords can be compromised.
It delivers passwords directly to their holders, with little chance for undetected compromise.	The system is vulnerable to people with specialized knowledge.

TABLE 8.3   User Generation, Pro and Con

Strong points	Weak spot
Flexibility for users.	Requires that users select passwords properly and change them often.
Useful when operations are widely scattered.	

easy to remember, and the holder need not write it down. Table 8.3 summarizes the benefits and shortcomings of user generation.

Nothing's perfect

The password is a basic means of access control, but like all security methods, it has some advantages and drawbacks.

Among the strongest points: A password works much like the combination to a safe. A few people can crack it, but effectiveness depends on controlling who knows the password or combination. How well the password system works depends mainly on how well you manage the system. If the system is well run, the password protection will usually be effective.

The biggest danger is from poor administration. If you and the users don't maintain strict control, the system can easily be compromised. A survey by the National Bureau of Standards found that most organizations use their passwords poorly. Among the most dangerous practices: changing passwords infrequently if at all and storing them in formats that leave them easy to detect by unauthorized users.

The system's effectiveness can also depend on how a password is assigned. Automatic generation provides for regular, automatic password changes. This system delivers the passwords directly to their users, with little chance for undetected compromise. On the other hand, little chance does not mean no chance. There are ways to detect an envelope's contents without opening it. Not everyone knows how to do it, but it's not impossible.

User-generated passwords provide more flexibility. Consider them, too, when your users are in widely scattered locations where direct delivery of new passwords may be impractical. The major weakness is that old security bugaboo, human nature. Ideally, users should change their passwords regularly and protect them from outside disclosure. In practice, an all-too-typical user will keep the same password forever and file it in his or her desktop Rolodex.

That brings up another aspect of human nature that often interferes with sound password administration. In selecting a password, you must avoid common terms that an unauthorized user could readily guess. At the same time, try to avoid overcomplicated passwords. As a writer for *Computerworld* magazine, David J. Buerger has put it, "while the best passwords are the hardest to remember, they are also the most likely to be written on a Post-It stuck to a PC."

Putting passwords to use

You can use passwords to control more than direct access to your computer system. There are many points along the access path where you might require a password for further progress. Among them:

- Entry to the building
- Entry to the terminal room
- Gaining use of a terminal
- The encryption interface unit
- Log-in
- File access
- Data item access

In a typical security system, you might require physical devices such as cards or keys to pass the first three access points. Then you could use passwords, alone or in combination with some other technique, to control log-in and file and record access.

In addition to identifying authorized users, you can use a password system to provide some protection against other types of threats. These include:

- *Browsing.* Using legitimate access to part of the system to gain access to unauthorized files.

- *Masquerading.* Claiming the identity of an authorized user after obtaining a password through wiretapping or some other means.

- *Between-lines entry.* Penetrating a system when a legitimate user is on a communication channel but is not using his or her terminal.

- *Piggyback infiltration.* Intercepting user-processor communication and returning messages that appear to be legitimate responses.

Effectiveness

Passwords are effective against these threats to varying degrees (see Table 8.4). They provide good protection against browsing when implemented at the file or record level. Passwords are almost completely ineffective against between-lines entry and piggyback infiltration. In these cases, the only way a password could be effective would be if you required one before every message was sent.

The Technology of Passwords

In order to be an effective deterrent, a password should be:

- Hard to guess
- Easy for the owner to remember

TABLE 8.4 Password Characteristics

Password scheme	Advantages	Drawbacks
User-generated selection	Easy to remember	Often easy to guess
System-generated selection	Hard to guess	Hard to remember (An expert may be able to deduce the generating algorithm.)
In effect indefinitely	Easy to remember	Vulnerable to automated and repeated guessing attempts
In effect for fixed term	Easy to remember if interval is a week or longer	Vulnerable if in effect for long periods
Changed after single access	Deters and detects intrusions	Hard to remember; a written version could be vulnerable
Size and alphabet	The longer the password, the more effective	The longer the password, the harder to remember
Information contents, such as authorization codes and check digits	Could aid in detection, particularly if the penetrator is unaware of the password structure	Makes passwords longer and harder to remember
Handshaking and dialogues	Resists exhaustive attempts	Time-consuming; requires more storage space

- Frequently changed
- Well protected

   Technology helps a password system meet these requirements. You'll often find these requirements self-contradictory, though, so technical choices must often be compromises. Available password technology includes:

- System-generated passwords
- Limited lifetime
- The password's size and alphabet
- Its information content
- Capability to carry on a dialogue with the user

Computer generation

   An example of a computer-generated password scheme is the random word generator developed to run on Honeywell's Multiplexed Information and Computer System (MULTICS). The random word generator forms pronounceable syllables and connects them to create words. A table of pronunciation rules is used to determine the validity of each construct. This system was developed to enhance the security of some MULTICS installations, such as the Air Force Data Services Center (AFDSC).

   The reason for generating pronounceable passwords is to make the assigned words easier to remember. This can reduce the temptation to write the words down. Of course, what one person considers pronounceable may be gibberish to another, but the system adheres to conventional rules of grammar. To enhance pronounceability, generated words may be presented to the user in hyphenated form. Examples are *qua-vu, ri-ja-cas, te-nort, oi-boay,* and *fleck-y.*

Besides being easy to remember, generated words must be hard to guess. To satisfy this requirement, the Air Force system gives the program the ability to generate a very large set of possible words in a random fashion.

The random word generator can generate words of any length, but words of five to eight characters are best. Longer words tend to be less pronounceable, while shorter words result in too few available passwords for a given system and its user population.

At the Air Force Data Services Center, use of the password generator is not mandatory. To minimize the problem of being given a password that to them is unpronounceable, users can reject the assigned password and elect to provide another. After nearly 18 months of operation, observers found that about half the system's users allowed the system to assign their passwords.

Limited lifetime

Passwords that remain in effect indefinitely are the most susceptible to compromise. They are particularly vulnerable to exhaustive randomized attempts to hit on an authorized letter combination. Making the length of the password reasonably long, locking out log-on attempts after several tries, and enforcing time delays between log-on attempts provide some defense.

Another shortcoming of passwords with indefinite lifetimes is the difficulty of detecting a successful compromise. Some systems prohibit a user from being logged onto the system from more than one terminal at a time. Others inform the user at log-on and log-off of the presence of other users with the same user name or identification number, and hence the same password.

Even if such system constraints are in force, the odds of a system penetrator and the legitimate user trying to use the same account at the same time depend on how long and how often each makes the attempt. Of course, to lessen the probability of detection in this manner, the penetrator may elect to use the system late at night when the legitimate user presumably is not on duty. As a deterrent against such threats, some systems include the last time logged on as part of the messages displayed when a user logs on. This presumably informs someone if such successful penetration has taken place. The best idea is to change passwords frequently. In the Air Force Data Services Center system, users are required to change their passwords every 6 months. The operating system enforces this requirement.

Biodegradable passwords

One-time passwords generally provide a higher level of protection. The system may select successive passwords from an internal list generated by a program or from lists or cards previously distributed to authorized users.

As one researcher has said, "If passwords are changed every time they are used, there is no more risk in writing down the password than in carrying a key to a locked room." Should loss or theft occur, prompt reporting would minimize the risks involved. Of course, the legitimate user would have to use the system often, or a successful penetration may not be discovered until long afterward.

To further reduce the risk of carrying a password openly, authorities suggest that the system print a list of passwords for each user. Only one word on the list would be the actual password, and the exact location of the valid password could vary from user to user. You could also encode the new password on a magnetic card.

In another study, a prototype system was designed to require that the card holder key in a secret password in addition to a password read from the card. Such combinations of authentication techniques may provide a higher degree of security than systems that incorporate only one such technique. The use of a manually entered password is necessary to prohibit unauthorized use of a lost or stolen card. At the same time, the password is of no use to a would-be penetrator who does not have the card.

Lawrence Livermore Laboratory's OCTOPUS network uses a password scheme similar to one-time passwords, incorporating a changing counter. A computer generates and authenticates all passwords. At each terminal session the counter increases the value of the password, and this new value is communicated to the user. If an expected value is skipped, it suggests that someone else has used the combination.

Another one-time system

One-time passwords are used in SWIFT (Society for Worldwide Interbank Financial Telecommunications), the worldwide banking system developed by the Burroughs Corporation. When a terminal is connected, the operator uses a 4-digit, one-time password taken from a pair of lists sent separately. For example, from the lists in Table 8.5, the first password would be 1245.

Additional security features in SWIFT include message sequence numbers and the generation of a 4 hexadecimal digit authenticator result. This number is generated by running the entire message text through the SWIFT authenticator algorithm. In addition, at log-off time the operator specifies the next log-on time. SWIFT will refuse any earlier log-on attempts.

Major drawbacks to one-time passwords are the cost and difficulty of distributing the lists to large numbers of users and users who get out of step in a

TABLE 8.5 Combining These Lists to Create a Password

List 1		List 2	
1	2	4	5
3	7	9	8
4	6	3	5

system with a heavy workload. Of course, in systems that incorporate counters or incremented passwords, the distribution problem is minimized.

One-time password schemes alone are not effective against the threat of between-lines or piggyback entry. For protection against these threats, you would have to authenticate messages by attaching one-time passwords to each. Encryption at the terminal level also is effective in this situation.

Physical characteristics

A password's physical characteristics include its size and makeup—the "alphabet," or set of characters from which it is made. The number of different passwords possible in a given scheme is called the *password space*. The PIN system typically uses a 4- to 6-digit number. Some computer systems accept passwords 8 or more characters long, with letters, numbers, symbols, and other characters permitted.

The likelihood that someone could systematically duplicate a password depends on the password's length, the size of the alphabet from which it is taken, and the time over which the attempts take place. It has been computed that a 7-letter password drawn from the English alphabet has a probability of no more than .001 of being recovered in 3 months of systematic testing. If you use the 128-character ASCII character set, a 5-letter password will do the same.

Encryption keys are similar to passwords, but an adequate key size involves added considerations. The size of the key space should be as large as possible, not only to discourage trial-and-error attempts but to provide for frequent changes and large numbers of users.

The effectiveness of encryption does not depend solely on the chosen key. It also depends on:

- The algorithm employed
- When the encryption takes place
- The criteria used to select the key

If you use only 4 digits when your algorithm would support more, your space is effectively reduced.

Information content

A password can provide more than just personal authentication. The University of Western Ontario's Generalized Information Retrieval System (GIRS) incorporates the use of assigned, functional passwords whose contents reveal the users' authorization levels. In particular, these passwords determine:

- Which subset of available processing functions can be exercised
- Which parts of records can be operated on by these functions
- Which records the user is privileged to work with

In this system an additional password is needed for authentication. The functional password is used by the information retrieval system to assess a user's authorization level or capabilities. This is not to indicate, though, that both functions could not be provided by one password.

Passwords also could be constructed to contain check digits or some other sort of self-checking code. Check digits already are successfully used in other environments. In one example reported by Alan Taylor, "The Pennsylvania Bureau of Sales and Use Tax some time ago adopted a Modulo-10 check digit to safeguard a seven-digit number. The technique it selected was to multiply the first digit by 7, the second by 6 and so forth until the last digit was multiplied by 1. It then used the Modulo-10 complement of the answer as the check digit and placed it after the seventh number."

Techniques such as this, combined with some elementary analysis, could help more sophisticated password systems discriminate between entry errors such as transposed digits and actual penetration attempts, particularly those that use exhaustive testing.

Handshaking schemes

Other types of authentication schemes are known as *handshaking* or *extended handshakes*. Some of these procedures directly involve the use of passwords; others can only marginally be considered password schemes.

The ADEPT-50 timesharing system incorporates a handshaking scheme. To gain admittance to the system, the user must supply information that includes user identification, the password, and accounting data. The terminal identification also is compared against an authorization list.

In several systems, handshaking is performed through a dialogue between the system and the user. The user may be required to answer questions such as a cat's name or astrological sign, asked in a semirandom fashion, or to supply additional passwords or account information. This is much like having several passwords, any of which may be requested in any order. It is even conceivable that the questions themselves could be chosen by the system user.

In another variation, the handshaking is accomplished by both the system and the user transforming a given number and comparing the results. The system presents the user with a pseudo-random number and requires that the user perform a specified mental computation on that number. It might be as simple as adding the hour of the day. The result is sent back to the computer which performs a comparable transformation and compares the results.

9

Securing
the Desktop

*Personal computers and even higher-powered
workstations have all but replaced the traditional
dumb terminal. That means you have to be smarter
about security, too. It doesn't necessarily mean that
these systems are less secure.*

When a Boston-based mutual fund company switched from a mainframe to
personal computers, its managers heard plenty of conventional wisdom. PCs
and other advanced workstations can never be as secure as the mainframe
and its dumb terminals, they were told.

The advice wasn't exactly wrong, but it wasn't exactly right, either. It's
true, large systems have significant advantages in both physical and technical security. But PCs and workstations have some points on their side, too.
The investment company discovered one advantage early on: the ability to
back up critical data to optical disks, which offer much longer useful-life
spans than magnetic media. "We're a lot more confident now that 10 years
from now, we'll be able to read the data," said one executive.

A Wisconsin firm certainly challenged conventional wisdom when it moved
its benefits and payroll applications from a mainframe to a local area network. Employees have easier access to the data, and it's easier to protect confidential information, the new system's manager contends. Instead of waiting
for reports from a distant computer center, employees can call the information directly to their desktops. This direct access might seem to present a
greater security risk, but it is offset by a major security advantage. Under the
old system, data passed through multiple processes and people, each offering
an opportunity for error and compromise. Now, the data go directly to a single employee's desktop with no midcourse handling.

You often have to create your own opportunities, but desktop systems do
offer many opportunities to improve security. More important than the differ-

ence in equipment is the ever-present human factor. In the words of one manager fresh from a downsizing experience, "Security is only as secure as the users," he said. "You can't protect the system from what the users do with it."

New Problems, Old Solutions

The fast-growing use of PCs, workstations, and networks has presented serious new challenges in computer security. Consider the case of an Arizona electronics company that downsized its financial records, parts inventory records, and other functions to a PC. When the company installed the new system, it made one dangerous mistake. Fortunately, it discovered the misjudgment before anything went wrong.

The company had placed the system server next to a well-used path through the building. That would have been only a minor problem with a terminal attached to the mainframe system. The system itself, plus the limited number of people who had access to it, reduced the possibility of stolen or altered data. With a PC sitting there, however, plenty of people had both the ability and the knowledge to misuse it. The company could have solved this problem by relocating the system or installing a password system; it chose the passwords. But even with a choice of physical and technical responses, this problem boiled down to people and their recently gained knowledge of how to operate a PC.

PCs present other threats as well, particularly when connected to networks. Increasing numbers of these networks are connected to telephone lines, the prime invasion route for outsiders. PC data is also vulnerable to simple but disastrous human error.

Not only is the data in danger but so are the PCs themselves. The Safeware Insurance Agency, a major insurer of PC hardware, reports that stolen systems represent the leading cause of loss among its clients; power surges and lightning damage ranked second.

Small systems, hidden problems

The full security implications of PCs and workstations are not always obvious. Particularly when people buy these systems for what they consider small-scale use, they may not realize they are acquiring some large-scale security problems. If there is a basic rule of PC security, it would be: *A small computer requires the same kind of security as a large computer—only more of it.*

Direct connections

Most computer security techniques have been developed with mainframes in mind. They are designed to protect large units with extensive files of critical information. There are a few mainframe techniques that can't be readily adapted to PCs. Many of the physical protection techniques devised for mainframes are based on having a single room, or even an entire building, dedicated to the computer's care and feeding. The techniques that protect these locations can't be adapted readily to the PC on every desk.

But that's the exception, and the standard methods may be easier to apply than you think. Most mainframe security techniques can be and must be adapted to the personal computers in your organization. At most, they need only be converted to their new, decentralized purpose. For example:

- Your password system must be as fully developed as the access-control system for a larger computer, including proper administration to make sure the passwords are not leaked or shared. You must assign passwords that someone else cannot easily guess, and you must change them regularly.

- You must maintain an audit trail to keep track of who has been using the system, when, and for what.

- You must separate the tasks performed by individual users and the types of data to which they have access. This is reasonably easy when each user has a truly personal computer with which to work. It becomes much harder when the computers are shared or hooked together in a network.

- Most of all you need a security policy that recognizes personal computers as important elements of your system.

The challenge of PC security

There is one significant difference between PC and mainframe security. PCs make it easier to bypass the usual security and management controls that can be imposed over their more centrally controlled big brothers. Their sheer numbers and generally accessible locations make it harder to limit access, control activity, and segregate duties. A report by Price Waterhouse identified these particular security threats from the spread of PC use (Fig. 9.1):

- Financial records can be modified, and you will have no record that it has been done.

- Limited storage space may mean some records are not kept in great enough detail.

- Access to information on personal computer disks—hard or floppy—is not easily controlled.

- Users may keep inadequate records and backups of their files and activities.

A burglary tool in the office

Vulnerable spots like these mean that having a personal computer in the office is like having your own in-house burglary tool. After all, it is the tool

Challenges of PC security

- Maintaining audit trails
- Controlling access
- Gaining users' cooperation

Figure 9.1   Networking and numbers add to the threat.

used by so many hackers on their cross-country invasions of defense computers, credit records and medical computers.

The PC's vulnerable spots also have a frustrating ability to multiply. A password that slips out today may be on a hacker's bulletin board tonight, available to thousands of would-be raiders. That's exactly what happened when the password to a major retail chain's credit records was compromised. It was a month before someone told the company what was happening. By then, illicit users had run up unknown numbers of false credit card charges and had access to the credit records of about 90 million people.

More ways to get in

Personal computers multiply your security problems because they multiply the number of sources from which a threat could arrive. What's more, the spread of small computers has been accompanied by the widespread knowledge of how to use them. Once you had to watch out only for a few knowledgeable computer specialists who worked in an easy-to-control environment. Now, nearly anyone has—or can easily get—the knowledge to bypass your controls and get into your system.

Computers make it easier to conduct many business operations that used to be nothing but boring drudgery. They also have made it easier for computer criminals to compromise these processes. Take accounts receivable, for example. A computerized receivable system can eliminate an intricate, cumbersome process—or at least make it a lot easier for the operator who must do it. The computer also can eliminate the many opportunities for error that go along with manual data entry. But for everything the computerized system lets you do, it also provides an opportunity for mischief by someone else:

- You can quickly enter payments, credits, and other changes to a customer's account. The criminal can take this same information out.

- You can make instant credit decisions by calling the customer's record to your personal computer screen. Someone else can make instant alterations the same way.

- You can transfer data from the receivables system to other programs such as financial and inventory records. A raider can follow the same route to these other accounts.

To shore up widely scattered weak spots like these, you must include the personal computer in your basic security assessments and policies. Treat the PC like an integral part of the system. That's what your enemies will do.

A Policy for PC Security

A sound security policy, properly implemented in practice, gives you a first big advantage over anyone who tries to misuse your computers. Simply put: You were there first. A good policy lets you anticipate raids on your computer instead of just reacting to them. In devising a good security policy for desktop computers, you should:

- Base the policy on an overall company plan for computer security. Think of workstation security as a major element in the larger plan.

- Include provisions for communicating your policy and for enforcing it.

- Include security in your purchasing plans. Try to avoid random selection of PC or network products that don't work well together. A unified system lends itself to a simple, uniform set of security procedures and equipment—it might also qualify for volume discounts on both purchases and maintenance agreements. Include provisions for cost-benefit analysis of prospective purchases. Once you have the equipment, put it to use maintaining an inventory of all your computer resources.

- Explain—clearly and completely—each employee's responsibilities for security. Observing proper security procedures should be part of each employee's job requirements.

- Explain the reasons for your controls, including their legal basis.

- Set standards for the use and management of computer resources.

- Provide central support to help users do their work more efficiently and securely. Make security and proper use an important part of the training program. Make sure there is help available in case of trouble. The employee who learns to use the computer properly and who doesn't encounter repeated bugs, is more likely to observe policies and avoid dangerous short-cuts.

- Write and post separate notices applying the overall security policy to each department. Specify what the workers in each operation should do to help maintain the security system.

Assign responsibility

Responsibility is an important element of PC security. Employees must take responsibility for their use of the computer, proper or improper. That responsibility should extend to their supervisors and managers, too. Ideally, you should create a sense of ownership. People who are responsible for a certain resource should come to feel that file is theirs. That should mean, of course, that it is theirs to protect and maintain, not to manipulate. It should mean that the people who use a resource should feel personally involved in its safekeeping.

Set priorities for the data to be protected and the proper safeguards to be installed for its protection. Don't limit your view to the data that is stored and used within your area of responsibility. Look beyond the office walls to the data that is transmitted to and from your department. Data transmission lines are among the weakest links. They're even weaker if you forget them in your planning.

Get managers involved

There are fewer managers these days who feel it's beneath them to operate a computer themselves, but there still are some who don't use computers regularly and who rely primarily on other employees. Even if they don't personally use computers very often, it's important to give them a basic understanding of how the equipment works and the role it plays in running your operation.

Encourage everyone to ask questions, either of your own support staff or of the dealers who supply the equipment. Both are supposed to be there to help. Take advantage of it. In particular, you can use your own experience and knowledge to help establish procedural security standards. It takes more management than technical skill to decide what duties should be separated and what an employee needs to know. You also can set up the policies and procedures for managing passwords and other procedural elements.

In a supporting role

The technical and physical requirements of desktop security may require other kinds of specialized knowledge, but a manager's touch still is required.

Assigning responsibilities, scheduling and budgeting activities, and analyzing the cost-effectiveness of a security plan are important management activities that organize the work of your technicians. It takes a good management head to build good organizational support for the full security program and to integrate security into all the company's operations.

Desktop Security Techniques

The security methods for protecting small computers aren't all that much different from those for larger, centrally located units. They just must be adapted to the large numbers and widely scattered locations in which personal computers are found.

Physical security

It's easy to give up on physical protection before you even get started. Certainly, physical control of a scattered group of small units isn't as simple as building a protective ring around a central computer. But it's not that much different, either. There have been few computer crimes in which the criminal has walked right up to a working mainframe to do the damage. In nearly every case the criminal has worked from a distance, entering the computer electronically over its communication lines. That's exactly the same problem you face with a network of personal computers connected over communication lines.

Many physical security techniques start with the basic locked door, backed up by other means to limit access. Personal computers used in sensitive applications also can be gathered into a central place where access is easier to control. This is particularly true of network servers.

The lock and key is the basis to another leading security approach: simply locking the computer. There are many locking devices available that will secure the computer to a table or lock up the keyboard when the unit is not in use. Another lock can control access to any floppy disks or other removable media that contain sensitive data. On one hand, a personal computer disk is such an efficient storage device for its size, your collection of all the company's most important records could go out the door in a briefcase, and not even a well-filled briefcase. On the other hand, the disk's convenient size makes it easy to lock up your stored data. Whether the disk is convenient to you or to the thief depends on how reliably your information is kept in secure storage when it is not in use.

Procedural methods

Procedural security is the form that most directly attacks the human element of computer security. Many more humans have access to personal computers than to any other kind. The basic security problem of a personal computer is that it's so easy for anyone with a PC and a smattering of computer literacy to overcome nearly any of the controls you have built into or around your system. Procedural controls help you meet this risk. Effective procedures may be difficult, but they aren't impossible. Here are some ways to attack the problem (Fig. 9.2).

Develop accountability for computer use. This is the official support mechanism for maintaining responsibility. It should be the main goal of your proce-

Procedural steps for PCs

- Establish accountability
- Maintain integrity
- Reinforce access controls
- Monitor activity

Figure 9.2 Procedural methods deal with the human element.

dural control system. With computers in the hands of so many new users, it's important to make it clear that the users are totally responsible for their data, equipment, and passwords.

Reminding users of their personal responsibility should be an important part of your training program. Issue frequent notices and post them on bulletin boards and include them in employee publications.

When a file is used in an individual computer, establishing accountability for the data can be easy. However, when users are hooked up to a network server, tracing responsibility can become infinitely difficult.

Maintain integrity. A system of user accountability also can help you implement controls to help maintain the integrity of your data. When many people use the same file, it often can be impossible to control the accuracy and proper use of that file. One way to make users responsible for their own work is to establish a procedure through which users make themselves and their intentions known before they can work with data from a central file. This check-in can be built into the system, or it can be as simple as being required to check out the disk from a library under the supervisor's control.

Another way is a variation on batch processing techniques. Each user who makes additions or changes to a central file enters these changes first onto a disk in the user's own computer. At the end of the day or some other appropriate period, the material from the disks is transferred into the central file. The disk files then are kept for their value in auditing. If you find the disk from which a questionable entry came, the employee who used that disk is clearly the leading suspect.

As an alternative, each entry added to the central file could be flagged with information to identify its source. Make sure, too, that everyone is required to make backup copies of their work and to keep necessary logs and documents.

Reinforce passwords.   Procedural controls for personal computers also should back up the access-control system. Here again, the personal computer you are trying to protect is part of the problem. It can be used to generate random password attempts, or a clever user can bypass its security control system.

Monitor activities.   A fourth procedural control for desktop computers is a system to help detect unauthorized activities. There are several personal computer activities with which you can effectively direct a surveillance system. One of these is the use of online systems. If the system keeps track of users, as it should, it then is up to you to read those reports once in a while.

Bring the employees themselves into the monitoring system. Each employee who logs on should be shown the last date and time the employee's password was used. The employee who suspects a misuse should be encouraged to report that suspicion instantly. In the same way, give each employee a regular printed log of a week's or a month's computer use.

Part of the employees' personal responsibility for their use of the computer should be the responsibility to report discrepancies in these use records. Many employees will respond favorably to this kind of responsibility. For those who don't, have fair but firm job rules in place to require that they uphold their areas of responsibility.

Technical methods

As with other forms of protection, technical controls are not a full answer to your problem, but they are part of it. That's particularly true of PCs because their scattered locations and the increasing sophistication of their users make technical solutions harder to implement and easier to evade. Within these limits, there are several technical solutions that can contribute to your overall strategy.

You will need technical means to back up your access-control system. The system should have internal controls to identify users, screen out the unauthorized, and restrict what authorized users are allowed to do. The internal controls also should shut down the system if someone makes more than two or three tries to enter a proper password.

Another effective built-in control is one that shuts down a workstation automatically if there is no activity within a certain period. This limits the risk that someone will take advantage of an open, unattended terminal.

Technical controls also can contribute to your authority over access to designated files. Encryption is a useful technical method, particularly for your most valuable data. Don't forget the encrypting effects of data compression programs, which are available for personal computer data files.

Built-in controls also can help impose identification and access procedures for the use and transfer of data and establish audit trails.

Another valuable built-in control is an error-checking mechanism that tests to see if an entered figure is within a certain range. A simple example is a date-checking routine that would reject an entry like February 30. You can apply the same idea to your payroll system. You should know, for example, the total amount you normally need to meet a payroll. Add allowances for vacations, normal overtime, and other contingencies. Program the computer to sound an alarm should a total payroll exceed that figure. It could mean nothing. Then again, it could mean that someone is trying to pad the payroll. This kind of built-in control also helps you maintain the reliability and accuracy of your data.

Another technique that can help you do that is an automatic mechanism for backing up personal computer data. Tape backup of a hard disk's contents is a leading example.

Preventing Loss and Damage

Where personal computers are concerned, the perils of lost and damaged data are much greater than the danger of theft or deliberate tampering. For every would-be computer saboteur, there are thousands of employees who have destroyed data just by pushing the wrong key at the wrong time.

Say, for example, your superiors ask you to retrieve a report in a hurry. You place the floppy in your disk drive, call for the file, and receive nothing but an error message. Is this a serious problem? It depends. If there's a backup available, you have a minor inconvenience. If there is no backup, you have a potential disaster. Who is responsible for making the backup? Chances are, it's you.

The importance of procedures

For reasons like this, procedural security is a major key to protecting data in corporate PCs. The employee who follows proper procedure can usually avoid errors and oversights that destroy valuable data. Note the *usually*. You can never prevent all human error. In fact, though you can't see it now, there was a human error made while typing the previous sentence. With good procedural security, however, you can avoid many errors, and you can have the chance, as I did here, to go back and correct the errors that do occur.

Since accountability is particularly important for personal computers, make it clear that the users are totally responsible for their data, equipment, and passwords. Make it equally clear that if they lose data because they fail to observe the proper procedures, they will be held responsible for the results.

How data get lost

When important information exists only in the form of magnetic impulses on a computer disk, many things can go wrong. Intentional theft and destruction are only two possibilities. Others include the following.

Hardware malfunctions.   A typical and very common example involves the hard work that goes flying off into data limbo because you had not yet saved it to disk when the power suddenly failed. A close second is the failure of a hard disk. No mechanical device works perfectly forever, and a hard disk is no exception.

Software bugs.   These can happen in any form of software, both commercial and locally written. Even the best programs can occasionally hang, forcing you to reboot the computer. To do so is, in effect, to create your own power failure.

Procedural errors.   As already pointed out, this is the area of greatest danger. Consider the user who formats a disk, then discovers it was the one that held the only copy of a key report. Closely akin is erasing a lot of files when you only intended to erase one. The asterisk wild card of DOS commands is particularly notorious for stimulating this kind of error.

Environmental hazards.   These include heat, humidity, and electrical malfunctions. They can also include sandwich crumbs and spilled coffee.

Procedures to protect data

It's one thing to say you're always going to do things right. You may resolve always to back up your work and never to use the FORMAT command on a hard disk. It is something else entirely to avoid these common faults—the fact that they are common is a clue to how difficult it is to maintain this kind of self-discipline. If you have trouble keeping yourself in line, think of the multiple difficulties produced by an entire staff of computer-using employees.

You will never eliminate human error. What you can do is implement procedural requirements that employees probably will observe most of the time. You won't prevent all loss, but you can minimize the loss, and that should be your objective. Your policy should include the following elements (Fig. 9.3).

Regular file backup.   Nothing provides better protection against lost and damaged data than having another copy available. It is comforting to employer and employee alike to find this resource there waiting for you when you need it. Many programs have automatic timed backup features. If they do, use them. You can set the program to make a new backup file at a preset interval, say, 15 or 30 minutes. If you have the feature set for 30 minutes, should there be a power failure or some other problem, the most you will lose is half an hour's work. The more critical the data and the harder it would be to restore, the more frequent your backup interval should be. If your operating programs lack this feature, try to instill it in the employees. Train them to save their work every 15 to 30 minutes or whenever they finish some logical work unit such as a page of a letter or one group of numbers in a spreadsheet.

Protecting data

- Regular backups
  - Servers by network manager
  - Workstations by individual users
- Automatic saves
- Safe storage

Figure 9.3 Expect to reduce error, not eliminate it.

Some programs also make their own backup files. Whenever you save a file, the previously saved file is saved with the extension .BAK or something similar. Other programs will make a backup copy of the file as it existed when you first began to work on it. That can keep you from wiping out good work by writing bad work over it.

Another backup procedure that should reduce data losses: Immediately after completing a project, have the user make copies of all work files on a separate floppy disk. Employees can manually emulate an automatic backup process by saving each version of the file on a separate floppy disk and using a new disk to save each successive version. That way, you can go back and recover any previous version of the file.

Label backup disks as such, and make it a policy never to disturb them unless they are needed for backup purposes. Otherwise, employees may mistakenly modify the backup copies, thinking they are new and available.

Hard disk backup. Along with backing up individual files, your policy should require regular backups of each computer's entire hard disk. DOS comes with BACKUP and RESTORE utilities, but there are many commercial programs that do the job better and faster. These are well worth the modest investments they usually require.

If your data is particularly valuable and subject to change, consider sequential backups for the hard disk as well. Back up the drive onto one set of disks. When the time arrives for the next backup, use a separate set. A third backup can use the original set of disks again, and from then on, you can alternate sets.

A hard disk backup takes some time, which means that it must usually be a planned event, and most users will procrastinate. Set a policy requiring backups at fixed intervals. Then do your best to enforce it. How often should this interval be? Some authorities suggest that you balance the cost of making the backup against the cost of restoring the data. They provide few instructions on how to compute either figure. A more practical approach: Determine the length of time you could afford to be without your data while your staff scrambles to recreate it. Schedule backups at least that often.

Safe disk storage.   Don't make a backup, whether of an application program, a data file, or a hard disk, and carelessly toss the backup disks into a drawer. Store backup disks at some distance from the computer, preferably in a location where a fire or flood that destroys the original material will not affect the backups. Make sure that location is protected from magnetic fields and other environmental hazards.

Hardware problems and solutions

Nothing is certain but death and taxes. Benjamin Franklin used those words to express his concern about the future of the young nation he had just helped to create. In this era of the personal computer, which even Franklin failed to anticipate, you could expand the certainties to include hard disk failure. Your hard disk will fail. Normally, it will run for many thousands of hours before it does so, but that is only delaying the inevitable. Since you cannot prevent this failure, you must do what you can to be ready when it happens.

That means regular backup, as just described. The best response to this most common PC hardware problem is the simple procedural precaution of backing up. There are also a few things you can do to protect a hard disk from damage and premature demise. Find out whether your disk automatically parks its heads when you turn off the power. Parking moves the read-write heads to a part of the disk that contains no data. That way, if the computer is moved or bumped and the heads scrape the disk, nothing of value will be damaged. If you do not have automatic parking, you should have a head-parking program. Users should run it just before they shut off their units for the night and just before a unit is moved.

Some damage and failure need not be permanent. There are several disk maintenance utilities that will diagnose hard disk problems and help you recover from apparent failures. Most of these are inexpensive and well worth their cost, particularly if they help you avert disaster some day. Just remember, they cannot save you from every mechanical failure. Only a fresh backup can do that.

Software problems

There is a lot of badly written software out there, no surprise. Consider, for example, the number of programs that give you no way to recover from the error signal that is sent when a disk is full. If there are any sadder words of tongue or pen, it must be these: File not found.

If a program does not allow you to retrieve both your data and your dignity from one of these errors, get rid of it. There are good substitutes for nearly every piece of PC software ever written. Buy a version that gives you a chance to insert a new disk and save your data. That should not be too much to ask of any program. It should not be an excessive demand, either, that a program provide some way to let you check the amount of disk space you have remaining.

Aside from these self-induced bugs, the major software problems on a PC will usually yield to procedural solutions. Consider this common problem: the accidental reformatting of a disk, hard or floppy, that contains critical data and that has not been backed up, of course. Doing this can be as simple as typing FORMAT C: when you meant to type FORMAT A. Newer operating systems and disk utilities include routines that you sometimes can use to recover from such an error. Another solution uses this technique: Go to the directory where FORMAT.EXE is stored. Type:

```
REN FORMAT.COM FORMAT!.COM
```

Then create this oneline batch file, called FORMAT.BAT:

```
FORMAT! A:
```

Including the exclamation point in the name of the original FORMAT program guards against invoking it by accident. If you merely type the command FORMAT, you will activate the batch file. It will make sure you confine your activities to the floppy disks you insert in drive A. If you actually want to use the renamed FORMAT!, perhaps when you really do want to format your hard disk, you must be emphatic about it. Another procedural method that can help protect you from software problems includes using the DOS ATTRIB command to make critical files read-only. That means they cannot be changed or erased or use one of the disk utility software packages that includes an undelete function.

Hazardous duty

A PC security program also should take into account the environmental hazards of office living. It's been said on the basis of first-hand knowledge that a spilled cup of coffee is a devastatingly efficient way to ruin a keyboard. Even a puff of cigarette smoke can do a surprising amount of damage if directed to the wrong place like a hard disk—another argument for the smoke-free workplace.

One of your major desktop security problems will be to protect the systems from all the hazards in their environment. This doesn't just refer to the traditional big three of fire, flood, and electrical disturbances, although any of them can readily do in a PC. The real hazards to personal computer operation are the little things. One of computerdom's great disaster stories tells of the disk full of painstakingly created data that was wiped out by a magnetic paper clip dispenser. If the magnet didn't do the damage, an ill-placed piece of dust could have.

A computer never was really designed to exist in the typical office environment. It's sensitive—perhaps unduly so—to radio speakers, fluorescent lights, coffee, smoke, and dust. You must be equally sensitive, searching out these sources of possible trouble and isolating the computers and disks from them.

Here's a way to make even coffee breaks more productive: Give employees ample opportunities—and strict instructions—to take their breaks away from their computers. Light up, if you must, at that time and place. Just don't do it near the computer.

Then, check out the fire and flood protection. And don't hesitate to invest in electric surge protection and uninterruptible power supplies.

Signs of a Good Program

Perhaps the best test of a good personal computer security program is the simple answer to this question: Have you checked up on your PC security program lately?

Personal computers add new dimensions to your security problems, and they're not always easy to solve. They also offer some features that can help make security easier and more effective. The best sign that you have a handle on this slippery problem is the simple fact that you give microsecurity the serious, regular attention it deserves. Other elements of a good program include

- Security considerations are included in your purchasing specifications.

- You have adequate controls to limit access to both files and equipment.

- You have an up-to-date inventory of your desktop computers and their programs and files. You know what they are, where they are, and how they are protected.

- You provide adequate supervision to make sure employees observe established procedures, particularly those that segregate and isolate their access to sensitive information.

- Employees, supervisors, and managers all are given personal responsibility for their computer use. This responsibility is clearly communicated and enforced, preferably with a written notice or agreement.

- The system keeps adequate records of computer use, and you regularly review these records.

- You have adequate provisions for backing up your data.

PC Security Techniques

Table 9.1 lists the baseline security techniques that are applicable to personal computers. these techniques are fully described in App. A. Table 9.2 lists selective techniques and the situations in which they might be advised.

TABLE 9.1   Baseline Security for PCs

Item	Class
Areas where smoking and eating are prohibited	Procedural
Assets accountability assignment	Procedural
Compliance with laws and regulations	Procedural
Computer program change logs	Procedural Technical
Computer security management committees	Procedural
Computer system password file encryption	Technical
Computer user trouble call logging	Technical Procedural
Confirmation of receipt of documents	Procedural
Contingency recovery-equipment replacement	Disaster
Cooperation of computer security officers	Procedural
Data accountability assigned to users	Procedural
Data file and program backup	Procedural Technical
Disaster recovery plan	Disaster
Discarded document destruction	Procedural
Electrical equipment protection	Disaster Physical
Electrical power shutdown and recovery	Physical Disaster
Emergency preparedness	Disaster
Employee identification on work products	Procedural
Exception reporting	Technical
Financial loss contingency and recovery funding	Procedural Disaster
Input data validation	Technical
Keeping security reports confidential	Procedural
Minimizing traffic and access to work areas	Physical
Minimizing numbers of copies of sensitive material	Procedural
Participation of computer users at critical stages of application development	Procedural

TABLE 9.1   Baseline Security for PCs (*Continued*)

Item	Class
Physical access barriers	Physical
Placement of equipment and supplies	Physical
Production program authorized version validation	Procedural Physical
Programming library access control	Physical
Proprietary notice printed on documents	Procedural
Protection of data used in system testing	Technical Physical
Requirements and specification participation by EDP auditors	Procedural Technical
Responsibilities assigned for application program controls	Procedural
Security for sensitive areas during attended periods	Procedural Physical
Separation and accountability of IS functions	Procedural
Suppression of incomplete or obsolete data	Procedural Technical
Vendor-supplied program integrity	Technical

TABLE 9.2   Selective Security Measures for PCs

Item	When to use	Class
Alternate power supply	When high service availability is required	Disaster
Completion of external input data	When incomplete information is input from external sources	Procedural Technical
Computer program quality assurance	When quality assurances are available	Technical
Computer security officer	When there are enough computer security resources to justify the position	Procedural Physical
Courier trustworthiness and identification	When couriers are used to deliver output	Procedural
Cryptographic protection	When you need the greatest protection of data	Technical
Data classification	When data sensitivity is variable	Procedural Technical
Delivery loading dock access	Where you require strict physical access control	Physical
EDP auditor	When you use internal audit resources	Procedural
Human subjects review	When research data deals with human subjects	Procedural
Independent computer use by auditors	For advanced audits	Procedural
Inspection of incoming and outgoing materials	When traffic is high and force of authority is advisable	Physical
Limited use of system utility programs	When general-purpose utility programs are in use	Technical Procedural
Monitoring computer use	When access is to be limited to employees	Procedural Technical
Personal data input-output inspection	When personal data is received from or sent to outside organizations	Procedural
Separation of personal identification data	When processing personal data	Technical
Sufficient personal identifiers for database search	When processing personal data	Technical
Universal use of badges	In cases of a large staff, heavy traffic, or many visits by outsiders	Physical Procedural

10

Securing the Local Area Network

The local area network is the key to enterprise network security, whether you're trying to install a security system—or evade one.

When subscribers to a computer security bulletin board were polled about their experiences with local area networks, a full 69 percent said they had experienced some kind of security problem. In more than half these cases, the loss was $10,000 or more (Fig. 10.1).

The ComSec BBS, run by a nonprofit organization of more than 2,100 computer security professionals, chose 300 of its members to participate in the

Losses per security incident

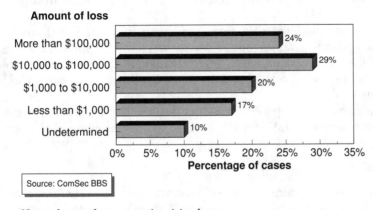

Source: ComSec BBS

Figure 10.1 Network growth accompanies rising losses.

online poll. The results paint the typical LAN as a highly vulnerable installation. In all, 55 percent of the respondents said security violations happen regularly in their systems. Among the poll's other findings:

- 59 percent of the respondents had been hit by a computer virus during the preceding year.
- In 9 percent of the virus attacks, losses exceeded $100,000.
- In 28 percent of the virus attacks, there were losses of $100,000 or less.
- 18 percent of the respondents had been victims of fraud by insiders.
- 16 percent were victims of fraud by outsiders.
- Only 7 percent said they had never experienced a security problem.

While it demonstrated the LAN's vulnerability, though, the survey also suggested a reason: Few of the victims had done very much to keep themselves from being victims. In other words, it wasn't the LANs at fault so much as the people who ran them. Supporting that conclusion are survey results like these:

- 41 percent described their existing security provisions as inadequate.
- 7 percent said they had no security measures in place at all.
- 26 percent characterized their organization's approach to security as lax. Some called it "reactionary."

The respondents' bad experiences ranged from minor incidents to industrial espionage. A financial institution reported a virus that tied up its ATM network for 2 days. A pharmaceutical company found itself the object of computerized attacks by activists opposed to the firm's use of animals for testing. Other victims lost software, data files, or both.

If there is good news in this survey, it is that two-thirds of the respondents thought their senior managers rated security as a high-priority activity. If that is generally true, it would represent a sharp increase from just a few years ago.

Still, many respondents said management in their organizations has been slow to recognize a need for better security. This even included some of the victims of the most costly attack. Many managers exhibited an old reaction: They wanted to cover up the incident to avoid the embarrassment of looking like victims.

And the survey sponsors had this prediction: The problem will get worse before it gets better. As LANs proliferate, so will the problem of securing them.

A Matter of Perspective

Back in the days of mainframes and dumb terminals, network security was not a big issue. Everything was private, proprietary, and internally controlled. There were few if any connections with the outside world.

Now, there are not only LANs, but they are increasingly connected to each other. Furthermore, they have direct links to the most important route of outside invasion: the telephone system. LAN security itself was once a relatively minor problem. Initially, most LANs were small, department-sized operations. However, that situation is changing, and security is becoming vitally important. Corporations are moving their most sensitive and critical data to networked client-server systems. Often, they fail to recognize that they are moving this material to a less secure environment. As these networks expand, they often outgrow the company's security system. These LANs are vulnerable not only to sophisticated outsiders but to unsophisticated everyday users.

Thomas Lunzer of SRI International sees the untrained user as a particular threat. "All too often, we see that users are undertrained in both security and the proper use of the system," he says. While outsiders will always represent a threat, the greater threat comes from accidental misuse. Robert Courtney, who runs a security consulting service in Port Ewen, New York, agrees. "I'm convinced that the crooks will never compete with the authorized LAN users who just make mistakes," he says.

Of course, there are always new challenges from those who invade your system on purpose. One recently reported problem involves vendors who go snooping around your network while installing or maintaining components. They want to find out who might be competing for your business.

The challenges of securing networks

Yet another consultant, David Ferris of San Francisco, points out that mainframes are generally secure largely because security is a recognized problem in that environment. LANs face much the same risks, but they aren't as well recognized. Ferris lists these as the main security issues facing LAN managers:

- *Password protection.* Many LANs implement it poorly at best. Users choose simple passwords, which they never change. They will walk away from their workstations without logging off, leaving live terminals abandoned.

- *File access.* Users often have unnecessary access privileges to critical programs and data files.

- *Remote connections.* This problem is a creature of telecommuting and the laptop computer. Tools that let remote workers connect easily with their employer's systems also let other people connect easily when it is not such a good idea.

- *Data integrity.* The information in data files should be accurate. In Ferris's words, it should mean what it purports to mean. There are two threats to truth in data: faulty logic injected by insiders and viruses planted by outsiders.

- *Reliability and availability.* The network and its resources should be there when you need them.

- *Disaster recovery.* Just as with larger systems, PC networks should be prepared for bomb threats, flooding, earthquakes, tornadoes, and hurricanes.

- *Legal liability.* The existing system of licensing PC software is horribly ill-suited to LANs, but mistakes—honest or otherwise—can land you in court. That can be a losing proposition even when you win.

- *Privacy issues.* The privacy of electronic mail communication is a growing area of litigation.

For every problem, a solution

A mainframe system takes care of many of these problems by keeping its processing, file integrity, and other security provisions within a closed system. A LAN lacks these automatic, built-in security features, but increasingly network operating systems and other facilities give you the means to provide your own protection. That throws the issue back to the familiar human factor. Effective LAN security has two main components (Fig. 10.2):

- Active management that takes specific, direct action to meet security challenges

- User education, to teach employees how to use their systems in a proper way

A management response

LAN managers have important roles in the security of their systems. Their main responsibility is to build into their networks the same kinds of security mainframes enjoy automatically. For example, the widely used Novell networks have account-control facilities that have vastly improved since Netware's earliest versions. These allow for much more effective password administration. You can also define many log-in parameters such as:

Pillars of LAN security

- Management
  - Password administration
  - Backup control
- User education
  - Build awareness
  - Teach techniques

Figure 10.2 Effective LAN security deals with the human factor.

- Identifying valid workstations and restricting the times at which they can provide access
- Enforcing a minimum password length
- Requiring that passwords be changed at fixed intervals

You can also beef up file access control, again by making good use of the tools you have available. Among these tools are encryption programs. You can use them to protect the file that records passwords—a natural target.

More fundamentally, you can manage file access by setting levels of security and assigning access privileges to individual users on the basis of their need to know. Again, most systems provide the ability to do this. The real challenge is to take advantage of it.

Remote access programs have password protection, too. Use it. Some also offer dial-back facilities that let you disconnect an outside call and dial back to verify that it comes from a proper source. For sales representatives and others who move around, you can use one-time passwords that are automatically generated and checked.

Users are the key to data integrity. Most errors creep in when they download portions of a database and add flawed data or mathematics. Sometimes, preventing this problem is a simple matter of definition. Specify, for example, whether SALES YTD refers to net or gross sales. Encourage users to check their reports against sources they know are accurate.

Backup is the key to network reliability, whether from failed components or natural disaster. The first order of business, of course, is to make the backups. Pay particular attention to file servers. The second order of business is to check the backups periodically. The third is to store them off site. Other available measures include:

- A help desk, readily available
- Good network management tools, but with access restricted to designated network managers
- Alternative routing around failed components
- Physical access controls over servers
- Uninterruptible power supplies

The importance of education

Managers must manage the network properly; users must learn to use it properly. User education is one of the most powerful weapons you have available against LAN crimes. You can solve many security problems through proper training and supervision. The most fruitful areas for training include:

- Educating employees about the security issues involved in their work
- Training users in how to properly use and protect their passwords

- Making people aware of the need to maintain accurate data and of the ways in which they can do this
- Educating users about the possible impact, personal as well as corporate, of illegally copying software
- Establishing and communicating a policy that internal e-mail messages are not private or secure
- Teaching employees the rudiments of e-mail courtesy and restraint

Technical Security for LANs

Network operating systems are the toolboxes of network security. PC workstations and their operating systems offer little security—and a lot of vulnerability—in a network setting. To secure the network, you should look first to the network operating system. For most network managers, that means one version or another of Novell Netware. But there are other possibilities including OS/2, Unix, and a host of Novell competitors. All offer some degree of security, and it's usually a high degree. The most important requirement is that you make use of it.

The Netware security system

Contrary to a widespread impression, Netware has always been a secure networking environment, and it's gotten more secure with each new version. With version 4.*x*, Netware security has become so comprehensive it can be discouragingly complex.

The basic Netware security scheme dates back to version 2.*x*. This early release provided three kinds of security measures:

- Log-in control
- File management
- Directory security

Overall responsibility for managing this security system went to the network supervisor. The supervisor was responsible for setting up user accounts, installing applications, and managing the security system. The supervisor could assign one of eight types of privileges, or rights:

- Read
- Open
- Search
- Write
- Create
- Delete
- Parental

- Modify

You could assign these rights to individuals or groups; in that case they were called *trustee rights*. You could also assign *directory rights,* in which a directory was assigned certain rights over the files within it. The combination of trustee and directory rights governed each user's access to particular files. Each directory had an *inherited-rights mask* (IRM). This served as a filter, controlling access to files and allowing users to exercise only the rights they had available.

A good start, but...

With this system, the supervisor could provide a secure environment for sensitive files, placing them in directories that limited access and at the same time limiting the authority of individuals and groups to see or alter these files. It was good, but far from perfect.

People soon found the imperfections. For example, with the help of a simple, easy-to-find utility program, they could change the names of files in Netware's bindery section. This would force Netware to reconfigure itself, and the user could gain entry as an supervisor. The invader could not only get into your system but could do so with enough apparent authority to steal or destroy at will.

The most recent releases in the 2.x series have addressed this problem. So has the more advanced version 3.x, the mainstay of most LAN installations today. The system of rights and privileges in version 3.x is an improved version of those originated in 2.x. The most important change has been to grant supervisors authority over individual files. In the previous version, they were able to establish access controls only at the directory levels; the files inherited their directories' controls. With 3.x, the supervisor can assign trustee rights to individual files. If necessary, you can bypass the directory security structure and establish finely tailored controls file by file.

From control to management

The security measures in release 4.x again follow the pattern of the earlier versions. In 4.x, however, the emphasis shifts from control to management. Furthermore, while the earlier versions were designed to manage directories and files on network servers, 4.x security extends across the entire network.

The instrument of these changes is Netware Directory Services (NDS), a global database with copies reproduced throughout the network. The access control of previous versions is still maintained at the file servers. NDS takes a broader view in which the server is one object within a larger security scheme. This object view is an important feature. NDS has its own system of directories, different from those used in earlier versions. All entities within an NDS directory are treated as objects. These include users, printers, file servers, and other elements of the system.

The NDS database establishes four levels on which to grant access rights to these objects:

- Directory
- File
- Object
- Property

The object rights are:

- Browse
- Create
- Delete
- Rename
- Supervisor

The property rights include:

- Read
- Compare
- Write
- Add or delete
- Supervisor

As with earlier forms of Netware security, you can use these rights to determine who will have access to a particular resource and what they can do with it when they gain that access. The distinguishing feature of the NDS system is that it goes beyond an individual server and lets you apply the security system anywhere in the network. That feature is particularly important in networks that have more than one server. Previously, you had to establish a separate security scheme, with duplicate sets of individual user accounts, on each server. The 4.x global approach lets you establish a single access-control scheme for one server, then place duplicates on the network's other servers.

The network supervisor is now responsible not only for the original NDS database but for all its clones throughout the network. Even so, the system makes it easier to meet that expanded responsibility. The supervisor can administer the full access scheme by entering the changes in a single NDS database. Other copies of the database then pick up the changes. You can administer several network objects, regardless of where they are located.

The NDS security is an addition to the earlier system and works in conjunction with it. Most of the old principles still apply. Most important, though the means to secure the network are present, it's up to you to take advantage of them. You must use the password and log-in system to identify who has access to the system. Then you must use the system of rights and privileges to determine what even an authorized party is allowed to do.

Netware security and viruses

You can use the Netware security system to help protect the network from viruses. If properly used, Netware's security system can go a long way to protect you from the typical virus attack. There are some openings for trouble, though—and human error can create even more.

As with other forms of Netware security, the tools are there, but they don't work unless you use them. There are two key ways in which you can use Netware security to protect yourself from virus attacks:

- Limit the right to modify an executable file.

- Create a pseudo-supervisor to minimize use of the main supervisor account.

Revoking modify rights

A Netware directory can hold rights to modify the files contained within it. This can make it a sitting duck for a determined virus, and all viruses are determined. The solution is to revoke any privileges assigned to directories that contain executable files.

An invading virus can easily get past any defenses you might try to put up using DOS. In particular, and contrary to conventional wisdom, it does little good to use DOS to change a file's attributes to read-only. Many viruses can infect read-only files. In fact, there's an easier invasion route than that. Many viruses are designed to activate DOS and change the attributes of a target file. The virus can reverse the very step you took to try to stop it.

On the other hand, there are few viruses that can get past the Netware system of directory rights. Revoking directory rights to modify a file is usually an effective defense.

Supervisory authority

The Netware supervisor's account is a powerful feature that comes with few built-in restraints. The supervisor, or anyone who successfully logs on under that name, can do just about anything—including overriding the entire security system.

Of course, most supervisors are qualified network administrators who know how to handle the power at their disposal. Often, though, you'll find that maintenance and support technicians use the supervisor's password to work on the system and diagnose problems. There are also viruses just waiting for these people to give them an opportunity. Often they lie in supervisors' PCs or on their floppy disks, waiting to take advantage of an error.

A virus can also create its own opportunities. In a typical scenario, the virus will cause a computer to hang. The frustrated user will call for help. A support technician will reboot the machine and log in under the supervisor's password. If things look good, and a well-designed virus will ensure that they do, the technician will pronounce the problem solved. Just to make sure, a test will be run with the user's account. Given that opening, the virus will spring joyously to all corners of the network.

The solution is to set up a separate account for service and support technicians, without the wide-ranging powers of the supervisors' account. Create similar accounts for the supervisors themselves. If you carefully allot the privileges granted to these accounts, you can give the individuals the privileges they need to do their jobs, without giving them all the power and peril that goes with the supervisor's account. Done properly, you can set up a system in which the full supervisor's password hardly ever needs to be invoked, even by the supervisor.

In an ideal allocation of rights, the pseudo-supervisor accounts will have trustee access to control access rights to all areas to which other users will have access. This lets the supervisor use the limited password to grant individual access to directories and files. These accounts should not include the right to modify directory rights. Someone who gains this kind of access could modify their own directory rights, including the right to modify executable files. This would defeat the purpose of the entire exercise. Give the pseudo-supervisor account no more than the right to read and scan at the directory level.

Network Security Basics

As they come from the box, most LANs provide little, if any, security. They provide the means to provide security, but it's up to you to make use of those tools. A full LAN security system should include:

- An availability system to make sure the network's assets are readily available to authorized users

- An access-control system that allows restricted data to be used only by authorized persons

- An integrity system that guards against modification of data, whether by accident or design

The first of these needs is often in direct conflict with the other two. The real challenge of network security is to lock the door, without slamming it so securely you unnecessarily hinder access to those who not only are authorized but have work to do.

One problem is that networked resources—by definition—are strung out all over the place. New forms of data communication bring together many activities that previously had been handled separately. At one time, data processing and office automation were separate fields. As time passed, it became increasingly hard to tell one from the other. Then PCs were added to the mix. Then, everything was wired into networks. The near future promises a merger of computers and telephones. The result is one multifaceted system where you formerly had several. These developments have had several consequences:

- They have combined and multiplied the risks associated with each of these previously separate components.

- There has been an increase in the number of communication channels that must be secured.
- Departmental distinctions within the organization have been blurred.

Not long ago, a computer security officer was responsible for a single, centrally located system. A department head might have responsibility for the security of a single computer or a small network. Now, both of you share responsibility for a networked system that can amount to a small communication conglomerate within your own company. Almost anyone in the office now has computing and communication power, to be used wisely or otherwise.

This creates a sense of diffusion within the organization that can easily outstrip the company's ability to manage it. Management includes security. Just as your expanding communication net requires tighter and better management, its impact on the organization can seriously curtail your ability to do it.

Electronic mail is a leading example. Like other kinds of networks, it is a communication system that has many points of access and a number of vulnerable spots. It may be convenient to send a sales order to be filled immediately or to receive reports with the most up-to-date information possible. But don't send a salary schedule by electronic mail. Don't transmit a facsimile of the blueprints for a major new product. Don't send sensitive information about your employees or customers. At least don't do so without encrypting it first. The same rules should apply to facsimile transmissions.

In fact, these rules should apply to any communication whose security is not absolutely certain. The first rule of communication security is to be careful what you send over the network. Don't assume it is safe from compromise. Assume that whatever you will transmit will arrive shortly on the desk of the person you would least want to receive it.

One reason communication networks have been so vulnerable is that many users don't understand how vulnerable they are. Many people rely solely on password systems because they truly don't know any better.

> **Action item**   Check out your own system. Does it rely on passwords alone, or is there something to back them up?

Have a Plan and a Policy

The key to protecting a computer network is to protect the components that are hooked into it. This means the protection measures that work for a network file server on one end of a communication link and a PC on the other also serve to protect the linked pair. The same is true of other PCs and peripherals attached to the LAN.

Any assessment of your vulnerable spots should include an assessment of your highly vulnerable network connections. Find these spots, checking both the communication lines and the physical locations they connect. Figure out what would happen to the company should someone exploit this weakness.

Identify the controls, both baseline and optional, that can be used to counter the threat.

> **Action item**   Make a detailed diagram of all the physical facilities in your system, including the workstations, servers, cabling, and other elements. Identify how each element is used and the policies under which it is operated. Not only does this give you a complete inventory of your linked resources, it gives you a better picture of your system and could indicate some ways to save costs. Then include these vulnerable communication links in your overall security plan. Look at:
>
> - How much the company relies on communication and how much it is likely to do so in the future
> - What kind of data is to be communicated over the network
> - Who will use this data, and what they will be allowed to do with it
> - The value of the data you are trying to protect
> - How much you can budget to protect this data

Resources for Network Assessments

The system diagram is one resource you can use to assess your position and plan for adequate network security. In one case such a diagram revealed some mysterious extra communication lines that appeared in none of the original system documents. Tracing these lines led to a pair of employees who had installed their own lines into their employer's network and were using it to run their own on-the-side business.

Include site plans in the security check. A poorly protected server can be the familiar weak link. Also look at the existing access control system and determine how well it governs individuals' use of particular files.

Basic Network Security

While network operating systems provide some degree of security, different types of networks provide different degrees of security. Generally, the most secure is a server-based system in which the critical files are all on a single computer. Physical protection is fairly easy, and you can concentrate other tactics as well on guarding this single resource. Least secure is a peer-to-peer system in which anyone has a chance to lose or damage a file.

Many LAN operating systems imitate the security features of their mainframe big brethren. If you are familiar with larger systems, you should have little trouble adapting to the LAN. On the other hand, if you lack that experience and your security needs are modest, you might find that these adaptations of large-scale systems offer more security and require more effort than you need.

Before you invest in network security, identify the threats your organization faces and prepare a list of baseline and additional security measures to meet those threats. Then, shop for a network security system that provides the measures you need. Anything more only makes things tougher on you, and on the employees who have to cope with an excessive security burden.

Among the security risks that might be particularly acute in a network setting are:

- *Password systems.* Passwords are the foundation of access control, but networks multiply all their weaknesses.

- *File access.* In all but the smallest networks, this will probably require multiple layers of access control.

- *Hardware problems.* Not only do many kinds of network hardware leave you vulnerable to unauthorized entry, but the failures of some elements can shut down an entire network.

- *The human factor.* As with every other kind of computer security, the most effective security program for a network must concentrate on the people who use it—or would misuse it.

Passwords

Passwords are the most common form of network protection; they are also among the weakest. One particular danger in a network setting: Some users write DOS batch files that include the passwords and log-on sequences. Since these batch files are in easy-to-read ASCII form, anyone with even a smattering of PC knowledge can read and use them. The use of a network transforms the "anyone" from a single user to plural possibilities. That means the password system requires tight administration and other forms of procedural and technical backup.

> **Action item** Have supervisors check each user for proper password behavior. Repeat the checks regularly enough to let people know you're serious.

Access control

Beyond the use of a password to admit a user to the network, you should establish multiple layers of access control. Most network systems call for user profiles to serve this purpose. The system restricts the files to which an identified user has access, then restricts the kinds of operations that user can perform on them. Among the restraints you may need are:

- *Who can log in.* This is the obvious password control: You want to confine access to authorized users.

- *What resources are available to them.* Certain files should be available only to certain users. You may also want to limit access to other resources such as modems and printers.

- *What they can do with these resources.* Some users should be allowed to add new data to a file; others only to read it. In some cases, unauthorized users should not be able to learn that the file even exists.

- *When access is available.* If all your operations take place during normal business hours, you may want to prevent access at other times.

- *From where access is available.* This restriction is useful if authorized users always log on from their own workstations. It can be a hindrance if the users must call in from various sites.

Authorization levels

These multiple levels of access are usually managed by assigning a particular access level to an individual's user identification. For example, the system administrator should have access to every asset in the network. If you have a small network used by people you know well, you might give this access level to everyone and save yourself many administrative headaches. In a larger group, only those responsible for running the system should have access to the entire network. Employees who work with particular parts of the business, such as accounts receivable or sales records, should be given access only to the directories and files that contain the data with which they work.

Even those who have access to particular files should be restricted in the type of access they enjoy. Some users can be given authority to add or modify existing data. In many other cases, it may be enough to let a user read the file without changing it. This reduces the chances of error and corruption as well as closing off an opportunity for mischief.

There is one type of file access control that doesn't always get the attention it requires. Many application programs produce temporary files. For example, when a word processor must handle a document longer than it can store in random access memory (RAM), it may create temporary files to hold parts of the document that aren't immediately being used. Another common form of temporary file is that found in a print spooler, waiting its turn to be printed.

Specify that all these temporary files be routed to a particular disk drive or directory. Then place that resource in a highly restricted category such as a Netware directory that imposes restricted access rights.

Securing Network Hardware

A network's hardware presents as many risks as its operating system and application software. Did you ever think of a printer as an access point? It's possible. Other weak spots include PCs and terminals, servers, bridges, gateways, modems, and cables.

Networked PCs and workstations

One particularly vulnerable point is the unattended personal computer, left running and logged on while its user steps out for a quick break. You can't do much to change this basic hardware setup, but you can attack this hardware problem with a procedural technique aimed at the ever-present human factor.

Action item   Establish policies, training, and posted reminders to help make employees aware of this danger.

At particular risk in a networked PC is the data its user may have down-loaded from a server or central database. This data may be well protected at its source but not while it resides on the hard disk of a workstation. Diskless workstations are one solution for this problem, but they do not always serve the needs of their users. You must balance the risk against the business needs.

Network servers

The server that holds all basic data files is the most secure form of network installation. It's obviously easier to protect your data when it is all in one place. However, there are two problems with that idea. The first is that the data doesn't always stay in one place. It often is downloaded for processing at the workstations. The second problem is that a network server often is not as physically secure as the larger systems that have traditionally performed similar services. These are often placed in locked rooms with restricted physical access; a network server is more likely to be out in the open. It may be even someone's personal workstation. Putting such a server in a locked office or closet is an easy, elementary security step.

Environmental security is also important. The power surge or spilled cup of coffee that knocks out a single PC is serious enough. When the PC is connected to a network, the same disasters could shut down your entire business. This is a particularly serious risk if the affected computer is the server.

Peril in printers

It's possible someone could steal your data by tapping the signal that flows through a printer cable. But why bother, when you can simply read the same material as it is committed to paper?

Most network printers are some distance from many of their users. When you send a print job to one of these printers, you don't always leave your desk right away to pick up the output. While this material sits at an unattended printer, anyone who can get to the printer can read your information.

You could buy a separate printer for each workstation, but that defeats one of the primary purposes of a network: the ability to share resources. Again, the best approach may be to attack the human factor and insist on such procedural steps as picking up sensitive printouts as they are produced.

Another printer-related threat is the phantom printer. Some invaders can arrange to have a nonexistent printer appear to be available to network users. Data sent to that printer flows directly to the invader instead.

Tapping the cables

Network cables are particularly weak in protecting data. You could be a victim of a digital version of phone tapping, or an intruder could simply monitor the stray electrical signals your cables generate.

This is a case where the risks can be over- and understated at the same time. On one hand, the idea of some kind of LAN wiretapper working in the basement is largely a romantic idea based on fiction, not reality. Most people who attack your system will use the means they know well, and few people are expert at this kind of snooping. On the other hand, the person who does have this knowledge is likely to be a professional, intent on stealing your most critical data.

The monitoring of stray signals requires sophisticated equipment, but some people have it. Professional network wiretappers have made use of network protocol analyzers. These are supposed to be maintenance tools used to diagnose transmitted signals. In the wrong hands, they can be used to disassemble the signals and reveal the data being moved.

One line of defense is to enclose as many devices as possible inside conductive containers that diffuse the signals to the outside. The other is like jamming a radio signal. You add enough spurious signals to the system to override any signals that might be useful to an outsider.

These technical means of prevention can be costly and hard to use. Before you go that route, make sure your analysis reveals a need.

Is encryption justified?

Encryption is a less costly alternative, but it still is not problem free. Encryption can present some particularly difficult problems for a cost-conscious manager.

Under most normal cost-benefit standards, this is an option to be used only where the files to be protected are unusually valuable. Its care and feeding are expensive, so it may not be practical for files of limited value. On the other hand, you may find it is the only practical way to protect data while it is in transit between your secured computer stations. If this data is valuable at all, you may have no choice but to accept the cost of encryption.

Make your decision carefully, and consider all the costs. For example, an encryption system almost always reduces the system's response speed. Someone must assume responsibility for protecting the encryption key. That's a particular problem if you have multiple users and a single key system. For networks, a public key system would let users encode their own work without the separate key necessary to decode it. There's also new equipment to buy— and you'll then need people to run and maintain it.

Other points to consider

- Maintain a standard procedure for installing new application software on the network. This can help avoid viruses and other infections. It can also avoid potential legal trouble from the use of pirated programs.

- Include network consultants in your security plan. Grant them only the access they need to do their jobs, and for the time periods the task requires.

Tips for a Secure Network

In an ideal world, users would faithfully observe all the policies and precautions, viruses would be eradicated, even ex-employees would have kind thoughts, and no one's e-mail messages would be exposed to general readership. In the real world, people make mistakes, new users must be trained, and the LANs configuration changes almost daily. You'll log a lot of nights and weekends just getting the LAN to work, much less maintaining its security. These tips sum up the process of meeting that responsibility:

- Train users. Let them know how important it is to log in and out properly and to keep their passwords secret.

- Manage software installation. A central authority should be responsible for all installations, ensuring that license terms are honored and that incoming material is free of viruses.

- Place servers behind locked doors.

- Scan regularly for viruses. Include all network nodes as well as the servers.

- Grant supervisor rights to as few people as possible.

- Change all the default passwords provided with applications or network operating systems.

- Use a front-end menu application with built-in password control. Use the menu to supplement the controls available through the operating system.

- When users close programs, return them to the menu, not to DOS. This reduces the opportunities for mischief. It also guards against damage caused by employees who get lost in the system.

- Maintain a log of employees who fail to log out properly, particularly after hours. Start with gentle reminders to offenders. If they still don't comply, consider this educational process: Close out their accounts, and force them to come to you to have them reactivated.

- Maintain audit records of who was using the network, when, where, and why. These records can be invaluable if you have to trace a problem to its source.

- Make backups daily. Store them off site in a secure and fireproof location. Along with them, store documentation on how your backup system is configured.

- Require password changes at fixed intervals. Require that the passwords be at least 5 characters.

- Control access to e-mail, and its folders and groups, just as you control access to other network resources.

- Make sure you receive immediate notice when someone leaves the company, regardless of the terms. Cancel that person's network access immediately.

- If your staff uses dial-in access, make sure you use all the security features available in the communication package. Include encrypted or hidden passwords and dial-back features. If the communication software lacks these, find an alternative.

- Use screen savers. They aren't really necessary to preserve modern monitors, but they protect against random eyeballing of critical data. Many also include password protection.

- Make sure people know what their available printing options are. Don't let print jobs be sent to nonexistent printers.

- Place printers that handle sensitive information in secure areas.

- Grant trustee rights only to people who truly need programs or information.

Going Wireless

Sometimes it's refreshing to find out there is little danger in some places where it would be expected. Wireless transmission is not free of danger—nothing is—but it is much more secure than first impressions might suggest.

That might seem strange to anyone who's tried to find the proper channel for a portable telephone or a garage door opener or to anyone who takes seriously those Federal Communications Commission warnings that electronic emanations from business computers can wreck nearby television reception. You tend to forget that protecting wireless transmissions is one of the oldest and best-developed forms of communication security. Some of the leading technology now in use was developed for military communications during World War II. Perhaps because they realize this, some of the most important users of wireless transmission are government agencies. They have accepted wireless networks as trusted means of communication. Financial institutions, which also seek high security, are also among the major users.

Three types of security

There are three different forms of wireless transmission:

- Infrared transmission
- Microwave transmission
- Spread spectrum

The three share many standard security features. In addition, each form and each vendor's implementation offer its own additional forms of security. Furthermore, there are as yet no accepted standards for wireless transmission. That leads to diverse products which require close examination to find a feature set that meets your need. You must compare various product's specifications for operating speed, price, and security features.

Infrared beams

Infrared light beams have attracted, and reflected, attention as a simple way to hook up a local area network. However, a major limitation is that an infrared transmission is a beam of light. It is thus easily interrupted, and it can't pass through walls. This limitation contributes to its safety, though. To intercept an infrared transmission, you must get close to it. Furthermore, common radio and wiretapping systems cannot detect infrared transmission.

Infrared systems come in two main types: line of sight and diffuse propagation. Line of sight is probably the more obvious method. It requires that the sending and receiving units be aimed directly at each other, no more than 80 feet apart. As a practical matter, a line-of-sight network must be within a single room. Anyone who wants to intercept a transmission would have to get directly in line with the transmission beam or would have to move the sensors and transmitters to point to the intercepting device. This would effectively shut down the network, and the invader would be left with nothing to intercept.

A diffuse propagation system makes use of reflective surfaces to extend the reach of an infrared transmission. Properly set up, an infrared signal can bounce off walls, floors, and ceilings to reach every receptor in a room, and perhaps in rooms beyond. Diffused propagation is naturally more susceptible to interception since the invader's unit need not be directly in a line of sight and will not interrupt the transmission.

Microwave transmission

The microwave system uses low-power radio signals on the 18-GHz frequency. Like infrared transmission, these signals are designed to stay within a confined area. They are broadcast at the lowest possible power, will travel no more than 200 feet, and will not pass through floors or exterior walls.

An outsider who wishes to tap into this network would need a large, high-gain parabolic antenna, then would have to find a way to place it directly adjacent to the network. Even someone working from inside would have to have the proper hardware to receive the signal. Making that more difficult is the proprietary status of this technology. It is available only in Motorola's Altair product line.

Also to prevent capture by unauthorized hardware, this system encrypts the data sent between control and user modules. The system generates a new encryption code for each transmission. The system also lets network administrators register each user module under a unique name; you would need a registered module to either transmit or receive.

Spread spectrum

Spread spectrum is the oldest and best-used form of wireless security. From soldiers in Europe and the Pacific to wireless LANs, spread spectrum has protected wireless communication from interference and interception.

The spread spectrum system distributes the signal across multiple broadcast frequencies. It can do this in either of two ways. The direct sequence method spreads the signals across a continuous band of frequency. Frequency hopping, true to its name, jumps from frequency to frequency. Either way, an interceptor must constantly change frequencies to keep up with the transmission, almost impossible unless you know the frequency changing code.

Spread spectrum systems have other security features as well. They use low transmission power to keep the signal within a limited area. In spreading transmissions over multiple frequencies, the system also effectively encrypts them. They also let a system administrator assign unique addresses to authorized units. Many spread spectrum products also let you establish a different frequency-spreading code to each network hub. Even an adjacent hub with a different code could not usefully intercept the transmissions. As a final security measure, someone who tries to enter the building to intercept wireless communication would somehow have to get in carrying a suspiciously bulky device.

As with all other forms of security, the inherent protection of wireless networks cannot do the job by itself. However, it does provide a level of protection you might not have expected, and used in conjunction with physical protection and network operating system security, it can be an effective means of protection.

Network Security Techniques

Table 10.1 lists the baseline security measures that are normally appropriate for network installations. Table 10.2 lists the selective measures that might be applied under the indicated circumstances.

TABLE 10.1   Baseline Security for Networks

Item	Class
Compliance with laws and regulations	Procedural
Computer security management committees	Procedural
Password file encryption	Technical
Computer system activity records	Procedural
Workstation access use restrictions	Physical
Computer use access-control administration	Procedural Technical
Computer user trouble call logging	Technical Procedural
Contingency recovery-equipment replacement	Disaster
Data file access control	Technical
Data file and program backup	Procedural Technical
Disaster recovery	Disaster
Electrical equipment protection	Disaster Physical
Electrical power shutdown and recovery	Physical Disaster
Emergency preparedness	Disaster
Employee identification on work products	Procedural Technical
Input data validation	Technical
Isolation of sensitive production jobs	Procedural Physical
Minimizing traffic and access to work areas	Physical
Minimizing numbers of copies of sensitive files and reports	Procedural
Passwords for workstation access	Procedural Physical Technical
Privileged information display restrictions	Technical
Security for sensitive areas during attended periods	Physical Procedural
Separation and accountability of functions	Procedural
Telephone access universal selection	Technical
Terminal log-in protocol	Technical

TABLE 10.2   Selective Security Methods for Networks

Item	Use when:	Class
Alternate power supply	High service availability is required.	Disaster
Computer security officer	There are enough computer security resources to justify this position.	Procedural Physical
Courier trustworthiness and identification	Couriers deliver output.	Physical Procedural
Cryptographic protection	You need the greatest protection of data.	Technical
Delivery loading dock access control	You need severe physical access restraints.	Physical
Dynamic password change control by user	There may be frequent interruptions in terminal use.	Technical
Limiting transaction privileges from workstations	The system permits multiple terminal access.	Technical
Monitoring computer use	Access is to be limited to employees.	Procedural
Passwords generated by computer	There are many remote terminal users.	Technical
Remote terminal user's agreement	Terminal users are outside your immediate control.	Procedural
Separation of equipment	You have large, complex systems.	Disaster
Separation of test and production systems	You have networks of multiple computers.	Technical
Workstation identifiers	High workstation security is required.	Technical
Universal use of badges	There is a large staff, heavy traffic, or many visits by outsiders.	Physical Procedural

Securing the
Enterprise Network

*When securing an enterprise network, the first rule is
that the old rules don't work.*

By definition, a local area network covers a local area. Not so the networks
that are sprawling across our enterprises today. The original local networks
are being connected into networks of networks. Furthermore, these expanded
networks connect a host of seemingly incompatible components: mainframes,
minicomputers, LANs, wide area networks, resources in other parts of the
country, and even resources in other countries. If the enterprise network is
notable for one thing, it is its diversity.

This diversity, both technical and geographical, means that all the familiar
rules of computer security must be rewritten, or at least heavily edited.
Mainframe techniques built around securing central locations are clearly
insufficient to secure a virtual computer that can encompass the entire organization. LAN techniques can do a good job of securing local networks based
on nearby servers, but securing the enterprise network requires that you
expand your vision by several multiples.

Securing an enterprise network can also be an exercise in frustration.
Often, you'll reach into your toolbox and come up empty. The tool you need
hasn't been invented yet. At other times, you'll have to shoehorn into place
security measures that clearly are ill-suited for the task at hand. You will
often have to deal with confused and frustrated users who see passwords, log-
in schemes, encryption, and other security measures as inhibitions on the
ability to do their own jobs.

If there's good news in all of this, it is that the basic techniques of computer
security are still valid. The enterprise network simply requires that you
adopt and adapt these, sometimes stretching them a little. It won't be easy,
but you can do it. In fact, you must do it. Enterprise networking will continue
to spread, with or without your participation.

Building an Enterprise Security Plan

To meet the widespread challenge of enterprise network security, start with a good plan. Include these elements:

- *Raise awareness.* Senior managers often are still unaware how important security can be. This is particularly true of the new perils you face as your networks expand. Provide for their education.

- *Adapt familiar methods to new needs.* Just because you decentralize the network, you need not decentralize security management.

- *Control file access.* The types of controls available over a LAN are even more important as the network expands.

- *Set priorities.* Concentrate first on the most likely invasion routes.

- *Audit the program.* Keep track of who is, or is not, behaving as they should.

- *Consider encryption.* Even when encryption is not practical on a LAN, it could be essential to an enterprise network.

- *Back up everything.* Make use of the decentralized environment to maintain duplicate copies.

- *Keep it simple.* Here is another built-in contradiction, but it's important. Encourage people to use their security measures by making them easy to use.

Spreading the word

With many members of top management, security is still a hard sell. This seems to be particularly true of those who control the finances. Even those who understand a need for security may not appreciate the scope required by the expansion of enterprise networks. It's up to you to make them understand.

Start with some ammunition. The Communications Fraud Control Association estimates that unauthorized access to computer and telephone systems costs victims $500 million a year. That's in the United States. Worldwide, the estimated loss is more than $2 billion. When the University of Texas conducted a survey of computer losses, it found that 43 percent of the firms that suffer a major loss never reopen. This is true whether the loss is to criminal activity or to natural disaster. Even among the firms that do manage to reopen, 90 percent are out of business within 2 years. That's not to say that the computer losses caused all those failures, but they certainly didn't help.

> **Action item**   Get top officials involved in planning for data security. This helps ensure that security plans are dovetailed with the organization's other activities. In addition, involvement is always a motivator; it works as well with senior executives as it does with lower-ranking employees.

This is essentially a selling job; technicians and security experts aren't always good at it. Still, it's necessary. If you're convinced certain security measures are necessary, it's part of your job to transfer that conviction to the people who make the final decisions.

Don't forget the rest of the organization. Selling security to the people at the keyboards can be as important as selling it to the people in corner offices. You cannot maintain a full security program without their cooperation. Ideally, they should become participating partners in protecting the resources for which they are responsible. You are no longer in an environment where you can control everything. You must get users to take charge of their own working environments. In particular, users need to learn to protect their own passwords. Carelessness in creating and protecting passwords is one of the biggest sources of loss.

Centralized security

Decentralized computing need not mean decentralized security. In fact, it's even more important that security be centrally managed. Training, planning, and management should all be consistent throughout the organization. Often, you'll have to teach users to help maintain the security system. They should have the advantage of consistent, easy procedures. You also may need a larger security staff. There are limits to your dependence on user cooperation. Someone has to manage computer security wherever the need exists. Spreading yourself too thin is a real possibility.

Setting priorities

You can't do everything at once. Attack the most urgent needs first. Usually, that will mean controlling access to workstations. Use keys, passwords, identification cards, or even biometric techniques to ensure that only authorized users can start up a system.

Establish the basic classes of network access:

- *The network supervisor.* This person needs access to all functions including the security system.

- *Administrative users.* This should be a small group given sufficient rights to maintain and support the network.

- *Trusted users.* These employees need and can use access to sensitive information.

- *Vulnerable users.* These employees do not need access beyond the strict confines of their responsibilities.

Access control is a balancing act. Authorized users should find it easy to gain access. Anyone else should find it very difficult. Striking that balance will always be a major challenge, and there's no magic formula. Just knowing the balance is necessary can help you achieve it.

Checking up

Creating the system is one thing; making it work is another. Auditing is the process of making sure your security measures work as well as you had hoped. Without being unduly intrusive, you want to make sure you know who is doing what with the network. The system should provide information like this that you can use to oversee the network:

- *A log of all attempts to gain access to the system.* This is one of the best ways to determine if your system is under attack. The more often you check this log, the more effective it can be.

- *A chronological log of all network activity.* Log every event, including identification of the users and workstations involved.

- *Flags to identify unusual activity and variations from established procedures.*

  Action item: Let people know you are keeping track. Don't hold it over their heads, but letting people know you are watching is the kind of security that helps keep honest people honest.

A larger role for encryption

The value of encryption in an enterprise network setting is that information obtained improperly will still be useless. Encryption can be a costly process that inhibits system performance. That limits its value in securing LANs and individual systems, but expanded networks can make it more worthwhile. The basic standard: Encrypt all sensitive information that travels along the network.

Basic backups

Backing up is the advice PC users so routinely ignore. That could be particularly serious on an enterprise network. Your network management plan should make someone directly responsible for backing up specific information resources.

Actually, the design of an enterprise network can help protect your data. The network involves so many bits and pieces that it's unlikely that all of them will go down at the same time. You can store duplicate copies of critical data at multiple points on the network.

On the other hand, a network's diversity can make backups more difficult. Particularly in a distributed system, parts of a database resource will be on different systems. These may not be alike or may not even have the same backup schemes. Distributed systems pose many difficulties besides this, however, and for most uses the best advice is to maintain and—regularly back up—a single database server.

Keeping it simple

The very nature of an enterprise network makes it complicated. Your security measures can be equally complex. Various components may have their own operating systems, access-control schemes, and passwords. While protecting this complex environment, you must also try to keep it simple. When a security scheme is too hard to use, people will find ways around it. For example, complexity in password administration leads to that stereotype security violation, the password on a sticky note. There are few simpler or surer ways to disable even the best security system

Several firms now make products that allow single sign-ons for diverse networks. These make it easy for security managers as well as users. You can manage the entire password system from a single location. Typically, this type of product will create a security kernel on each workstation. It contains encrypted versions of all the usual passwords, identifications and log-on sequences used around the network.

A user need only pass the initial sign-on routine. Once authorized, should the user need a particular resource, the sign-on software can provide transparent access to its part of the network.

Major Security Functions for Networks

The National Institute for Standards and Technology (NIST) has developed what it calls *Minimal Security Functional Requirements for Multi-user Operational Systems*. The security precautions it lists are not always unique to enterprise networking, but NIST has developed a useful checklist of the functions you should consider in planning a security system. The major functions are:

- *Identification and authentication.* Uses a password or some other form of identification to screen users and check their authorization.

- *Access control.* Keeps even authorized users from gaining access to material they should not see.

- *Accountability.* Links the activities on a network to the user's identity.

- *Audit trails.* Determines whether a security violation has occurred and what if anything was lost.

- *Object reuse.* Ensures that resources can be secured in the hands of multiple users.

- *Accuracy.* Guards against errors and unauthorized modifications.

- *Reliability.* Protects itself against monopolization by any user.

- *Data exchange.* Promotes secure transmission over communication channels.

Identifying the user

In the enterprise network, as in most other installations, user identification is necessary but not sufficient. An identification and authentication system usually relies on passwords, though it can use other clues such as badges and biometric measurements. None of the rest of the security system will work unless you can first make sure that you can determine whether a would-be user is authorized to be there.

Gaining entry should not be enough. Once a user is admitted, the system still should govern each person's access to information. Popular network operating systems have the means to do this, and so do many PC applications, particularly database management systems. Use privilege-control management to make sure a user has access to what he or she needs to do the job, but nothing else. You can often do this by assigning predefined sets of privileges to particular job responsibilities.

Recycling objects

Network users often share their files. The goal of object reuse controls is to make sure that they do so peacefully and that they do not compromise security in the process. For example, some programs leave data in memory after they have been shut down. Another user should not be able to retrieve that data. A similar problem involves documents waiting in a print queue. If another user needs access to the data, it should be governed by the access control and permission scheme.

Right the first time

Ensuring accuracy can be one of the toughest challenges in network security. No one should be allowed to modify data except under the most carefully controlled conditions. Be sparing with your use of this privilege. Don't leave an exposed system or application program where viruses can lodge. Protect the operating system, too.

One way to do this is to give each vulnerable file an encrypted check sum that is updated with every legitimate use. Whenever someone opens the file, check the sum against the previous version. If you do not see the expected increase, that's a sign of tampering or illegitimate use.

Of course, you should also encrypt and protect the file that records the check sums.

Principles of Network Security

There are many technical steps you can take to achieve an advanced level of network protection. For example, you can equip workstations, networked PCs, and other remote devices with self-identification devices. These are circuits that will respond to interrogation commands and transmit an identification code for the device. This code may be a simple identification scheme that merely identifies the type of device, or it may be a security code that uniquely identifies the individual unit.

It can be a useful safeguard against an unauthorized terminal or device masquerading as an authorized one. This is most likely to occur on switched networks because of the ability to communicate between arbitrary points. However, even in a hard-wired network, an impostor terminal might be attached by some means such as a wiretap.

Such a code lets you identify the device that is trying to gain access to the network, but it does not tell you who is using that device. The use of a built-in code to identify a terminal or personal computer does not provide much security if an eavesdropper can determine the code by prying into the terminal or by wiretapping. This user could then falsify the code using a device of his or her own. To prevent this, place the circuits that generate the code in a tamper-resistant housing. Then encrypt the transmissions.

The role of encryption

Protecting data transmission is only one possible role for encryption in an enterprise network. The most important is to protect passwords and their generation and recording systems. These are glaring weak spots in the typical network.

You can also use encryption to preserve the confidentiality of information transmitted between computers and remote terminals. In addition, it can help guard against threats like wiretapping, electronic eavesdropping, misrouting, substitution, modification, and injection of messages. Data files also can be safeguarded by encryption techniques.

Encryption algorithms can be used to create digital signatures, which can help verify the identity of message senders and recipients.

Protecting identity verification

When passwords or other information known to an authorized user are entered into a system, it is possible for a penetrator to intercept that information by wiretap or some other means. The penetrator then can use that information to impersonate the authorized users.

To guard against this threat, the keyboard or terminal used to enter the secret information should be safeguarded against tampering. Encryption then can be used to protect the information from the point where it leaves the keyboard or terminal and is transmitted to its destination. If you already are using encryption to protect the working information transmitted to and from the terminal, this same capability may be suitable for protecting the verification information.

The encryption process used to protect the verification information must provide for the information to be coded differently with each transmission. Otherwise, a penetrator might record the encrypted information from a point in its transmission path and fool the system simply by injecting the same encrypted information without ever having to decrypt it. Encryption systems generally have provisions for achieving the required variability.

When a personal attribute is used to verify an identity, a set of measured values is obtained and digitized and used for comparison with a reference profile. This information, in clear form, can be used by a skillful penetrator to simulate the data obtained from an authorized user. To guard against this, the device which measures the attribute should be safeguarded against tampering so the measured data cannot be taken while it is in the clear. Encryption can be used to protect this information during transmission.

Verification systems based on personal attributes are configured in a variety of ways. In one configuration, the measuring device sends the measured values to a central system where the reference profile is stored and where the comparison takes place. In this case, the measured values should be encrypted for transmission to the central system.

In another configuration, the reference profile is sent to the measuring device with the comparison taking place in the device. In this case the reference profile should be encrypted to prevent a penetrator from being able to inject a reference profile of his or her own.

Also, the device will produce a pass-fail signal, based on the results of the comparison, and this will be transmitted elsewhere, such as back to the central system that controls network access. This pass-fail signal also should be encrypted. Otherwise, a penetrator might be able to simulate this signal and produce a false pass response without ever having to deceive the measurement device.

Generally, the personal attribute sensing device will be either an integral part of a remote terminal or will be closely associated with such a terminal. Precautions should be taken to assure that equipment enclosures are tamper protected and that there are no exposed leads that would let a penetrator tap sensitive information.

Digital signatures

One form of authentication is the digital signature, in which the sender of a message attaches a coded identification to the message, enciphered in such a way that only the intended recipient can decipher it and verify the identity of the sender.

One way to do this is based on using individual station identifiers in the process of encrypting keys, which in turn are used to encrypt messages between the stations. Because of the hardware arrangements and operating procedures used with this system, it is possible for a sender to encipher a signature or any other message in such a way that only the prearranged recipient can correctly decipher it.

Digital signatures also may be achieved through public key encryption. In such a system, the encryption key differs from the decryption key, and knowledge of the encryption key does not result in knowledge of the decryption key. In a public key system, users may freely publicize the keys for encrypting messages that are to be sent to them; they keep secret the corresponding decryption keys.

The encryption and decryption procedures for some public key systems are inverses of each other. In normal practice, a message would first be enciphered for transmission and then be deciphered upon receipt to recover the information. However, the procedures in these systems may be applied in the reverse order, first using the decryption procedure to conceal the information and then using the encryption procedure to recover it.

A secure digital signature can be achieved this way: Assume that user A wants to send a secure digital signature to user B. A first passes the signature through A's own private decryption procedure, which in effect leaves it in unintelligible form. A then enciphers the signature in this form using B's public encryption procedure for privacy and sends it to B.

B first deciphers the signature using B's secret decryption procedure. B then applies A's public encryption procedure and recovers the digital signature. In practice, it is preferable to apply this process to entire messages rather than just the authenticating signature to keep a valid signature from being attached to a falsified message.

Range of capabilities

Once the identity of a user has been established and authenticated, he or she may be granted access to the network and may request the use of various available resources. These resources consist of various entities such as host computers, areas of main memory, files, programs, auxiliary memory devices, and instructions. They often are referred to as *objects*. Users must have proper authorization to be granted access to these objects. Each user has an associated set of access privileges to which he or she is entitled. This may be called the *capability profile*. Similarly, each object has associated with it a set of requirements for its use, which may be called an *access requirement profile*. An access request is authorized when the requester's capability profile matches the objects' access requirements profile.

An object may have many ways in which it can be used, such as reading data from a file, writing data into a file, carrying out a transaction, executing a program, compiling a program, or invoking various operating system routines. Thus, there is a range of capabilities associated with an object, not all of which may be authorized for use by every user. You can visualize this situation as a three-dimensional array, with users along one dimension, objects along another, and capabilities along the third.

Levels of access control

You can also visualize access control and privacy protection in three levels: memory, procedure, and logical. Access control at the memory level regulates access to memory in terms of units of memory. Concern at this level is with defined regions of memory rather than with its contents. This protection applies to the contents only while they remain in the defined region. Protected regions of memory typically are defined by the means of memory-bound registers or storage protection keys that control access to the bounded memory regions.

Access control at the procedure level regulates access to procedures, where a procedure is a set of programs and associated data. Access control at this level is concerned with the conditions under which programs can pass control from one to another. That is, the execution programs must be monitored in terms of calls, returns, and the passing of parameters.

Access authorization principles

Access control can be governed by a set of principles like these:

- *Least privilege.* No requester has any access privileges that are not required to perform the function—in other words, a need-to-know standard. As a corollary to this, access to resources should be compartmentalized whenever this separation adds to security.

- *Least common mechanism.* These are minimal shared or common mechanisms, other than those that expressly are there for security purposes.

- *Reference monitor approach.* Access controls are always invoked, isolated from unauthorized alteration, and accredited as being trustworthy.

- *Object versus path protection.* Protection can be provided to the object itself, the path to the object, or both. The network aspects are almost entirely path-oriented protection.

Composite authorizations

Nearly every computer transaction involves several entities. These could include a person, a terminal, a host computer, and a process. Each of these entities must be authorized either to receive, process, or transport the information being handled.

The logical intersection of these authorizations will establish the level of information which can be sent by this sequence of entities, but a further step-by-step authorization check also is necessary to ensure that only the proper entity or entities are the ultimate recipients of the information. For example, one entity may be authorized to process but not to copy the information.

In some instances, the request will be connected to a host that will, in turn, need access to other resources on the requester's behalf. Authorization is a larger problem than authentication since the latter is strictly binary at each intermediate requester. In contrast, the authorizations of each intermediate requester may differ, as may the authorization needs when information is processed at different nodes along the chain.

You can take either of two approaches:

- Continually subsetting the authorizations as necessary so the final privileges are the intersection of those of the original requester and all intermediate nodes. This will ensure that no intermediate node gets any information for which it is not authorized.

- Handling the authorization iteratively on a pairwise basis, so the nth level will provide any requested information for which the $(N-1)$th is authorized and leave the burden of further controls on passing of data to the host. This procedure allows the use of statistical programs, in which specific details are lost in favor of summaries. For example, the system might respond with the average value of a group of data but not with a specific value within the group. Of course, you still would be vulnerable to a cleverly devised statistical request.

Access to the authorization mechanism

The authorization mechanism is called upon whenever a user presents an access request for an object. The mechanism must therefore be readily accessible for frequent use. There also will be occasions when the mechanism must be modified to reflect changes in status for users and objects. This mechanism has a critical security function, and it must be properly protected from unauthorized modifications.

Guarding the Gates

One of the most vulnerable spots in a network is the system that administers the passwords. On many LANs, including both Ethernet and Token Ring systems, the passwords are transmitted in plain text that anyone with a little gumption and knowledge can intercept and use. The same is true of passwords transmitted by remote log-in and file transfer protocols. An invader can capture such a password to gain access to the network. Once inside, the invader also usually knows how to obtain the necessary privileges to see and modify even the most sensitive files.

Furthermore, someone who gains access to one machine on the network can often find easy access to others. A server may be set up to automatically accept commands from a designated group of "trusted" workstation or another server. An invader who gains access to one of the trusted machines then can use that authorization to gain access to the server.

Enterprise networks compound the problem because they usually involve multiple networks and protocols, each with its own passwords buzzing around the network. You have to assume that anything transmitted on the network—including the passwords—is open to interception.

Junkyard dog

A major challenge in securing an enterprise network, then, is to protect the password system. You must ensure that someone who uses a password is truly authorized to use it. One of the primary standards for authenticating identities is Kerberos. Developed at the Massachusetts Institute of Technology to protect its own network, Kerberos is named for the mythical three-headed dog that supposedly guards the gates to Hades. The MIT implementation can do much the same job on any network that uses the TCP/IP protocol. Kerberos uses encryption technology to require that a user and the system prove their identities to each other before they exchange data. It also helps keep unauthorized parties from eavesdropping on the data exchange.

Tickets and keys

In uncounted spy novels, two figures meet in a dark place and exchange cryptic remarks. "How about them Bucs?" asks one. "Only if it rains in Cleveland," replies the other. This exchange constitutes a password and countersign—the exchange of shared secrets. In this way, they confirm each other's identities. Kerberos also relies on shared secrets called *keys.* Used in conjunction with a parallel system of tickets, the system lets a user prove his or her identity to a server, using a Kerberos server as a third-party intermediary.

A key is a string of characters used to encrypt a message. Kerberos uses several types of keys. Client and server keys are both persistent; they stay in effect until someone changes them. There is also a session key that changes after every communication session. This key is known only to three entities: the client, the server, and Kerberos itself.

The user takes on the role of client. Before it can gain access to the system, the client must establish its password. The Kerberos server stores the password in encrypted form. The encrypted client password becomes the client key.

Like an airline traveler, the client must obtain a ticket to each network destination it wants to visit. To obtain a ticket, the client enters a password at its workstation. In response, client software forwards at the client's request a *key distribution center* (KDC) on the Kerberos server. The KDC responds with a message encrypted in the client key, the key that was derived from the client's password. By successfully decoding the message, the client verifies that it is indeed who it says it is. In this exchange, only the encrypted messages travel across the network. In particular, the client's password never has to make that perilous trip.

The travel agent

Having decoded the message, the client forwards the ticket request and proof of identity to a ticket-getting service (TGS), which functions something like a network travel agency. The request includes encrypted proof of the client's identity. The TGS uses a combination of the client's key and its own to obtain a ticket for each machine to which the client requires access. Then TGS returns the ticket to the client system, this time with proof of the server's identity encrypted in the combined client and server key. This information and a time stamp are enclosed within the ticket.

The client then can use the ticket to gain access to the desired resources. To further verify its identity, the client must submit a key matching the one encoded inside the ticket. The ticket must also be used within a short time after it was issued. Usually, software on the client's workstation will handle this process automatically.

The client can also ask for assurance that the server is authentic, not an impersonator. To do this, the client can issue a challenge, which can be a time stamp or a random number encrypted in the combined client and server key. An authorized server will decode this information, increase the time or number by 1, encrypt the new signal, and return it. The client then can encrypt the return message and compare it with the expected response.

It doesn't do everything

Like any dog, Kerberos can be a loyal, reliable servant. But while you can train it to recognize its master, there are things it never can do. Specifically, Kerberos is an authentication service. It verifies identities. It can determine who someone is, but it has nothing to say about what that person can do. That's a job for an access-control and privilege system.

Kerberos also has this in common with all other security measures: Even the best are not perfect. The exchange of encrypted messages make useful interception difficult, but there are ways an expert, determined invader could overcome the system. It also does nothing to protect passwords from that ever-present peril, human carelessness.

Hardware Security for Networks

Whenever you connect to networks, you need something with which to connect them. These connecting points can be vulnerable, but they also offer opportunities to add security to the enterprise network. Once, these interconnection devices came in distinct categories. Though later developments have erased the clear distinctions, these classes do still exist:

- Hubs are simple wiring centers, convenient places to make connections. They are often used to connect the nodes of a local area network.

- Bridges are nearly as simple but are intended primarily to connect multiple LANs.

- Routers are more intelligent. They have the power to intercept messages and forward them only to their intended destinations instead of broadcasting them to the entire network. Their main use is in linking LANs to larger enterprise networks.

- Gateways add the power to translate data formats. That's why you'll often find them at the intersections of LANs and large-system networks.

This clear division no longer exists. Hubs have taken on many of the characteristics of higher classes and have become known as "smart hubs." Routers are becoming the technology of choice in many installations that once would have used bridges. These smarter connections offer many advantages, including two that directly relate to security:

- They are selective in switching messages, sending them only along routes that lead to the intended destination. That means data traveling the network are less exposed to compromise.

- They can incorporate encryption, authentication, and other security schemes to help thwart invaders.

Hubs getting smarter

Typical of recent trends is the smart hub. No longer just a place to plug in cables, this increasingly brainy connection can include several kinds of security provisions. Hubs are particularly well suited for these tasks. They serve as focus points for LAN management, and they usually are installed in protected locations. The hub also intercepts user communications before they travel too far across an unprotected network.

For example, 3Com has developed a LAN security architecture (LSA) specifically designed to turn its hubs into management and security centers. You can set up this system to deliver data only to users who prove their identities and demonstrate a need to know. LSA also lets administrators create closed user groups, improves password protection, and disconnects unauthorized users.

Ungermann-Bass includes security in a concentrator module you can add to its high-end hub. You then can program the concentrator to accept only the messages from designated workstations, blocking out all other sources.

Securing Unix and Open Systems: What Can You Do?

Sooner or later, the enterprise network will take you to the world of Unix and open systems. Some professionals worry that adding open systems to a network will leave it open to security risks. That's possible, but as with LANs, Unix does offer the tools to build secure networks. The main requirement is that you use them.

Unix security isn't as easy as securing a LAN. There are several reasons:

- Netware's security features are familiar and widely used. Many network managers are less familiar with the Unix counterparts.

- Unix is often found in open systems that offer remote, direct dial-in access.

- There are no generally accepted standards under Unix for access control, setting privileges, or auditing the system. Some standards are being developed, though.

- The people who know Unix tend to know it very well. If motivated to do so, they would know how to exploit its weaknesses.

One way you can make Unix more secure is to institute mandatory access controls. These can be similar to those imposed under Netware, with access rights assigned both to users and to files. Users should not have the authority to change either.

You can also subdivide access to the Unix root, which governs its access-control system. Unix file systems are organized much like DOS directories: a tree system with a root directory at the top. Within the Unix root directory are the privileges to conduct 20 to 30 functions. Only a few people need access to them all. Allot these privileges carefully, according to each user's need.

Unix security also responds to many universal techniques, the most important of which is proper password administration. If your system is connected to the Internet, forbid the use of the file transfer program FTP. In particular, avoid the variety known as *anonymous FTP*. It provides direct, anonymous access to the files on remote computers. It's also a good idea to limit yourself to only one connection with outside systems.

Securing the Telephone

Telephony is one of those concocted words that makes you wonder, where did it come from, and how can we send it back? Unfortunately, it's now a vital part of a network manager's vocabulary.

For better and for worse—and it truly is some of both—the variety of devices now connected to the typical enterprise network includes the telephone. That's particularly important because the phone is the most popular route for invading a computer network.

Large-scale networking has always depended heavily on telephone lines. The wide area network (WAN) is usually based on telephone services. When you link the LANs and WANs in your organization, you inevitably connect your enterprise network to the public telephone system. Furthermore, new products are blurring the line between voice and data communication. Both serve the same body of clients in the same locations, and both use wiring to do it. Add the digital technology in the newest PBXs, and the underlying technology is similar.

Unfortunately, there is another common trait: exposure to fraud. In fact, Paul Merenbloom, a network manager and *Infoworld* columnist, identifies four vulnerable spots that could compromise a phone system:

- Direct inward system access (DISA)
- Unsecured voice mailboxes
- Unsecured systems
- Insider information

As telephone systems and computer networks are linked together, these same four threats can imperil the enterprise network.

Direct-dial trouble

DISA is a popular system because it saves companies money on long-distance phone charges. It's popular with another group, too: hackers who can use it not only to invade your system but to get there at your expense. Several telephone equipment suppliers are now advising their customers to discontinue their DISA services.

Hackers have also learned to use unsecured voice mail systems as a way to gain illicit access to a company's internal telephone system. Many voice mail systems let a caller press the zero to leave messages and get assistance. In some of these systems, pressing the zero plus a trunk access code puts the caller in a position to make outward calls from your telephones. Naturally, the phone company bills you for the calls.

What you can do

In ways like these, networks have become the unwitting tools of phone fraud, but there are several things you can do:

- Get a list of all the test mailboxes used by the vendor. Change their passwords.
- If you can avoid it, don't allow outward dialing for a voice mailbox. If you truly need this service, program the PBX to limit the exchanges and area codes to which calls can be made.
- Make all passwords at least 5 digits long. Six or more is better.
- Change passwords every 60 to 90 days.
- When you create new voice mail accounts, avoid the temptation to use the box number as the initial password. This is much too obvious.
- Don't assign numbers to unused mailboxes. This may seem like a convenience for future expansion, but it is also a heavily traveled invasion route.

Securing the Client-Server Database

The word went out some time ago that a popular database server used in client-server applications was not really suited for client-server duty. It offered no way to centrally manage the security of each server installation. You could set up individual security schemes on each server, but in one organization that maintained database files on 16 different servers, that was turning out to be a critical problem. Just as frustrating: While the maker of one component of the client-server system said it was willing to work on a solution, the makers of other components were busy denying responsibility.

If any one application characterizes the enterprise network, it is the client-server database. If any one thing characterizes the client-server database, it is its split personality.

The system is centered on a database server, where you can store large bodies of information in a database management system (DBMS). At each workstation, a separate application runs as a client. When an employee needs information from the database, he or she enters the request into the front-end client system. The client then passes the request to the back-end server, usually using structured query language (SQL). The server processes the request and sends the requested information back to the client side, where the employee can work with it. The client and server software can, and often do, come from different vendors.

From a security standpoint, the client-server database has a great many advantages. The main body of data remains in a central server. The only data that travels over the network is in response to client's requests. Though the main object of this feature is to minimize network traffic, it also has the effect of minimizing exposure. Furthermore, SQL has a substantial built-in security system comparable to those in network operating systems. You can use SQL commands to identify users, control access, and grant and revoke varied types of privileges to use selected parts of the database. Though SQL is primarily a data management language, it has more commands to govern access control than to manage data.

Nevertheless, the client-server system has also shown its weaknesses. The SQL security commands work only one database at a time. If your data is distributed among several servers, the administrative burden is also multiplied. Furthermore, the multivendor environment makes it hard to bring about solutions. The organizations involved in the dispute mentioned earlier had to deal with three different parties: those responsible for the client system, the server system, and the operating system. The division can be an internal problem, too. Often, database and network security are in the hands of two different people.

Principles of Database Security

The typical user of a client-server database must pass through two levels of security: at the network and at the DBMS. That isn't as good an idea as it might seem. For the user, it can be the kind of awkward, difficult experience many people try to avoid and evade. At the operating system level, the employee as usual must enter a password or provide some other form of identification. Connected with that password is a set of privileges to conduct certain kinds of operations on certain categories of data.

DBMS security

If the network's security scheme grants the user access to the database server, the DBMS security kicks in. Just like the network operating system, a DBMS controls access by setting up a system of user accounts.

Again, the user must enter a password and gain acceptance at the server. In some systems, the DBMS processes the password already entered to gain entrance to the network, but other installations require a second password. Using the same password is a big convenience for administrators and a benefit to the users as well. It does have the effect, though, of removing one level of security. Someone who breaks into the network then can have unchallenged access to the database.

Database privileges

In most DBMS systems, you can grant privileges on two levels: system privileges and database object privileges. System privileges govern your access to the DBMS as a whole. For example, the DBMS will usually have a provision that lets an authorized user create a new table. Other system privileges include the ability to create, alter, and drop the accounts of database users, or to create or drop various database objects including the database itself.

This is a powerful feature you can use to administer the overall security of a database server. With most systems, you can create custom accounts to conduct specific management jobs such as authorizing users, organizing the database, and backing up files. With different administrators for different functions, you can create a system of finely tailored access privileges .

Object privileges

An SQL database is a collection of tables. Not all the data have to be in the same table; the essence of a relational database is to relate multiple tables. Everything, though, is in some form of a row and column format. Someone in the organization owns that table. Initially, the owner is the person who created it. In practice, that usually will be the network administrator. If you own a particular asset, you may grant other users the privileges of access to your data. You can grant privileges for any table or view you have created. A view is a selected portion of a database table. These privileges come in several varieties:

- *Select* lets the newly privileged user see but not alter the data in your table or view.

- *Insert* lets the user add new rows or records to the table. A personnel clerk would use this privilege over the roster table to add new employees to the list.

- *Update* grants permission to edit existing data.

- *Delete* confers authority to delete existing rows or records, as you would do to the roster table when an employee leaves the company.

- *Alter* gives the user permission to change the structure of the table, such as by adding, deleting, or renaming columns.

- *Index* grants the authority to create an index. This is a database management function that has no direct bearing on security.

- *References* controls the ability of one table to refer to data in another.

- *Execute* controls the ability to execute a procedure.

Granting privileges

As owner of a table, you can grant varying powers to individual users. For the purpose of an SQL database, every individual has both a user name and a password. First, you must identify an authorized user. This SQL command does that:

```
SQL>    GRANT RESOURCE
2       TO ADDIE
3       IDENTIFIED BY SHEPHERD;
```

(The SQL> and the subsequent line numbers are prompts provided by the SQL database system; these vary from system to system. The semicolon is the standard closing punctuation for an SQL command.) The individual is now known by the user name ADDIE, and her password is SHEPHERD. You can assign user names and passwords to the other employees as well.

Having given Addie her identity, as far as the database system is concerned, you can grant her whatever privileges you care to delegate. If Addie is a department head, she needs the privileges necessary to manage a table that contains her departmental employee records. If that table is named ROSTER, you can:

```
SQL>    GRANT ALL
2       ON ROSTER
3       TO ADDIE;
```

This command gives her the full list of privileges, including reading, adding, deleting, and altering the structure. You might want to grant one further type of authority by using this command instead:

```
SQL>    GRANT ALL
2       ON ROSTER
3       TO ADDIE
4       WITH GRANT OPTION;
```

Now, Addie has the authority to grant access privileges to other users. She can grant only the privileges she has herself. For example, she might want to give her office clerk the authority to view the roster table and to add and subtract new employees as they join and leave the company. The command would go like this:

```
SQL>    GRANT SELECT, INSERT, DELETE
2       ON ROSTER
3       TO MISTY;
```

Thus, the employee with that user name could view, add, or remove employee records. She could not change any of the data, though.

In addition to privileges over tables, some SQL databases let you assign privileges over individual columns. That's a dubious advantage, though, particularly if holders of the privilege use it with less than absolute care. For example, you can invite all manner of trouble if someone who holds privileges over only a column or two tries to insert a new row into the table. The results vary; none are good. Usually, you can use a view to meet the same objectives, with less uncertain results.

The view as a security device

In an SQL database, the view is important for many reasons, not the least of which is security. By assigning privileges, you can individually control the actions each employee is authorized to take with your data. You can use the view to control the data on which those actions can be taken. An SQL query usually retrieves selected elements from one or more database tables. For example, a table called ROSTER might contain employees' names, job assignments, and department numbers. A second table called DEPTS could contain the department numbers and the supervisors' names. You could retrieve the names and specialties from the first table, then use the department numbers from the first table to look up the supervisor's names in the second. The SQL query would go something like this:

```
SQL>    SELECT NAME, SPECIALTY, SUPERVISOR
2       FROM ROSTER, DEPT
3       WHERE ROSTER:DEPTNO = DEPT:DEPTNO;
```

The result, reported back to the client station, would be a virtual table that uses selected parts of the source tables: the names, specialties, and supervisors. It offers a look at only the data requested by the query.

The view makes this virtual table permanent. It stores and names the query that created it. You can then use the view's name in an SQL query, just as you would use a table's name. You can also grant privileges for its use. The view's value in security is its ability to provide a precisely defined look at data. Say, for instance, the ROSTER table has a column that lists every employee's salary. You probably don't want this data to be open to general viewing, even by people who are privileged to see other elements of the data. Accordingly, you create a tight scheme of limited access to ROSTER. Then you can be much more liberal in granting access to a view that omits the less sensitive data.

Managing privileges

It's easy enough to set up a system of privileges for a few people, but the job gets harder as the number of privilege holders increases. An extended enterprise network could become a rat's nest of different rights to do different things to different resources. The job of managing all these varied permissions can easily outstrip the ability to handle it. When that happens, the access-control system can easily become a liability instead of an asset. There are two ways you can get a handle and keep a firm grip: grouping and role playing.

Many operating systems and DBMS installations let you establish groups of people who all have the same permission requirements. Often, these are employees in a single department or a particular job specialty. Instead of creating an individual account, you establish an account under a group name. Then, you assign a set of privileges to the group. Once the group has been established, you need not go through the process of establishing privileges for each employee. Instead, you assign the employee to the privileges, by assigning the employee to a group that has the proper assortment.

Most database servers come with a preinstalled group called *Public*. Every user is in the *Public* group and enjoys whatever privileges you may assign to that group. Naturally, you'll want to keep them limited. If you want to grant added privileges to an individual employee, you can assign that employee to a more privileged group or grant the privileges directly to the employee.

The role system is a variation on grouping. Instead of granting privileges based on an individual's overall responsibilities, it grants them on the basis of whatever activity they happen to be performing at the moment. To create a role system, you start by defining the roles. Usually, these are defined by application. When a user starts a particular application, the system grants a set of privileges associated with it. If the user is authorized to work with that application, the user enjoys the privileges associated with that application.

The advantage of a role system is that the grants of privileges are dynamic. An application's privileges are available only to people who are actively working with the application. The privileges expire when the user leaves the application. The drawback is that you must tightly control access to privileged applications.

Managing resources

In addition to managing access to the system, DBMS security must control the use of system resources. If available, use the resources of your DBMS to establish interval controls. These limit the length of time an individual can claim access to the CPU without interruption or the number of disk activities allowed per transaction.

Without these limits, a user—deliberately or by accident—could throw the system into an endless loop that would deny everyone else access to the database. Users who interrupt a transaction could leave critical assets locked and unavailable to anyone else. Just a single complex transaction could impede the system's performance for other users.

Only a few DBMS servers have interval controls to prevent this, but if you have them, use them.

Getting Together on Security

There is no standard pattern for client-server DBMS installations. There is one scheme that's in wide use, though, as organizations move away from their large systems toward networked database servers. This is a transitional system with a server-based DBMS handling new and downsized applications. Meanwhile, a large-system DBMS continues to store legacy applications and larger databases.

Though SQL is supposed to be standardized, in practice it comes in many variations. This is particularly true of the security commands, which vary widely from system to system. Different systems have different combinations of security features and use differing commands to invoke them. Then there is this added complication: Network and database security are often administered by different people.

On one hand, security over the database installations is often the responsibility of the database administrator. Not only must this figure maintain security on a variety of systems and platforms. This DBMS administrator is responsible for the entire database system, not just its security. Furthermore, the administrator may have to deal with a separate official, who is likely to be a security professional, with responsibility for network security.

There are few management tools available to establish unified management over this doubly diverse field. There are few standards to guide you, either. Instead, an organization in this position usually develops an ad hoc security plan that administers each DBMS separately. The typical plan follows these two basic steps:

- Determine what you need.
- Then figure out how you can get it done.

Facing frustration

This can be a frustrating experience. For example, one New York City bank maintains two DBMS systems. One is an IBM DB/2 installation running on a mainframe. The other is the Microsoft/Sybase SQL Server running on a LAN. Each DBMS has its own security system, and the LAN operating system presents a third. These systems present no common platform from which to administer a single security scheme.

Situations like this are difficult—and common. The bank has responded with a plan that seeks to make maximum use of all the security features each system has to offer. For example, it is able to use the DB/2 security system down to the table level, where the LAN system picks up the load. There is a similar working relationship using SQL Server security. This means, however, that an employee who has the rights to see information from both databases must penetrate three security schemes: the network's, the server's and the mainframe's.

This approach to security is not entirely a bad thing. Implementing security one DBMS at a time helps promote a *granular* approach that fine-tunes each user's access rights. Still, this type of system can produce a great deal of confusion, for users and more important, for the people who have to maintain the security system. Faced with this situation, administrators are often tempted to take shortcuts. With multiple checkpoints available, they decide to enforce security more rigidly at one point than at the others. Typically, they exert their tightest controls at the LAN, then assume that anyone who can cross that point successfully is also entitled to use the database. This plan is weak because there are so many ways to evade LAN security.

Drawing the line

An alternative is to impose security most strongly at the system level. Again, you make the assumption that anyone who can pass the main security barrier is entitled to use the database. This is where large systems still have an advantage. Compared with LANs, their security systems are strong enough that the basic assumption is safer.

Action item   Wherever you decide to draw the line, you must draw it somewhere. Determine the point at which you want to exert your main access control, and set up your main line of defense there. You can still set up additional security checkpoints further into the system, but their roles should be to back up the initial screening.

Choosing security measures

A second point is to be selective in what you try to control. Only a few highly sensitive databases require row-by-row oversight, and most of these belong to the government. Refer again to your initial assessment and review your most serious protection needs. Then concentrate your effort and assets on meeting those identified needs. You can pick from the security measures listed in Table 11.1.

TABLE 11.1   Security Checklist for Distributed Databases

Local Area Networks

- Encrypt passwords that are transmitted over the network.
- Associate passwords with time stamps and adapter addresses.
- Provide screen locking.
- Require that users sign on again if the server becomes unavailable.
- Require that users sign off when leaving their workstations.
- Forbid sign-ons while the system is being maintained.

File Access Control

- Define file access rules for both physical and logical drivers and at the subdirectory and file levels.
- Make sure file-level security will support file-name wild cards.
- Access rules should not have to be rewritten if you move groups of files or directories.
- Limit the number of current users at the subdirectory and file levels.
- Limit LAN administration to a single server.
- Report all access attempts to the resource owner.

Server Security

- Prevent all input to the server without a valid ID. Impose this requirement on the mouse as well as the keyboard.
- Maintain backups of the entire server operating system as well as data files.
- Run scheduled, unattended backups of the server.
- Use disk mirroring for quick recovery.
- Establish scheduled server-controlled backups of the workstations.

Securing Multiple Servers

- Do not require that employees use unique IDs and passwords for each server. Provide a one-stop log-on.
- Maintain local control of remote access.
- Give the administrator the power to determine whether the access rules for a particular file will apply to copies of that file or to information extracted from it.

12

Managing the Enterprise Network

*There's a simple way to manage networks. Or maybe
it's a way to manage simple networks.*

Not long ago, the organization's most valuable people included the network whiz who could set up a Novell LAN and actually make it work right. Today, the criteria for valuable people are much tougher to meet. A LAN can include several types of systems. Then, that LAN can be part of an enterprise network.

The enterprise network places new demands on the people who manage it. The focus shifts from managing individual networks to managing an enterprise network with multiple systems. You must take charge of all these divergent systems. What's more, you must cope with different layers of networks and network management. You may well have one management system at a central point, supporting multiple management systems in individual departments.

That demands not only good people but good management tools (Fig. 12.1). Therein lies a problem. The ideal enterprise network tool kit would make television's *Home Improvement* look underequipped. Such a tool kit does not yet exist. It's being created, but if enterprise network managers have one common lament, it is the lack of tools to manage their expanding areas of responsibility.

Needs to Be Met

You will have to make best use of the resources that are available and hope that the future brings better tools—quickly. It is almost impossible to manage a large enterprise network without automated help. The network product marketplace does offer some help. LAN operating systems let you see perfor-

Network management tools

- You need a lot
- You have a few
- A wish list:
  - Remote management
  - Management applications
  - Better monitoring
  - Automated administration

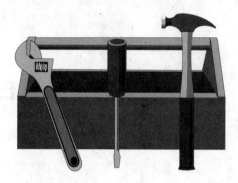

Figure 12.1 Perhaps the biggest current obstacle to enterprise networking is a shortage of management tools.

mance statistics and account for the network's use. From a remote location you can control terminal servers and bridges; these, too, report traffic conditions and errors. Add-on equipment is available for existing networks that are short of management ability.

After all this, there is still a shortage of network management tools. Networking technology continues to expand beyond the ability of existing resources.

There are still plenty of needs a network management system must meet. They include these technical needs (Fig. 12.2):

- *Chain reaction failures.* You need to know how a failure in one part of the network might affect the total operation. Suppose there should be a bug in the database software that keeps track of network addresses. It could block access to critical services like backup systems, but at the same time it could hide this problem from the monitoring system. You need cross-checks and consistency checks to detect this kind of problem.

- *Traffic congestion.* Like even a well-designed highway, a network can suffer from traffic jams. If several network elements fail simultaneously, the load of blocked and diverted traffic can bring the system to a halt. Adding to the congestion: the messages the network generates to report the problems.

- *The unexpected.* A network hit by unexpected events must be able to help itself. It should manage and reroute traffic to avoid trouble spots. The system must also react properly to duplicate messages or messages from questionable sources. Most systems use timeouts and retransmissions to deal with these problems. Another approach is to display a status flag that warns of impending problems.

Burning technical issues

- Multiple failures
- Congestion
- Unexpected problems
- Local and central management
- Protocols
- Testing
- Growth
- Adaptability

Figure 12.2   These are only some of the needs you must meet through network management.

- *Centralized and decentralized management.* Central management can also create a central point of failure. Decentralized management can be a source of inconsistency. In an enterprise network, you are likely to have elements of both, with their combined drawbacks. You must decide who should be responsible for managing such things as database consistency, standby systems, and database updates. Another decision: Who should receive status information and error messages? Often, a local group can take care of problems in its own system. There are other times when central management is more effective.

- *Protocol standards.* The choice of a network management standard—or none at all—can either improve management or make it harder. If you base the system on standards, you must be sure the entire system follows them. Otherwise, it might interpret nonstandard messages in strange ways. You must also make sure you can support the standards you want to maintain. On the other hand, standards make it easier to integrate network management with the network as a whole.

- *Testing.* The network management system should include test points, including interfaces, snapshots, and tracing.

- *Growth potential.* The management system should adapt to traffic growth and the addition of new nodes and networks. It should also incorporate new technology as opportunities arise.

- *Adaptability.* The network management system should adapt to system changes. It should accept new features and technology easily and with little disruption.

Nontechnical issues

- Software distribution
- Error response
- System configuration
- Security

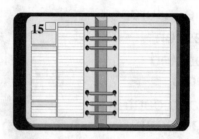

Figure 12.3 Management includes problems like these as well.

Management issues

Those are the technical issues. Enterprise network management involves many management issues, too. These include (Fig. 12.3):

- Software distribution and version control
- Error response and correction
- Managing the system's configuration
- Security and access control

Managing software distribution

There has always been one good reason to manage software distribution and to make sure everyone uses the same version: to avoid cluttering the network with different formats and commands. However, there's another reason that has little to do with the software itself. Unlicensed software can bring warrant-wielding detectives to your door, demanding stiff penalties. Viruses are also threats.

You now can manage software upgrades from a central location. From this single distribution point, you can copy the software to remote file servers and local disks. Like the old movie cliché of synchronizing watches, you can program the network to make the change at a preset time. If you are updating a distributed database, for example, install two copies—one old, one new—at each location. At the appointed time, the network will switch en masse from the old system to the new.

There is one big danger with this method. It presumes that every element will immediately make the switch. There are many reasons that may not happen. One server may lose its power at a critical moment, or its hard disk may be full when you try to load the new version. It will miss the mass upgrade, yet the system may assume that all went well. That single out-of-sync server can cause major disruptions.

Action item   Make software distribution a two-step process. Distribute the software, and wait for confirmation that every node has received the transmission. Then trigger the simultaneous changeover.

The transition becomes trickier if you must upgrade transaction processing systems. A failure, or even a brief interruption, while a transaction is in progress could divide parts of that transaction between the new and old databases. One solution is to include version information on all data transmissions. You can then program the system to reject transmissions based on outdated versions.

The dual-software method can also help you fight off bugs and viruses. If you keep a previous version on the system, you can fall back on it should the new software develop a serious problem.

Shooting troubles

The largest bin in your management tool kit will contain tools to find and correct problems. All but the smallest networks require automated procedures to report errors, manage backups, and do similar jobs. You will also need one or more qualified people to use these tools. On a small LAN this may be a part-time job for a single in-house expert. As the enterprise network grows, it will require more people, doing more specialized jobs.

Network management software can augment your staff and keep its numbers within reasonable limits. The jobs it can do include:

- Identifying and correcting problems
- Logging and reporting events
- Controlling operations

The software records problems as they arise. Depending on the type of problem, it may notify the network manager. Other types of problems, or those that exceed stated thresholds, are reported to central management.

The software may also have an echo mechanism or some other way to monitor resources like gateways and file servers. It notifies the appropriate manager when one of these resources fails.

When there is a problem, the software usually sounds an audible alarm. It puts up a display that describes the problem and its location. Management software can also point out the likely cause and suggest what the manager should do to isolate and correct the problem.

The system can collect these reports, creating a history file for each network element. The log can include information about the nature of the problem, how it was resolved, vendor contacts, and other information that might be helpful in the future.

Logging errors

Beyond these problem-solving messages, management software can report on other events that can affect the network and its performance. It can chart peak volume times and notify you when it detects new addresses on the system. It can direct this information to a printer or disk file.

TABLE 12.1   Management and Support Checklist

What type of support do you now offer to network users?
What parts of this support are: ■ Centralized ■ Decentralized at the department level ■ Decentralized at an intermediate level
What levels of support are available and appropriate at the departmental level?
What additional options are available for supporting the enterprise network? ■ Existing services ■ Outsourcing
Which networks are mission critical? How do you provide for the necessary level of support?
What provisions should you make for: ■ Maintenance ■ Disaster relief

The system should let you use this information to generate periodic reports, such as a log of network operations over the previous 24 hours.

Operator control

The system should respond to your queries about the status of any device attached to the network, including workstations, bridges, and gateways. Some of these elements may maintain their own records. For instance, a bridge can incorporate the Simple Network Management Protocol (SNMP). You then can use SNMP to query the bridge for its operating statistics on traffic, errors, and unusual events.

Another useful function tests the path between two workstations. This is particularly useful when there are repeaters or bridges between the stations.

Managing Configuration

Configuration management lets you learn and control what kind of software is on what systems. It helps you maintain an approved software list and look for exceptions, whether authorized or unauthorized.

Configuration management software also helps you keep track of how each element of the network is configured internally. You can use it, for example, to find out whether a PC on a department's LAN has the memory, processing power, and disk capacity to run a particular application. This information is particularly valuable to the technical support staff. You can solve many problems by analyzing and correcting a computer's configuration.

One decision you must make is where on the network to store user applications. Standard LAN practice is to place them on servers, where the connected workstations can share them. This is the easiest approach to manage since it sharply reduces the number of software copies you must manage. The licenses for network software often assume this kind of configuration.

There is an alternative, but you might not want to consider it very seriously. This is a scrubber program that automatically erases unauthorized software, wherever on the network it may be. It eliminates much of the need to manage software installations by the simple expedient of eliminating the software. This is like using a club when the appropriate instrument would be a scalpel. A scrubber indiscriminately wipes out all exceptions to the authorized list. It doesn't allow for flexibility in managing software installations. Ironically, while it restricts your flexibility, it is vulnerable to manipulation by a determined user.

SNMP: Simple Management?

You face enough challenges managing a diverse network. At least, you can install a single network management system.

That isn't as easy as it might sound. Diverse networks come with diverse management systems. Network managers haven't been eager to fight these. Furthermore, as wiring hubs became popular, they also became logical sites for network control. They are the logical places to install a standardized network management system. There are several candidates for that honor, including proprietary systems, IBM's NetView, and Digital Equipment's tool set. For a mixed environment, there is only one serious candidate: the simple network management protocol (SNMP).

First things first

SNMP has its roots in open systems and TCP/IP. True to its name, its designers set out to keep things simple. They started by responding to their customers' top priority in network management: fault isolation. SNMP can immediately flag a defective router, for example. This used to require repeated tests until you found the culprit. This emphasis on fault detection dovetailed with the growing interest in network hubs. The hubs provide a logical administration point, and hub makers began to incorporate SNMP into their products.

This has been a key to the system's growing popularity. It is inexpensive. It does the most-needed jobs. It is easy to install and use. It is available in a growing number of products. At last count, more than 350 network products had incorporated SNMP. These include most key network components like routers, intelligent hubs, bridges, and servers. You can choose from more than 50 network management stations that use SNMP to collect information about your network and display it on a central console.

For example, one user reports that he and 10 managers can use central consoles to view graphic representations of their network. They can communicate with SNMP-equipped routers and hubs to learn their performance and configuration. They can also receive warnings of network events.

Since SNMP is a nonproprietary standard, an SNMP management console can work with nearly any device, from any vendor, that also uses SNMP.

Feeling insecure

SNMP is winning widespread popularity for managing internetworks, but it does have some drawbacks. Security is one of the most serious. In its basic form, SNMP does not offer any significant level of security features. It has a series of SET commands you can use to help control network use, but these commands themselves are not secure; any knowledgeable person can change them. Some network managers say they don't even implement the SET commands because they are not secure.

Vendors have been addressing the problem with a variation called *secure SNMP*. This near standard is not designed to be a stand-alone SNMP upgrade but is intended as part of a more broadly based improvement called the *simple management protocol* (SMP). Secure SNMP adds two important security features to the original management package:

- An encryption service based on the Data Encryption Standard.
- An authentication service called *Message Digest Algorithm 5*. It places an authentication stamp on each network packet to guard against alterations by unauthorized users.

Adopting secure SNMP would also mean adopting SMP, which has several features that strengthen your ability to maintain network management.

Bulk transfer of management information lets you download a full suite of management information at one time. This overcomes a limitation of SNMP, which asks only for one piece of management information at a time. This could lead to an extended exchange of information; at an extreme, this could swamp the network in its own management data.

SMP also provides for event-driven management, a feature that reduces network traffic. A remote agent will signal the management console only when it has something to report.

Networking and Security

Conventional wisdom holds that networks lack many security and data integrity features of large systems (Fig. 12.4). Even on a mainframe with dozens of dumb terminals connected, all the processing takes place on one machine. All the screen handling, program logic, referential integrity checks, security checks, and similar functions are done on the mainframe. The terminal simply provides a view into that bigger machine.

Many developments are combining to change that picture. Ease of use has become important, illustrated by the spread of graphic interfaces. Databases that once lived on large systems are moving to network servers. There's a movement in the opposite direction, too, as stand-alone PC databases migrate into client-server architecture.

Confidential information could be reasonably well protected when it

Network security challenges

- Physical protection
  - Servers
  - Connectors
- Access control
  - Passwords
  - Dialbacks
- Encryption

Figure 12.4 No system offers ironclad security, but even a far-flung network can come close.

resided on a single large system with its multiple built-in protective mechanisms. That information is much harder to protect now that PCs and networks have entered the picture. DOS, the prevailing PC operating system, has almost none of the technical checks and balances that large systems provide. Another serious problem is that desktop workstations are physically more accessible than their larger counterparts.

That does not prove the case for mainframe security. It just means that networks often lack built-in security measures. System administrators must provide them. You can't sit back and let a downsized system take care of its own security. You must actively provide it. But you can do that.

It's probably true that if you need ironclad protection for truly sensitive data, a LAN may not measure up to a well-protected mainframe. Still, it is possible to achieve a high degree of security, even in the open environment of an enterprise network. For example, Amoco maintains sensitive information on a Chicago-based network. That network must be available to dial-in access from employees across the country. Borrowing from mainframe technology, the company began a call-in system. An inbound caller cannot immediately gain access to the full network. The system accepts the caller's log-in information, hangs up, and redials a telephone number associated with that identification.

Protect yourself

An enterprise network requires that you manage your own security. That kind of active self-protection would be necessary with any kind of system. A network whose managers want to control dial-in access is in much the same position as a large system that requires the same controls. Physical protection is another common concern for systems of all sizes. Just as large systems are located in secure, dedicated rooms, a LAN can also be physically isolated. You can place power supplies and hubs in locked closets; file servers can go in secure rooms. The networked PC workstations, then, present little more security risk than dumb terminals connected to a mainframe.

Selective security

The placement of your assets can also boost security. You might want to run application programs on desktop computers but keep the data itself on a larger, better-protected system. In particular, large corporate databases are remaining on the main computers, with access provided by gateways and similar communication links. This pattern may have only a little to do with security. One small college, for example, is installing an extensive network system but has left student grade and financial records on its mainframe. The primary reason, officials explain, is the mainframe's ability to handle the sheer volume of data. Security is a secondary benefit.

System security

Network operating systems and allied utilities are increasingly providing security features the PC operating systems do not. There are programs to scan for viruses. There also are utilities that can restrict access to specified directories or files. Most network operating systems, including Netware and Vines, include account control features that restrict users to particular workstations and particular times.

You can use these features to keep people from logging in from home or after hours. For example, you can use an account-control feature to permit log-ins to the finance department network only during normal working hours. This helps keep unauthorized users—from inside or outside the company—from looking at the corporate books.

In addition, most network operating systems let administrators set up different levels of access to files and data. While users may need access to certain types of corporate data for instance, they won't need the ability to change or delete that data. Granting them read-only access to those files protects the data from both deliberate and accidental modification.

Unlike DOS, some computer system operating systems also have built-in security features. Unix and OS/2 control access and limit the permitted types of use of designated directories and files. OS/2 also can restrict the number of licensed application programs that operate on a network. This helps you prevent the use of pirated software.

The human factor

The real security challenge for a network administrator is to manage the human factor. PC users constantly frustrate security professionals with their less-than-careful habits. In particular, those who have come to regard PCs as truly personal tools may not understand that in a networked environment, they may become responsible for corporate data that needs more protection.

For that reason, many security experts and PC managers say user education is a critical part of their security policies. Training is a high priority, concentrating on such subjects as how to recognize hazards and observing security procedures. One bank's security training program includes sessions in such subjects as managing change.

The idea behind this: A new network is a major change in the way an organization does business. A system is most vulnerable at times of change. It's a time when errors are frequent. A new program disk may contain a virus. Access controls may not yet be in place or may not work properly. The training is intended to help managers monitor and educate their employees more closely during this period. Says one PC manager, "Users need to understand that even transferring a file from a floppy disk to their hard drive is a significant change in their system."

That means there is a potential hazard they should be trained to recognize. This is one area where IS professionals can continue to use their talents in a networked environment. They can maintain the security, validity, and integrity of the data. This lets the users go about their own jobs.

The ease-of-use factor

This division of labor can help overcome another security problem. Maintaining a high degree of security in a networked environment can conflict with a major objective of downsizing: ease of use. Users often aren't receptive to institutional security procedures. There's more than personal preference involved here. Often, obtrusive security measures can keep people from doing their jobs effectively. The security features that keep out the bad people can be just as effective—and frustrating—at keeping out the good people. Some computer security professionals don't like to concede that point, but they must.

> **Action item**   Make a list of ways you can carry out as many security measures as possible at the network level rather than at individual workstations. This can include the use of a security-conscious operating system and keeping critical components within locked rooms.

Involve the users

Another important measure is to involve the users. To resolve conflicts between security and ease of use, many organizations have set up cooperative working arrangements. There, users can discuss their needs and problems with security and systems professionals. This process can break down resistance and build cooperation by helping each side understand the other. It also gives the participants a sense of ownership in the downsizing project. There's no better way to build enthusiasm and support (Fig. 12.5).

Where teamwork counts

- These must work together:
  - System features
  - Physical security
  - Threat analysis
  - Training and procedures

Figure 12.5 Security measures must work as a system, not as individual components.

Hackers and viruses

The two most heavily publicized types of security problems—hackers and viruses—are also among the least serious threats to most systems. Security experts estimate that the country holds only a handful of hackers of the type who might cause deliberate damage to a system. The number of actual virus infections also does not match the apparent threat.

A Protection Strategy

People think of crimes as committed by mysterious strangers: shadowy muggers or scheming hackers. But whether in computers or other areas of life, most crimes are committed by somebody the victim knows. In business, that usually is an employee. The second most likely cause of data loss is the simple accident: the mispunched key at a critical moment or the cup of coffee spilled on a floppy disk.

Even so, when it comes to computer security, many corporations focus on protecting themselves from outsiders rather than insiders. Corporations spend much money on expensive security systems when they might better spend their time more productively: making sure passwords are properly used, educating their employees on the need for security, and ensuring that backups are performed regularly.

The first question

How much security do you really need? That's the first question to ask when planning for network security. Its answer depends on the answer to another question: "What would the damage be if the most sensitive information on my LAN were compromised?"

If the answer is "Not much," you may need only to warn your workers not to write their passwords on sticky notes. If the damage would be severe, you must do more to make sure your network is secure. What and how much you must do depends on several things: security features in the network operating system and applications, physical protection of the server and communications media, and the kinds of threats you face. Many users do not view all these items as a whole. In part, that's because vendors tend to offer piecemeal solutions. These products can respond to one security threat easily, but your system probably has holes somewhere else.

Action item   Make an assessment of what levels of security you truly need to protect your network.

Rating your risks

Developing an effective protection strategy requires that you identify the specific risks you face. Classify your PCs and networks based on how they are used. Their use usually is an index of the security threats they present. You then can develop a security plan that responds to those risks. This could range from locked rooms for a network carrying a payroll application to regular virus detection on a PC used mainly for word processing. One company has developed a three-level system for classifying PCs and networks:

- Systems that handle highly confidential data such as client records and information on corporate strategy
- Midlevel systems handling information whose disclosure would not be a serious threat but whose loss would cause problems
- Systems that hold only departmental files and personal work

Once it has established the security classification, the company institutes security measures to match. The top-category systems get a security package that includes passwords, data encryption, and audit trails. These systems are also physically secure and isolated from other networks. At the middle level, where loss of data is the greatest threat, the company requires password access to sensitive files and limits transfers of files and programs. Regular backup is also a priority here. Bottom-level systems are often individual PCs, where the emphasis is on regular virus scanning. Some of these also require password access.

What You Can Do

Whatever the system, security problems tend to fall into the same few broad categories. Many problems of PC network security are just the same as those of mini and mainframe security. A few preventive measures will take care of most potential security problems. The major challenge is to make administrators and users aware of the potential problems and inform them of the tools available to solve them.

The two best steps an organization can take are to make regular backups and to set up a system of passwords. Take the time to make sure you have backups that are both available and safe. In particular, regular backups help with the small, everyday problems of lost files and data.

The password is probably the most important security measure you can take on any system: Says one security consultant, "Your system security is only as good as the password." Though you'll encounter resistance and evasions, enforcing good password choice is a high-payoff security measure. Most outsiders who get into business systems do so by defeating password systems.

There are programs that will run through a password file looking for the most-used ones. Hackers use these programs to find passwords they can use to break into your system.

> **Action item**   Use the same programs to identify easy-to-guess choices within your own systems. Then get them changed.

People: The critical factor

Whatever the protection plan, it ultimately will depend on people, not technology. User-education will always be an important element of any security program. The most serious threat to your system comes from inside, not outside. That threat is much more likely to be accidental than deliberate. Most hazards involve acts like accidentally erasing a file—things that are preventable with proper precautions. Proper training can teach and motivate employees to take those precautions. For example, you can't back up all the files on individual systems from a central location. It's the users who must do that. Consider regular seminars on the personal aspect of computer security. Back them up with a regular newsletter or with articles in other company publications.

Involving employees

These measures still won't work if they appear to the employees like edicts handed down from the mountain. Individual departments, and individual users, are intimately familiar with their operations, including the dimensions of any conflict between security and ease of use. Contrary to some managers' cynical expectations, most employees want to do their jobs effectively. They will resent any security measures, imposed from above, that keep them from doing it. Involve employees in these discussions. Solicit their ideas for striking the balance. Not only will you have the benefit of their knowledge and understanding, but you will have the enthusiastic participation that comes from a sense of ownership in the results.

Avoiding overreactions

There is a so-called newspaper effect that causes many system administrators to worry most about the most highly publicized external threats. This means they give too little attention to the basic measures, like backups and passwords, that can protect them from the more serious internal threats (Fig. 12.6).

On a percentage basis, the threat from viruses is minuscule. Carelessness and ignorance by honest employees make up the largest menace to informa-

Don't be fooled by publicity

- Major causes of loss:
  - Accidents
  - Dishonest employees
- Minor causes of loss:
  - Viruses
  - Hackers

Figure 12.6 For most organizations, the most highly publicized threats are really the least serious.

tion security. An estimated 80 percent of all damage is caused internally. Still, the virus threat is real, and it feeds on user carelessness. The threat can become more serious when a networking project progresses from LANs to WANs. Departmental LANs are closed systems; many have no external gateways at all. Once you go through a gateway to an enterprise network, you've multiplied the number of people who can possibly gain access to your data.

A well-managed password system is the best defense. A survey by the Executive Information Network showed that 55 percent of all computer security losses could be attributed to errors or omissions. Dishonest and disgruntled employees accounted for 25 percent of losses. External threats such as natural disasters caused the remaining 20 percent. That leaves only 5 percent for all other causes, including invasions by outsiders.

Common-sense protection

Viruses are a case in point. They happen, but only a minority of all PC users have been victims. One generally recommended protective measure is to get software only from reputable vendors, buy it shrink-wrapped, and avoid public-domain software and shareware. If you must download bulletin board programs, try to limit yourself to those whose source code is available. This lets the system administrator examine the code for oddities.

Since even commercial software has been known to conceal viruses, users should run virus-scanning software at least once a month—more often if users are adding software or sharing a PC. One word of caution: Virus-scanning software works well and is constantly being improved, but it is not foolproof. Don't rely on this strategy alone.

13

The New Epidemic of Viruses

Worry a little about viruses planted by outside thrill-seekers. Worry a lot about new breeds of viruses whose aim is to cause you specific damage.

Over the years, hackers and viruses have gotten publicity far out of proportion to their numbers (Fig. 13.1). The image of disrespectful youth playing games with your system created more than a little fear. That was dangerous in itself because in overreacting to the threat of these public-domain viruses, many system managers underreacted to threats that were less well publicized but were much more serious.

PCs infected by viruses

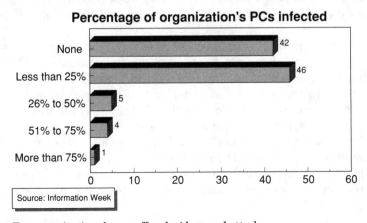

Figure 13.1 Few organizations have suffered widespread attacks.

Now, the picture has changed. Some of the newest forms of viruses are much more than pranks. Computer criminals have changed the virus into a digital sneak thief that can be a very efficient agent of industrial espionage. Invaders are no longer using these just to cause inconvenience or to send little worms crawling across your screen. They are using viruses to steal. Some authorities no longer refer to these new strains as "viruses," instead using terms like "attack software" or "malicious code."

Viruses Programmed for Theft

Take the case of a delayed-action virus that was planted in the accounting system of a large corporation. When several employees left the company, they left something of themselves behind. Several months later, this computerized memento submitted a fake invoice. Typical of most successful computer thieves, the ex-employees knew their target very well. They had programmed the invoice with all the proper sign-offs and authorizations, and they had kept the amount just below the level that would have triggered a higher level of review. The virus submitted the bill, the accounting system paid, and the money landed in a Swiss bank account. At last report, the perpetrators were still at large.

Cruisin' for a bruisin'

This company was the victim of a *cruise virus,* named after the missile of the same name. It has much in common with other viruses, worms, Trojan horses, and similar invaders, but it has this mark of distinction. Most of the older electronic invaders selected their victims at random. A cruise virus is aimed at a specific target.

Attack software like this can enter a network through any of the usual channels, such as infected disks from an unpoliced bulletin board or handed out at a user group meeting. It can exploit the carelessness of a single person, working at any point on the network. Once inside the network, it can make its way to the target point. It doesn't have to work quickly. The fake invoice virus made its bogus transfer at a preset date and time, long after it was planted.

Another characteristic of attack software is that it sends messages back to its master. Almost all these programs work by impersonation. There is one version that masquerades as a sign-on screen. Users think they are entering their passwords in response to the usual system prompts; in reality they are broadcasting the passwords to an outsider. Eventually, the virus owner can usually learn the system administrator's password and use it to damage parts of the network that normally are beyond reach. Other variations can collect enough encrypted traffic to insert fraudulent messages into the network traffic. An intruder using this method can impersonate a network manager and trick other users into divulging secret file access information.

Launching the attack

Often, the person who plants such a virus will simply offer it to the public domain, in hopes that someone in the target organization will inadvertently introduce it into the network. If not, the invader will try again.

Once inside, the virus begins to send its reports back to its master. In the case of an insider who knows the system, the sponsor may need little more than verification that the virus has made it inside. An outsider with less knowledge may receive data on the system makeup and types of protection.

Once the virus reaches its target, it usually does its work as quietly as possible. A virus planted by an amateur will gleefully plant a "gotcha" message on the victim's screen. Professional attack software will do as much as possible to avoid attention. It will usually remove itself after a successful attack or even after a certain number of failed attempts. It will not affect any processes other than those necessary to meet its objectives. It's entirely possible you may never know you were attacked.

Viruses Log In

The cruise virus is only one of several new types of infection against which you must be on guard. In particular, there are new strains that attack the weakest outposts of local area networks. Ironically, this is often the point at which the network seems strongest: the log-in process.

A successful attack must get past the access-control system. It only makes sense to erect your first barrier there. In addition, many network administrators expect too much of access control. They presume that nothing can get past. In reality, many viruses are designed so their first task is to get past. Not only that, but they seek to emulate a highly privileged user, the better to gain access to network resources. For this purpose, viruses that attack personal computers and their networks work with the interrupts used by legitimate hardware and software to gain access to the PC's central processing unit. For this purpose, there are two main types of viruses:

- Boot sector viruses that load into memory and infect the hidden system files. They usually use the low-level interrupts that are available before a system executes COMMAND.COM.

- File viruses infect other system and application files. They generally use higher-level interrupts available after COMMAND.COM has been executed.

Making their marks

Because they work with higher-level interrupts, file viruses are usually easy to detect—even though it sometime happens the hard way. In a Novell network there are two functions, NETX and IPX, that often use the same interrupts as the viruses. When this happens, the results can vary, but the leading possibilities include these:

- Neither of the competing parties can prevail, and the workstation will hang.
- The viruses will prevail, and the workstation cannot establish a network connection.
- NETX and IPX will prevail, ejecting the virus from the network.
- NETX and IPX cannot load.

The last result is the most serious. When the user follows normal instincts and tries to reboot, the virus could become memory-resident, able to infect network files. Fortunately, this is also the least likely possibility.

Boot sector attacks

More dangerous is the boot sector virus, which is unlikely to create such visible conflicts. A boot sector virus can gain access through an infected disk or over the network. Either way, the virus loads itself into memory when the system starts up. It then can locate and modify the two hidden system files that run a DOS workstation.

The virus will then try to duplicate itself on every floppy disk that goes into the machine. If the floppy is itself a bootable disk, the virus code will replace its boot sector. That means any time you use that floppy to boot a machine, you will load the virus instead of the system files you expected. Usually, everything appears normal while this is happening.

While a boot sector virus can easily infect multiple workstations, a Netware server is less vulnerable. Netware uses a different file structure than DOS, so a boot sector virus does not have direct access to a server's drive. The virus does have the power, however, to damage data on workstation drives, and in some cases it could find its way into a server's DOS partition.

A History of Virus Infections

Though viruses are being used in inventive and dangerous new ways, they have been around for a long time. A virus was demonstrated in a research setting as early as 1974. Academic papers on the subject began to appear about 10 years later, and viruses themselves began to spread widely about 1986.

Some of the first viruses were devised by programmers to relieve the stress and tedium of their work. They would engage in "core wars," hiding and concealing their colleagues' work. Tracy Kidder described one such round of friendly sabotage in his 1981 book *The Soul of a New Machine*. The victims of these early viruses were systems professionals, fully able to defend themselves and, when so inclined, to retaliate. The game in Kidder's book came to a sudden halt when a secretary became a victim. The technicians realized they had harmed a victim who was unable to protect herself or fight back. They voluntarily cut back on their high-tech games.

The next wave of viruses appeared on college campuses, also among knowledgeable professionals. They were also relatively benign. One, named after *Sesame Street's* Cookie Monster, would pop up on the screen, demanding a cookie. Users learned that when they typed the word "cookie," the program would be satisfied for a while. By 1986, however, viruses began to attack the computers of less knowledgeable users, and with more damaging effects. One of the first to gain wide publicity was the 1987 Christmas Card virus, which printed extensive and unwelcome greetings on thousands of computers.

Many people first learned about viruses in November 1988, when computers connected to the Defense Department's Arpanet data communication network ground to a halt. Arpanet is a data communication network used by the institutions to exchange research data. It is part of a government Internet communication, then a little-known network of government and university scientists, now considered the prototype of a nationwide information highway. The cause, it was quickly discovered, was a virus, a program planted in the system and designed to replicate itself on computers throughout the network.

Strictly speaking, this was not a virus but a *worm*. A virus spreads by infecting other programs in a computer or network. A worm just spreads without affecting other programs. Either way, the effects on the computer's user are much the same, and invasive programs of all kinds have been collectively referred to as *virus*.

Regardless of its label, this infection was relatively benign. One authority termed it simply a nuisance. No data was destroyed, and the virus did not penetrate the military's highest-security communication links. Even so, the virus shut down about 6,000 computers, most of them at federally connected research centers.

The source of this invasion was Robert Morris, a college student and ironically the son of a Defense Department computer security expert. The student planted the virus as an experiment. The experiment failed in a spectacular way. The student injected the virus from a computer on the campus of Cornell University, connected to a system at the Massachusetts Institute of Technology. He said later he chose the MIT route to hide his identity. As Arpanet users made contact with the MIT system, the virus spread itself to their computers as well. The virus was programmed to reproduce itself slowly. Instead, it developed a capacity for explosive growth that brought thousands of systems to a virtual halt within an hour. The student had to admit his role in order to bring the invasion under control.

Repeat attack

Within a month of the Arpanet virus attack, the Pentagon announced that a similar attack had forced it to temporarily disconnect its Milnet communication system from Internet. Milnet carries unclassified military information.

In this case, the Pentagon ordered the shutdown after learning that an unidentified intruder had gained entry into a defense contractor's system. In a parallel to the earlier case, the intruder apparently had used a Canadian university as the gateway in much the same way as the MIT computer had been used earlier.

A year later

One of the government's responses to these attacks was to form a Computer Emergency Response Team (CERT). CERT, based at Carnegie Mellon University, is a team of experts formed to help network managers cope with security violations.

In a report 9 months after the Arpanet attack, CERT had this to say: "Many computers connected to Internet have experienced unauthorized system activity." These invasions took place "over a period of several months," the team continued, and "that activity is spreading." A similar report came from the National Computer Security Center, a computer security arm of the National Security Agency. "Poor security practices contributed to the spread of the virus on Internet last year," the report said, "and those practices are still there."

Eugene Spafford of Purdue University restated what has been a familiar theme of computer security professionals: "The problem with security is not with the network itself," he said. It is with the people who run the network. For example, in an academic setting, systems managers often hesitate to adopt stricter security measures because of the burdens they would impose on users. "What's needed," Spafford said, "is a heightened awareness of what security is all about, at the individual sites."

Friday the 13th, the sequel

As if on cue, those reports were followed by the discovery of a virus known, variously, as *Columbus Day, Friday the 13th,* or *Datacrime.* October 13, 1989, was a Friday, the day after Columbus Day.

Computer owners were warned to be braced for a virus that would be activated that Friday. If a computer was infected, this virus already had attached itself to application files and was programmed to erase the boot sector of a personal computer's hard disk. Without the data in that sector, the computer could not tell where to find any of the programs or data on the disk. The only way to find these files again was to reformat the disk. This, ironically, would erase every file on the disk.

Another virus, to be triggered the same day, would cause application files to swell in size until they were too big for the computer's memory. Fortunately, the existence of both viruses was well known in advance of the fateful day, which passed with little incident. Some firms used antiviral programs to scan their files for evidence that they had been altered by a virus. That proved to be a time-consuming process, though, and many computer users were forced to back up their data—thus overcoming another common human failing.

The backup system was simple enough. Since most viruses attach themselves only to application files like spreadsheets and word processors, the data files remain untouched. Users could back up their data files, then when the threat was over, reinstall their application programs from the original uninfected disks.

More infections

More recently, some viruses have appeared to represent social or political causes. A No Nukes virus has appeared more than once at Internet installations, particularly those operated by the National Aeronautics and Space Administration (NASA). It penetrated systems by identifying multiple accounts that bore the same user identifications and passwords.

In Europe, many hospitals and other medical installations welcomed a new program that would help them assess a person's likelihood of contracting AIDS. Within the program was a virus that destroyed both data and programs or altered file directories so data could not be found. Unlike most virus-bearing programs, the AIDS program was professionally packaged and marketed. Apparently, someone had devoted much effort and expense to the project and had used commercial mailing lists to distribute the product.

This virus was at least semibenign. It would warn a victim that data was about to be destroyed. It also announced that you could avoid this fate by sending a payment to an address in Panama. Authorities viewed this as a form of extortion; the Cleveland resident charged with circulating the program apparently viewed it as a way to enforce payment from users who had received unsolicited copies of the program.

In what it planned as a public service, the U.S. Census Bureau compiled a collection of its statistics and distributed them to public libraries throughout the country. Two days after the disks had been mailed, the bureau discovered that they had been infected by a virus.

The Michelangelo fizzle

The record for press coverage per infected site probably belongs to the Michelangelo virus of 1992. Word went out that computers all over the country would be brought down by a virus set to be triggered on the artist's birthday. The fateful day came, and nothing much happened. The Michelangelo virus now ranks as one of computer history's most notable flops. It's still uncertain whether the virus was overpublicized or whether the publicity spurred most computer owners to protect themselves. Both were probably true to some extent.

The incident did make many people newly aware of the need for computer security. It also demonstrated that you need not panic. More people were able to put the virus threat in perspective. The fear of such public-domain viruses has subsided to a more rational level, more conducive to rational, effective responses. The stage has also been set, though, for the newer forms of professionally planted viruses characterized by their mean streaks.

How Viruses Spread

A virus is a form of Trojan horse, an invasive program that sneaks into a system within a seemingly legitimate program, then emerges to attack the system. The virus has an added dimension: the ability to duplicate itself and spread into other computers on a network.

With exceptions like the AIDS computer virus, which was disguised as a commercial product, a computer virus normally enters a system in one of four ways:

- *Through the exchange of infected disks.* For example, a friend may give you a game disk that you run on your own computer or one that belongs to your company. The virus will leave a copy of itself on the host computer. More than one security expert has likened sharing a disk to sharing a hypodermic needle. In that sense, a computer virus is spread much like the AIDS virus in humans.

- *By downloading an infected program from an electronic bulletin board.* Most of these programs have been screened for viruses. That is particularly true of "shareware" programs, which are for sale and which have supporting organizations behind them. Bulletin board operators are also well aware of the problem and try to immunize their systems. Even so, an occasional virus does slip through.

- *Through the exchange of infected files on a network.*

- *Through specific acts of sabotage.*

Spreading around

Once inside a system, a virus begins to make copies of itself. These clones spread to other host programs, often on other computers. Sometimes these new viruses do their damage immediately. In the case of the Friday the 13th virus, there was an internal logic bomb, designed to be activated the first time an infected program was run after the designated date.

The Internet viruses have circulated primarily through networked minicomputers, but the personal computer has become an increasingly popular target. PC networks are particularly vulnerable. A virus can be planted in the network through an infected disk, or it may arrive over the network. The virus duplicates itself and attaches its clones to files that are sent out over the network. Users who share these files also contract the virus.

Many types of infections

Viruses are the product of inventive minds. It should be no surprise, then, that they come in a seemingly limitless assortment, with new varieties arriving all the time. In fact, the variety is so great that viruses defy classification. The types of countermeasures available against them is equally diverse. It is possible, though, to identify a few basic characteristics. You can identify a virus by:

- The type of disruption it causes
- The type of computer system it infects
- Which part of the system it infests

Friendly viruses?

Some viruses are hostile and cause serious damage. Others are almost amusing. A few, like the Cookie Monster mentioned earlier, reside in the system and make an occasional appearance. The Christmas Tree virus is another example.

The authors of these viruses have no hostile intents, and their products don't deliberately cause damage. In some cases, though, a programming error will produce drastic, unintended effects. The Arpanet virus spread infinitely faster than its author anticipated.

Other types of viruses alter data files. They will find a spreadsheet file, for example, and change a number or relocate a decimal point. This type of virus is small and hard to detect. It makes simple changes that could throw off an entire chain of calculations. Another even more serious type is the virus whose intent is to cause severe damage. This is the type of virus that will make files disappear or disable the computer entirely. The latest versions of these viruses are direct instruments of computer crime.

Which system?

The IBM PC and its innumerable successors and clones, are the most likely targets of a virus. More than 70 percent of all reported infections have involved these computers. The Apple Macintosh, second in popularity with buyers, is also second in popularity with virus authors. For some time, many users believed that the Mac was not susceptible to viruses, but the authors of new strains have proved them wrong.

The Unix operating system has also been identified as highly vulnerable. Unix is also the operating system of choice in many enterprise networks, particularly those based on open systems. Unix has attracted particular attention because its Berkeley version 4.3 was the system invaded by the Arpanet virus.

Some critics of Unix have argued that the system is too complex, and fully securing a Unix system is beyond the ability of many users. Many users, however, were able to avoid the Arpanet virus through what has been described as a simple technique: closing a trapdoor in the electronic mail facility. That solution does require programming. Meanwhile, developers have been working on improved versions of Unix that meet security standards established by the National Computer Security Council.

The Arpanet virus also established another first: It infected both the Digital Equipment Corporation VAX systems and Sun Microsystems computers. Most previous viruses had been able to infect only one basic type of computer.

Where viruses attack

A virus's point of attack is related to its purpose. Some of the most destructive viruses attack the boot segment of a hard disk. This is where the computer looks for instructions when it first is powered up. If it cannot find these instructions, it can do nothing further. Other viruses attack operating system files or infect application programs.

One early virus, known as the *Pakistani Brain* is a boot segment virus that hides itself well. It copies the boot segment to another part of the disk, then copies itself into the original boot segment and to other parts of the disk. The areas occupied by the virus are flagged as unusable, so the computer will pass them over when looking for places to write new data. This pattern, typical of boot segment viruses, makes the infection almost impossible to detect. Anyone who uses a disk diagnosis program to examine the boot segment will find the original, which is unchanged but has been moved and is inoperable. This type of virus affects the computer's startup mechanism. The machine is left much like a car with a faulty starter.

Destruction is even more difficult than detection. Several vaccination programs have been developed to counteract boot segment viruses. Only a sophisticated programmer knows enough to write this kind of virus. That same programmer would readily know how to fool a vaccination program into thinking it had removed the virus, which would remain alive and ticking. One particularly mean trick: when you try to boot the computer from an uninfected disk, the virus will infect that disk while making it seem that you now have a clean system.

Another class of viruses alters the operating system, the program that controls electronic traffic within the computer. A virus that infects the operating system can operate at a very basic level of the computer's controls. If a boot sector virus is like damaging a starter, an operating system virus is like cutting the brake lines.

Normally, when you fire up the computer, the boot system initiates the operating system, which consists of one or more program files. The virus can attach itself to these files and gain control of nearly any part of the computer operation it chooses, such as disk access or file copying. A well-conceived virus can introduce errors in such a way that the operator believes they are his or her own fault.

Some viruses will attach themselves as extra system files, hidden from normal directory listings. Others will replace the entire operating system with one tailored for mischief.

System viruses don't usually spread rapidly within a single computer. There usually is only one operating system to serve as a host. They can infect the system files they find on floppy disks, however, or can extend to other computers on a network.

A virus that does spread rapidly is one that alters application programs: spreadsheets, word processors, and the like. How many programs can such a virus infect? How many do you have in your computer? The virus can infect them all, in minutes. A virus can even infect the programs used to diagnose and remove viruses.

These viruses spread easily to other computers. They can travel over networks or hide themselves in files downloaded from electronic bulletin boards. Once in your system, they may lie dormant for a while until some signal triggers them. These are among the least sophisticated viruses to be found, but they are also among the most dangerous. That's because there are so many of them, and they can spread so rapidly.

The Life Cycle of a Virus

A virus has three distinct stages of life:

- It enters the host system and locates a receptive home.
- It reproduces itself within the system.
- It is activated to perform the task for which it was designed.

Gaining entry

A virus may enter a personal computer system when the user inserts an infected disk. It may also arrive by way of a file downloaded from a bulletin board service. Once in the system, it searches for a suitable host. In the case of an operating system virus, for example, it would search for the operating system programs. It then would either attach itself to a host program or replace that program entirely.

This is your first chance to detect the virus. It is not necessarily your best chance. To the ordinary user, the system looks unchanged. Sometimes the infected program is changed in size from the original, but often it is not. An experienced computer hand can detect the virus by examining the program's code. The virus is probably designed to take control of one or more of the program's basic functions, such as initialization and setup, main operations, input and output, and termination. It will do so in a way that the program retains control of its display and other visible aspects of its operation, so the infection will not be obvious to the user. A sophisticated analysis of the program code can detect these activities.

As the program operates, the virus searches for receptive hosts to which it can spread. An initialization sequence, disk access, or some other program activity may trigger the search. If it finds a host, it can reproduce itself there. If not, it can return the operation to the host program and remain dormant until another search is triggered.

Sometimes there is one clue that such a search is in progress. There may be an unusual amount of disk activity during the program's operation. Operators should become familiar with the normal operation of the lights that indicate disk access and should report any apparent deviations from a normal pattern.

Spreading the infection

The virus begins the second phase when it begins to reproduce itself. As it takes its cues from the host program, it looks for other suitable hosts. These can be other applications on the same disk, system files on a floppy disk inserted into the computer, or files on networked computers. At this stage, the virus's limited activity makes it hard to detect. It stays within the host program, only occasionally looking out for a new host. If it finds one, it inserts a copy of itself into that host. If not, the virus retreats into the original host program. Either way, there is a minimum of activity, and the computer operates much as its operator expects.

A well-designed virus is designed to carry out this phase of its activities as unobtrusively as possible. A lot of self-discipline is also often programmed in. A virus that discovers a disk full of suitable hosts will usually be programmed to restrain itself and avoid extensive activities that would attract the user's attention. Instead, the virus will choose to infect only one or two of the available candidates, waiting for other opportunities to reproduce itself elsewhere.

Becoming active

A virus is easiest to spot when it is too late: when it has been activated. The original virus, or one of its duplicated clones, will decide to perform the job for which the virus was designed. The virus may display a greeting on your screen, or your computer may suddenly go dead as vital parts of its operating system or hard disk memory are erased. The virus often will send a message in this vein:

As you read this, your hard disk is being trashed.

In a variation on that theme, one virus sends a bouncing ball across your screen several times before it renders your system useless. Another produces an animated cartoon in which bugs eat the contents of your screen. Some viruses are just ruthlessly efficient: They destroy what they have set out to destroy and don't bother with notice or warning. Others are subtle, doing their damage in small increments over many months.

The virus must be programmed to operate when it receives a certain signal. The Friday the 13th virus attached itself to application programs. Then it was activated by the first use of that program on or after the designated date. In a form of direct retribution, another virus was triggered by a search of the user's data files. The virus was activated whenever it found the name of a certain company in the file.

Does Immunization Work?

The Arpanet virus had many effects among the computer-using community. One was to spawn an infant new industry, marketing *antiviral immunization programs.* These are programs that launch search-and-destroy missions in a computer system, seeking out viruses and trying to disable those it finds. There is even a Computer Virus Industry Association (CVIA) composed of firms which market antiviral products.

On the surface, the antiviral program may seem like a good idea: electronic preventive medicine. In truth, the best defense against a virus is to avoid it in the first place. The next best is to kill it at an early stage, before it has had a chance to spread and certainly before it has been activated. An antivirus program can't help much until the second stage.

Not too many years ago, there were those who believed the cure of an antivirus program could be worse than the disease. This was particularly true when this was a fledgling industry that turned out many poorly written products. The risk is less today, but it is never completely absent.

Antivirus programs are inherently risky. They work on the same vital computer resources as the viruses: disk sectors, operating systems, and the like. Any program that works at this basic level is hazardous. There are some reports of poorly programmed immunization programs that have themselves run amok, knocking out computers and destroying the data they were supposed to protect. Today, a more mature industry has minimized these dangers. Antivirus marketing still seems to be a mixture of hype and legitimate protection. Even so, prevention remains a better choice than any attempted cure.

If you are considering an antiviral program, there are four things to remember:

- While computer owners initially underreacted to problems of computer security, there have been some overreactions to the virus scare. If you take reasonable precautions, such as backing up your data and other measures to be discussed later in this chapter, you may not need to accept the risks of an antiviral program.

- The more reliable and reputable the source, the more likely an immunization program is to be safe and effective. Look for programs that have undergone rigorous scientific evaluations at major universities or other recognized research facilities. The CVIA has developed a standards and testing program. Contact the Computer Virus Industry Association, 4423 Cheeney Street, Santa Clara, CA 95054. (Telephone: 408/727-4559; Modem: 408/988-4004) The industry trade magazine *Computers & Security* also evaluates immunization programs.

- Don't expect this or any other form of technology to do the entire job for you. A virus is a product created by people and allowed into your system by human error or omission. There is still no antiviral product which is so fail-safe it allows you to ignore the human factor. CVIA describes these programs as providing a margin of safety, not absolute insurance against disaster.

- Look for programs that actively monitor the system for virus activity. Those that simply scan disks can return false alarms and miss some viruses. Also, virus writers are familiar with scanning programs and can write their products to evade detection.

The Best Way to Protect Yourself

There are few better ways to protect yourself from a computer virus than with an effective security policy, firmly enforced (Fig. 13.2). This policy should include all the available procedural, physical, and technical protections. Some of these are of limited use against viruses. For example, a data encryption program would do little to combat a virus that invades a boot sector or operating system and never reaches the encoded data files. At the same time, some simple security techniques as in the following examples can overcome even the most sophisticated viruses.

Regular backup

Had the proverb about being easier said than done not already been written, it could have been applied to PC backups. Backups are such an effective way to protect both programs and data that they should be a mandatory part of every security policy. Yet they seem to violate some basic element of human nature. Backups are easy. They are also rarely done.

Actually, there are two types of backups, and only one requires an employee's active involvement—that is, to back up your data onto tape, disk, or some other medium from which you can recover it should it be lost, damaged, or altered. Maintain two sets of backup media. One should hold the most recent backup. Then, when making the next backup, use another tape or set of disks. The third backup can then use the first set of disks. That way, should a file be invaded, you have two chances to find an uninfected original.

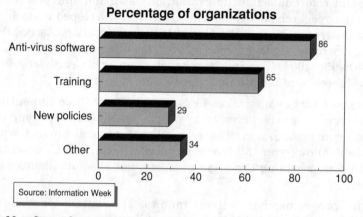

Figure 13.2   Most firms rely on antivirus software.

The second type of backup consists of the original, factory-fresh versions of your program disks. The first thing you should do when you receive a new program is to write-protect every disk. You'll have to violate this rule occasionally to accommodate those last vestiges of copy protection that insist on writing your name on the program disk. In any event, provide the write protection at the earliest possible moment. The second step is to make and store copies of these disks. Never, even by accident, copy another program onto one of these disks. Should an application program become infected, you again have two chances to replace it with a clean original. Do the same with DOS or other operating systems. A system with a hard disk should never be booted from a floppy. Allow an exception only if the rare case that you cannot start the machine any other way. If you have one of the surviving all-floppy systems, boot only from the write-protected original operating system disk.

Isolating one computer

Every floppy disk inserted into a networked computer should first be screened for viruses. You won't catch them all, but you still can save yourself the misery of falling victim to a known, avoidable attack. Set aside one system for this screening process. Make sure it is never connected to a network.

Electronic bulletin boards

Viruses have been particularly tough on shareware, the low-cost marketing method through which you can download a program from an electronic bulletin board, try it, and pay for it if you like it (and if you're honest). The bulletin boards have been major sources of virus infections.

Most shareware programs are clean. So are their public-domain cousins, distributed without charge through the same bulletin board networks. Still, there have been enough network-borne virus infections to make downloading risky. The safest policy is that no one should be allowed to download bulletin board files. Such a policy might seem unfairly tough on the shareware operators who depend on this method of distribution, but if security is vital, it may be your only recourse.

The next best policy is to allow downloading only in controlled circumstances. Stick with well-established services that have the means to police their files and keep viruses out of their offerings. When in doubt, don't hesitate to contact the bulletin board operators to find out how secure their files are.

On the home front

Increasing numbers of employees are doing their work on home computers. The growing legions of portable computer users fit into this category. There also are active *telecommuters,* or employees who simply take a little work home once in a while. This kind of homework can benefit a company in many ways, but it is also a well-known infection route. One of your program disks might be infected with a virus downloaded onto a home computer.

Your security policy should monitor and control the flow of data between work and home. The simplest and most effective control is that no program disks should leave the office, or be brought in. These are the most likely sources of infection. Employees still can carry data disks back and forth. These can be infected by viruses, but the risk is low.

Other steps

Other steps you can take include:

- Do not use a system disk to copy or transfer application programs.
- Do not insert the system disk from one computer into another.
- Do not exchange disks with other users.
- On a DOS system, note the size of your uninfected system file COMMAND.COM. Check regularly for any changes.
- Do not execute programs that come from unknown sources.
- If you believe a system is infected, let it share nothing more than airspace with any other computer.

Recovering from an infection

In spite of your best efforts, your system could be infected anyway. Cleansing your system is a difficult job at best, but it can be done. It certainly must be done if you expect to use the system again.

As with most human ailments, early detection vastly improves your chances of a cure. The longer a virus exists, the more it can multiply. This is particularly true if it has the chance to spread over network connections or onto numerous floppy disks. The more the virus reproduces itself, the lower your chances of weeding out every copy.

Dealing with bad disks

When you first suspect a virus has attacked, isolate the computer and any disks that have been used in it. Do no further processing. Confine access to those who are necessary to locate and remove the virus.

Ideally, you should try to locate every disk that might have been used in the computer during the last 6 months. Make up a large rubber stamp that reads "Possibly Infected," and use it on every disk. Reformat or destroy these disks unless you are sure you can meet both of these conditions:

- The disk contains only data and no system or application program files.
- The virus is not one that attacks the boot sector.

Restoring the system

Shut down the computer, and reboot it, using a write-protected original operating system disk. Then, follow either of these sequences:

- If you believe the virus has attacked the boot sector or system files, restore the operating system files from the original disk. In a DOS system, the SYS command does this. Do the same with any system files on floppy disks, other than the protected original.

- If the virus may have infected application programs, you must go further. If you do not already have backup copies of your data files—as you should—boot your backup program from its original disk, again write-protected. Back up the data files, but not the executable program files. Then, reformat the hard disk.

Now, recopy the backed up data files. Restore the system and application files by installing them from their original disks.

These steps usually will work unless the virus has become well established. Keep the infected system isolated, and monitor its performance for evidence of revival. If these steps fail to completely remove the virus, it may be worthwhile to try an immunization program or to consult a security expert.

Finding the source

Don't stop with restoring the system to service. Try to find out how the virus came to be there in the first place. Then try to establish and improve the security measures that will keep this from happening again.

14

A Disaster
Need Not Be
Disastrous

No place on earth is immune from natural disaster.
How well you survive depends on how well you
can expect the unexpected.

A noted social scientist once visited the newsrooms of several metropolitan newspapers to study the decision-making process that went into selecting and presenting the news. The results of her work are open to criticism; she seems to have gathered reams of statistically significant data without ever achieving a real understanding of what she saw. Nevertheless, she nailed down one important point: For a news organization, expecting the unexpected is simply part of the normal routine.

Protecting a network from natural disaster is a lot like that. There are earthquakes and fires in California. Hurricanes strike Florida, the Carolinas, and the Gulf Coast. A building is bombed in New York. Floods swallow Mississippi River farms and towns. In the Silicon Valley, along the San Andreas Fault, they wait for the Big One. Somewhere in the world, a large building is on fire. There always seems to be a disaster happening somewhere. You may not know exactly what to expect, but you always have to expect something.

As usual, a network is more vulnerable to disaster than a mainframe, with its central location and tight control. Managing a network inevitably involves dealing with chaos—and that's before the disaster strikes. Furthermore, there are more things that can go wrong with a LAN than with central or stand-alone systems.

Dealing With Disaster

Among recent history's most famous disasters was the bomb that exploded in New York City's World Trade Center. When employees evacuated the offices of one financial services firm, they left behind about 70 PC networks. The company could never have anticipated this particular incident, of course, but nevertheless it was prepared. The organization had made regular backups of the server disks and had stored the backup tapes off site. A contingency site was available until employees could return to the building, and the staff had collected enough information to duplicate the original system.

This was hardly mainframe-level security. Users were responsible for backing up their own workstations. Some had, some hadn't, and many of the backups were in desk drawers made inaccessible by the bombing. The servers had backup power protection, but only enough for about an hour. Traditional systems professionals might scoff at these limitations, but there was a reason for both decisions. The company was not in a position to monitor the software and backup status of thousands of individual workstations—a problem you don't have when everything is on a mainframe. The backup power supply was intended to ensure an orderly shutdown, not to keep the networks running nonstop. These systems met their prime objective: The system was back in service within 24 hours.

LANs Have Special Needs

Preparing a network to withstand a natural disaster has much in common with preparing a larger system. There are two major differences, though, that can make LAN disaster planning a much different experience:

- Mainframes are centralized; LANs are decentralized.

- The mainframe environment is stable; networks are ever changing.

Protecting a mainframe is easier, simply because you have a greater degree of control. You know exactly where the data are stored. That makes it a lot easier to back up and recover.

In this respect, a network server is much like a mainframe. You can keep tabs on its contents and make sure it is regularly backed up. The problem is with the individual workstations. Though many network management tools are available and they are constantly being improved, few if any yet meet the need for monitoring the contents of every disk on every station. You have to depend on individuals to back up their own systems, and that often means you must rely on the unreliable.

The plan is: there is no plan

Probably the more important difference, though, is that a network is a constantly changing environment. The plans you make today may not fit the need tomorrow. Applications, configurations, and critical data can change so often and so quickly that a recovery plan can become obsolete almost as soon as it is written.

That means planning for network disaster relief is a process, not a project. You never finish the job. You must constantly test your plan and correct the problems you discover. The financial service company from the World Trade Center learned the value of constant testing. Even before the disaster it had identified many human problems that would interfere with a prompt recovery. Even among people who made backups, some were saving the oldest copies and losing the newer versions.

Another firm had a policy of regularly backing up its servers, including those that served a crew of application developers. Then a test showed that the backup files contained program source code that was more than a month old. The programmers had found the network too slow for their liking, so had been saving their most recent work on their own workstations instead of on the server.

> **Action item**   Make users responsible for their own data. Challenge them with this standard of performance: If you would lose your files this instant, how long would it take you to get back into production? The answer should be no longer than it would take you to restore their server to full operation.

Minor disasters, major problems

Not all disasters make headlines. Your next threat may be as localized—and as serious—as a power surge that knocks out a critical server. In terms of numbers, fluctuations in the local power supply are a much more serious hazard to networks than any kind of major disaster.

For example, one organization recently suffered a direct lightning strike on the local power lines. Because the firm had installed uninterruptible power supplies (UPSs) on most of its PCs and telephones, it was able to maintain its usual level of customer service until the power was restored. When an unprotected computer lost its hard drive, line suppressers were able to isolate it and keep the electrical problem from spreading to other systems.

The makers of UPS hardware are increasingly responsive to network needs. Once designed to protect single computers, these systems now include software that can close files, log-out users, and otherwise shut down the network automatically. UPS software also can provide for power management from a single location. For example, Netware comes with an optional Netware Loadable Module (NLM) that lets you monitor your servers' power levels and temperatures.

Still, electrical protective devices are not the complete answer. For example, there is no way in which a power management system can complete a half-finished update of a database. That is particularly important in accounting or transaction processing applications where an addition to one database table should have a corresponding subtraction from another. Make sure instead that your database applications will either complete the transaction or roll it back completely.

Network Security Resources

Though networks can be hard to protect, they also give you many useful tools to overcome the difficulties. The most important asset is a good installation. If your network is sound and reliable from the outset, it is less likely to malfunction when minor problems arise. Even the best-designed networks are no match, though, for the hazards of major disasters. You must make maximum use of the available tools to minimize the effects and get yourself back into business.

> **Action item**   Take inventory of the tools you have available. Determine whether these will meet the need or if you should add more tools to your network kit (Fig. 14.1).

Regular backup

This is a simple and obvious step, characterized by frequent errors and omissions. You have the ability to make regular backups and to store them in safe places off site. If all else fails, your backup data will be there waiting for you—if you bothered to create it in the first place.

A good backup system will let you copy data to a variety of media and to restore any portions that have been lost. Magnetic tape has the low cost and high capacity you need for a typical network installation. You can buy ready-made backup systems that include tape drives and the necessary software, or you can put something together out of individual pieces.

Reliability is sometimes a problem with backup systems. Make sure you follow all the system's prescribed procedures, including regular tests to compare the backup with the original data. Remember, too, that the most serious reliability problem originates with people, not systems.

Network disaster control

- File backups
- Redundant storage
- Emergency power
- Offsite resources
- Utility software

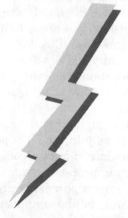

Figure 14.1   Networks often give you the means to create these assets.

Redundant servers and disks

Many systems intended as network servers now include higher levels of back-up by duplicating data on redundant hard disks. There are at least three levels of protection available:

- *Server redundancy* maintains the duplicate files on a completely different system. For example, Netware SFT III provides for server mirroring. It links two servers via a high-speed connection so if one fails, the other can keep the network running.

- *Disk redundancy* maintains the duplicate files on separate disks in the same system. It is naturally more vulnerable than server redundancy, but it is also less expensive. *Disk mirroring* maintains the duplicate data in a drive on the same bus adapter; a *duplex drive* uses a separate adapter and provides a bit more security.

- *RAID technology,* for redundant arrays of inexpensive disks, has become a standard feature of many file servers. RAID can cover many things, including disk mirroring or duplexing. Most often, though, it means that if the server loses a single hard disk, there are at least two others that will keep going. This form of protection is less effective than other systems, and it has no particular price advantage, but it is widely available in standard network products.

Power backup and conditioning

A UPS can keep a computer going when the power fails. The least expensive can keep things going long enough to let you shut down the system with some measure of control. Only the most expensive are designed to keep you in service for long periods. If you need your system at all times, such as to maintain customer service, the better systems can be worth the investment.

Line conditioners and surge protectors can't replace a shut-down power supply, but they can provide more stable power. Link conditioners smooth out the power flow, while surge protectors block voltage surges that exceed specified values.

Document the system

Since a LAN configuration changes so often, it's important to keep a full, timely record of its configuration. If you have to rebuild the network after a disaster, you will need this information to do it.

Also provide instructions on how to recover from a network crash. Since you never know who might have to take on this task, make sure even the Complete Idiot can understand the instructions. It isn't necessary to invest in specialized documentation or publishing tools for this purpose alone. The word processors and illustration tools you already have available are probably good enough. Invest your money instead in a professional technical writer; programmers too often lack the specialized communication skills this project requires.

Off-site resources

There are two types of off-site resources that could prove invaluable should you have to recover from a major disaster. Both were originally established with mainframe support in mind, but many now support networks as well.

An off-site storage facility will put your backup tapes in secured, climate-controlled storage. They will pick up your tapes on schedule and deliver them on demand. Their response times vary, though; make sure you include your requirements in any contract.

A *hot site* is a place to set up shop should your regular quarters be unavailable. You can expect to find a network with file server, PC workstations, and communication abilities (Fig. 14.2). You must keep your hot-site plan up to date with changes in your network. Remember, too, that in case of a widespread emergency hot-site services may be at a premium. As a backup to this backup, have an emergency equipment acquisition program in place. Arrange an open purchase order with a reliable vendor to be activated should you need it. It pays to sign up in advance since a widespread disaster could strain suppliers' stocks. It also pays to make advanced arrangements with data recovery services, which often can restore data from damaged disks or tapes.

> **Action item**   Set up your own backup supply of servers, workstations, and key components you can use to repair loss or damage. This is a good use for outmoded equipment that still can be pressed into service in a pinch.

Utility software

Common PC utility software from Central Point Software, Symantec, and other vendors can also be invaluable in an emergency. They have the means

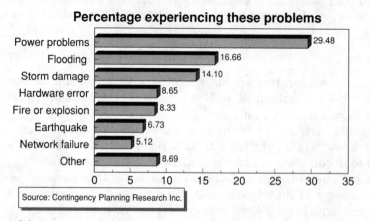

Why organizations use hot sites

Percentage experiencing these problems

Power problems: 29.48
Flooding: 16.66
Storm damage: 14.10
Hardware error: 8.65
Fire or explosion: 8.33
Earthquake: 6.73
Network failure: 5.12
Other: 8.69

Source: Contingency Planning Research Inc.

Figure 14.2   Other reasons include evacuations, relocations, and riots.

to restore lost files and repair damaged disks. There is also an abundance of other troubleshooting tools such as diagnostic software and cable testers. Network management software is also a necessary emergency resource.

A Guide to Disaster Planning

Products and services can help you recover from a disaster, but none of them can replace good planning. Like the backup disks left in the World Trade Center, you can have a perfect backup that you can't use. Otherwise healthy businesses have failed because they couldn't reopen their doors and their systems quickly enough.

Though it's hard to write a disaster plan for something as fluid as a network, it's necessary to have a plan in place. Yesterday was none too soon to start writing it.

Ideally, when you design a network, its disaster recovery plan should be part of the design. LANs and internetworking tend to spread on their own, and the outset is the best time to get a handle on their security. You can also make sure the new installation is made up of standard, readily available equipment. Of course, you don't always have that advantage. What you can do is to assess your current situation, using network monitoring tools to take inventory of what you have. Then use that knowledge to build a plan that will avoid disaster if possible and recover from it if necessary.

Approaches to disaster planning

Disaster planning is a kind of insurance. When you face a risk, the prudent thing to do is to ensure against it. A disaster is just that kind of risk. We have come to depend on our computers. The possibility that we could lose them is a risk against which we must protect ourselves.

In fact, if you ask an insurance carrier about disaster coverage, it will probably insist, as a condition of its coverage, that you take adequate steps to prevent the loss. There are several ways to minimize a risk:

- Avoid it. This is the simplest and most effective—if you can pull it off. Protect your equipment and data against any kind of risk you can reasonably anticipate. A good security plan is a major part of this protection. Include protective measures against natural disasters, storms, and even deliberate sabotage.

- If you can't avoid the risk, reduce it. It isn't always—or even often—possible to eliminate a risk completely. It still makes good sense, though, to do what you can to minimize the risk.

- Try to control the damage should the disaster happen in spite of your best efforts.

- If all else fails, learn to live with it. Have a contingency plan ready to be put into practice. If you have a limited budget, concentrate on protecting the resources that would be hardest to replace. You might also assume a risk that is unlikely to happen.

All four elements have their places in a good disaster plan. You can't anticipate every possible disaster, much less avoid them all. To some extent, a disaster control plan must count on reducing some risks, confining the effects of others and accepting still others. The plan should be based on a cost-benefit analysis that weighs both the likelihood and the seriousness of any particular loss.

First, of course, it's necessary that you have a plan. And while it's true that any plan is better than no plan at all, a good plan is better yet. A good plan can meet two very important objectives:

- Minimize the impact of a disaster on your ability to conduct business.
- Enjoy a speedy recovery to normal operations.

Assessing the threats

Just as with any other element of a computer security plan, the first step should be to assess the threats you face. Among the most common disasters that can strike a computer system are:

- Fire
- Power failures and fluctuations in the available power supply
- Interference from outside electrical sources
- Interruptions in gas, water, and other utilities
- Mechanical failures
- Sabotage

Then determine the possible consequences of these disasters. Among the leading possibilities:

- The loss of vital business records such as accounts receivable, customer orders, or product development plans
- The loss of communication systems
- The possible failure of computer security systems
- The inability to use important programs
- An extended period of operating at less than normal efficiency

In other words, base your control and recovery plan on an assessment of what you stand to lose and how you might lose it. The plan should present an organized approach to containing the damage and getting back into operation. As a longer-term goal, but as soon as possible, the plan should provide for resuming full normal operations. It should also be based on a thorough comparison of the costs and benefits of available security measures.

A set sequence of events

It's been estimated that the average company can remain in operation 4.8 days after its computer goes down. That's more time than you may have thought you had to get a backup plan into operation before those long odds cited earlier start to take effect. It's probably less time than you'll need if you haven't already developed an adequate contingency plan. Then too, your company may not be average.

After a disaster, the company will go through a predictable series of events. They will happen with or without a plan. It's much better, of course, that you plan for them instead of just letting them happen. Major steps in the sequence include:

- The disaster itself.

- The immediate response. Employees on the scene should begin a standard response procedure that will include protective measures to minimize the damage and notifying key officials. These officials then will supervise the formation of a recovery team.

- An assessment of the impact. Determine what you've lost and what you must do to recover.

- Returning to operation. Have backup resources available to replace both your data and the equipment you need to process it. Get the company into an emergency operating mode as soon as possible.

- Making a full recovery. Replace and repair damaged resources, and get back to full normal operation.

    Action item   Build a scenario like this, tailored to your own needs and operations.

The goals of the plan

Another major element of your disaster control planning is to decide exactly what you hope to accomplish. The major objective, of course, is to get back into operation again, as quickly, smoothly, and inexpensively as you can.

Within that overall objective are several component goals that include the specific details of what you hope to do. Among them:

- Develop a plan that can readily be implemented. When the time comes, you will have to execute your plan, probably under the worst possible circumstances. Develop it with ready implementation in mind. Make regular trial runs so you can be sure the plan will work and your employees will know what to do.

- Restore vital operations and resources as quickly as possible. You must get the company operating again as soon as you absolutely can, even if it is initially on a limited, emergency basis.

- Your plans, and the postdisaster resources you will use, should be compatible with your normal operations. Assuring this kind of compatibility can be a difficult proposition since you may not have identical equipment and other resources available as a backup. Achieving it could be the key, though, to restoring your most critical operations.

Nothing on this list will be easy. You face a complex problem of trying to find adequate backup resources that will replace—in a useful way—those you might lose in a disaster. You might find yourself renting time on a different type of computer than the one you normally use or hooking up to a completely different type of communication system.

This will mainly be a management problem, though, not a technical one. The most common reason disaster plans fail is that the company looks for technical solutions and pays too little attention to the need for good management.

Your success will depend primarily on how well your people contribute to the effort. Even before the disaster, you must convince them to maintain adequate backup copies of their work. You and other managers must learn to anticipate a disaster, not just to react to one.

As a Philadelphia insurance company learned after a major fire, the human factor can affect a disaster plan in totally unexpected ways. Security consultants who were called to the scene found the insurance firm's senior executives in varying states of shock. It would be several days before the people who had to lead the company out of the disaster would again become the decisive, effective executives they normally were.

What Makes a Good Plan?

The consultants involved in the Philadelphia fire had written a disaster plan for the company—in fact, they had written several. But this incident proved the adage that the best-laid plans of mice and men are usually just about equal. They hadn't planned on the executives' limited ability to take charge. And the plans did not account for one major short-term contingency: At the time the fire broke out, the company was 3 days away from completing its conversion to an entirely new system. Both systems were left entirely useless. To make things worse, the firm had a data processing subsidiary that might have provided a backup. That unit had recently moved and was not available.

A new plan was devised on the spot, and it worked. The job of recovery was divided into six chunks, each of a size that even a dazed executive could manage. One person was put in charge of each operation. The six areas were:

- Securing the site, restoring records, and overseeing salvage work
- Communication and information, including notifying the public and heading off rumors
- Negotiating with the insurance carriers
- Locating a new facility
- Acquiring new equipment
- Restoring normal operation

Action item Set up your own division of responsibilities—before it becomes critical.

Preparing to fail

The plan worked, and the company enjoyed a healthy recovery. Its success illustrates what might be the most important feature of any good disaster plan: It should provide for its own failure. No matter how hard you try—and you should try hard—no plan can cover every possibility. No one at this company anticipated that the fire would break out in the middle of a conversion, and with no relief in sight. Yet one of the first things salvaged was a workable plan.

The fact that plans had been developed, even if they weren't directly useful, probably helped. Even when an unexpected problem forces you to change or abandon a plan, you should be able to build or adapt from your existing plans to meet the actual circumstances.

Your plan should include a built-in means to make this adaptation. Provide an administrative mechanism to review your situation, and make adaptations as they are needed. If for some reason you must build a whole new plan from scratch, your original should at least establish a method for doing that. Beyond that, the plan should include a variety of available options. The proper response to a limited emergency is not the same as the right way to handle a total disaster. Give yourself a list of possible actions, and provide the means to take them. Then in an emergency you can select the individual actions that best respond to the situation at hand.

Other qualities to have

Other elements of a good plan include:

- *Provisions to test and refine the plan.* It should call for regular training exercises. If these show any need for improvements to the plan, make them.

- *Provisions for maintaining the plan.* Employees should be trained to execute their roles in the recovery process.

- *Support from top management.* That's a cliché, but it's true.

The Planning Process

Developing a disaster plan is a major project, involving many complex decisions about costs, benefits, probabilities, and contingencies. Perhaps the best way to develop a plan in these circumstances is a system development life cycle approach. This is simply a matter of working from beginning to end, one logical step at a time.

The first step should be a thorough cost-benefit analysis. Assess the threats and their likely consequences. Determine the value of each resource you are trying to protect, and compare with the cost of protecting it. As a second step, decide which activities and resources are most vital to your operation. Set priorities that will emphasize the most essential resources first. Both considerations—protecting the most valuable resources and those most vital to your operation—will form the basis of the third step: Actually developing the plan.

Identifying the dangers

You can't proceed very far with any of these three steps until you know what dangers you face. You can't anticipate every disaster, nor can you tell in advance what the results of even a predictable disaster might be. Still, you can develop an idea of what is likely to happen. There's a good chance your plan will fall close enough to actual events to serve as a springboard for an effective response.

Consider the types of disasters most likely to happen, and for each work up a scenario that includes:

- The likely length of the interruption. If it's unknown, say so.
- The operations that might be affected.
- The types of equipment you might have to repair or replace.

For each possible scenario, determine what you would require to recover. Applying the priorities you have determined based on the value of the resource and how essential it is. Lay out a step-by-step recovery process, including:

- The priority of each activity
- Who will take charge
- Procedures for notifying key personnel
- How to implement a backup plan
- The location of the command post and other key operating centers

Testing your plan

Before you proceed any further, examine each element of the plan. Each possible response should specify:

- *What must be done.* The plan should provide as many details as possible about the exact procedure to be followed. Even if you must adapt these procedures to meet actual disaster conditions, these details will give you a place to start.
- *When must it be done.* Establish the proper sequence of each step. If a deadline is required or if the step is a prerequisite to some other action, specify these requirements clearly.

- *Who must do it.* Someone must be in overall charge of the recovery effort. And, as was done in the Philadelphia disaster, each major operation should have an individual who is fully responsible for completing it. Also identify the staff resources to be assigned to each person.

- *How it should be done.* Describe the methods to be followed and the standards to be met.

- *What is needed to do the job.* Determine the amount of money, people, and other resources that must be applied to the task.

Finding Backup Resources

Data managers who have hot remote-site backup facilities available give these centers great credit for peace of mind. In several of the disasters mentioned earlier in the chapter, the companies shipped tapes to remote hot sites, then found they could get their main computers up and running and would not need the remote services. Even so, the managers almost universally expressed gratitude for the peace of mind of hot-site insurance. This was one less thing they had to worry about, at a time when they had a lot to worry about.

A typical backup center might look like the one maintained near Seattle by Weyerhaeuser Information Systems. It is a 450,000-square-foot building where large computers made by all the major manufacturers can be found. Most of the time, they just sit, waiting for a disaster to happen somewhere else. Like many companies that build facilities like this, Weyerhaeuser first established the center to meet its own needs. Later, it decided to make the center available to other business customers. For example, several customers called the center after a utility vault fire knocked out six major transmission cables and blacked out a 50-block area of Seattle.

What seemed like minor electrical disturbances at a North Carolina textile company caused major damage. All the disks had been knocked out of service, and their data was unavailable. While service technicians worked on the damaged equipment, the company put its contingency plan into effect. Smoothly, and with only a few hitches, the shipping center fell back to a manual system until the computer was back in service. This is an example of one of the simplest possible types of backup resources: Doing it with whatever you have left.

> **Action item** Identify any backup resources that you can develop and maintain within your own organization. These home remedies could be the easiest and least expensive solutions to a problem. The one big requirement is that they survive the disaster.

You may require something more, and that could easily mean you must depend on outside resources, either in other branches of your own organization or from sources beyond the company. There are several possibilities, as follows.

Cooperative agreement

There's a tradition in the newspaper industry that if one newspaper suffers a disaster that knocks out its printing facilities, another newspaper usually will furnish its resources to help out—even if the other paper is a direct competitor. Computer users could try to arrange something similar. You could form a mutual-aid agreement with other computer owners. If one goes down, the others will temporarily pick up the slack.

This can be a useful, inexpensive option. The main problem is to find other companies whose systems are compatible with yours. You also must acknowledge that this is just an arrangement to maintain your most vital operations through the worst early days. It's not likely that anyone would have the unused capacity to support an entire second company over a long term. That means you must identify your most critical priorities and make mutual arrangements to handle them.

Hot and cold sites

In a scene that resembled a "bugout" from M*A*S*H, the computer staff of a Los Angeles-based restaurant chain suddenly found itself working in Dallas for a few days. The occasion was a test of the company's ability to establish operations in a remote site should its main facility suffer an earthquake or some other disaster. The plan called for quickly relocating the operation to a part of the country not likely to be affected by the same disaster. Several services have been set up, offering themselves as disaster relocation centers. In other cases, a company may establish its own.

The center may be a shell, or *cold site,* offering only a building with the necessary electrical and communication connections. The building is designed so necessary equipment could be installed quickly.

The more popular option is the *hot site,* where the vendor has a computer system already set up and running. This is a costly option, and you must be careful to find a compatible system, but many companies are choosing it, particularly when large amounts of money are at stake.

Duplicate facilities

At a Massachusetts manufacturing plant, a storm knocked out power just as the company was preparing to run the payroll. The company that hauled its backup tapes to Rhode Island and made use of a duplicate facility that happened to be available in an affiliated company. This shows you don't have to be big to maintain this kind of backup—but you do have to be part of a fair-sized organization. This type of company can set up a mutual-aid system within its own subsidiaries and affiliates. The systems and procedures may well be much alike, solving compatibility problems and giving you most of the advantages of working in-house. If money is an object, the developing network technology may give you a low-cost alternative. You can simply direct your work to a part of the network that is still in operation. You may face problems of limited capacity, but you should be able to get your most important work done.

Action item   Take stock of the outside resources on which you might be able to rely in an emergency.

Testing the Disaster Plan

The first test of your system will not go well. That's why you test it after you install it. Many computer security experts share one big worry: that even among companies that have developed disaster plans, few have tested their plans to find out what's wrong with them. The choice of words is deliberate. You do not test your plan to find out *whether* it has any defects that must be corrected. You test it to find out *which* defects still require your attention.

The work of developing an adequate disaster plan literally never stops. You must test it regularly to find its weak spots and train the employees who must implement it in an emergency. You also must continually update it to account for new equipment and techniques. If you install a new bank of microcomputers, for example, a plan originally developed for a central mainframe will not be much good.

The charmed third try

A battery maker centered in Madison, Wisconsin, conducts an annual exercise in which the data processing operation is relocated to a backup site near Chicago. It has been the kind of experience you can also expect.

The first year nothing went well. The staff was able to get the operating system to operate, but it was unable to produce any useful work. The second year, several test production runs were successfully completed, but lack of a full communication system kept the test from being a success. The third year, everything finally went well. The first two tests could not be classed as failures. Each taught lessons that were applied to the succeeding years' improvements.

Another company has established a corporate hot site for its varied divisions and affiliates. It's designed to be used when needed by any operating group that suffers a disaster. The backup center staff conducts tests twice a year to make sure the center is ready. The individual subsidiaries are encouraged to test their own contingency plans just as often.

Disaster simulations

A program that hasn't been adequately tested is a program that easily could fail when you need it the most. This is true of plans much less elaborate than those you might find in major corporations. Depending on the type of plan you have, there are several ways to test it.

GE, for example, conducts full-scale disaster simulations, testing the staff's performance against deadlines for restoring particular operations. These probably will give you the best picture of how well the system—and staff—would respond in a real emergency.

A less disruptive alternative is to walk through the plan at night or on a weekend when you have the chance to stop and deal with any hitches that develop. The problem with this approach is that real emergencies don't proceed at such a convenient time, nor can they be handled at a leisurely pace.

Evaluating the results

The test of a good program is whether it adequately protects and restores the functions you have identified in the plan, particularly the high-priority ones. The results of the test should tell you how close you have come to this goal. Use the plan itself as a checklist. Go over each function, and see how well the system actually performs with respect to that need. Note the areas that need improvement. Then improve them.

Don't limit your examination to the computer system alone. Include related functions such as communication lines and instruction manuals. Determine, too, whether all the information in databases and other storage can be retrieved.

The human element is an important part of the system, too. Make sure all the employees who will be involved in executing the plan have been thoroughly trained in their duties. Use the plan as a training guide, and include disaster control in every appropriate orientation and training program.

Points to consider

Here is a checklist of points to consider in planning a disaster relief program or in evaluating your present one. The results may not make you feel very comfortable. Nearly every plan has shortcomings of some kind, and even the good plans require regular checkups and maintenance. Treat testing as a learning experience. It's a whole lot better than learning the hard way—in a real emergency.

- How well could your company function if a disaster struck right now?

- Is your plan adequate to recover the information, communication links, and other assets connected with personal computers?

- Do you know the kinds of disasters that are most likely to affect you?

- Have you assessed the probabilities and the consequences of each?

- Are one or more responsible persons assigned specific responsibility for establishing and maintaining a disaster control plan?

- Have you developed specific policies on how to conduct disaster control and recovery?

- Has your plan been adequately tested, and is there a plan for regular tests?

- Are changes in the plan adequately explained to the people who will be involved?

- Do you know exactly what to expect at your backup site?

- Do you have adequate backups to all your material, and are they stored in a safe place?

15

Electronic Mail and Other Legal Problems

If you have no other reasons to protect your system, consider the legal liability that could come from not protecting it.

An electronic mail supervisor at a California computer equipment company had been told employees' e-mail exchanges were strictly private. It came as a shock, then, when she discovered her supervisor poring over reams of downloaded e-mail messages.

The e-mail supervisor protested loudly, and predictably she was fired. Just as predictably, she took the company to court. The ultimate ruling came down in the company's favor: Employees have no right to expect privacy in their correspondence over employer-provided e-mail systems. This ruling, in the first e-mail court case on record, established a principle all employers can profitably adopt. It was only the beginning, though, of a new wave of legislation that could make e-mail a bottomless pit of civil and criminal liability.

For example, a major oil company was sued recently, accused of fraud in selling its solar energy subsidiary to an electronics firm. The suit contended that the oil company knew well its solar products were not commercially viable but withheld that information from the buyer. In support of that claim, lawyers introduced messages it had obtained in some way from the oil company's e-mail system. In one, an executive appeared to acknowledge problems making the transition from lab to manufacturing plant; another referred to the solar technology as "a pipe dream."

That was neither the first nor the last time e-mail messages have figured in court cases against their creators. E-mail messages figured in the Iran-Contra scandal. When two computer firms squared off over charges of stolen trade secrets, an executive's e-mail messages were auditioned for a smoking gun role.

Furthermore, e-mail is just the tip of another legal iceberg: the entire issue of maintaining personal privacy against the burgeoning banks of personal information that is finding its way into computerized form.

E-Mail and Employee Privacy

In the case of the surprised supervisor, the court had the right answer. Contrary to what they expect, employees have no legitimate right to expect privacy when they use their employers' internal e-mail systems. Few legal authorities have contested that point, though they add the proviso that it applies only to internal e-mail systems. These are the employer's systems, not the employees'. This means any employer can solve its basic e-mail privacy problems with a simple, widely accepted response: Adopt and publicize a policy that clearly states that e-mail messages are not private.

This policy should not be so crude that it simply states the employer's rights and interests. It should consider employee reactions, too, particularly their concerns about big-brother spying. A policy that effectively strikes a balance between employer and employee concerns is this one, adopted by the Nordstrom's retailing chain:

> Electronic mail is a company resource and is provided as a business communication tool. Employees with legitimate business purposes may have the need to view your electronic mail messages. It is also possible that others may view your messages inadvertently, since there is no guarantee of privacy for an electronic mail message. Please use your good judgment as you use the electronic mail system.

There is one important caveat: This policy will apply only to internal e-mail communication. Should the communication leave the boundaries of the company's control, the federal Wiretap Act comes into play, restricting the ability to intercept messages. The Wiretap Act involves consent, warrants, and any number of unsettled issues. The only safe assumption is that you cannot legally intercept external communications. Internally, though, all you need to establish your rights is to assert them.

At the same time, employees must learn to exercise restraint in their messages. There is something about an e-mail system that seems to encourage "flaming." Many e-mail users become prone to using insulting, intemperate remarks they would never utter over the telephone or in person and certainly would not commit to paper. These could be the source of personal embarrassment, legal liability, or both.

That means a second response is also in order: Make it clear that you do not approve of intemperate e-mail language. Provide training in e-mail etiquette, and take action when anyone's coarse, accusatory language interferes with the proper exchange of information and ideas.

Action item   Issue the two policies, one stating that e-mail is not private and the other forbidding intemperate language. Include both subjects in employee orientation and other appropriate training.

The issue of good faith

All your problems should be so easy to solve. All you need to do is establish a couple of clear policies and make sure employees understand them. There is a deeper issue here, though, and you can't paper over it with policy statements. That is the issue of trust and good faith.

Look again at the case of the surprised supervisor. It all started when she was told e-mail messages were private. She had an understandably strong reaction when she found out otherwise. That was the real issue in this case. It wasn't the simple question of whether internal e-mail communication is private—it clearly is not. The real problem was that the supervisor felt betrayed. Had the company acted openly and honestly from the outset, it's likely there would never have been a court case to add to lawyers' billable hours.

Uneasy feelings

Modern management is built on trust and cooperation, between people at all levels. Employees should work as teams, with members feeling free to contribute their ideas. A supervisor's duty is not to act as a boss but to support and assist the employees.

At least, that's the way it's supposed to work. It's based on a well-proven premise: that the vast majority of employees take gratification from doing their jobs well and want to do them even better. Unfortunately, American business is still full of managers and supervisors who act as though they believe all employees are slackers and cheats, if not downright dishonest.

You can't generalize about employees either way. There are enough dishonest and vengeful employees to make internal security the most important component of computer security. There also are more than enough capable, honest employees to justify participatory styles of management. Studies have shown that suspicious supervisors and managers cost their companies money. Their organizations have more absenteeism, more theft, less quality, and less efficiency than those that show more respect for their best people.

Computerized oversight

Supervisory style becomes a privacy issue when management uses computer technology to monitor employees. There are right and wrong ways to do this, and suspicious supervisors invariably choose the wrong way. They track keystrokes and examine e-mail messages for evidence of lax behavior or—gasp—insubordination (as they define it, of course).

Among the most glaring examples is data entry, the sweatshop industry of the computer age. Some systems monitor every keystroke, flashing warnings should the operator fall even a few strokes behind. These electronic overseers add immeasurably to stress levels that will ultimately be reflected in higher health insurance costs.

This is only the most widely noted example of surveillance. When *Macworld* magazine surveyed more than 300 American companies, 21.6 percent of the respondents acknowledged that at some time or other they have conducted searches of employee computer files, voice mail, electronic mail, or other communications. Often, there were good reasons: to investigate thefts, review performance, seek missing data, and guard against illegal software. Even when justified, though, there still are the right and wrong ways. Otherwise, an employee might have a case for invasion of privacy or unjust discharge. To ensure that you're doing it right, adopt a monitoring policy that includes these provisions:

- The company reserves the right to examine employees' computer files and messages when there is a substantial reason to believe this investigation will lead to information regarding theft or some other criminal behavior.

- The company reserves the right to monitor employees' performance. This monitoring will be limited to 2 hours per week.

- Performance monitoring will measure long-term performance over a day, week, or a month, not individual keystrokes.

- Employees will be judged on the results they produce, not the effort they extend.

   Action item   Set the example in establishing a working environment where, in the absence of contrary evidence, employees are treated with trust and respect.

Privacy and the Public

A Louis Harris poll released late in 1993 indicates that most Americans are "very concerned" about the privacy of their personal records. Furthermore, a follow-up poll identified specific types of businesses where Americans want their privacy to be protected. Leading this list, in order of expressed concern, were:

- Banks
- Health insurance carriers
- Hospitals and clinics
- Credit card issuers
- Life insurance firms
- Stockbrokers
- Long-distance telephone carriers
- Direct mail

In all eight categories, more than 75 percent said privacy was at least somewhat important; in all but direct mail, a majority called privacy very important.

On the strength of these results, companies have been asked to adopt voluntary codes of fair information practices. These would let customers see and correct their records and would prohibit practices like selling mailing lists without the customers' consent. There is pending legislation in the hopper that would require these practices.

Reforming health records

These poll results are part of a trend in which the public has shown increasing discomfort about the amount of computerized personal data being collected about them. They don't just fear that the collecting agency will misuse the information but that inadequate safeguards will grant access to others with even less noble motives.

As if to demonstrate that these worries are justified, shortly before the poll results were announced, the Internal Revenue Service reluctantly announced that 368 employees had taken advantage of "ineffective security controls" to snoop through individual returns at the agency's Atlanta office. Most of the errant employees had simply gone exploring through the files of friends, relatives, neighbors, and several celebrities. There were five employees, though, who had used their illegal access to create fraudulent returns and trigger undeserved tax refunds.

The widely asked question after the announcement: "If the IRS can't protect its files, what can we expect from others?" In fact, the employees beat a system that meets nearly all the applicable federal security standards. It controlled access using passwords and user profiles, and file privileges were limited according to job descriptions. The IRS said it discovered the improper activities by using software that could detect suspicious-use patterns.

Health care and privacy

Another major privacy concern was raised by President Clinton's proposal for health care reform. The proposal envisioned a computerized system of patient records doctors could use to record medical histories, improve diagnoses, prevent harmful drug interactions, and avoid unnecessary tests. It would be a networked system, linking various databases that contain this information. This system could do much to reduce costs, but it immediately raised another question: how well this data could be protected.

Then there is the story of the South Carolina junkyard owner who purchased the patient records of a retiring physician. He sold former patients copies of their records; later he sold the entire batch to a new medical practice. This was an extreme case, but privacy advocates worry about practices like these:

- Hospitals that hold free health clinics to acquire participants' names for their mailing lists
- Physicians and pharmacists who let market research firms examine their records

- Court rulings like one by the Ohio Supreme Court, which found nothing wrong in a police department's computerized collection of pharmacists' patient records

Developments like these have spurred calls for stronger laws to govern the use of personal information. With or without new legislation, there is every reason to expect that more people will express their privacy concerns in the form of lawsuits. I can give you even more reason to maintain a high level of security over the records you maintain: It's not only important to protect yourself against loss but you must also protect anyone whose records happen to be in your files.

The Current State of the Law

Only a few years ago, not too many states had statutes on their books that specifically governed computer crime. The federal government had none. That picture has since changed greatly. Nearly every state has a computer crime law on the books, and Congress has adopted at least three acts that relate to computer security.

The first federal computer crime law was adopted in 1984. This statute, part of a larger act, was primarily a measure designed to establish a precedent for computer security legislation. This law made it a felony for anyone to fraudulently gain access to a federally owned computer to retrieve classified information or data protected by federal privacy or credit disclosure laws. (While granting an individual access to his or her own credit files, the law restricts disclosure to third parties.) It also created misdemeanor offenses for unauthorized trespassing into government computers or computers containing information regulated under the privacy and credit laws. This act did nothing to outlaw unauthorized access to privately owned computers.

The broadest federal legislation was the 1986 act. This act protects "federal interest" computers against unauthorized access and similar activities. The federal interest of this act includes more than government-owned systems. A broad definition includes any computer used to process data for the government or its contractors. The law also can be extended to computer abuse that crosses state lines.

A third major act was the Computer Security Act of 1987. Its purpose was to establish a nondefense counterpart for existing laws that protect classified information. This act defines and protects "sensitive, but unclassified, information." The act makes each federal agency responsible for identifying its own computer systems that contain sensitive information. It gives the National Bureau of Standards the mission of developing standards and guidelines for federal computer systems security. These standards form the basis of federal policy for computer protection of unclassified information. The Department of Defense remains responsible for protecting national security information.

The 1986 act in detail

The 1986 Computer Fraud and Abuse Act is the federal act that most directly affects private users. It applies to federal interest computers including those used by the government or by regulated financial institutions, such as banks, savings institutions, and stockbrokers. An invasion of a computer may also attract federal interest if it is "one of two or more computers used in committing the offense, not all of which are located in the same state." If a computer falls under that definition, these activities are outlawed:

- Knowingly gaining unauthorized access, or exceeding authorized access, to obtain national security information. This offense is actionable if the offender has any reason to believe that information will be used to harm the United States or gain an advantage for a foreign nation.

- Intentionally gaining unauthorized access and obtaining personal information contained in the records of a financial institution, credit card issuer, or consumer reporting agency.

- Intentionally gaining unauthorized access to a federally owned computer.

- Intentionally gaining unauthorized access to a federal interest computer for fraudulent purposes. This section applies if the offender gains anything of value beyond the use of the computer itself.

- Intentionally gaining access to a federal interest computer and altering, destroying, or damaging information when the act causes certain specified losses. Among these losses are the potential impairment of medical diagnosis or treatment.

- Knowingly, and with intent to defraud, trafficking in any password used for computer access where this act affects interstate commerce or the computer is used by or for the federal government.

The law also specifies penalties for these offenses and gives primary enforcement responsibility to the Secret Service.

Noncomputer laws

Several other federal laws can also be used against computer crime. In fact, many authorities claim there is little need for new computer-specific legislation. Existing laws, properly applied, are enough to do the job. One of these is the federal wire fraud statute, which in essence forbids fraud by telephone. In one case prosecuted under that act, a management company with a federal contract began to suspect that an unauthorized person was using its time-sharing system and was about to download a copy of a system program. By tracing telephone calls and inserting a "spy" function into the system, investigators were led to a former employee who had once been responsible for the system's security. The ex-employee was indicted for using interstate telephone calls to defraud the company of its property rights in the system program. An appeals court rejected the defendant's contention that the government had violated federal wiretap laws and his constitutional right against unreasonable search and seizure.

State Laws on Computer Crime

Most states also now have laws that govern computer crime. Several states have adopted the model Consumer Systems Protection Act as their own; others have extended existing theft or fraud statutes to include these acts when committed by computer. These statutes and their interpretations are always subject to change, but the list of state statutes includes these:

Alabama. It is against the law to deliberately gain or attempt unauthorized access or to read or modify programs or data. It is also an offense to destroy this data or to disclose or use it. It is a felony to remove data in a way that causes physical injury.

Alaska. It is a criminal offense to gain unauthorized access to a computer or cause it to happen and to obtain information or enter false information with an intent to either damage or enhance a personal data record.

Arizona. A person can commit computer fraud in the second degree by intentionally gaining access to, altering, or damaging a computer system or its contents without authorization. The fraud is considered first degree if it is done with intent to defraud.

California. It is illegal to gain unauthorized access to a computer system. A violation also occurs if an unauthorized user should alter, damage, delete, or destroy the system or its contents. It is also illegal to use the system to commit fraud, extortion, or theft or to take copies of unauthorized materials or to use computer services without permission. Another offense is to disrupt computer services knowingly and without permission. The law applies to those who assist others in violating the act.

Colorado. It is a crime to knowingly use any computer system with the intent to defraud or to obtain money, property, or services by false pretenses. It is also illegal for anyone, knowingly and without authorization, to use, alter, damage, or destroy any computer.

Connecticut. State statute forbids "computer-related offenses," which include intentional unauthorized access, theft of computer services, and the interruption of computer services. The act must be intentional and can be excused if the individual reasonably believed he or she had authorized access. It is also a crime to misuse information from a computer system.

Delaware. It is a crime here to gain unauthorized access; to do so with the intent of obtaining unauthorized services, programs, or data; to transmit or copy data from another system or to alter or damage data. The statute provides grounds for civil suits as well as criminal penalties.

Florida. It is an offense to gain unauthorized access and a separate offense to intentionally make modifications, commit fraud, or obtain property. Also illegal: unauthorized modification or destruction of data, programs, or documents and theft of trade secrets.

Georgia. The law forbids deliberate unauthorized access to commit fraud or to obtain money, property, or services under false pretenses. It is also an offense to deliberately damage or destroy a computer or its contents or to try to do so. Reporting of known violations is mandatory.

Hawaii. It is an offense to gain access with the intent to defraud; to obtain money, property, or services through computer abuse; to gain access with the intent to obtain unauthorized information; or to introduce false information that causes damages.

Idaho. It is a crime to gain unauthorized access for fraudulent purposes or to obtain money, property, or services by fraud. It is also illegal to alter, damage, or destroy any computer asset, system, or network.

Illinois. It is against the law to use a computer to gain unauthorized access; alter or destroy programs or data without permission; knowingly use, alter, damage, or destroy a system in a deceptive scheme to obtain money property or services; or to use a computer fraudulently. Victims may collect civil damages.

Indiana. It is a felony to knowingly or intentionally alter or damage a computer program or data without permission. Computer trespass is an offense. It is also illegal to intentionally access a computer without the owner's consent.

Iowa. A person who gains access without authorization is guilty of a misdemeanor. Access that causes damage is a felony. A separate section forbids computer theft.

Kansas. This statute defines computer crime as willfully and without authorization, gaining or attempting to gain access to, and damaging, modifying, altering, destroying, copying, disclosing, or taking possession of a computer or its contents. It is also illegal to use a computer for fraudulent purposes or to exceed the limits of authorized use.

Kentucky. Unlawful access is an offense. It is also illegal to do so for fraudulent purposes or to alter, damage, or destroy a computer system. It is also illegal to attempt to do so.

Louisiana. The law forbids offenses against intellectual property or against computer equipment or supplies. It is also illegal to deny authorized users the full and effective use of their systems. A separate provision provides penalties for computer fraud.

Maine.   A theft of services statute has been interpreted to include computer services.

Maryland.   There are penalties for illegal access to a computer or network. A "continuing course of conduct" is defined as a single offense.

Massachusetts.   Larceny statutes have been amended to include computerized data and trade secrets.

Michigan.   It is an offense to gain unauthorized access for fraudulent purposes or to obtain money or property.

Minnesota.   It is a criminal offense to damage a computer system or software. It is also an offense to intentionally alter a computer system without authorization. Separate sections make it a crime to gain unauthorized access to obtain services or property or to deprive an owner of computer assets.

Mississippi.   It is illegal to commit computer fraud or to obtain money, property, or services by false or fraudulent conduct. There are also penalties for unauthorized computer use.

Missouri.   It is illegal to commit computer fraud or to obtain money, property, or services by false or fraudulent conduct. There are penalties for unauthorized computer use and for tampering with intellectual property.

Nevada.   It is an offense to unlawfully use or destroy a computer. Unlawful use includes modifying or copying programs or data. It is also illegal to misuse or destroy computer property or to unlawfully use or deny the use of a system or network. Penalties are more severe if these acts are committed with intent to defraud.

New Hampshire.   This state's laws generally forbid knowingly gaining unauthorized access to a computer system and theft, interruption, misuse, or unauthorized disclosure.

New Jersey.   There are no criminal statutes, but a victim of computer crime may seek civil remedies, including compensation for loss or damages.

New Mexico.   Unauthorized computer use is illegal. So is unauthorized access with fraudulent intent.

New York.   Unauthorized access is illegal when the computer is equipped with a means to deny unauthorized access. Other provisions forbid computer trespass, tampering, and altering or destroying data or programs. It is also an offense to duplicate computer-related materials without permission or to possess material that was improperly obtained.

North Carolina. It is a felony to gain unlawful access with intent to steal or defraud. There is an exception for educational testing materials. It is also illegal to deny access to an authorized user or to maliciously threaten to damage a computer or related materials.

North Dakota. It is illegal to commit computer fraud; it is a lesser offense to gain unauthorized access without further criminal intent.

Ohio. There are criminal penalties for unauthorized use or access, and for denying use and access to authorized users. A general theft statute may also apply to computer crime.

Oklahoma. Defined computer crimes include unauthorized access, modification, destruction, or theft. Proof that any of these acts were committed is prima facie evidence that they were done intentionally.

Oregon. Computer crimes include knowingly gaining unauthorized access for fraudulent purposes and alteration, destruction, or damage of computer property. Unauthorized access by itself is a lesser offense.

Pennsylvania. It is an offense to gain access with fraudulent intent or to alter or destroy property. It is also illegal to deliberately interfere with a system's operations or to damage or destroy any part of a system. It is also against the law to publish passwords, user names, and other identification codes.

Rhode Island. This state's statute forbids computer crime but provides little further definition. It specifically forbids access for fraudulent purposes or for alteration, theft, or destruction.

South Carolina. Computer hacking is specifically forbidden in this state. It is also illegal to gain unauthorized access or to alter, destroy, or damage computer resources.

South Dakota. This statute includes circular language that makes it an offense to use a computer unlawfully. The "use" in this provision includes unauthorized use, alteration, or destruction.

Tennessee. A computer crimes act provides penalties for fraudulent schemes and for intentional alteration or destruction.

Texas. It is an offense to breach a computer security system. This includes giving out a password or other identification. "Harmful access" is also an offense.

Utah. It is an offense to gain, or attempt, unauthorized access to a computer program and to damage, alter, destroy, disclose, or modify that program. It is also illegal to use a computer to gain unauthorized access to another computer. Also forbidden are fraudulent access and interference with authorized users.

Virginia. This state has a wide-ranging statute that forbids provisions for computerized fraud and theft. A trespassing offense includes removing data, even temporarily; causing a computer to malfunction; altering or erasing data; causing physical damage or injury; and making unauthorized copies. The law also has a privacy section that forbids obtaining information without permission. Also illegal: theft of computer services and trespassing with the intention to use a computer to cause physical injury. There is a 5-year statute of limitations. The law also provides a basis for civil action.

Washington. Access without authorization is treated as trespassing. Other crimes committed at the same time can also be prosecuted.

Wisconsin. It is an offense to modify, destroy, gain access, take possession, copy, or disclose restricted access codes or other restricted information or programs and supporting documents. Fraudulent action makes the violator subject to greater penalties. A violator can be sued, and the court can restrict the individual's future use of computers.

Wyoming. The law forbids actions against intellectual property, specifically including damage or modification to computers.

Now, About Your Responsibilities

Many laws now protect your computer resources, but probably just as many impose obligations and responsibilities. In fact, if there's no other reason to establish a sound computer security program, this side of the law provides one. The implication for computer owners of all kinds: Just as computer criminals can be held responsible for their acts, you can be held responsible for the ill effects of your own computer use. The possibilities are as infinite as the present and potential uses of the computer.

Computers are governed by a large, varied, and growing network of laws and regulations. In a report on computer-based national information systems, the Office of Technology Assessment (OTA) found 14 areas of law and regulation that somehow involve themselves with computerized information.

There actually are many more. The OTA cited only the regulations, statutes, and constitutional provisions that have widespread general application. If you're in a regulated industry like banking or insurance, there are many more requirements to be considered. Many demand that you maintain a secure computer system.

Take banking, for example. Your records must be accurate, customers' funds must be kept safe, and confidential information must be protected. All these requirements in turn impose a requirement that you maintain a secure computer system. If the computer doesn't maintain the necessary level of accuracy and security, you can't hope to do it.

In any business, you face not just a single law or policy but a haphazard collection of legal and regulatory requirements. Among the OTA's findings:

- There appears to be neither a strong trend nor sentiment at present among policy makers in favor of a uniform federal information policy that would encompass all the problems that could arise from the many possible uses of data systems.

- There are numerous laws and regulations, some overlapping and some potentially or actually conflicting, that directly and indirectly affect the users of information systems, the consumers of information services and the subjects of personal information data banks.

- There is a lack of congressional focus on information policy as such, and consequently the emerging issues are not being directly addressed.

One reason there is no central government policy on information is the First Amendment. It was written to guarantee free, unregulated exchanges of information and ideas. Any government action in this area carries the automatic threat that it could intrude on First Amendment rights.

Another reason is that no one has really tried to set up a central government policy. Various pieces of the computer security question are being studied in increasing detail. A few authorities have taken an overall view.

In his book *Why Information Systems Fail,* Henry Lucas reported on a detailed quantitative study of how information systems affect corporate decision making and on the problems connected with implementing a system. Other authors, like James Rule and Abby Mowshowitz, have done philosophical and historical analyses of automated information systems and their effects. Several other authors have concentrated on particular subjects. Privacy has been one of the most thoroughly studied: The National Academy of Sciences, the Department of Health and Human Services, a Privacy Protection Study Commission, and a series of congressional hearings have dealt with the subject.

What the rules require

The laws and policies that do exist tend to focus on the design, use, and operation of information systems. Their goal is to ensure that the system does what's expected of it, reliably, securely, efficiently, and within the expected time. Fortunately, these tend to be the same kinds of things that concern many users, too. The system designer who meets one set of needs probably will do well with the other at the same time.

These specific, often technical, types of requirements can have much broader significance. Take, for example, several incidents in which air defense computers have falsely detected apparent missile attacks.

Susan Nycum, the computer law expert who headed the OTA study committee, once listed three hypothetical incidents in which computers could be at fault: a midair plane crash caused by a fault in the control system, a subway train switched into the path of another oncoming train, and workers splattered with molten steel. A while later, Michael C. Gemignani, dean of science and humanities at Ball State University, suggested that Nycum's disasters weren't all that hypothetical. He listed several real events, including a near collision of two airplanes, a computer error that closed some nuclear plants, and a false alarm of nuclear war—all attributable in some way to computer failures.

All are cases in which the details of computer operations—the main subjects of laws and regulations—can literally have widespread impact. Areas of concern cited by the OTA include:

- The safety and reliability of the air traffic control system
- The reliability, security, and controllability of military command and control systems, existing and proposed
- The security of large-scale electronic funds transfer systems
- The reliability, accuracy, and responsiveness of the social security information systems

In each case, notes the OTA, we need secure, reliable operation—and face serious consequences if we fail.

Secondary effects

These are only the primary effects. By increasing the amount of information we collect, and by making it easier to collect, store, and use that information, the computer can create new areas of conflict. For example, the automated systems developed to store and spread criminal justice information can help bring about arrests and prevent crime. They also spur legitimate worries about the individual rights of honest citizens whose names find their way into these systems. The use of electronic mail means speedier communication—and less privacy for our mail.

If anything, we face more rules in the future that can demand secure, reliable computer systems. Issues like the suggestion for a national identification card to help spot illegal aliens, the spread of electronic fund transfer systems, and the drive for a national information highway all present new things to worry about—with the possibility of new laws and regulations to deal with these worries.

Where You Could Be Held Liable

A Vermont building contractor met with his banker to discuss future financing for his work. To his surprise, the banker pulled out a notice from a reputable credit reporting service. It said the contractor had recently filed for bankruptcy. Naturally, the contractor was granted no loan that day. He hadn't filed for bankruptcy, either.

The credit report was wrong. The bankruptcy petition had actually been filed by a former employee of the contractor. But before all that was straightened out, the incident had become a landmark Supreme Court case. The major issues: whether the credit bureau was guilty of libel, and the degree to which the erroneous report was protected by the First Amendment. The high court ruled that the First Amendment reserves its greatest protection only for comments on subjects of public concern. An erroneous credit report circulated only to about half a dozen of the service's clients hardly qualified for that protection.

This is only one example—although a leading one—of a problem that takes you beyond security precautions that are designed to protect your interests. You also can be held responsible for protecting the interests of the employees, customers, and other parties who are the subjects of your computer files.

There are many ways in which you could be held liable for the accuracy and reliability of your computer system, and the list seems to be growing all the time. For example:

- There was a rash of cases for a while in which innocent people were tossed into jail because a computerized criminal information system falsely identified them as wanted fugitives. Part of this problem has been laid to laxity by the police in using the computerized information; part of it also appears to lie in inaccurate information in the computer.

- A Louis Harris poll in 1984 showed that even then, more than three quarters of all adult Americans worried about computerized information that could invade their privacy.

- After a major New York bank installed an electronic mailing system that linked more than 500 personal computers, it found many employees afraid to use the system to its full capacity. They were afraid the system would not adequately protect the confidential and personal messages.

- Dr. Willis H. Ware, a Rand Corporation computer security expert, suggests that you should be held legally liable for contributory negligence should someone else be victimized because your computer is unlawfully entered.

More problems coming

In its report on national information systems, the Office of Technology Assessment expressed a common view: Things will get worse, not better. The OTA found these developing problems:

- New technology, and new applications of existing techniques, will produce new kinds of information files, all carrying the threat of misuse and faulty security.

- The individual who furnishes information for one purpose—a credit application, for example—can be surprised to see this information retrieved and used later by someone else for an entirely different purpose.

- Computers have made surveillance easier. The OTA group worried that even a legitimate use, such as screening for improper telephone calls by employees, could easily be abused. It could raise the issue of civil rights in a new form, the report suggested.

All these are current issues—yet the OTA was reporting on them as early as 1981.

Existing standards

The OTA has mainly been concerned with the impact of computers on the right of personal privacy. This is only one of many sets of ways in which you may be responsible to outside interests as well as your own. There are many federal laws and regulations that could impose this kind of external responsibility. Among them:

- *Securities and Exchange Commission regulations.* There have been several cases in which computer files have been misused to gain information for "insider trading" and other improper activities. The SEC also is officially worried about the use of computer files to influence decisions by stockholders.

- *The federal privacy act.* This legislation applies mainly to federal agencies, but it also suggests standards for private organizations to follow.

- *Banking laws and regulations.* These include Federal Reserve rules that govern all credit transactions and electronic fund transfers.

- *Regulations on foreign trade and other overseas activities.* A leading manufacturer recently paid $1.1 million in fines after one of its customers turned out to be an agent of the Soviet KGB. Exports of many computer products are restricted for national security reasons.

- *Product liability laws.* At the familiar bottom line: More and more people are doing more and more to demand that your computer is secure and reliable. And it's not just for your own protection.

What Are Your Legal Requirements?

Many security managers take a follow-the-leader approach. They tend to rely on the proven, established controls that everyone else uses, too. There are at least a couple of reasons for that. One is the simple fact that proven techniques are just that: proven techniques. Another is the legal duty of care. Whether you regard a programmer as a professional, a skilled technician, or something else, the work will be judged against the prevailing practices in the field. The obvious safe course is to let these practices prevail in your own work, too.

You can be held liable for the losses another party suffers because of an act of malice on your part or because of negligence in recklessly disregarding the consequences of what you do. The average careful person isn't likely to have either of these problems. The real legal danger for most people is from failing to take due care for the interests of the other party. In such a case, the first requirement is that you observe the accepted standards of your field. That alone may not be enough, though. The computer industry's established practices may form an initial frame of reference against which to judge your own efforts to maintain accuracy and security, but the circumstances may demand that you go even further. In fact, you can learn something from an unfortunate tugboat captain.

The captain's story goes back to 1928 when his tug, the *T.J. Hooper,* ran into a storm while towing a string of barges along the New Jersey coast. Two of the barges sank, and before this disaster at sea had run its course, it had become a landmark court case.

In a ruling by the famed federal judge Learned Hand, the tug's owners were held responsible for the loss because they had failed to put a weather radio aboard the *Hooper.* The weather radio was a new high-tech device in 1928, but a few ship owners had installed them. Several skippers who heard the weather reports the day before the storm prudently headed for port while the *Hooper* sailed blindly into disaster.

It didn't matter, said Judge Hand, that the weather radio was an innovative device and its use was not yet an established industry practice. "A whole calling may have unduly lagged in the adoption of new and available devices," said the judge, "and there are precautions so imperative that even their universal disregard will not excuse their omission." That ruling has strong implications for people who work with today's innovative technology. It's not enough just to observe standard practice if there is some further step you could take to avoid the damage.

Providing a bailout

Judge Hand did recognize that we can't always predict and prevent every possible problem. It is our responsibility, though, to provide some form of relief from the unexpected. In nautical terms, he put it this way:

> We need not hold that a barge is necessarily unseaworthy because she leaks in a gale; the heaving and straining of the seams will often probe weak spots which no diligence can discover. It is, however, just against this possibility that pumps are necessary.

Debugging a program is much like building a ship. There are times that in spite of your best efforts you won't discover a weak timber or a program bug until it turns up under the stress of long-term service. Your duty is to do your best to find and correct the weak spots before they cause trouble. It is also often your duty to stand behind your product when the weak spots do appear—in other words, to give your customers some pumps.

What kind of care is due?

The kind of care you owe the other party depends on the circumstances, and there are very few firm guidelines. In a case similar to the *Hooper* incident, it was argued that an airline should have installed radar to prevent a collision. That was in 1948, and the court rejected the argument that a commercially feasible radar system had not yet been developed.

In 1977, another airline was held responsible for the loss suffered by a bank in a robbery of the airline's storage room. The airline had taken the standard precautions of posting an armed guard in front of a locked, unmarked door, but the court ruled that taking those industry-standard measures was not enough to relieve it of responsibility.

In the computer field

The requirements are even less clear in applying the legal concept of due care to computer services. One point is reasonably well established: The basic requirement of due care doesn't change just because a computer is involved. In other words, a computer error is no excuse.

For example, a finance company computer repeatedly cranked out notices that a customer's car payments were past due. The system automatically forwarded these notices to the customer. Twice, the customer came in to display canceled checks for the disputed payments, but the computer continued to report them as overdue. Finally, on the basis of the computer reports, the finance company repossessed the car. When the shocked customer sued for damages, the company claimed it was the equally innocent victim of a computer error. The court didn't buy it:

> [The finance company] explains that this whole incident occurred because of a mistake by a computer. Men feed data into a computer, and men interpret the answer the computer spews forth. In this computerized age, the law must require that men in the use of computerized data regard those with whom they are dealing as more important than a perforation on a card. Trust in the infallibility of a computer is hardly a defense when the opportunity to avoid the error is as apparent and repeated as was here presented.

"It is clear," says SRI International commenting on this decision, "that excessive reliance on computer data without proper safeguards to ensure the reliability and accuracy of the information may constitute the failure to exercise due care, and in some cases may even result in the award of punitive damages," above those the courts grant to cover the actual loss.

Professional standard?

SRI feels that at a minimum "there is clearly a duty to exercise reasonable care in using computers." Depending on the contract terms involved, "a higher standard of care may be required of suppliers of computer services." If programmers and other experts offer professional services to their clients, they may also be held to professional standards of care and performance.

This point is drawn from one of the many cases in which an installed computer and program failed to do the job its buyer expected. The buyer argued that from the time the system was installed, through the unsuccessful debugging process, and until the parties broke off their relationship that the vendor was in the role of a professional, much like a physician or lawyer. And as a professional, the customer continued, the vendor was guilty of malpractice. The court rejected that argument, as several other courts also have done. As SRI points out, though, the decision actually was a refusal to acknowledge a professional relationship under the circumstances of this particular case. Different facts could produce a different decision.

Goods or services?

Being treated as a professional could have its advantages. It is less likely you would be held to strict liability for losses that are not necessarily your fault. The strict liability doctrine has been developed primarily for physical goods. Under the traditional legal approach, it would not apply to work you do under a contract for professional services.

There are two main problems here. First, legal experts strongly disagree about whether data processing should be treated as goods or services. Second, traditional legal approaches don't always lend themselves very well to new technology. SRI suggests a third approach in which the decision is not automatic: Make an ad hoc decision in each case whether it involves sales or services and, thus, what kind of liability there might be.

Talk it over

None of this offers firm guidelines to the security manager who would rather avoid the fine details by keeping the case out of court in the first place. There is one thing, though, that you can do to help stay out of this legal maze: Do everything you can to make sure your information is accurate and your product reliable. Don't settle for the standard, conventional approaches. If there is something you can do to improve your performance, do it.

> **Action item**   Have a serious talk with a knowledgeable attorney about the types of products or services you offer, the language of your contracts, and your resulting status under the various liability laws. There are many choices to be made, and most of them are tradeoffs. Make sure you understand exactly what you would gain or lose from each option.

Your responsibility for accuracy

Regardless of the standards of care and liability to which you are held, one thing is clear: You must do your best to make sure any information that comes from your computer is accurate, before you rely on that information.

The mistaken repossession was a case in point. Another example is found in the periodic reports required under federal securities laws. The company's management has a duty to maintain accurate records, and anyone else has a duty to verify the information that management supplies.

Various provisions of securities laws impose liability for making false or misleading statements or for leaving out significant information. A company reporting to SEC has a legal duty to maintain accurate records and prepare accurate reports from them. Many other laws also require accurate record keeping. For example, after an embezzlement cost a bank $21.3 million, a stockholder in the bank filed suit. The suit claimed, in part, that management had failed to institute internal controls that were required by law—and might have prevented the loss.

Certainly, you should maintain a control system that makes sure your computer produces accurate and reliable information. These include controls on who can gain access to the computer and on who can use or alter the information stored inside. Audit trails should be established to create written evidence of who made what transaction. SRI has this advice: "Electronic record keeping systems are only as trustworthy as the people who use them, and it is imperative that a security system be established to help preclude unauthorized persons from gaining access to the computer or altering information in the system."

The Law and Liability

Some insurance companies now offer what they call *computer malpractice policies*. Their purpose is to protect computer owners from claims that arise from computer-created errors. Actually, says Boston attorney Robert P. Bigelow, "malpractice is a fancy term for a particular kind of negligence." Strictly speaking, he explains, anyone who acts negligently in building, selling, or programming a computer could potentially be held liable for any financial or physical losses that occur when the system doesn't work the way it should.

So far, says Bigelow, computer errors have produced only a few negligence suits and even fewer successful ones. That's primarily because negligence is hard to prove. Still, in this litigation-conscious era, many computer users do worry about the risks they face from computer malfunctions. After all, an error could put a company out of business, and if the error was due to your mistake, the resulting lawsuit could put you out of business.

And when there's a fear of such large losses, the insurance industry will not be far behind, offering policies against those losses. The malpractice policies now being offered are in addition to the general liability policies most companies carry. They're designed to protect against risks that can't easily be seen or anticipated.

For example, a software company might sell a program that not only fails to work properly but destroys some of the user's vital data in the process. If the user can demonstrate a serious loss and prove that the software supplier was negligent, the supplier might have to pay for such things as the cost of replacing the lost data and the user's financial problems while the information was not available.

Suits like this might become more common, many experts believe, as more and more small businesses turn to personal computers to manage their finances. Unlike the traditional corporate computer buyer who has staff experts to help decide on mainframe purchases, the small-business owner tends to rely heavily on the promises made by computer and software sellers. Judges also tend to be more sympathetic to smaller users.

Protecting yourself against liability and other legal problems is a major part of computer security, and it's a part you should not ignore. Security isn't just a matter of protecting yourself from the misdeeds of outsiders or even of your own employees and associates. To err is human, and one major part of your security program should be to protect yourself from your own mistakes. It's also important to protect yourself from other kinds of legal liability, like invading someone's privacy or violating a constitutional right.

A complete computer security program must consider every kind of loss you might suffer. A lawsuit may be unlikely, but should it come—and should you lose—it could be a serious loss. Guard against this kind of loss just as strongly as you would protect yourself from other kinds of losses.

Learning from mistakes

In 1977, a mortgage company that held a $28,000 note found the debt wiped out by the Arkansas Supreme Court. Due to a computer error in calculating the payments, the company had inadvertently charged an illegally high rate of interest. It was an honest mistake, but the company still was penalized.

This is just one of many ways in which a computer and its software can malfunction, often with disastrous results. Take a typical situation in which a programmer makes an error. The programmer is reasonably skilled and has no intention of causing any harm, and any warranty on the program has elapsed by the time the damage is done. Even under these reasonably favorable circumstances, computer lawyer Susan Nycum lists at least five different ways the programmer or the employer could be held liable for the results: express and implied warranties, third-party contracts, negligence, and strict liability.

Express warranties.   The company that agrees to supply a program or service signs a contract with the user. In microcomputer practice, the contract usually is a license agreement that spells out the conditions under which the customer may use the program. It also usually specifies the terms under which the company offers a warranty on the product.

Such warranties usually have stated limits. They are valid only for 90 days, or some other time period, and they are typically limited to replacing the defective program. The company will voluntarily accept no liability for any ill effects on the user's software or business—consequential damages in legal terms. Usually, says Nycum, provisions like this are enough to protect the company from consequential damages, but that may not always be the case.

In particular, she says, you could be held liable for any promises you make, or even suggest, outside the contract. For example, if your advertising suggests a certain level of performance, your product had better provide it. You also could be held liable if the bug slipped through a quality control program that wasn't up to normal standards. In circumstances like these, the company could even be held liable for damages to someone other than the customer.

Implied warranties. Not all warranties are written into contracts. The law also imposes implied warranties to meet the interests of public policies. There are two major types of implied warranties:

- *Merchantability*. The program should be suitable for the general types of purposes for which computer programs normally are used.

- *Fitness*. The program also should be suitable for the customer's specific intended use.

You can disclaim these warranties in the contract, a tactic that sometimes works—and sometimes doesn't. State laws vary on this subject. You also might avoid liability if the customer makes a belated complaint, misuses the program, is also guilty of negligence, or voluntarily assumes the risk of an accident.

Third-party contracts. You might find yourself liable to someone other than your customer. If a third party suffers loss due to a fault in your program, that party might have the right to sue. The basis of such a suit would be an argument that the program really was written for the third party's benefit.

Nycum feels few third-party suits could succeed, though, unless the program actually was written to be used by the third party. What this means in practice, though, is that if you are sued, it probably will be for some other reason.

Negligence. This isn't based on any kind of contract. The basic question is simply this: Did you do anything—or fail to do anything—that caused harm to someone else? If so, you can be liable for that harm. On the other hand, if you can demonstrate that the harm came from some other source—a power surge, perhaps, or bad input by the customer—you can just as easily avoid liability.

This is based on an old common law theory: You owe your customer a certain minimal duty of care. Just what that duty might be depends on the circumstances. Most likely, says Nycum, the programmer will be held to a standard of care typical of the profession—doing what most members of the profession would do. Or, since programmers lack full recognition as professionals, the standard might be that of a trained expert. If so, the programmers might find themselves in much the same position as accountants, for whom there are established limits to their liability to third parties.

Another possible standard: In some circumstances where a computer could cause airplanes to collide or nuclear plants to go out of control, the courts might consider the program to be an inherently dangerous instrument. If so, its use would require the highest possible degree of care. Nycum also classes this idea as unlikely. More realistically, she says, such a program would probably be treated like a painter's scaffold: dangerous only when it's improperly built or used.

Strict liability. This is a legal catch-all under which you could be held liable even after exercising all possible care. While this may sound unfair on the surface, it is based on three sound principles:

- If you make a product, you're in a better position than anyone else to reduce any hazards, and you should be given every possible incentive to do so.

- Some problems can't be completely avoided. In that case, you can distribute the cost of the necessary insurance among all your customers.

- A person who is seriously injured isn't always able to prove negligence by the responsible party.

This is the theoretical foundation of a modern legal phenomenon: the product liability suit. The idea is that if you are held strictly liable for the performance of your product, you'll make good use of your unique ability to avoid errors, and you'll take out insurance on any liability you can't absolutely prevent. You'll also be expected to warn your customers of any such remaining hazards.

There's also a legal precedent for imposing liability for defective design, and a faulty program easily could be considered a bad design.

Avoiding liability

The standard way to reduce your liability for a defective product is to include a disclaimer in the contract. Talk with your attorney about the right language for your particular needs, but a typical disclaimer has three major clauses that read something like this:

> The supplier does not make any express or implied warranties, including but not limited to the implied warranties of merchantability and fitness for a particular purpose. In no event will the supplier be liable for consequential damages, even if the supplier has been advised of the possibility of such damages.
>
> The customer agrees that the supplier's liability hereunder for damages, regardless of the form of action, shall not exceed the total amount paid for the product. This shall be the customer's exclusive remedy.
>
> There are no understandings, agreements, representations, or warranties, express or implied (including any regarding the merchantability or fitness for a

particular purpose), not specified herein, respecting this contract or equipment hereunder. This contract states the entire obligation of seller in connection with this transaction.

At some time or other, lawyers point out, all of these typical clauses have saved someone's hide. The first tries to limit the extent of any warranty the company might offer. Its main object is to disclaim any warranties other than those the supplier has specifically ordered.

In the second provision, the customer agrees to accept a limit on the amount of damages should the program prove faulty. In this case, the limit is to refund the price of the program.

The third clause makes the point that if there is any agreement between the seller and the buyer, it has been written into the contract. Verbal agreements and, most important, verbal disagreements don't count.

Clauses like these work in some cases—and are useless in others. In one of the first court cases to involve a computer warranty, a Pennsylvania automobile dealer contracted with a major computer firm for both the hardware and software to process the dealer's business records.

The system was installed with great hopes, and the dealer canceled its contract with the timesharing service it had been using. A year later, though, the new system still wasn't working right. The supplier's representatives still were working hard and earnestly trying to solve the problems, but the dealer was experiencing serious problems of his own. He rejected the machine and sued for damages.

Although the contract included most of the standard disclaimers, the court made a substantial damage award. The basis of its ruling was that the dealer never had accepted delivery of the computer. The court also held the supplier to a verbal promise, not included in the contract, that it would provide programming services to the dealer.

One conventional legal response to this decision was that the supplier should have included in the written contract a section that disclaims any oral promises that might have been made. A more reasonable view would be not to make any promises you aren't prepared to keep. A similar approach to the total problem of liability would be this: Provide the necessary contract disclaimers—they might help and can't hurt. More important, do everything you can to make sure your products work properly.

How to Protect Privacy

Several years ago, the Internal Revenue Service decided it had a problem. It felt, with justification, that self-employed individuals are major sources of tax losses because they don't report their full incomes. One big reason for the problem is that none of the established income-reporting systems, such as the W-2 forms or the information returns on other kinds of income, give the IRS an adequate way to check the tax returns against other income reports.

Seeking to fill this gap, the IRS launched several plans. In one, the agency purchased commercial mailing lists targeted at high-income recipients and began to check the returns of people on the mailing lists. In another, it asked state licensing agencies to report on people who take out occupational licenses or register expensive cars. The IRS also would be part of a plan under which government agencies would have almost unlimited instant access to the computerized records of seven major credit bureaus.

These plans ran into strong opposition. To a large extent, the opposition was based on the general idea that the government should not have unrestricted access to information about our private lives. It stems from abuses in the Vietnam era, when it became apparent that just the collection of personal information could inhibit the free expression of unpopular views.

A right to privacy

A right to personal privacy appears nowhere in the Bill of Rights or anywhere else in the Constitution, but the Supreme Court ruled in 1965 that it does exist. It's inherent in other specified rights, including the First Amendment's right to free expression. There is legitimate reason for concern that the unrestricted collection and use of personal information could run afoul of the Constitution, and not just where the IRS is concerned.

That's only one dimension of the problem. Robert Ellis Smith, editor of the *Privacy Times*, strongly opposes the widespread use of credit bureau reports. Invasion of privacy is a major concern, of course. But what he calls the "most shocking aspect" of the plan is that the credit-reporting business "has a poor reputation for maintaining the accuracy of its information."

The mailing list plan encountered similar opposition, and it came from members of the mailing list industry itself. The names that appear on a high-income mailing list are mostly those of high-income people, industry members pointed out, but the selection process is similar to the statistical technique used in public opinion polling: It includes a known margin of error.

That means many of the names are there by mistake, the list managers said. The lists are considered accurate enough for commercial purposes, but the managers expressed doubt that they should be used in tax law enforcement. Many innocent people could find themselves facing IRS investigations.

This issue was hotly debated for a while and has since faded away. Still, it illustrates two separate but related burdens on anyone who maintains computerized information about private individuals. You must:

- Be careful that you do not improperly invade your subjects' privacy in collecting, using, or spreading your information. This includes protecting it from unauthorized access.

- Take care that any information you publish is accurate. At the extreme end of this process there could be a libel suit.

Long-standing issues

Problems of personal privacy existed long before the computer. Parties to the debates have raised a multitude of issues, including these:

- *Government intrusion.* The extent to which the government can intrude—physically or electronically—in the lives of individuals. This was the subject of the 1965 Supreme Court decision. It affirmed the right of married couples to practice birth control, overturning a Connecticut statute that prohibited it. It is also a very current issue. The main line of objection to Clipper Chip encryption is that it would leave an opening for the government to eavesdrop on private transmissions.

- *Communication surveillance.* The government's right to intercept communication by reading mail and monitoring telegraph traffic, by wiretapping telephone conversations or by using "mail covers" to keep records of who sends letters to whom. This issue is becoming more important with the development of new computerized communication systems.

- *First Amendment rights.* The right to a free, uninhibited exchange of ideas.

- *Privileged communication.* The traditional rights of professionals to receive personal information in confidence, and the less well established right of news reporters to withhold the identities of their sources.

The OTA committee observed after it compiled this list, "These examples not only convey the historical nature of privacy debates but also the extraordinary range of issues encompassed by the term."

Where computers are concerned, the range hasn't been quite as broad. The issue of the government's use of information in private files has only recently been raised. Before that, the main discussion was concerned with private use of the same computerized collections.

Congress has considered several other privacy issues in the last few years. They include wiretapping, psychological testing of government employees, and the use of lie detectors. The problem has become so large that early in 1984, a subcommittee of the House Committee on Science and Technology recommended that a national commission be established to examine it. As proposed, the commission would "examine the vast set of interrelated issues surrounding the security and privacy of computer/communications systems, especially those that transcend either the jurisdictional boundaries of federal, state and local government agencies or public and private sector interests."

Legal limits on data collection

In an attempt to limit the amount of data collected by government agencies, Congress specified in its 1974 Privacy Act that any collected data must be "relevant" to the reasons for which it is collected. That's proven to be a weak provision. A study commission found that government data collection decreased after the law took effect, but not by very much.

A dispute between the Labor Department and a major insurance company brought private information collections sharply into the picture. Labor was investigating possible charges that the company had engaged in discriminatory hiring. As evidence, it requested the company's computerized personnel records. Without the computerized files, Labor probably would never have made such a sweeping request. The task of analyzing the same information on paper records would have been nearly impossible.

In a similar fashion, the computer has added new elements to the overall privacy debate. It once was assumed that the information collected about an individual was given up voluntarily and usually in exchange for some reciprocal benefit. Filling out a loan application in order to get the credit is a classic example. More recently, though, privacy experts have been concerned with information collected without the subject's knowledge. The computer makes it easier to store, analyze, and trade this kind of information. The systems that can spread information about an individual also have a particular capacity to spread misinformation.

The mailing list problem

The mailing list is an example of how things have changed. At one time it was considered a reasonably benign type of information collection. At worst it did no harm. Now, however, the picture is different. Even without the IRS program, private users have put pressure on mailing list suppliers for a greater degree of selectivity. They want specialized lists of high-income people, for example. In response, list making has become more sophisticated.

A political solicitation list may contain information about a person's memberships, religious beliefs, charitable contributions, income, and support for various causes. A modern political organization could use such information to predict your likelihood to support a certain candidate or issue. A targeted mailing list could be prepared accordingly.

Controls lacking

As the OTA committee noted, even before the IRS episode:

> Such personal information, which is often collected without the consent of the subject through the exchange or purchase of mailing lists...assumes the character of a political dossier. It is not clear that existing controls, either over the use of such data systems for purposes beyond computing mailing lists or over the original collection of the information, are adequate to deal with the increasing capability modern technology offers to collect data and compile such lists.

Advancing computer technology will expand this kind of information collection, the OTA group predicted:

> Point of sale systems are an example of this trend. A sale made at a store and recorded through a terminal will collect a variety of information about a customer, such as what was purchased, the exact time and location of the transaction and possibly the customer's financial status. This will not only be recorded at the bank...but may also be retained by the store management for its own use, or perhaps even sold to third parties.

Lost forever

Once information reaches this open market stage, there are few controls over its further distribution and use—or misuse. Credit bureaus and mailing list operators sell information. Once it has been sold, they have no control over how it is used. Managers of large corporate information systems face the same kind of problem, particularly if many employees or even outside users have access to the data.

The problem is not just adequate security against unauthorized use but adequate control of authorized use. Your security system must be concerned with who is authorized to use your data and what uses they may make of it. The challenge will grow as we develop data communication systems with easy access over internal communication lines. A local area network, one of the simplest and most centralized forms of data communication, still offers multiple-user access to large amounts of data—exactly what such a system is designed to do. Your system should be as effective against these authorized users as it is against unauthorized raiders.

Other rights at stake

Privacy is just one of the individual rights a computer security manager may have to protect. The government currently faces a serious First Amendment question of how and whether to regulate new electronic means of communication: The relative freedom of print media or the regulated atmosphere of broadcasting and communication utilities like telephone and telegraph companies, or the Postal Service.

The AT&T breakup, and all the confusion it brought, actually started with a simple idea: A company that has a monopoly on the means to carry information should not also be in the business of originating that information. There's too much danger that it would favor its own information sources and would block transmission of competitors' data. That idea obviously has been imperfectly put into practice, but it is a major part of the First Amendment debate.

Also important to a data security manager is the Fourth Amendment, which forbids unreasonable search and seizure. The OTA group found three major problem areas here:

- The use of personal and statistical data contained in automated information systems as a justification for search and seizure. For example, a police officer might feed the known characteristics of a suspect into a database full of personal information on a great many people. The system then would provide a list of people who have those characteristics.

- The seizure of information as personal property, particularly when it appears in electronic form.

- The use of automated information systems as a tool for search-and-seizure operations.

Regulating computers

The AT&T case represents an attempt by the courts and the Federal Communications Commission to draw a line between two classes: services and technology. The FCC decided communication services should continue to be regulated but the technology to originate and process information should not. It was a good idea in theory, regardless of its outcome in practice.

That's part of the constitutional problem, of course, but it also relates to the regulatory problems the computer can create both for the government and for you.

Banking presents at least two regulatory challenges. Some large banks have developed elaborate data processing systems to support their operations. They've found that the sale of their systems and services to smaller banks can be very profitable sidelines. In the banks' view, of course, selling such services is a natural extension of their normal banking activities. Others take a much different view: that the big banks are using their massive financial resources to enter an entirely new field, in competition, of course, with the bureaus.

An allied problem is that of branch banking. Computers and electronic communication systems are breaking down many of the barriers that long have restricted the spread of branch banks and have served as barriers to interstate banking. An electronic fund transfer can speed a transaction to a distant central office before you can say, "This bleeping machine didn't return my card."

The rapidly growing electronic mail services present even more problems. There's the natural danger of unauthorized access, but even authorized access raises some legal problems. For example, the "mail cover" in which investigators check the envelope but not the contents has been accepted as an activity that requires no search warrant. In electronic mail, though, there's no real distinction between the "inside" and the "outside" of the letter.

What Can You Do?

Computers are now being bought by people who know little or nothing about how to use them. A computer isn't just a household appliance you can plug in and use right away. The computer is really a huge bank of tiny switches that are either on or off. The ways in which the program and the user manipulate these switches determine how the computer does its work. An error at any point in the process can cause the system to go haywire.

Sometimes the crisis is due to an error by the operator. At others it might be an outside factor like a power failure. At still others, the problem might be with the computer or the program. There are four main points at which you can introduce an error into a program:

- When the basic algorithm, or program structure, is created
- When the programmer codes the algorithm into a high-level language like C or BASIC

- When the compiler or interpreter translates the programmer's work into machine language

- When the machine language program actually operates the computer's internal switches

In other words, whatever can go wrong, will (Murphy's law). The sheer numbers of codes, instructions, and switches present a multitude of possibilities for error.

Even this list doesn't exhaust the possibilities for a computer-connected lawsuit. Many people have found themselves in court when their products didn't do what the customers expected. An overstated sales pitch is one way to make a sale that leads to the courtroom, but customers can be disappointed in many more subtle ways. For example, a program's practice in rounding off figures could mean many dollars to some users. Or the program may work properly but take an unacceptable length of time to do it.

Prevention: The best policy

The first and best way to avoid this situation is to do everything within your power to make sure a program or file you maintain is efficient and bug free. Plan it well, and test it thoroughly. There's no test that can give ironclad assurance that it will catch all the bugs. It can't hurt, though, to be able to show that you met all the expected standards for program testing. It can hurt even less if you've exceeded them.

The second method—and next to the best—is to include the right language in your customer contracts. A contract disclaimer can't turn falsehood into truth, or vice versa, but it can help guard against those risks for which you have no other means of protection.

A third method: Communicate with your customers and employees. Make sure you understand what they expect of you and that they understand what you can do. In particular, avoid overzealous sales pitches that can create false expectations.

If you are selling a computer-related product or service, communication also is important after the sale. If something does go wrong, do your best to reach a mutual settlement before someone takes the case to court.

Protecting yourself from liability problems is much like protecting yourself from any other kind of computer security problem. In protecting your own interests, you also do a lot to protect the people whose names, data, and interests are represented in your files.

However, good security is only a start. It isn't enough to protect your files from errors and misuse caused by someone else's improper activities. You also must protect yourself and others from errors that are not due to someone's misuse. To meet your full legal and moral responsibilities to the outside world, you do your best to make sure the system is accurate and reliable under any circumstances you might encounter.

Prevention through maintenance

You probably appreciate the value of a sound preventive maintenance program for your major mechanical and electrical equipment. Well-scheduled prevention can catch small problems before they grow into big emergencies. The same preventive attitude should be the first step toward a reliable computer system. Physical security and environmental controls have been discussed earlier as basic security tactics. They can be valuable for preventing liability problems as well.

You've no doubt heard—perhaps you have first-hand knowledge—of how a misplaced speck of dust can mess up a floppy disk or cause a hard disk to crash. Its effects on mainframe disks can be just about the same—but usually larger. It stands to reason that dust control should be one of the first items on any preventive maintenance program for computer media. Good housekeeping thus becomes an element of a computer security program. It's doubly important if there's a hard disk in the picture. The dreaded head crash that destroys 10 kilobytes at a single blow can usually be avoided simply with good maintenance.

Regular physical checkups are important to your media. If you find dust, tears, or rough edges, copy the contents to a sound disk or tape—immediately if not sooner. Check the media storage, too. Make sure your disks and tapes are protected from dirt, magnetic fields, and other hazards.

One thing you might not have thought of: Clean out your disk boxes and other storage containers. Their object is to keep dust out. But dust and other bits of debris often find their way inside anyway. A regular cleaning can prevent some major damage.

A healthy environment

Beyond that, filters in the ventilating system and similar measures can help reduce the risk. While you're at it, establish and enforce the necessary rules to keep food and drink out of the computer room—and out of the computer.

These are examples of environmental controls that are necessary to your computers' welfare and reliability. Cooling, ventilating, and electrical systems designed specifically for computer use may cost more than their household or office counterparts, but they also must perform better and more reliably. A shutdown in the air-conditioning could be uncomfortable to you. It could be devastating to your computer.

That's exactly what happened when the cooling system failed at a major airline's computer reservation system. The computers shut down and took millions of dollars worth of business with them. At least two securities exchanges have suffered major losses for similar reasons.

Your computer may not handle the major volumes that these enterprises require, but your resources are valuable to you. Compare that value closely with the cost of proper environmental controls. Even short of a computer that goes down like the *Titanic,* you could suffer from rust, corrosion, condensation, deteriorated media, and premature failure of your circuit boards.

The air-conditioning system that's adequate for personal comfort may not be adequate for your computers. Check to make sure it has the capacity and reliability you need. Look for durable components, selected for long life, mounted in shock-resistant enclosures that open easily for service access. Look for similar features in other building equipment.

Then let the computer help protect itself. Set it up to monitor the state of its environment and to turn the right switches or sound an alarm when things go wrong.

A

Eighty-Two
Control Tactics Analyzed

A security program is really an organized collection of tactics, tailored to the organization's vulnerable areas, the value of the resources to be protected, and the cost of implementing each measure.

Earlier chapters have included lists of possible tactics, organized by function and whether they should be treated as baseline or selective measures. This appendix describes these tactics in detail.

You cannot possibly adopt all 82 of these security measures. Some will not fit your needs, and many of those that do fit will not be cost-effective. You should select those that are best for your needs using the baseline system: plan to adopt baseline measures unless there is a valid reason not to do so and adopt those selective measures that are suited to your needs.

This list is taken from *Computer Security Techniques,* a report prepared for the Justice Department by SRI International. Table A.1 is a guide to help you understand the listings.

Alternative Power Supply

Objective Avoid destruction of assets and business interruption.

Description A power supply independent of the public utility source for uninterrupted service is provided by batteries charged from public utility power providing a few minutes of independent power or by an independent power source such as a diesel generator for long durations. An alternative source of energy, such as a diesel generator without batteries but with adequate power quality regulators, can be used when uninterrupted service is not important, but long durations of outage are harmful.

This control is needed only where power is sufficiently unreliable relative to the seriousness of computer failure or unavailability. The location, environment control, and access security are important to ensure integrity of the alternative power equipment and fuel. Periodic full tests are important for maintenance. Some organizations use the independent source as the primary supply and the public utility as a backup. One organiza-

TABLE A.1   Guide for the Listings

Item	Description
Control title	A descriptive name for the control.
Objective	Control objective stating the type of adversity dealt with.
Description	A description of the ideal control function based on observations at field sites.
Variables	Varying specifications to be determined in particular cases.
Strengths	The particular positive values of the control in field sites.
Weaknesses	Possible undesirable effects of the control, including the creation of additional vulnerabilities or failure to reduce target vulnerabilities.
How to audit	Role of the auditor in testing and reporting the effectiveness of the control.
Purpose	Which security functions are performed, such as deterrence, detection, prevention, or recovery.
Control area	The particular area of the computing environment in which the control is implemented.
Mode	The type of control and the way in which it is implemented.
Area of responsibility	Functional activity that has responsibility and accountability for the assets the control protects.
Cost	Cost of the control and its operation, on a scale of low, medium, and high. A low-cost control probably would not appear as a line item in an annual budget. A medium-cost control would be a line item, and a high-cost control would have a material effect on a budget.
Principles of note	Control principles exemplified by this item.

tion has located a new computer center at a site between two public electric power grids and obtains power alternatively from both to reduce the likelihood of public power failure.

Variables   Type and size of alternative supply, switching equipment, location of equipment and fuel, computing equipment and facilities to be supported, testing frequency.

Strengths   Electrical damage to computer equipment and loss of data can be prevented with uninterrupted power supplies.

Weaknesses   The cost can be prohibitive for large systems.

How to Audit   Auditors should require a demonstration of alternative supply use. An independent power engineer should be called in for periodic inspections. Fuel supplies should be checked periodically for supply levels, quality, and safety.

Purpose   Recovery

Control Area   Computer system

Mode   Hardware

Area of Responsibility   Computer security

Cost   High

Principles of Note Limit of dependence on other mechanisms.

Areas Where Smoking and Eating Are Prohibited

Objective Avoid destruction of assets and business interruption.

Description Smoking and eating are not permitted in computer equipment areas. Prevention requires signs, written policy, enforcement, and penalties rigorously applied. In addition, personal grooming to eliminate long hair and loose clothing should be voluntarily practiced to avoid interference with moving parts of peripheral equipment and personal injury.

Variables Designated areas, signs, policy.

Strengths In addition to obvious benefits, prevents smoke detection and water detection alarms from being triggered unnecessarily; also increases worker productivity somewhat.

Weaknesses Poses an inconvenience for employees; might require the establishment of a separate lounge area. If lounge area must be outside the security perimeter around the computer room, physical access to the computer room might be compromised. Heavy smokers might not be able to work in this environment. Disciplinary measures will need to be defined and enforced.

How to Audit Observation that this policy is actually being followed.

Purpose Prevention

Control Area Computer center

Mode Policy

Area of Responsibility Operations

Cost Low

Principles of Note Acceptance by personnel.

Assets Accountability Assignment

Objective Prevent asset responsibility loss.

Description Specific data producers, computer users, and computer center staff are assigned explicit ownership or custodial accountability and usage rights for all data, data handling and processing capability, controls, and computer programs. This can be done by establishing policy; establishing meaning of ownership, usage, and custodianship; and requiring that forms be completed and logs made designating and recording such accountability for data and programs and copies of them in all locations and for specified times. For example, one organization has a set of booklets for each data activity area stating ownership, usage, custodial, and control requirements. Another organization has this information as part of its policy manual.

Variables Owners, users, custodians, data, programs, responsibilities, accountability, sanctions.

Strengths Accountability for assets is basic to their security. Accountability assignments also make clear who is responsible and accountable for each control and its effectiveness and overall adequacy of protection.

Weaknesses   If accountability assignments are not kept up to date with changes in assets and organizations, confusion and a loss of accountability can occur. Strict accountability can result in a structure that inhibits one owner from assuming responsibility for another's assets when emergencies or sudden changes occur.

How to Audit   Questionnaires and interviews should be used to assure accountability of all assets and discover any inconsistencies or lack of awareness of assignments in compliance with policy.

Purpose   Prevention

Control Area   Management

Mode   Policy

Area of Responsibility   Management

Cost   Medium

Principles of Note   Accountability.

Automation of Computer Operations

Objective   Prevent unauthorized computer activities.

Description   Computer operations should be made as automatic as possible, using such capabilities as production, program and test program libraries, automatic tape library management, reduction of job control by punch cards, and computer operator activity logging.

Variables   Availability of computer operations software package, high volume of activity justifying use of automated methods, amount of routine production activity.

Strengths   Reduction of manual procedures generally results in improved control of computer operations activities. Reduction of staff reduces exposure to accidental or intentionally caused loss, provides motivation to use automated operations packages beyond other considerations of cost-effectiveness.

Weaknesses   Concentration of trust among fewer people might result in less exposure to loss but potential for larger losses if they occur. It becomes more difficult to separate job duties among fewer operations personnel.

How to Audit   Observe erasure activity and location of degaussing.

Purpose   Prevention

Control Area   Computer center

Mode   Manual procedures

Area of Responsibility   Operations

Cost   Low

Principles of Note   Accountability, instrumentation.

Completion of External Input Data

Objective   Prevent modification, disclosure, or unauthorized use of obsolete or incomplete input/output data.

Description   If missing essential data are still missing beyond a time limit, take steps to obtain the appropriate data. Within the criminal justice environment, a request for disposition information is issued when a particular record has remained incomplete beyond a time limit.

Variables   Types of external data, time periods, methods of completion, forms design.

Strengths   Acts as an error correction/detection control identifying records for which important information is still missing after a certain period of time (the update could have been misplaced, processed incorrectly, inadvertently omitted, etc.). Preserves personal privacy, ensuring that incomplete records, which might have misleading decisions based upon them, are reduced. The control also helps keep records up to date.

Weaknesses   Administrative overhead associated with requests for information, when the information might not yet be available, might be a burden to the data supplier who might not be able to easily provide the information requested or who might not provide it because it is too costly. Unless data suppliers have a good reason for providing additional information, they might ignore requests for additional information. Information providers might no longer be able to provide information (because of funding and other reasons). Resolution might involve significant liaison efforts and problems in different levels and branches of government.

How to Audit   Review policies and procedures for requesting additional data. Identify certain records (preferably based on a random sample) that are in need of follow-up and determine that the proper requests have been made.

Purpose   Prevention, detection

Control Area   Computer center, application systems

Mode   Manual procedures, application system

Area of Responsibility   Users, computer operations, development

Cost   Low

Principles of Note   Independence of control and subject; completeness and consistency; instrumentation.

Compliance with Laws and Regulations

Objective   Avoid violations of laws and regulations.

Description   A statement regarding the new or modified system's compliance with relevant laws and regulations must be provided in requirements and specifications. Direct quotes from laws and regulations regarding EDP security and privacy applying within a legal jurisdiction, or those that might apply, should be included.

Variables   Legal and regulatory requirements for inclusion of statutes, laws, and regulations.

Strengths Provides management with increased assurance that an application system is in compliance with relevant laws and regulations, thereby reducing the chances that management liability and other sanctions might be applied.

Weaknesses Unless reviewed by a lawyer or some other knowledgeable person and compliance assured by audit, the control can become merely a perfunctory piece of paperwork where the blanks are filled in regardless of compliance with laws and regulations.

How to Audit Examine documentation for statements regarding compliance, i.e., did the system designers actually have cause to represent that the new system was in compliance? Discuss the applicable laws and regulations with corporate legal counsel and system designers.

Purpose Prevention

Control Area Application system

Mode Manual procedures

Area of Responsibility Legal counsel, development

Cost Medium

Principles of Note Simplicity, universal application, accountability.

Computer Program Quality Assurance

Objective Detect computer, application, and communications systems and operations failures.

Description A testing or quality control group should independently test and examine computer programs and related documentation to ensure integrity of program products before production use. This activity is best authorized by software development management or by the quality assurance or test department. Excessively formal program development standards should be avoided. Basic life-cycle procedures should be established before more elaborate practices are required. However, compliance with the established standards and procedures should be strongly enforced.

Variables Quality assurance resources available, procedures, staff charter and size, sign-off forms design.

Strengths A consistent compliance with good controls design offsets computer programmers' resistance to independent observation of their work.

Weaknesses Imposing too much discipline too quickly on applications programming staff can cause negative reaction. Quality assurance programmers are difficult to motivate.

How to Audit Operational audits should be performed by EDP auditors with extensive experience and reputation as competent computer programmers.

Purpose Prevention

Control Area Application system

Mode Manual procedures

Area of Responsibility Development

Cost High

Principles of Note Acceptance by personnel, least privilege, accountability.

Computer Programs Change Logs

Objective Detect computer, application, and communications systems and operations failures.

Description All changes to computer programs are logged in a permanent written document. The log can be used as a means of ensuring formal approval of changes.

Variables Log content, assignments, and accountability.

Strengths Review of the purpose, time, type, and individuals who made changes is facilitated. This control aids in researching problems that occur. Utility programs that maintain program libraries in the computer are useful; they can automatically log change activity.

Weaknesses Enforcement to ensure completeness is difficult.

How to Audit Visual review of logs and random verification of changes.

Purpose Detection, prevention

Control Area Development

Mode Manual procedures

Area of Responsibility Development

Cost Low

Principles of Note Accountability.

Computer Security Management Committees

Objective Prevent loss of security support.

Description A high-level management committee is organized to develop security policy and oversee all security of information handling activities. The committee is made up of management representatives from each of the parts of the organization concerned with information processing. The committee is responsible for coordinating computer security, reviewing the state of security, ensuring the visibility of management's support of computer security throughout the organization, approving computer security reviews, receiving and accepting computer security review reports, and ensuring proper control interfaces among organization functions. It should act in some respects similar to a Board of Director's Audit Committee.

Computer security reviews and recommendations for major control should be made to, and approved by, this committee. The committee ensures that privacy and security are part of the overall information handling plan. The Steering Committee can be part of a larger activity within an organization to carry out the function of information resource management. For example, in one research and development organization, an oversight council made up of representatives from organizations that send and receive databases from the R&D organization was established. They are charged with oversight responsibilities for the conduct and control of the R&D organization relative to the exchange of databases. Especially important are questions of individual privacy concerning the content of the databases.

Variables   Level and participation of Steering Committee members, objectives and charter of the Steering Committee, powers and advisory capacity of the committee.

Strengths   A Steering Committee visibly shows the dedication and support of security by top management to the entire organization. Security activity is organized on a top-down basis. A committee that crosses organizational lines can better ensure the consistency of security across the interfaces and the consistency of attention to security in all information-processing-related functions. The Steering Committee can consider security and privacy within the context of other issues confronting the organization. Policies and procedures can be more effectively enforced. The committee approach can avoid the control of computer security by technologists who tend to be limited to technical solutions to security problems.

Weaknesses   A computer security management Steering Committee could add a level of undesirable bureaucracy. Control procurements and decisions can become time-consuming and expensive because of approvals necessary from a high-level committee. Individual managers might attempt to avoid the responsibility for security by assuming that the Steering Committee absolves them of such responsibility.

How to Audit   Review decisions of the committee and its work products. The head of EDP Audit should be a member of the Steering Committee.

Purpose   Prevention, deterrence

Control Area   Management

Mode   Policy

Area of Responsibility   Management

Cost   Low

Principles of Note   Completeness and consistency, accountability.

Computer Security Officer

Objective   Prevent inadequacy of system controls.

Description   An organization with sufficient computer security resources should have an individual identified as a computer security officer. In small organizations, the individual appointed might share this responsibility with other duties. In large organizations, one or more full-time employees should be assigned computer security administration responsibilities. The computer security officer should ideally report to the protection or security department covering the entire organization. This provides proper scope of responsibility for information and its movement throughout the organization. For practical purposes, the computer security officer often functions within the computer department. Job descriptions are highly variable; examples can be obtained from many organizations with established computer security officers.

Variables   Computer security resources, functional and administrative position and reporting, job description.

Strengths A computer security officer provides a focus for the formal development of a computer security program.

Weaknesses Line management might attempt to transfer their responsibilities for security to the computer security officer.

How to Audit The computer security officer's activities should be audited according to his job description.

Purpose Prevention

Control Area Computer center, applications systems, computer system, programming and maintenance, management

Mode Manual procedures

Area of Responsibility Computer security, management

Cost High

Principles of Note Control and subject independence, acceptance by personnel, sustainability, accountability.

Computer System Password File Encryption

Objective Prevent unauthorized computer access.

Description The password file in the computer system contains master copies of passwords to verify correct identification and password input from terminal log-ins. This data file is one of the most sensitive in the entire computer system and must be properly protected. Passwords in the file should be individually encrypted using a one-way encryption algorithm, i.e., the password can be encrypted but there is no reasonable means of decryption that would be computationally feasible given the current state of the art in switching speeds and cryptanalysis. When a password is entered from a computer terminal, it is immediately encrypted using the same algorithm and compared with the encrypted form of the master password for matching. In this manner, clear text passwords reside within the computer system for the shortest possible amount of time.

Variables One-way encryption algorithm, change control of passwords in the encrypted password file.

Strengths Unlimited levels of protection are possible, depending on the strength of the cryptographic algorithms.

Weaknesses Modification of the encryption algorithm computer program could cause a total compromise of the system and would not be detected easily.

How to Audit Analyze the cryptographic algorithm program to ensure its integrity.

Purpose Prevention

Control Area Computer System

Mode Computer operating system

Area of Responsibility Computer security

Cost Medium

Principles of Note   Override capability, avoidance of need for design secrecy, least privilege.

Computer Systems Activity Records

Objective   Detect unauthorized system use.

Description   Most computer systems produce a number of system activity logs, journals, and exception reports. Such recordings should be periodically and selectively examined both manually and through automated means looking for key indications of possible unauthorized activities. Such recordings on tape, disk, and sometimes paper listings should be archived for a reasonable period of time, and records should be kept to ensure that no reports are missing.

For example, printed console logs should be on continuous forms. Any breaks in the forms should require signature indicating integrity of operation and no missing pages. In one computer installation, the console logs are examined on a sample basis monthly. All logs should be dated and timed with an indication of operational personnel on duty at the time the logs were produced. It might be necessary to keep manually written logs of some computer operation activities to compare with or complete the automatic logging of system activity.

Variables   Types and contents of activity recordings, mode of recording and archiving of records, archive cycling periods, analysis methods and frequency.

Strengths   Activity records might be important for evidence in litigation and insurance claims. Accountability of employees can be better assured. Recovery from contingencies can be facilitated.

Weaknesses   Large amounts of systems resources can be consumed in the recording and analysis. Large volumes of data might discourage manual inspection.

How to Audit   Periodic sampling and evaluation of recordings should be performed. Recordings represent an important audit trail for auditing various applications and computer usage.

Purpose   Detection

Control Area   Computer system

Mode   Computer operating system, computer application systems, manual procedures

Area of Responsibility   Computer security, operations

Cost   Medium

Principles of Note   Control and subject independence, completeness and consistency, instrumentation, accountability.

Computer Terminal Access and Use Restrictions

Objective   Prevent unauthorized use of computer terminals.

Description   Access to the use of all terminals owned or under the control of the organization should be restricted to authorized users. This can be done by physically securing rooms in which terminals are located and, where justified, by using metal key or electronic key locks to activate terminals. Terminals within security perimeters that are used frequently can be turned on at the beginning of the work day and left unlocked throughout the business day, then locked again at the end of the business day. Those terminals that are used only occasionally can be left locked except during use at any time of day. It also might be advisable to use various commercial locking devices to prevent terminals from being removed from assigned areas.

Variables   Physical security barriers around terminals, terminal locking mechanisms, procedures for locking and unlocking terminals and physical access areas, manual or automatic logging of usage at or within the terminal.

Strengths   The need for security can be impressed upon terminal users through secure locking capabilities.

Weaknesses   Physical security can sometimes be difficult to enforce in the informal environments in which terminals are frequently used.

How to Audit   Periodically observe terminal areas to ensure that physical security procedures are being used. Review the administration of key access control devices.

Purpose   Prevention

Control Area   Computer center

Mode   Manual procedures, hardware

Area of Responsibility   Security, computer security

Cost   Low

Principles of Note   Least privilege, limit of dependence on other mechanisms, instrumentation, accountability.

Computer Use Access Control Administration

Objective   Prevent unauthorized computer access.

Description   People wishing to have access to a computer system or to change their mode of access and authorized privileges must go through a formal procedure administered by a computer user coordinator. Usually one or more special forms must be completed indicating the type of request and providing for authorizing signatures of appropriate managers. A specific document stating the conditions of access and privileges should accompany the authorization form. The person gaining access should be required to sign his name indicating that he has read and understands the conditions of access and limitations. The computer user, administrator, or coordinator can be in the data processing department or in a department where computers are being accessed.

Variables   Assignment of user coordinator, forms and agreements designed, authorization procedures, administration and record-keeping of access authorizations, coordination with computer operations staff for assignment of access in the computer system.

Strengths   Separation of duties between computer users and computer service providers is enhanced. The use of signed forms and agreements documents provides accountability and deterrent values.

Weaknesses   Adds complexity and bureaucracy, especially in small informal organizations.

How to Audit   Examine the coordinator's administrative activities and records to ensure proper management authorization of forms for access. Trace changes made to access authorization by interviewing computer users and operations staff.

Purpose   Prevention, deterrence

Control Area   Computer center, management

Mode   Manual procedures, computer operating system

Area of Responsibility   Computer security management, operations, computer users

Cost   Medium

Principles of Note   Override capability, least privilege, control and subject independence, instrumentation, accountability.

Computer User Trouble Calls Logging

Objective   Prevent overlooked security problems and detect potential adverse side effects of changes to computer systems and other elements of the operating environment.

Description   All calls from users and staff regarding problems with a computer and communications systems are logged detailing the caller's name, the time and date, and the nature of the problem. A brief disposition report is then prepared for each problem report. A manager reviews each of the problem disposition reports to determine that the problem has been satisfactorily resolved and also to determine that there are not any adverse impacts of the solutions provided (e.g., a correction of the operating system can have some side effect with a security or privacy implication). The reviewing manager also determines whether or not the responding operating person taking care of the problem was within bounds of authority. Simple requests for information are not considered problems within this procedure.

Variables   Logging assignments, forms design, review process.

Strengths   This practice forces user and staff liaison people to justify their actions and to document each correctional action that they have taken. The log can be analyzed by performance monitoring and by system development people for possible improvements of the current operating environment.

Weaknesses   Preparation of logs and brief reports is time-consuming and takes talented and knowledgeable people away from their other duties. Users might abuse the problem reporting system whenever they wish to get operation management's attention.

How to Audit   Review a sample of logs detailing all problem reports received. Examine problem disposition reports. Interview managers who review the disposition reports.

Purpose   Prevention, detection

Control Area   Data center

Mode   Manual procedures

Area of Responsibility   User (responsibility to report problems); operations.

Cost   Medium

Principles of Note   Instrumentation, accountability, auditability.

Confirmation of Receipt of Documents

Objective   Prevent disclosure, taking, or unauthorized use of documents.

Description   The confirmation process consists of verification of receipt of documents. Confirmations of delivery can be made by obtaining master files of names of input/output documents and their addresses, performing a selection of a sample of addresses by running the master file on a computer separate from the production computer or at least at a time different from normal production work. Confirmation notices and copies of the documents are then sent to the addresses to confirm that the documents are correct and that they received the documents as expected. Confirmation of smaller volumes of documents can be done easily on a manual basis. Receipt forms are used by recipients of particularly sensitive documents and returned to the sender to confirm correct report distribution and encourage accountability.

Variables   Area of responsibility, type of reports, frequency, sample type and size, acceptable percentage of response, exception action, forms design.

Strengths   An audit department's use of confirmations to determine the correctness of customer's balances in banking is well known. The use of confirmations in the insurance industry also is occasionally practiced. This suggests the possibility of extending the confirmation techniques as a general control to be used in a wide range of applications. Receipts increase assurance of confidentiality. Printing receipt forms embedded in a computer output to be returned to senders might be more efficient.

Weaknesses   The possibility of building the confirmation process into the application might not be desirable, because it might compromise the independence of confirmation control. Return of forged receipts can be accomplished. Failure to trace and recover missing receipts can cause rapid deterioration of control.

How to Audit   This control is used as an audit tool. Review number and nature of confirmation—related activities for costs and benefits. Sampling of receipts and sensitive report deliveries can confirm correct procedures.

Purpose   Detection

Control Area   Application system, computer center

Mode   Manual procedure

Area of Responsibility   Audit, output control

Cost   Medium

Principles of Note   Auditability, accountability, instrumentation.

Contingency Recovery Equipment Replacement

Objective   Recover from business interruption.

Description   Commitments should be obtained in writing from computer equipment and supplies vendors to replace crucial equipment and supplies within a specified period of time following a contingency loss. Some vendors will commit to replacement of their products within a reasonable period of time and will specify that period of time as a commitment.

For example, in one computer installation a vendor agreed to replace a central processor within five days and a second processor, if necessary, within 10 days. The paper forms supplier agreed to deliver a two-week supply of all special forms in the same time frame. In contrast, other vendors would not guarantee replacement times but would only indicate that best effort would be provided with a priority over other normal product deliveries. Emergency ordering procedures should be established as part of a contingency recovery plan.

Variables   Willing vendors, delivery time constraints, content of binding letters of agreement.

Strengths   Vendor commitments provide a means of planning alternative data processing until equipment and new computing capabilities have been restored.

Weaknesses   The legal value of vendor commitments is not known. A payment in return for commitments might be required. A false sense of security might be produced because other contingencies can interfere with vendor commitments.

How to Audit   Auditors should periodically confirm the validity of agreements to be sure that they are still in effect. Agreements should be reviewed with legal counsel. Commitment periods should be checked relative to other contingency recovery plans.

Purpose   Recovery

Control Area   Computer center

Mode   Policy

Area of Responsibility   Management

Cost   Low

Principles of Note   Sustainability, accountability.

Cooperation of Computer Security Officers

Objective   Prevent inadequacy of system controls.

Description   Maintaining an effective computer security function can be enhanced by exchange of information with computer security functions in other outside organizations. Local computer security organizations can be developed within a city, a part of a city, or regionally. Monthly or other periodic meetings of computer security officers can be held to exchange useful information and experience. A hotline communication capability can be established for exchange of information on an emergency basis to provide warning of possible mishaps or losses. It is important to limit the details of information exchanged to ensure that confidential controls information is not disseminated to unauthorized parties.

Variables   Identification of cooperating organizations, types of information exchanged, procedures.

Strengths   This cooperation provides an opportunity to share important experiences and information and develop professional relationships that strengthen the career path of computer security officers.

Weaknesses   Too much information regarding an organization's security can become known to unauthorized persons.

How to Audit   EDP auditors should become involved in such outside organizational activities.

Purpose   Detection

Control Area   Management

Mode   Manual procedures

Area of Responsibility   Computer security

Cost   Low

Principles of Note   Overt design and operation, least privilege.

Correction and Maintenance of Production System

Objective   Protect against unauthorized program or data modifications.

Description   In spite of implementation and strict enforcement of security controls and good maintenance of application and systems programs, emergencies arise that require violation or overriding of many of these controls and practices. Occasionally, production programs will fail during production runs on the computer. This can happen on second and third shift, during periods of heavy production computer activity. If a failure occurs in an important application production run, it is frequently necessary to call upon knowledgeable programmers to discover the problem, make a change in the production computer program, make changes in input data, or make decisions about alternative solutions (e.g., reruns using previous versions of the production program).

When such emergency events occur, all necessary and expedient measures must be taken including physical access of programmers to computer and production areas, access by such programmers to data files and production programs, correction of production programs, and ad hoc instructions to operations staff. During any of these activities, it is necessary for a trusted individual in computer application production work to record all of the events as they occur or shortly thereafter.

Following the termination of the emergency, programmers should be required to make the necessary and ordinary permanent changes that might have been made on a temporary basis during the emergency and document the emergency actions. This usually requires updating and testing production programs and the normal process of introducing tested updated programs for production use. After an emergency and before permanent corrections have been made, the production application program should be treated in a suspicious mode of operation requiring increased levels of observance by users, production staff, managers, and possibly EDP auditors. These extra efforts should continue until confidence has been built up in the production activities through acceptable experience.

Variables   Emergency maintenance procedures, documentation of actions, past recovery procedures.

Strengths   Flexibility in handling emergency production situations and having security-related procedures and continuing levels of security at highly vulnerable times is important.

Weaknesses   Providing a formal method of handling emergency repair might encourage the excessive use of emergency repair procedures.

How to Audit   This control should be audited during emergency work periods by assigning EDP auditors to oversee emergency procedures and production work using patched computer programs. The basis of decisions to make emergency repairs should be examined for correctness and consistency.

Purpose   Recovery

Control Area   Computer center

Mode   Manual procedures

Area of Responsibility   Operations

Cost   Medium

Principles of Note   Override, least privilege, accountability.

Courier Trustworthiness and Identification

Objective   Preventive disclosure, taking, or unauthorized use of documents.

Description   Couriers frequently are used to distribute computer output reports to computer users. Couriers must be especially trustworthy, have a background investigation similar to that for computer operators, and be bonded. A new courier should be personally introduced to all those persons to whom he will be delivering computer output and to all persons from whom he will be receiving materials for delivery. Couriers should be required to use signed receipts for all transported reports. Couriers should be required to keep all reports in their personal possession in properly locked or controlled containers. All users should be informed immediately upon the termination of any couriers delivering or picking up reports. Couriers should carry special identification to show that they are authorized to function in claimed capacities. Telephone calls in advance of delivery of highly sensitive reports should be made to recipients of those reports.

Variables   Courier background investigations, identification procedures, design of receipt forms, delivery procedures, logging procedures.

Strengths   Procedures ensure positive accountability by receivers and senders of reports as well as couriers.

Weaknesses   Because couriers are generally low-paid employees, their potential for trustworthiness sometimes is reduced. Bonding of such employees is imperative.

How to Audit   Couriers periodically should be followed in their delivery work and be observed. Their activities should then be compared to receipt documents.

Purpose   Prevention

Control Area   Computer center

Mode   Manual procedures

Area of Responsibility   Input and output, computer users

Cost   Low

Principles of Note   Control and subject independence, limit of dependence on other mechanisms, instrumentation, accountability.

Cryptographic Protection

Objective   To prevent compromise of data.

Description   A high level of data communications and storage protection can be obtained by using the Data Encryption Standard (DES). However, effective encryption key management is essential. Frequently, applications do not require this level of encryption, and much simpler forms of encryption can be used. Data compression is a particularly simple form of encryption that also increases the efficiency of data storage. Data compression can be achieved by eliminating redundant information (spacing, etc.) and by encoding data fields. The cryptanalysis work factor should be determined and compared to the value of compromising the data being protected.

Variables   Selection of data for encryption, selection of encryption methods and products, key management.

Strengths   Encryption provides varying amounts of protection to data in communication circuits and when stored in computer readable form. Its strength depends on the work factor of cryptanalysis and the effectiveness of key confidentiality and administration.

Weaknesses   Weak encryption or powerful encryption but weak key confidentiality and administration can provide a false sense of security.

How to Audit   Periodic audits should be performed to determine the proper application of cryptographic protection, the effectiveness of the key confidentiality and administration, and independent verification of unauthorized decryption work factor.

Purpose   Prevention

Control Area   Computer center

Mode   Hardware

Area of Responsibility   Computer security

Cost   High

Principles of Note   Least privilege.

Data Accountability Assignment to Users

Objective   Prevent asset responsibility loss.

Description   Users are formally assigned the responsibility for the accuracy, safekeeping, and dissemination of the data they handle. If the data processing department does not handle data properly, then it is up to the users to require corrections. Organizationally, users provide a data processing department with the resources to assist them with their functions. In terms of controls, users should be able to tell data processing what is required in terms of data accuracy, relevance, timeliness, handling procedures, etc.

Variables   Identification of users, responsibilities, documentation of procedures, policy.

Strengths   Explicit accountability ensures correct processing. Failures can be identified more easily.

Weaknesses   Users might not be knowledgeable enough to determine that data are inaccurate or improperly handled. This control requires that users have at least a fundamental understanding of computer security and privacy issues and controls. This control might run contrary to many current organizational structures, where data processing in some sense controls the users.

How to Audit Review organizational assignment of responsibilities for computer security and privacy matters. Discuss with both user and data processing management their mutual responsibilities regarding computer security and privacy. Review procedures in which users correct records, control the dissemination of records, and otherwise actively participate in the enforcement and design of computer security controls.

Purpose Prevention

Control Area Management

Mode Manual Procedures

Area of Responsibility User

Cost Low

Principles of Note Simplicity, independence of control and subject, accountability.

Data Classification

Objective Prevent compromise of data.

Description Data can be classified at different security levels to produce cost savings and effectiveness of applying controls consistent with various levels of sensitivity of data. Some organizations maintain the same level of security for all data, believing that making exceptions is too costly. Other organizations might have only small amounts of data of a highly sensitive nature and find that applying special controls to the small amount of data is cost-effective. When data are classified, they can be identified in two or more levels, often referred to as general information, confidential information, secret information, and other higher levels of classification named according to the functional use of the data, such as trade secret data, unreported financial performance, etc.

Variables Amounts of data at various levels of sensitivity, potential controls, cost savings for no classifications or several levels of classification, policies concerning security for each level of classification.

Strengths Separate security treatment of data at different levels of security can result in control cost savings when the volume and concentration of sensitive data warrant special treatment. Otherwise, savings can be made by reducing control exceptions.

Weaknesses Classification of data can easily result in excessive complexities in data handling and processing.

How to Audit Review classification policy and sample data for audit trail testing of controls.

Purpose Prevention

Control Area Management

Mode Policy

Area of Responsibility Management

Cost Low

Principles of Note Cost-effectiveness, simplicity, least privilege, minimization of exceptions, accountability.

Data Files Access

Objective Prevention of unauthorized access to, modification, destruction, and disclosure of, and taking or using data stored in computer systems.

Description Every data file stored in a computer system that could result in a significant loss if compromised through modification, destruction, disclosure, taking, or use should be protected by having access restricted based on a secret password known only to authorized persons and computer programs. File access should be restricted further by mode of access allowed: read only, append only, modify only, file name change, file access control change, or some combination of these modes.

Commercial file access control computer program packages are available for some makes of computer systems to provide this protective feature. The operating systems of some makes of computers have this capability integrated into the system. Specific resources such as magnetic tapes and disks also can be controlled. Access controls should also include the journaling of accesses to provide audit trails and should produce a set of journal reports and exception reports, for example, of all unauthorized attempts to access specific files. The administration of assigning access rights and password assignments is important for the effectiveness of internal computer controls.

Variables Selection of computer program package or implementation of operating system programs, administration of access control, forms design, identification of data files to be protected, identification of authorized file accessors.

Strengths Employees, knowing that their activities are controlled and monitored, are deterred from engaging in unauthorized activity. Journals and exception reports can be used to investigate suspected unauthorized activities or to obtain evidence of known or suspected activities.

Weaknesses Computer program commercial packages or other programs for file access control might degrade system performance.

How to Audit Review system journals and exception reports to determine that proper actions have been taken. Test file access control for effects of unauthorized access. Review file access control administration.

Purpose Prevention

Control Area Computer system

Mode Manual procedures, computer operating system

Area of Responsibility Computer security, operations

Cost Medium

Principles of Note Least privilege, control and subject independence, completeness and consistency, instrumentation, acceptance by personnel, accountability.

Data File Access Subcontrols by Job Function

Objective Prevent unauthorized access to data.

Description Different types of database read and update privileges are given to employees with different job functions. Data field read privileges can be granted or not depending on user job function. Likewise, update privileges might not be granted, or might be granted only for certain data fields within certain types of records of a database. For instance, clerks handling mailing-related matters would be permitted to update only the address field. This control results in division of labor and separation of duties.

Variables   Date file access control capability, identification and authorization of users, data files and fields within data files, administration.

Strengths   Collusion is made necessary and more difficult when privileges for file and field access are directly related to an employee's job duties. Employees are prevented from altering fields in records that do not come within the domain of their jobs. Privacy and confidentiality are preserved when persons who do not need to be able to access certain fields are prevented from doing so; browsing is prevented.

Weaknesses   Users must be uniquely identified with passwords and identification user words for this control to be applied. Significant system overhead might be associated with the authorization. If someone is unavailable, then another person who might not have the same privileges might need to perform the other's duties; this could lead to sharing of passwords and other circumventing of controls activities.

How to Audit   Ask employees to demonstrate certain system capabilities, if possible, asking them to do things that they properly should be prevented from doing. Care should be taken that internal system alarms triggered by such testing do not cause problems. Discuss with applications management and systems designers the segmentation of personnel duties within certain applications areas and the separation of duties enforced by the procedures.

Purpose   Prevention

Control Area   Application systems, computer systems

Mode   Manual procedures

Area of Responsibility   Computer users, management, development operations

Cost   Medium

Principles of Note   Least privilege, independence of control and subject, accountability.

Data File and Program Backup

Objective   Prevent loss, modification, disclosure, or destruction of data assets.

Description   The current form of every data file that might be needed in the future should be copied at the time of its creation, and the copy should be stored at a remote, safe location for operational recovery purposes. It is advisable to store several copies, one immediately available in the computer center, another available some short distance away, and a third archived at some remote distance for longer term storage. Periodically updated data files should be cycled from the immediate site to the local site to the remote site by data file generations (father, grandfather, etc.).

   In addition, copies of the computer programs necessary to process the backed-up data files, documentation of the programs, computer operation instructions, and a supply of special printed forms necessary for production running of the programs also should be stored at a remote, safe location. This hierarchical arrangement of backup data files provides for convenient restarting of production runs in case of damaged or missing files. More serious problems that could result in loss of local backup data files can be resolved by using copies of remote backup data files. When a backup file is returned to the computer center for use, there must be assurance that it also is backed up safely with another copy.

Variables Data files to be backed up, higher hierarchical arrangement in locations of backup files, cycling frequency and methods, archivable record-keeping, security of backup facilities.

Strengths Defensive depth of backup provides a significant increase in assurance of recovery that addresses small as well as large contingencies. Recovery from backup files is commonly done under abnormal conditions that usually accompany recovery efforts. These conditions increase the likelihood of loss of the backup files. Therefore, it is important to have at least secondary backup in addition to primary backup files.

Weaknesses Operational complexity in moving backup files from one stage to the next at a multiplicity of backup sites can increase the opportunity for human errors or intentional acts of sabotage or theft. Multiple backups might produce complacency and cause degeneration of computer center procedures. There is an increased exposure to loss in transporting files to the remote sites.

How to Audit An audit should periodically include the actual demonstration of recovery from each level of backup. Inspection of backup sites should be conducted to ensure their secure states.

Purpose Recovery

Control Area Computer center

Mode Manual procedures

Area of Responsibility Operations

Cost Medium

Principles of Note Defensive depth sustainability.

Delivery Loading Dock Access

Objective Avoid destruction of assets and business interruption.

Description The loading dock area is made secure with the use of a window and an intermediate holding room. The window is used by truck drivers when they wish to speak to someone from the facility, have receiving papers signed, and gain authorization for access to the intermediate holding room. An employee from the inside can release the lock on a door opening on the loading dock from the holding room. The truck driver can unload supplies or other items onto the dock and into the holding room without having access to any other areas of the building. When the delivered material is entirely within the holding room, and when the delivery man has gone, the outside door can be locked again by the employee at the receiving window. Then an inside door leading to the holding room can be unlocked and opened for the movement of the material to its proper storage/use location.

Variables Facility layout, staffing in area, volume of materials.

Strengths Prevents unauthorized persons from gaining access to facilities through the loading area. Allows receiving clerk to stay physically separated from the driver/delivery workers (employee safety is the concern here). Permits received materials to be inspected in a locked room prior to movement to operational and storage areas of a data processing center. A bell at the receiving window can be used to summon a clerk, thus eliminating the need for the window to be manned on a full-time basis.

Weaknesses Holding room can take up a large amount of floor space, which could be used for other purposes. Receiving window, related doors and locks, plus additional walls incur additional costs. Only large data processing centers probably have the volume of deliveries to justify such an expenditure.

How to Audit Examine facilities to make sure that the appropriate loading dock access controls are in place. On a surprise basis, watch a delivery to make sure that specified procedures are being followed.

Purpose Prevention

Control Area Computer center

Mode Manual procedures, hardware

Area of Responsibility Security, operations

Cost High

Principles of Note Simplicity, least privilege, independence of control and subject, universal application, sustainability.

Disaster Recovery

Objective Recover from business interruption.

Description Every computer must have a written disaster recovery plan and a recovery management team. Primary and backup managers must be assigned specific responsibilities for each aspect of recovery from all types of partial or complete disasters. Each aspect of the disaster recovery plan should have assigned a specific individual responsible for its execution. Separate individuals should be assigned to coordination, systems support, hardware recovery, facilities, administration, scheduling, communications, documentation and supplies, backup data files and security recovery funding, insurance, personnel, historical recording of events, and public affairs.

Priority processing needs of all time-dependent applications to be recovered after a disaster must be identified. This requires that all computer users specify the importance of their computer applications, processing requirements and alternative means of processing, and consequences of failure to process. Data processing management is responsible for meeting the crucial needs of computer users in the best interests of the organization. Priorities will assist in the scheduling of processing when it is restored. A designated person should provide liaison with users informing them of special needs and the status of processing of their work. A detailed history of the recovery process must be documented and recovery activity verbally reported during the recovery process.

After recovery, the historical documentation should be analyzed to determine how future contingencies can be better handled and to handle insurance claims recovery and any litigation that might follow a disaster. Every job function should be analyzed relative to its performance during and prior to a disaster. Measures of importance and priority of functions should be determined and documented in the plan.

Variables Identification of anticipated disasters, applications and their priority for recovery, staff assignments, disaster and recovery plan, type of data processing backup site, documentation and distributions, identification or arrangement of alternatives, data processing capabilities during recovery, and arrangements for alternative services, such as communications, transportation, security guards, equipment, supplies, facilities, and personnel.

Strengths   Flexibility in plans facilitates meeting a wide range of contingencies. A documented recovery plan provides for a means of practicing and testing all recovery procedures. Potential threats that can provide a means of adding controls to reduce risk should be identified. Setting priorities of applications provides users with perspective on the importance of better applications recovery needs. Application of limited area processing resources can be more effectively planned. Communication among recovery managers helps ensure smooth and minimum cost recovery. Documentation of recovery activities encourages responsibilities and accountability among managers and workers. Job function analysis facilitates management's quick mobilization of vital personnel and resources in the event of a disaster. Management can more easily and effectively assign work to employees during recovery. A disaster plan reduces the likelihood of confusion. Use of a disaster recovery contact list provides for speedy notification of vendors, suppliers, and customers who can take appropriate action to assist or reduce loss.

Weaknesses   Documentation of a backup plan can produce complacency unless the plan is frequently reviewed and tested. Documented backup plans also can become quickly outmoded. Ranking of priorities of applications can cause ill will and disputes among computer users. The preparation of historical documentation can be distorted or incorrect and result in reduced capability to file loss claims with insurance companies or provide defense in litigation or governmental hearings. Documented recovery plans that have not been tested can quickly become too detailed or inappropriate for recovery.

How to Audit   Disaster recovery plans should be studied to ensure that they are still current. Proof of testing plans should be documented and reported. Scenarios of possible disasters can be generated and theoretically played against the disaster recovery plans to ensure their adequacy. Application priorities can be verified through auditors responsible for the audit of specific functions of an organization dependent on computer services. Examination of historical documentation recovery experience should be performed to note any changes necessary in disaster recovery planning for the future.

Purpose   Recovery

Control Area   Management

Mode   Manual procedures

Area of Responsibility   Management

Cost   High

Principles of Note   Simplicity, override capabilities, limit of dependence on other mechanisms, completeness and consistency instrumentation.

Discarded Document Destruction

Objective   Prevent disclosure, taking, or unauthorized use of documents.

Description   Input/output documents, including any human readable documents or nonerasable computer media (carbon paper, punch cards and tape, one-time-use printer ribbons), should be reviewed for potential loss sensitivity and appropriately destroyed when no longer needed. Appropriate protection of materials awaiting final disposition should be used. Logging of all actions to ensure an audit trail and adherence to rules is essential. Strict assignments of tasks and accountability are essential. Documents such as obsolete system development materials, test data and manuals, and obsolete criminal histories should be considered.

Variables   Secure storage facilities, method of destruction, e.g., mechanical (shredding), chemical, or burning; logging method; marking documents for disposition.

Strengths   Provides complete accounting for all documents. Reduces exposure to loss in facilities and trash. Makes facilities less cluttered and reduces fire hazards. Reduces cost of storage.

Weaknesses   Expensive errors could result from discarding valuable documents. Sensitive documents are concentrated in one area and in one activity.

How to Audit   Examine trash for sensitive documents. Examine sensitivity criteria for appropriateness. Observe storage and destruction areas. Do sample confirmations of destruction based on destruction log.

Purpose   Prevention

Control Area   Computer center

Mode   Manual procedures, hardware (shredder)

Area of Responsibility   Input/output

Cost   Low

Principles of Note   Least privilege, completeness, and consistency.

Dynamic Password Change Control by User

Objective   Prevent unauthorized use of passwords.

Description   Users are allowed to change their passwords any time once they have logged in to the system. A parameter can be set at log-in time or at any time during a logged-in session that prevents changing a password. This would be useful in the case where an individual logs in to the system, gets up and leaves the terminal for a short period of time, and does not want anyone to come along and change the password while he is away. The user must enter a new password twice to prevent an incorrect password entry caused by a typing error. If the second password is not the same, the user must begin again.

Variables   Password change protocol

Strengths   Provides flexibility for users.

Weaknesses   User motivation is difficult.

How to Audit   Conduct live test of the change procedure.

Purpose   Prevention

Control Area   Computer system

Mode   Computer operating system

Area of Responsibility   Computer security

Cost Low

Principles of Note Instrumentation, accountability.

EDP Auditor

Objective Prevent inadequacy of system controls.

Description Organizations with internal audit resources should establish EDP audit expertise within the internal audit function. In small organizations, general auditors can acquire EDP knowledge and skills. In larger organizations, full-time EDP audit specialists should be established to carry out EDP audits and assist general auditors in financial audits.

Variables Amount of audit resources, regulatory or legal requirements for internal audit.

Strengths Management can be assured about adequacy of computer security and auditability of systems and can be notified on a timely basis of vulnerabilities.

Weaknesses EDP auditors might not be given sufficient responsibilities and resources to perform an adequate job. EDP auditors might fall behind in state-of-the art EDP audit practices and tools.

How to Audit Periodic external audits should report to management on the adequacy of internal EDP audit capabilities and practices.

Purpose Detection

Control Area Computer center, computer system

Mode Manual procedures, computer application system policy

Area of Responsibility Management

Cost High

Principles of Note Auditability, instrumentation, sustainability.

Electrical Equipment Protection

Objective Prevent damage to equipment.

Description Every item of computing equipment that is separately powered should have a separate circuit breaker in the electrical supply for that equipment. Alternatively, equipment can be supplied with other protective mechanisms from power failures or other electrical anomalies. Circuit breakers should be clearly labeled for manual activation. The locations of all circuit breakers should be documented and available in disaster and recovery plans.

Variables Identified equipment, types of protective devices, assignments of accountability for activation, location, redundant transformers, documentation.

Strengths Individual devices can fail and be switched off without having to cut power to other devices. Failures can be localized as well as more readily detected. Device configurations can be changed more readily, avoiding excessive time in diagnosing electrical problems and reconfiguring electrical systems to suit new equipment setups.

Weaknesses Additional opportunity to tamper with equipment is possible.

How to Audit Electrical switch boxes and circuit breakers should be examined periodically.

Purpose Prevention

Control Area Data center

Mode Hardware

Area of Responsibility Operations

Cost Medium

Principles of Note Override capability, limit of dependence on other mechanisms.

Electrical Power Shutdown and Recovery

Objective Prevent damage to equipment.

Description Emergency master power-off switches should be located next to each emergency exit door. The switches should be clearly identified, and easily read signs should be posted giving instructions for use of the switches. Activation of any of these switches should be followed with reports documenting the circumstances and persons responsible for their use.

Alternative power supplies should be tested on a periodic basis. The power supply should be used during the test for a sufficiently long period of time to ensure sustained operation under emergency conditions. Fuel supplies for alternative power should be periodically measured, and the quality of the fuel tested. Pumps, switches, and valves for switching from alternative fuel tanks also should be tested periodically. In one computer installation having an uninterruptible power supply, two independent, separately located oil tanks are used. Either tank can independently supply the entire uninterruptible power supply. Each tank is filled by a different oil company. Two diesel generators and engines are also installed for backup purposes.

Variables Number and location of master power-off switches, power-down and power-up operation instructions, frequency and extent of alternative power system testing, redundancy of power generators and fuel supplies.

Strengths Easily identified power-off switches are valuable for firefighters, rescue workers, and others in the event of emergencies. Testing facilitates preventive maintenance work and familiarizes staff with emergency procedures. Redundancies in alternative power supplies increase assurance of emergency recoveries.

Weaknesses Unauthorized or accidental use of power-off switches can cause extensive damage to computer equipment and loss of data. Intentional use of power-off switches could assist in gaining unauthorized entry to computer facilities. Cutover to alternative power supplies might result in interruption of service and inconvenience to users. Redundancy increases the complexity of alternative power systems. This increases maintenance problems and likelihood of failures.

How to Audit Periodically examine logs and question all switch activations. Ensure proper posting of identification and warning signs at switches. Observe testing of alternative power supplies and review testing logs. Review maintenance logs for excessive maintenance as an indication of possible problems.

Purpose   Prevention and recovery

Control Area   Data center

Mode   Hardware

Area of Responsibility   Operations

Cost   Medium

Principles of Note   Override capability, limit of dependence on other mechanisms, instrumentation, sustainability.

Emergency Preparedness

Objective   Prevent human injuries and other damages from contingencies.

Description   Emergency procedures should be documented and periodically reviewed with occupants of areas requiring emergency action. Adequate automatic fire and water detection and suppression capabilities are assumed to be present. Reduction of human injury is the first priority, followed by saving other important assets. Emergency drills that enact the documented procedures should be periodically held. It should be assumed that occupants of an area in which an emergency occurs do not have time to read emergency procedures documents before action. Procedures should include activation of manual alarms and power shutoff switches, evacuation routes, reporting of conditions, safe areas for regrouping, accounting for all occupants, use of equipment such as fire extinguishers to aid safe evacuation, and actions following complete evacuation. A hierarchy of emergency commands should be established with backup assignments.

Emergency drills should be organized to minimize loss of crucial activities such as computer operation. Close supervision of drills by managers who are aware of practice or real emergencies is necessary. Large, clearly visible signs providing basic directions are required. For example, locations of fire extinguishers, portable lights, and emergency switches should be identified clearly with signs that can be read from likely positions of occupants. First aid kits should be available in regrouping areas. Emergency food, water, tools, waste disposal, waterproof equipment covers, communication and sleeping supplies should be available for prolonged emergencies. All civil ordinances and insurance policy requirements equipment.

Variables   Frequency and extent of drills and briefings, content and location of written procedures, manual alarms and switches, evacuation routes and regrouping areas, signs, command assignments, amount and locations of emergency equipment.

Strengths   The safety of occupants from injury is the primary purpose of this control. Employees will have more positive feelings about their employer's concern for their welfare, and alertness to potential emergencies is maintained.

Weaknesses   Drills can become too commonplace and not taken seriously. Emergency equipment and supplies can deteriorate. Written procedures become obsolete. Emergency switches can be accidentally or maliciously activated.

How to Audit   Observe drills, review written procedures, check signs and equipment.

Purpose   Prevention

Control Area   Computer center

Mode   Manual procedures, hardware

Area of Responsibility   Computer security, operations

Cost   Medium

Principles of Note   Override capability, completeness and consistency, acceptance by personnel, sustainability.

Employees Identification on Work Products

Objective   Detect unauthorized activities of employees.

Description   All computer operators and other employees should have standard identification in the form of official names, numbers, or passwords. This identification is to be entered into all records, data input, and activity logs and journals to identify workers associated with all work products. Identification can be accomplished by manual signatures of keying of identification into equipment keyboards. Data entry clerks should be required to initial all forms or batch control forms used for data entry and enter identification into computer input data. Computer operators should sign computer console printer listings or enter their codes through console keyboards indicating the starting and ending of work periods.

Variables   Form of employee identification, entry of identification, manual verification of correct identification activity.

Strengths   Manual identification on forms can be compared with identification entered into computer systems to match times and work products. Incentives for higher quality and quantity of work are possible when work products are identified by individual worker. Tracking of errors and unauthorized activities is facilitated.

Weaknesses   Possible forgery can result in errors in accountability for unauthorized activity.

How to Audit   Spot checking of employee codes with immediate supervisors. Sampling of computer output by audit trail back to source data handling.

Purpose   Detection, deterrence

Control Area   Computer center, applications systems

Mode   Manual procedures, computer application system

Area of Responsibility   Operations

Cost   Low

Principles of Note   Control and subject independence, least privilege, instrumentation, acceptance by personnel, accountability.

Exception Reporting

Objective   Detect computer, application and communications systems, and operations failures.

Description   Exception reporting on a timely basis should be built into the computer operating system, utility programs, and application systems to report on any deviation from normal activity that might indicate errors or unauthorized acts. For example, if a user defines a data file that allows public access, a message will be printed out warning the user, and possibly the operations staff, that the file is not protected.

Exception reporting should occur when a specific control is violated, or the exception report can constitute a warning of a possible undesirable event. Exception reports should be recorded in a recoverable form within the system and when necessary for timely action, displayed to the computer operator, or, in case of on-line terminal use, displayed to the terminal user.

Variables   Actions requiring exception reporting, method of reporting exceptions, procedures for taking action on exceptions reported.

Strengths   This control is automatic and reduces the likelihood of human error in handling exceptions.

Weaknesses   Frequent or voluminous exception reports can result in lack of sufficient attention.

How to Audit   Tests that force exception reporting should be run, and actions taken should be reviewed.

Purpose   Detection

Control Area   Computer system.

Mode   Computer operating system, computer application system, manual procedures

Area of Responsibility   Computer users, operations

Cost   Medium

Principles of Note   Override capability, minimization of exceptions, instrumentation.

Financial Loss Contingency and Recovery Funding

Objective   Recover from business interruption.

Description   Self-insured organizations, such as government agencies, should be available for prolonged emergencies. All civil ordinances and insurance policy requirements equipment.

Variables   Frequency and extent of drills and briefings, content and location of written procedures, manual alarms and switches, evacuation routes and regrouping areas, signs, command assignments, amount and locations of emergency equipment.

Strengths   The safety of occupants from injury is the primary purpose of this control. Employees will have more positive feeling about their employer's concern for their welfare, and alertness to potential emergencies is maintained.

Weaknesses   Drills can become too commonplace and not taken seriously. Emergency equipment and supplies can deteriorate. Written procedures become obsolete. Emergency switches can be accidentally or maliciously activated.

How to Audit   Observe drills, review written procedures, check signs and equipment.

Purpose   Prevention

Control Area   Computer center

Mode Manual procedures, hardware

Area of Responsibility Computer security, operations

Cost Medium

Principles of Note Override capability, completeness and consistency, acceptance by personnel, sustainability.

Employees Identification on Work Products

Objective Detect unauthorized activities of employees.

Description All computer operators and other employees should have standard identification in the form of official names, numbers, or passwords. This identification is to be entered into all records, data input, and activity logs and journals to identify workers associated with all work products. Identification can be accomplished by manual signatures or keying of identification into equipment keyboards. Data entry clerks should be required to initial all forms or batch control forms used for data entry and enter identification into computer input data. Computer operators should sign computer console printer listings or enter their codes through console keyboards indicating the starting and ending of work periods.

Variables Form of employee identification, entry of identification, manual verification of correct identification activity.

Strengths Manual identification on forms can be compared with identification entered into computer systems to match times and work products. Incentives for higher quality and quantity of work are possible when work products are identified by individual worker. Tracking of errors and unauthorized activities is facilitated.

Weaknesses Possible forgery can result in errors in accountability for unauthorized activity.

How to Audit Spot checking of employee codes with immediate supervisors. Sampling of computer output by audit trail back to source data handling.

Purpose Detection, deterrence

Control Area Computer center, applications systems

Mode Manual procedures, computer application system

Area of Responsibility Operations

Cost Low

Principles of Note Control and subject independence, least privilege, instrumentation, acceptance by personnel, accountability.

Exception reporting

Objective Detect computer, application and communications systems, and operations failures.

Description Exception reporting on a timely basis should be built into the computer operating system, utility programs, and application systems to report on any deviation from normal activity that might indicate errors or unauthorized acts. For example, if a user defines a data file that allows public access, a message will be printed out warning the user, and possibly the operations staff, that the file is not protected.

Exception reporting should occur when a specific control is violated, or the exception report can constitute a warning of a possible undesirable event. Exception reports should be recorded in a recoverable form within the system and when necessary for timely action, displayed to the computer operator, or, in case of on-line terminal use, displayed to the terminal user.

Variables Actions requiring exception reporting, method of reporting exceptions, procedures for taking action on exceptions reported.

Strengths This control is automatic and reduces the likelihood of human error in handling exceptions.

Weaknesses Frequent or voluminous exception reports can result in lack of sufficient attention.

How to Audit Tests that force exception reporting should be run, and actions taken should be reviewed.

Purpose Detection

Control Area Computer system

Mode Computer operating system, computer application system, manual procedures

Area of Responsibility Computer users, operations

Cost Medium

Principles of Note Override capability, minimization of exceptions, instrumentation.

Financial Loss Contingency and Recovery Funding

Objective Recover from business interruption.

Description Self-insured organizations, such as government agencies, should be assured of readily available emergency funds for contingencies and recovery. Specialized EDP insurance is available and should be considered when insurance covering other types of losses in a business might not apply. Financial risk protection should cover asset losses, business interruption, and extra expense resulting from contingency recovery. Organizations not self-insured should bond all employees against fraud in high-risk areas of data processing activities. Blanket bonds will normally cover this activity.

Variables Organization insurance practices, lines of credit and availability of emergency funds, size of potential losses, and deductible amounts.

Strengths Protection against financial loss by sharing risks is an important business protection.

Weaknesses Insurance must not be used as an alternative to good security.

How to Audit   The insurance or self-insurance program should be reviewed periodically. Assistance of experienced risk and insurance experts should be used.

Purpose   Recovery

Control Area   Management

Mode   Policy

Area of Responsibility   Insurance

Cost   High

Principles of Note   Cost-effectiveness, minimization of exceptions, limit of dependence on other mechanisms.

Human Subjects Review

Objective   Prevent disclosure and unauthorized use of personal information.

Description   An independent review board (Human Subjects Review Board) reviews all proposals in an organization concerning treatment of subjects in studies. The board is made up of members of the parent organizations, some from the department in question, and some from outside the department. The charter of the board is to determine whether the subjects of a study will be put "at risk" or "at a disadvantage" because of participation in the study.

   The manner in which individual privacy (data confidentiality) is handled is a key issue. The board reviews the original plans of the project, the mode of operation, and justification of any risks to ensure that the potential benefits of the activity outweigh the potential costs. The board also has the responsibility to evaluate the staff decisions. The reason for this evaluation is that not all problems can be anticipated by the board. Three areas of qualifications are examined: (1) sensitivity to issues of privacy; (2) personal values; and (3) general competence and ability to cope with unforeseen problems. All decisions are documented.

Variables   Organization, criteria for acceptable activities, powers.

Strengths   An independent review is made at the beginning of the project. The review is made by peers and includes intangible factors.

Weaknesses   Control depends on the quality of board members, and sometimes not all problems are found.

How to Audit   Review minutes of the board meeting and any privacy problems that do occur.

Purpose   Prevention

Control Area   Management

Mode   Manual procedures

Area of Responsibility   Users

Cost   Medium

Principles of Note   Independence of control/subject, accountability.

Independent Computer Use by Auditors

Objective   Prevent interference with auditing.

Description   Audit independence can be considerably enhanced by using a computer not associated with the data processing activities being audited. Otherwise, if the same computer is being used, then the computer should be used in isolation from all other activities. Where data tapes are being audited, they can be taken to a service bureau to perform audit activities.

Variables   Computer availability, computer system compatibilities, computer audit activity.

Strengths   Use of an independent computer can provide the EDP auditors with more direct computer operation experience, adding to their capabilities. Audit computer use might avoid conflicts of overloading of the computer system being audited. The transportability of data from one computer to another can be validated.

Weaknesses   Unless a separate computer is readily available, the cost of audit can be prohibitive. Movement of sensitive data from the computer center can expose them to new vulnerabilities.

How to Audit   Investigate possible systems interconnections and ensure their independence.

Purpose   Prevention

Control Area   Computer system

Mode   Computer applications system, manual procedures

Area of Responsibility   Audit

Cost   Medium

Principles of Note   Cost-effectiveness, least privilege, control and subject independence, limit of dependence on other mechanism, auditability.

Independent Control of Audit Tools

Objective   Prevent interference with auditing.

Description   Audit programs, documentation, and test materials are kept in secure areas by the internal auditors. Audit programs do not remain in the data center tape library. The audit programs are not kept on disk or in any other way kept on the system where they might be subject to tampering.

Variables   Storage area, materials stored, auditors accountable.

Strengths   Preserves independence of auditors.

Weaknesses   It can be inconvenient for auditors to keep their materials in a secure place. An installation might have a policy that no tapes are to leave the tape library unless they are to be transferred to another computer center; this practice would then require exceptions to such rules.

How to Audit   Ascertain that all audit materials are maintained under the direct control of auditors, not the persons being audited.

Purpose   Prevention

Control Area   Computer center

Mode   Manual procedures

Area of Responsibility   Audit

Cost   Low

Principles of Note   Independence of control and subject, least privilege.

Input Data Validation

Objective   Prevent loss, modification, disclosure, or destruction of data assets.

Description   Validation of all input to a computer system should be performed in both applications and computer operating systems to assist in the assurance of correct and appropriate data. Validation should include examination for out-of-range values of data, invalid characters in data fields, exceeding upper and lower limits of data volume, and unauthorized or inconsistent control data. Program errors dependent on the content or meaning of the data also can be checked. For example, inconsistent criminal justice disposition data relative to previously entered dispositions can be flagged for manual checking and correction.

Variables   Validation checks, error actions to be taken, locations in processing sequences for validation activity.

Strengths   Early validation of input data can result in prevention of error propagation.

Weaknesses   Excessive computer resources may be used for infrequently occurring errors.

How to Audit   Review systems design documentation to determine that input data controls are appropriately designed into the system. Run tests using erroneous data to check on the functioning of validation controls.

Purpose   Prevention

Control Area   Application system, computer operating system

Mode   Computer operating system, computer application system

Area of Responsibility   Computer users, operations, input and output.

Cost   High

Principles of Note   Simplicity, override capability, minimization of exceptions, completeness and consistency, instrumentation, auditability.

Inspection of Incoming/Outgoing Materials

Objective   Prevent unauthorized taking and facility damage.

Description   Certain materials and containers are inspected, and entry or departure is restricted. Within constraints of all applicable laws and personal privacy, guards would prevent movement of materials and inspect contents of closed containers into and out of sensitive areas. Materials can include tapes, disks, listings, equipment, recorders, food and beverages, chemicals, and such containers as lunch boxes and briefcases. Some unneeded materials could be kept stored outside for later retrieval by owners. Authorization forms can be used to control movement. Spot checks and posted signs rather than continuous inspection may be sufficient.

Variables   Materials, authorization, degree of inspection.

Strengths   Prevents unnecessary or dangerous materials from entering areas. Reduces suspicion of otherwise trusted persons. Reinforces restrictions for unauthorized persons.

Weaknesses   Might reduce employee efficiency and freedom.

How to Audit   Observe inspection post activity. Attempt violation of rules (with great care).

Purpose   Prevention

Control Area   Computer center

Mode   Manual procedures

Area of Responsibility   Security

Cost   High

Principles of Note   Consistency and completeness, sustainability, acceptance by personnel.

Isolation of Sensitive Computer Production Jobs

Objective   Prevent compromise of data.

Description   Some production systems, such as those producing negotiable instruments or processing personal information (as in organized crime intelligence files) are sufficiently sensitive to potential loss to require special handling. Such systems should be run on dedicated computers or only share computer systems with harmless or other trusted applications. For example, data communications access might be shut down during such a job. Some sensitive systems can be run at times when general activity is minimal, such as on Sundays, and run by an operations team especially held accountable for the operation. Extraordinary physical and computer security measures can be taken during the job run. Special marking can be done of all materials used.

Variables   Selection of sensitive applications, operational circumstances during job runs, operations staff selection, identification of materials used.

Strengths   Concentration of security resources is possible. Minimizes exposure to sources of loss. May increase operational efficiency.

Weaknesses   Might introduce inefficiencies in scheduling production. Targets for compromise become obvious.

How to Audit   Rank and compare sensitivities of all production jobs. Observe special production runs and check on compliance with documented procedures.

Purpose   Deterrence, prevention

Control Area   Computer center

Mode   Manual procedures

Area of Responsibility   Operations

Cost   High

Principles of Note   Least privilege.

Keeping Security Reports Confidential

Objective   Prevent disclosure, taking, or unauthorized use of documents.

Description   Computer security requires the use and filing of numerous reports, including results of security reviews, audits, exception reports, documentation of loss incidence, documentation of controls, control installation and maintenance, and personnel information. These reports are extremely sensitive and should be protected to the same degree as the highest level of information classification within the organization. A clean-desk policy should be maintained in the security and audit offices. All security documents should be physically locked in sturdy cabinets. Computer-readable files should be secured separately from other physically stored files and should have high-level access protection when stored in a computer.

Variables   Security documents, safe storage containers, access authorization.

Strengths   The security function in an organization sets an example for the rest of the organization by appropriately caring for confidential information.

Weaknesses   Keeping security information under a high degree of protection makes the information difficult and time-consuming to use.

How to Audit   The auditors should periodically make an operational audit of the computer security program, including the safe storage of security documents.

Purpose   Prevention

Control Area   Management

Mode   Manual procedures

Area of Responsibility   Computer security

Cost   Low

Principles of Note   Completeness and consistency, accountability, least privilege.

Limit Transaction Privileges from Terminals

Objective   Prevent loss or destruction of assets, prevent unauthorized browsing of system files, prevent "hacking" (trying commands just to see what will happen), prevent system crashes caused by unauthorized use of certain systems commands.

Description   In addition to controlling resources (files, off-line data storage volumes, etc.), the transactions that a particular user is permitted to initiate are limited. What the system commands that a user can use or is informed of is controlled by the user's job duties. Thus, the system level and application commands, such as reporting who is currently logged into the system, are restricted on a need-to-know basis. Logs can be kept for all attempts to use an authorized system command; this can be used to determine who needs training or perhaps disciplinary action.

Variables Transactions to be limited, assignment of privileges to users.

Strengths Prevents users from performing unauthorized acts, including examination of file names of other users and other system-related commands. Without these systems transactions, compromise of the operating system and other such abuses are made significantly harder to accomplish. Because the system commands are monitored and controlled by the computer, they can be sustained and enforced.

Weaknesses Might unduly restrict users' ability to perform their jobs, especially if the users are programmers. Undue restriction might result in reduced productivity and increased levels of frustration. Determination of what commands should be restricted might be involved and time-consuming.

How to Audit Examine system commands permitted for certain groups of users for reasonableness. Review requests for changes in systems command privileges for authorization and need. If available, examine logs for unauthorized attempts to use systems commands that certain users are not permitted to use.

Purpose Prevention

Control Area Computer systems

Mode Computer operating system, computer application system

Area of Responsibility Operations management

Cost Medium

Principles of Note Simplicity, least privilege, independence of control and subject, sustainability.

Limited Use of System Utility Programs

Objective Prevent unauthorized program or data.

Description Most computer installations have one or more system utility programs capable of overriding all or most computer system and application controls. In some computer installations, one such computer program is called Superzap. In one large computer installation, five such utility programs were found. These programs should be controlled by password or kept physically removed from the computer system and the program library and physically controlled so that they are available only to a limited number of trusted, authorized users. Occasionally, if the programs are made available on-line, they can be protected by special passwords required for their use. Changing the name or password frequently is another way to better safeguard these on-line programs.

Variables Utility programs in use, residence of utility programs, operating system features.

Strengths Limitation of availability of system utility programs forces programmers to use more accepted means of accomplishing their purposes that can be more safely done under the controls of the system.

Weaknesses Limitations in the use of existing utility programs might encourage programmers to develop their own programs that are not under the same controls as the utility programs.

How to audit   Operational audits should include the examination of physical and internal computer control of utility programs.

Purpose   Prevention

Control area   Programming and maintenance

Mode   Manual procedures, computer operating system

Area of responsibility   Operations

Cost   Low

Principles of note   Override, least privilege.

Low Building Profile

Objective   Avoid destruction of assets and business interruption.

Description   Buildings housing computer systems and the computer facilities should be unobtrusive and give minimum indication of their purpose. There should be no obvious signs identifying computing activities outside or inside buildings. Buildings should look unimpressive and ordinary relative to nearby buildings. Building lobby directories and company telephone books should not identify locations of computer activities except for offices and reception areas that serve outsiders (users, vendors, etc.) and are located separately from operational areas. Physical access barriers, including access control signs, should be reasonably visible, however.

Variables   Building materials, windows, location relative to other functionally related areas, prestige and image value, safety.

Strengths   A low profile reduces the likelihood of attention by destruction-minded outsiders. Such attention tends to be directed away to other more visible targets.

Weaknesses   A low profile might reduce the business promotion values and inconvenience visitors, vendors, delivery people, and others who have a legitimate need to find computing facilities.

How to audit   Observation by those familiar with computer locations. Tests by persons unfamiliar with computer locations.

Purpose   Deterrence

Control area   Computer center

Mode   Manual procedure

Area of responsibility   Management, security

Cost   Low

Principles of note   Avoidance of need for design secrecy, completeness and consistency, least privilege.

Magnetic Tape Erasure

Objective   Prevent compromise of data.

Description Computer centers should have magnetic tape erasure devices, commonly referred to as *degaussers,* for the erasure of the contents of magnetic tapes. Such devices should be kept under strict control of the computer centers. Preferably, the device should be kept in a locked cabinet and authorized for use by selected individuals. The device should also be kept a significant distance away from magnetic tape storage areas. An erasure service should be offered to computer users, and an option for tape erasure should be made available on magnetic tape disposition forms providing a date upon which erasure should be performed. All magnetic tapes used for temporary storage (scratch tapes) should also be routinely erased before reuse. Dual control or separation of functions should be established to ensure that tapes containing valuable information are not mistakenly erased without authorization.

Variables Location of equipment, procedure for use, erase disposition service.

Strengths Routine erasure of tapes might prevent obsolete data from being used. Erasure of tapes can also be done at the time they are cleaned. High-speed degaussing devices, even when placed near magnetic tapes in storage, do not threaten magnetic media. A log can be used to record all degaussing.

Weaknesses The ease with which large amounts of data can be lost requires great caution.

How to Audit Examine documentation of procedures to erase sensitive information. Observe the handling of erasure activities.

Purpose Prevention

Control Area Computer center

Mode Manual procedures, hardware

Area of Responsibility Operations

Cost Low

Principles of Note Override capability.

Minimize Traffic and Access to Work Areas

Objective Prevent unauthorized access to sensitive areas.

Description Employee and vendor work areas and visitor facilities should be located to minimize unnecessary access. Persons should not have to pass through sensitive areas to reach work stations. Sensitive functions should be placed in low traffic areas. Traffic points through security perimeters should be minimized. Employee convenience facilities such as lavatories, lounges, lockers, and food and drink dispensers should be located to minimize traffic through barriers and sensitive areas. Toilets outside of security perimeters, such as in lobby and receiving areas, are essential. Areas with many work stations should be separated from areas with few work stations. For example, computer peripheral equipment requiring human operation should be in rooms separate from computer equipment requiring little human attention.

Access authorization should be granted on a privileged basis. Three access levels can be granted: general, limited, and by exception. General access is granted to those whose work stations are in a restricted area. In a computer room, this includes computer operations, maintenance staff, and first-level supervisors. Limited access is granted for specified periods of time to those responsible for performing specified preplanned assignments, such as auditors, security personnel, and repair or construction crews.

Finally, exceptions can be made in emergencies as long as those having access are escorted and after which extraordinary measures are taken to ensure integrity of the area. Application programmers no longer need access to computer rooms except on an emergency basis. Systems programmers need access on a limited basis. Visitors should be restricted entirely from computer rooms unless by exception and are accompanied by a high-level manager who explicitly accepts responsibility and is personally accountable. Other sensitive areas, such as programmers' offices, job set-up areas, and data entry work areas, should be similarly restricted to authorized access. Signs identifying limited access areas should be posted, and rules should be strictly enforced.

Variables Functional relationships of computing activities, work assignments, logging accesses, building constraints, worker efficiency, space size requirements, security level differentials, and assets values.

Strengths Unauthorized physical access is one of the greatest security vulnerabilities and is effectively reduced by careful placement of computing activities. Potential for criminal collusion is reduced. In addition, worker efficiency and productivity can be increased when interaction and communication among employees engaged in different activities are not essential. The number of security officers can be decreased.

Weaknesses Employees and managers might resent restricted movement. Reduced interaction and communication among creative people may reduce their performance.

How to Audit Observe traffic and work areas, study functional relationships, and perform traffic analysis.

Purpose Deterrence, prevention

Control Area Computer center

Mode Hardware

Area of Responsibility Security, management

Cost Low

Principles of Note Least privilege, minimization of exceptions, accountability, sustainability.

Minimizing Numbers of Copies of Sensitive Data Files and Reports

Objective Prevent loss, modification, disclosures, or destruction of data assets.

Description The number of copies of sensitive tape, disk, or paper files should be minimized. Destruction dates should be specified and destruction instructions followed. It might be advisable to destroy most paper copies of files on the basis that the information can be retrieved and reprinted from computer media when necessary. This is based on the concept that files stored in computer systems and computer media are generally often more secure than on paper. Normal backup procedures often require that several copies of computer media files be made and stored at different sites.

However, some files might be so sensitive that numerous copies in different locations can contribute seriously to their exposure. As many as 20 to 30 copies of computer-stored files can be produced in a single year in a large computer installation. The organization primarily accountable for highly sensitive information should have control and logs of all copies and their locations. Adequate backup must be balanced with the exposure danger of multiple copies and backup procedures.

Variables Selection of data for special copy control, copy logging procedures, dating for destruction, assignment of responsibilities and accountability.

Strengths Reduction in storage space and orderliness of facilities might be enhanced.

Weaknesses Retention of minimum numbers of copies of records might weaken the backup capability.

How to Audit Selective examination of storage areas looking for sensitive records and comparing to logging forms should be done periodically.

Purpose Prevention

Control Area Computer center

Mode Manual procedures

Area of Responsibility Operations, input/output, computer users

Cost Low

Principles of Note Simplicity, least privilege, completeness and consistency, accountability.

Monitoring Computer Use

Objective Detect unauthorized activities.

Description On a random or periodic selective basis, communications between the host computer and remote terminals are monitored. File names and contents are examined. Such monitoring must be limited to computer activity that is established for business purposes only to avoid privacy invasion. The usage is logged and analyzed to determine that the user is only doing actions that have been explicitly authorized.

Variables Selection basis, monitoring and examination methods and assignments, exception reporting.

Strengths Allows management to determine that computer/communications resources are being used as authorized. Allows management to take evidence of activities of persons they suspect of some wrongdoing. Allows management to determine how certain users interact with the system toward improving services (response time, application, ease of use, etc.). Useful as an audit tool. If users are aware that the activity exists, then they might be deterred from engaging in certain types of acts.

Weaknesses Could be used by unauthorized persons to spy on and/or harass users.

How to Audit Use the same procedures for other auditing matters. Identify individuals who engage in this activity and review their work.

Purpose Deterrence, detection

Control Area Computer system

Mode Manual procedures, computer operating system

Area of Responsibility   Computer security, operations

Cost   Low

Principles of Note   Simplicity, independence of control and subject, instrumentation, accountability.

Participation of Computer Users at Critical Development Times

Objective   Prevent inadequacy of system controls.

Description   Computer users, including those providing input data and using computer output reports, should supply explicit control requirements to systems analysts and programmers who are designing and developing application systems. Users also should be required to explicitly agree that necessary controls have been implemented and continue to function during production use of the system and programming maintenance.

Variables   Policies and procedures, forms for control requirements statements, responsibilities and accountability for adequacy of controls.

Strengths   Users' understanding of their own applications is enhanced significantly when control specifications are required from them. Users are placed in a position where they can make better decisions regarding the appropriate controls in some aspects of applications and determine recovery time requirements. Users become knowledgeable of and sensitive to the needs for computer security and privacy. Sharing of responsibility and accountability for control is enhanced. Separation of duties is also enhanced. Completeness and consistency of controls are more ensured.

Weaknesses   Users might not have sufficient expertise to identify necessary controls. Systems development procedures become more complex.

How to Audit   Review systems design and development procedures at points where users are to be involved. Interview users with respect to their participation, understanding of their role, and awareness of the potential for controls in applications systems.

Purpose   Prevention

Control Area   Systems development

Area of Responsibility   Users, development

Cost   Low

Principles of Note   Independence of control and subject, completeness and consistency, acceptance by personnel, accountability.

Passwords for Computer Terminal Access

Objective   Prevent unauthorized computer system access.

Description   Secret passwords are commonly used for access to computer systems through terminals. However, there is wide variation in the procedures for password administration. Passwords are normally accompanied by a protocol of exchange of recognition between the user and the computer, including the input from the user of a project or account number and a password. Normally, one or more users are working with the computer under a single project or account number. Occasionally, only one password is used for a group of people as well. However, each user should have his own secret password. In some cases, each user can select his own password, and it is known only to him and stored in the computer system. Others select their passwords but must receive approval of them from the computer security coordinator to ensure that they are appropriate and not easily guessed.

Some organizations use computer programs to produce appropriate, easily remembered, but somewhat random passwords. In other cases, passwords are chosen by a computer security administrator and assigned to users. And finally, passwords can be generated automatically by the computer system and assigned to users. Another variation is the assignment of a password to a user with instructions that he is to use his password for initial access, at which time he must then change his password in the computer system. He should be prevented from using the initial password again.

Frequently, privileged passwords are identified in the computer system so that systems programmers and others requiring password access allowing a wider range of system usage and use of special commands can carry out their work. It is generally accepted that passwords should be changed among a group of computer users who might share their passwords every time an individual leaves the immediate group by terminating his employment or given new assignments. Privileged passwords should be changed more frequently than others. Passwords also should be changed whenever there is any indication of possible system abuse or compromise.

If passwords are manually conveyed to users, it should be done in confidential, sealed envelopes personally delivered by a trusted employee or orally in face-to-face conversation in confidential surroundings. A receipt should be received from the user indicating that he has received and accepted a new password and agrees to keep it confidential. These receipts should be kept on file by the computer security administrator. It is best to keep no paper record of passwords, and the master password file in the computer system should be encrypted or otherwise protected. If a password is forgotten by the user, then it should be removed from the computer system and a new password should be assigned. The user should destroy any written record of the password once memorized, and severe penalties should be enforced for writing or revealing the password. An alternative is to keep a record of passwords locked in a safe place such as a vault. This can be done by the project leader for each group of users and is more desirable than having a centralized record of project numbers.

Variables   Password selection, password length, change frequency, record keeping.

Strengths   Secret passwords provide the equivalent protection of combinations for vault access that has long been accepted as safe access to valuable assets. The strength of the password system is primarily dependent on the length of passwords and the password administration.

Weaknesses   The primary weaknesses of password systems concern the administration and discipline with which passwords are used and kept secret by users and administrators and the characteristics of the log-in procedure that limits the likelihood of password compromise.

How to Audit   Auditors should periodically examine the journaling of password activity, looking for unusual patterns. They should observe the password administration to ensure compliance with procedural policy. They should also periodically observe terminal areas to ensure that controls are in place and working.

Purpose   Prevention

Control Area   Management

Mode   Manual procedures

Area of Responsibility   Computer security

Cost   Medium

Principles of Note   Least privilege, independence of control or subject, instrumentation, acceptance, accountability.

Passwords Generated and Printed by Computer in Sealed Envelopes

Objective   Prevent disclosure of passwords.

Description   User passwords are provided by a computerized random number/letter generator and printed directly through sealed envelopes, using the same carbon paper in envelope techniques that are used for many direct deposit receipts. These sealed envelopes are delivered directly to the user without the password ever having been seen by humans. Because the user expects a new password at a certain time, a missing envelop will be noticed, and the previously generated password will be canceled and reissued. Similarly, if an envelope is opened or has evidence of tampering, then the password is canceled and reissued. Receipts are returned to ensure delivery.

Variables   Frequency, computer security during password generation.

Strengths   Prevents persons involved in the password administration area from using passwords without the user's knowledge. Ensures that passwords are distributed on a regular basis without compromise.

Weaknesses   Known techniques can be used to read passwords within these envelopes without having to destroy the seal.

How to Audit   Witness the generation and distribution of sealed password envelopes. Examine the envelopes to determine the ease with which the passwords can be discovered without having to break the seal. Discuss with operations management the pros and cons of assigned versus user-chosen passwords.

Purpose   Prevention

Control Area   Computer system

Mode   Computer application system

Area of Responsibility   Operations, computer security

Cost   Medium

Principles of Note   Least privilege, independence of control and subject.

Personal Data Input/Output Inspection

Objective   Prevent disclosure or unauthorized use of personal information.

Description   An organization that receives or disseminates databases from or to outside sources should have an input/output control group. This group checks the databases when they are received and disseminated. It checks for the inclusion of improper data fields, such as individual names and social security numbers. Also, more sophisticated checking of the relational aspects of the data field is done to determine whether individuals can be identified by combining information from multiple fields. The group screens all files to be received and investigates anomalies. A log is kept of all activity.

Variables Organization, specific rules, approval and logging forms.

Strengths Potential privacy and confidentiality problems are caught early before data are made available to outsiders. This group also examines data to see that they meet the organization's standards with respect to items such as format, content, and value.

Weaknesses High-level people are required to review the databases.

How to Audit Compliance review of existing databases and review of criteria used by the group to evaluate the databases.

Purpose Prevention

Control Area Computer center

Mode Manual procedures

Area of Responsibility User

Cost Medium

Principles of Note Independence of control/subject, compartmentalization, accountability.

Physical Access Barriers

Objective Prevent unauthorized physical access to sensitive areas.

Description Physical access through a security perimeter from a less sensitive area to a more sensitive area or between areas where different privileges apply must be limited to as few openings as possible. The remaining barrier between openings should be made of sufficiently sturdy materials to resist entry. Openings should have entrance controls consisting of one or more of the following methods:

- Sign in/out log
- Challenge of unauthorized entry by authorized persons
- Challenge access by posted signs
- Mechanically or electrically locked doors
- Guards (local or remote using CCTV)
- Mantrap (double) or turnstile doors

In computer centers, limited access should be maintained for all areas except public entry lobbies, lavatories, lounges, food areas, and all areas outside of the outermost security perimeter. There should be a central administration of access throughout a computer center. Procedures must be documented and include exception condition procedures. Emergency exit doors must be provided for safety and to comply with ordinances and insurance requirements.

Variables Location of access, type of access constraints, authorization procedures, logging accesses, strength of barrier materials.

Strengths Access control prevents unnecessary movements of people as well as unauthorized accesses for security purposes. The practice of a secure procedure for gaining access maintains a vigilance and security awareness among authorized persons. It also discourages malicious persons.

Weaknesses   Controls reduce efficiency. There is a danger of mismatching stringency of controls and actual needs. Sustaining adequate levels of effectiveness is difficult unless automatic barriers are used.

How to Audit   Frequent testing by making unauthorized access attempts (without force) and challenging a sample of persons in limited access areas should be done.

Purpose   Prevention

Control Area   Computer center

Mode   Manual procedures, hardware

Area of Responsibility   Security

Cost   Medium

Principles of Note   Least privilege, override capability, completeness and consistency.

Physical Security Perimeter

Objective   To avoid destruction of assets and business interruption.

Description   The physical perimeter within which security is to be maintained and outside of which little or no control is maintained should be clearly established. All vital functions should be identified and included within the security perimeter. Physical access control and prevention of damage immediately outside security perimeters should be carefully considered.

For example, physical barriers should extend to the base floor and to the base ceiling around sensitive areas. Areas beneath false floors and above false ceilings must be controlled consistent with the control of working areas between them. Important equipment, such as electrical power switching and communication equipment and circuits, must be made secure and included within the security perimeter.

Employees and on-site vendors should be made aware of perimeters on a least-privilege basis. The perimeter should be easily discernible, simple, uncluttered, and sufficiently secure relative to the value of assets inside the perimeter. Drawings and specifications of the perimeter should be available and used for planning any facilities changes. Additional barriers between areas with different security requirements within the exterior barrier also should be established.

Variables   Placement of perimeter, perimeter barriers.

Strengths   Consistency and completeness in physical security will ensure maximum protection. Modification of facilities can be made without compromising security.

Weaknesses   Cooperation among all parties involved might break down and limit effectiveness. An obvious perimeter might attract undesirable attention.

How to Audit   Physical inspection of security perimeters should be done periodically, and physical barriers should be tested.

Purpose   Prevention

Control Area   Computer center

Mode Hardware

Area of Responsibility Security

Cost High

Principles of Note Completeness and consistency, minimization of exceptions, isolation, compartmentalization.

Placement of Equipment and Supplies

Objective Avoid destruction of assets and business interruption.

Description Equipment, such as telephone switching panels and cables, utilities, power and air conditioning plants, computer devices, and supplies, such as paper, cards, chemicals, water, tapes, and disks, should be placed or stored to ensure their protection from damage and minimize the adverse effects they might have on other items. Dust, vibration, chemical effects, fire hazards, and electrical interference are produced by some equipment and supplies, and they should be kept separate from equipment and supplies affected by these phenomena. Items requiring special safeguards should be isolated to reduce the extent of required safeguard coverage. In multifloor buildings, vertical as well as horizontal proximity should be considered.

Variables Equipment and supplies, nature and extent of separation requirements and limitations, functional relationships.

Strengths Cost of protection can be reduced. Damage can be reduced and isolated. Traffic can be reduced in some cases.

Weaknesses Distances and barriers between functionally related items might reduce efficiency. For example, small supplies of paper might be needed close to printers because of the remoteness of the primary storage. Traffic problems might arise, such as the need for access within the security perimeter by telephone repairmen.

How to Audit Observe placement of equipment and supplies and conduct vulnerability analysis.

Purpose Prevention

Control Area Computer center

Mode Hardware

Area of Responsibility Computer security, operations

Cost Medium

Principles of Note Control and subject independence, limit of dependence on other mechanisms.

Privileged Information Display Restrictions

Objective Prevent unauthorized data disclosure.

Description Programmers, users, and others who have access to computer databases are allowed to view only the data that pertain to their own job functions. Other data that might be resident on computers, outside the purview of an individual's job duties, are not available, nor is the knowledge of such data available. For example, database data item descriptions have only subsets of the data supplied to particular individuals. Assistance programs, system documentation, and the like are specially tailored to the needs of different groups of individuals with different duties.

Variables   Design of database index and tables of contents displays, access administration.

Strengths   If users, programmers, and others with access to the data do not know that certain data types are available, then they are prevented from perpetrating abuses associated with these data. Similarly, if these individuals do not have documentation or other information regarding these data, although they know these data exist, they are prevented from perpetrating unauthorized acts.

Weaknesses   Time-consuming and expensive to maintain separation of reference information of the data resident on computerized systems. May not facilitate certain efficiencies to be discovered and implemented.

How to Audit   Review systems design documentation to determine that individuals are not provided with more than the requisite information. Review systems development guidelines. Test access controls.

Purpose   Prevention

Control Area   Application system, computer system

Mode   Computer operating system, computer application systems

Area of Responsibility   Computer security, development

Cost   High

Principles of Note   Simplicity, avoidance of need for design secrecy, least privilege, acceptance by personnel, minimization of exceptions.

Production Program Authorized Version Validation

Objective   Prevent unauthorized program or data modification.

Description   The authorized versions or copies of production programs, according to identifiers, are checked with a list of authorized copies and changes made to the production programs to determine that the version of a production program to be run is authorized. Update of the list is part of the ordinary maintenance process of production programs. Separate test and production program libraries are maintained.

Variables   Identifiers, procedures, exception handling.

Strengths   Prevents unauthorized versions of the production programs from being executed when used in conjunction with other related controls. Accidentally running a test version or an old version of a production program can be prevented and detected using this technique. Unauthorized versions of production programs can be similarly detected and prevented from being run.

Weaknesses   Requires that the list of authorized change data and identifiers be protected from unauthorized changes. Adds additional complexity to the maintenance and production running procedures. The process might have to be disabled for recovery or emergency purposes.

How to Audit Logs showing all exceptions (compile dates that do not match) should be examined regularly; additionally, it should be determined whether action has been taken to follow up on all instances where a match between the list of authorized versions does not match identifiers.

Purpose Prevention, detection

Control Area Computer center

Mode Manual procedures

Area of Responsibility Operations

Cost Low

Principles of Note Minimization of exceptions, instrumentation, auditability.

Programming Library Access Control

Objective Prevent unauthorized access to sensitive areas.

Description Computer program libraries containing listings of programs under development and in production and associated documentation must be protected from unauthorized access. In larger organizations, a full-time or part-time librarian can be used to control access, logging in, and logging out all documents. The program library should be physically separated by barriers from other activities. Documents should be distributed only to authorized users.

It might be necessary to enforce strict access control to programmers' offices as a means of protecting programs and documentation. Programmers should have lockable file cabinets in which they can store materials currently in use. A clean-desk policy at the end of each working day might be justified as an extreme measure. Program and documentation control is particularly important when using or developing licensed software packages because of the strict contractual limitations and liabilities.

Variables Resources available for program library access control, barriers surrounding the program library and programmers' offices, policies and procedures regarding protection of documentation and program listings.

Strengths Demonstrates the importance of computer program assets to the organization. Provides separation of duty among programmers to ensure that programmers have access only to the documentation and programs within their areas of responsibility.

Weaknesses Restrictions on access might stifle communications and creativity of the programming staff.

How to Audit Observe operation of the program library, make unexpected visits and observations of programmer offices, review procedures and policies for restricting access.

Purpose Prevention

Control Area Programming and maintenance

Mode Manual procedures

Area of Responsibility Development

Cost Medium

Principles of Note Least privilege, control and subject independence, acceptance by personnel, accountability.

Proprietary Notice Printed on Documents

Objective Prevent disclosure or unauthorized use of documents.

Description Sensitive and valuable documents have a classification (e.g., "sensitive," "private," "proprietary," "confidential," "for authorized parties only") or an explicit warning indicating that the information is the property of a certain organization, that it should be handled according to special criteria, that it is not to be used for certain purposes, etc.

One site chose to print confidential in the middle of the page; although this made reading a bit more difficult, it prevented people from cropping the record and photocopying it to remove any indication that it was confidential. Another approach is to have the computer print appropriate words on only sensitive output. (This has the advantage of warning display terminal users that the information should be specially treated.) Policies and procedures must also be written.

Variables Selecting documents, wording, how printed, rules of use, owner's interest.

Strengths This control reduces ambiguity associated with the use and dissemination of sensitive information, provides concrete evidence that steps were taken to control information (this may be of use in court), and can be used to control use of proprietary software. Likelihood of privacy violation can to some extent be avoided or lessened. Use of copyright or trademark laws may reduce unauthorized distribution and usage of sensitive information.

Weaknesses Errors of omission become more severe.

How to Audit Examine samples of output to see that they contain an appropriate notice. Discuss the wording of such notices with legal counsel. Determine that the notice cannot easily be stripped from the output.

Purpose Deterrence

Control Area Computer center, application system

Mode Manual procedures, application system, computer system.

Area of Responsibility User, legal, computer security, operations, input/output.

Cost Low

Principles of Note Minimization of exceptions, compartmentalization, acceptance, sustainability, auditability.

Protection of Data Used in System Testing

Objective Prevent compromise of data.

Description   Application and test programmers usually need test data to develop, debug, and test programs under development. In some cases, small amounts of fictitious test data can be generated independent of users and production data. However, many application programs require significant amounts of test data that are exact copies of a full range of production data. Test data are frequently obtained as samples or entire files of production input data currently being used or recently used for the application being replaced or as output from other preprocessing computer programs. There is sometimes significant exposure by providing real, current production data to programmers.

Often data can be obtained from obsolete production input data files, but in some cases even these data might be confidential. Customers for whom production programs are being developed should be made aware of the exposure problem, and advice and assistance should be obtained in producing test data in the least confidential but expedient manner. Sensitive test data should be treated with the same care as equivalent production data. In any case, development and test programmers should not be given access to real production files in a production computer system except in the case of emergency and then under highly controlled conditions.

Variables   Selection of test data procedure, physical and logical handling of test data.

Strengths   This control can greatly reduce the exposure of an organization to a wide range of errors, omissions, and intentional acts. It also imposes a beneficial discipline on development and test computer programmers.

Weaknesses   Providing separate test data might be particularly expensive and not necessary in every case. Good decisions require the knowledgeable participation of customers for whom computer programs are being developed. This is sometimes difficult to obtain. Test data also might not be sufficiently representative. Production runs masquerading as test runs to expedite work is a possible problem.

How to Audit   Auditing requires a detailed knowledge of programming and testing practices and detailed observation of the software development life cycle.

Purpose   Prevention

Control Area   Operations

Mode   Manual procedures

Area of Responsibility   Development

Cost   Medium

Principles of Note   Least privilege.

Remote Terminal Physical Security

Objective   Prevent unauthorized access to sensitive areas.

Description   Physical access barriers, accountability for use, and resistance to visual and electromagnetic monitoring of terminals and local communication loops are maintained and periodically reviewed consistent with security of the computer system being used from the terminal. Terminals are frequently owned or are under the control of computer users and often do not come under the jurisdiction of computer centers supplying services. Therefore, this control is directed to users or indirectly to computer center employee functions as liaison to terminal users and has the authority to disallow system access from any terminal where acceptable controls are not in place. Signed agreements are used to enforce the requirements.

Resistance to visual or electromagnetic monitoring can include line-of-sight barriers to prevent reading of displays from a distance and placing terminals sufficiently removed from a security perimeter so that electromagnetic emanations would be costly to monitor. Securing of work papers and terminal media should also be ensured. Locks on terminals, clearing of work areas after use, and bolting of terminals to fixed objects might be considered.

Variables   Barriers, usage logging, distance to security perimeter, control of visual media, terminal locking mechanisms, mechanisms to prevent removal of equipment.

Strengths   Security consistency can be maintained over all system use. Losses are probably more likely to occur around terminals and during usage because people in positions of trust concentrate at terminals. Security reviews by computer center security staff facilitate independence and objectivity.

Weaknesses   Cost of security, remoteness, and informal environments make controls difficult to maintain. Portable terminals increase difficulty of security.

How to Audit   Review remote terminal inspection reports. Examine usage logs at terminals and compare with system-produced logs. Conduct surprise audits at selected sites where problems are reported.

Purpose   Detection, prevention

Control Area   Computer center (and its extensions)

Mode   Manual procedures

Area of Responsibility   Computer users

Cost   Medium

Principles of Note   Least privilege, completeness, and consistency.

Remote Terminal User's Agreement

Objective   Prevent assets responsibility loss.

Description   All remote users are required to sign a user's agreement before they are permitted to use system resources. The agreement covers who shall pay for systems-related expenses, identifies physical location and relocation of terminals, establishes maintenance and service of equipment, assigns training of users, states hours of usage, instructs on further dissemination of information obtained from the system, details proper usage of the system, assigns physical security of terminals and other equipment, states service provider rights to deny service and to inspect equipment, establishes insurance coverage and liability for losses and renegotiation of the agreement, and other related matters.

Variables   Form design and content, accountability for administration, period of agreement.

Strengths   Clearly delineates the rights and obligations of both the service user and provider. Serves as an authoritative source for resolution of disputes between users and service providers. Allows service providers to sensitize users to security and privacy concerns before users can do work on the system.

Weaknesses Legality of certain provisions might be in doubt and might require attention of legal counsel. Certain users might believe that the agreement does not suit their circumstances and might wish to modify the agreement or eliminate it entirely. Agreements might need to be renegotiated in light of additional legislation, regulation, or management decisions.

How to Audit Examine user agreements for reasonableness and to make sure that they are still current. Consult with legal counsel about the enforceability of various clauses in the contract. Visit user sites to determine that the terms of the contract are being met.

Purpose Deterrence, recovery

Control Area Computer center, management

Mode Manual procedures

Area of Responsibility Legal, user, computer security, operations

Cost Low

Principles of Note Simplicity, independence of control and subject, accountability.

Requirements and Specification Participation by EDP Auditors

Objective To prevent inadequacy of system controls.

Description EDP auditors should participate in the development of requirements for important applications systems to ensure that the audit requirements in applications systems are adequate and that adequate controls have been specified. EDP auditors should be required to sign off on all formalized application system requirements and specifications.

Variables EDP audit resources, procedures specifying EDP audit participation, forms for signoff.

Strengths The auditability of application systems is strengthened and can reduce the cost of both internal and external audits.

Weaknesses It might be claimed that excessive participation by EDP auditors could result in a loss of independence, because the EDP auditors must also evaluate the adequacy of implemented controls.

How to Audit Audit management should periodically review EDP auditor participation and ensure that all significant application systems receive audit attention.

Purpose Prevention

Control Area Programming and maintenance

Mode Manual procedures

Area of Responsibility Audit

Cost Medium

Principles of Note Auditability, accountability, control and subject independence, completeness and consistency.

Responsibilities for Application Program Controls

Objective Prevent inadequacy of controls.

Description The inclusion of controls in application programs should be explicitly ensured and documented starting with design requirements and continuing through specifications development, production, and maintenance stages. The responsibility for adequacy and types of controls should be shared among EDP auditors, systems analysts, computer programmers, users, and data owners. Explicit documentation of controls is essential to ensure completion of their implementation, test, development of operational procedures, to carry out the intent of the controls, and to ensure their integrity during change and maintenance.

Variables Documentation procedures and forms, policy.

Strengths It is difficult to document explicitly all controls that must be in application programs. However, establishing the procedures to ensure that controls are adequate and included in applications provides assurance that applications will be adequately controlled.

Weaknesses Controls that are not adequately supported by computer program application users will not be effective, and sufficient budgeting of money and resources will not be provided to adequately complete the specified controls.

How to Audit Auditors' participation in design requirements and postimplementation testing for compliance with specifications.

Purpose Prevention

Control Area Programming and maintenance

Mode Manual procedures

Area of Responsibility Development, computer users

Cost High

Principles of Note Completeness and consistency, instrumentation.

Secrecy of Data File and Program Name

Objective Prevent loss, modification, disclosure, or destruction of data assets.

Description Names for data files and computer programs are necessary for computer program development and documentation. They are also necessary for job setup and in some cases for computer operation. However, file and program names need not be known by those people who are in a transaction relationship with the computer system and not concerned with programming of computer applications. Therefore, a different set of terminology, and naming of entities should be developed for documentation of users manuals and for transaction activities.

Variables Selection of systems, naming conventions.

Strengths   The least-privilege or need-to-know principle significantly reduces the exposure of sensitive assets. Separation of duties must also include the separation of information.

Weaknesses   Having two sets of names for computer program application entities complicates communications between programmers and users.

How to Audit   Examination of computer program documentation and user documentation can indicate that different naming conventions are being used.

Purpose   Prevention

Control Area   Application system

Mode   Manual procedures

Area of Responsibility   Development

Cost   Low

Principles of Note   Least privilege, control and subject independence.

Security for Sensitive Areas During Unattended Periods

Objective   To avoid destruction of assets and business interruption.

Description   Sensitive areas during unattended time should be made physically secure with locked doors, significant barriers, and automatic detection devices for movement or natural disaster losses. Periodic inspection by guards and closed-circuit TV monitoring are also important. In addition, sensitive areas not generally visible to others should never be occupied by a lone employee for safety and prevention of malicious acts. Some computer-related work areas such as the computer room are occupied by employees at all times. Other areas and some computer rooms are left unattended for varying periods of time from several hours per day to only 1 or 2 days, such as holidays, each year. Safeguarding when employees are present and not present represents significantly different security requirements.

Variables   Detection and suppression equipment (vendors of equipment can assist in selection), guard inspections, periods of unattended time.

Strengths   Adequate control of unattended areas will ensure consistency of security.

Weaknesses   Unattended sensitive areas are particularly vulnerable, and automatic monitoring might not be sufficiently comprehensive to cover all contingencies.

How to Audit   Auditors should periodically inspect unattended areas during times in which they are unattended.

Purpose   Detection

Control Area   Computer center

Mode   Manual procedures, hardware

Area of Responsibility   Security

Cost   Medium

Principles of Note   Universal application, completeness and consistency, instrumentation.

Separation and Accountability of EDP Functions

Objective   Prevent loss of security support.

Description   Holding managers accountable for the security in the areas they manage requires that these areas be clearly and explicitly defined so that there is no overlap or gaps in managerial control of EDP functions. EDP functions should be broken down into as many discrete self-contained activities as is practical and cost-effective under the circumstances.

Besides being a good general management principle to maintain high performance, it also provides the necessary explicit structure for assignment of controls, responsibility for them, accountability and a means of measuring the completeness and consistency of meeting all vulnerabilities adequately. Separate, well-defined EDP functions also facilitate the separation of duties among managers, as is required in separation of duties of employees. This reduces the level of trust needed for each manager. The functions of authorization, custody of assets, and accountability should be separated to the extent possible.

Variables   EDP functions, accountability policy.

Strengths   This separation reduces the possibility of accidental or intentional acts resulting in losses. It forces the need for collusion among individuals who may attempt unauthorized activities. More efficient EDP functions are possible. The possible loss of control is inhibited from migrating from one function to another.

Weaknesses   Increased complexity of EDP functions could result from excessive separation of functions, making the application of individual controls more difficult. Small shops may not have adequate numbers of employees to support extensive separation of duties.

How to Audit   Managers of EDP functions should be interviewed and their charters examined to ensure adequate separation and effectiveness of functional interfaces. Interfaces should be reviewed for consistency and completeness.

Purpose   Prevention

Control Area   Management

Mode   Policy

Area of Responsibility   Management

Cost   Low

Principles of Note   Limit of dependence on other mechanisms, completeness and consistency, accountability.

Separation of Equipment

Objective   Prevent damage to equipment.

Description   Different types of computer equipment (central processors, disk drives, tape libraries, terminals consoles) each require different environments for optimum operation and different numbers and types of people in attendance. Therefore, they should be placed in different rooms with appropriate separation walls, distances, and accesses. For example, printers create dust and vibration from paper movement and should be separate from disk and tape drives that are sensitive to air quality and vibration. Central processors are normally unattended and should be in a low traffic environment.

Variables   Equipment configurations, size of spaces available, traffic patterns.

Strengths   Reduces repairs, avoids excessive environment and traffic controls.

Weaknesses   Increases expenses of facilities changes when new equipment is acquired.

How to Audit   Participate in facilities design. Review usable space.

Purpose   Prevention

Control Area   Computer center

Mode   Hardware

Area of Responsibility   Computer security, operations

Cost   High

Principles of Note   Simplicity, sustainability.

Separation of Personal Identification Data

Objective   Prevent disclosure or unauthorized use of personal information.

Description   For databases that identify individuals as well as contain sensitive information about individuals, the database is separated into a file of personal identifiers and a file of data with an index linking the identifiers with the data.

Variables   Justification for separation, method of separation.

Strengths   Physical separation of data fields ensures that privacy of individuals will not be compromised, even if other controls are compromised. It is required by law (Title 28) in criminal justice agencies and possibly in other situations.

Weaknesses   The process is complex and requires significant administrative procedures. Special systems procedures might be needed.

How to Audit   Review how files are set up and check records that log destruction of link files.

Purpose   Prevention

Control Area   Application system

Mode   Manual procedures

Area of Responsibility   User

Cost   Medium

Principles of Note   Independence of control and subject.

Separation of Test and Production Systems

Objective   Prevent loss, modification, disclosure, or destruction of data assets.

Description   When an organization is large enough to have need for more than one computer, there is a distinct advantage to limiting the development and test to one computer system and production work to another computer system. Further separation of activities can also be achieved by using multiple production systems and even multiple test systems where each application is run on a separate computer system. Likewise, each group of programmers could do testing on separate computer systems. The cost benefits of large size and high memory capacity would be lost, but applications could be more nearly matched to the appropriate size of computer and memory. Compilers may be moved to the test system.

Variables   Size of test and production workloads, available computers, location of development staff.

Strengths   Separation of systems reduces the possibility of accidental or intentional programmed access to production files and programs. It separates the duties of operations staff from development staff and reduces the likelihood of system crashes on the production system. The data processing organization can orient the systems configurations and mode of operation to that of the specific purpose of the system. This also forces a more formal approach to the movement of test systems to the status of production systems. The test computer can also provide backup for production computers.

Weaknesses   The increased complexity of operating more than one computer for different purposes increases other loss exposures. Operating systems and configurations will require compatibility.

How to Audit   This control can be audited to ensure that the production system is not being used for test or programming development purposes and that the test system is not being used for production purposes by examining usage logs and sampling output reports and the use of output.

Purpose   Prevention

Control Area   Computer center

Mode   Policy

Area of Responsibility   Operations, development

Cost   High

Principles of Note   Control and subject independence.

Sufficient Personal Identifiers for Database Search

Objective   Prevent disclosure or unauthorized use of personal information.

Description   To reduce the probability that an erroneous match between personal data and identification will occur, a sufficient set of personal identifiers is required before searches are permitted. Using techniques for the location of a personal record involves the ranking of several matches or near matches on several fields, such as name, date of birth, race, and sex. Because the erroneous identification, such as a criminal history or other record for an individual, can involve potential harm to the individual, the probability of a correct match should be very high. One installation identifies a sufficient set as complete name including known aliases (or maiden name if applicable), race, sex, and date of birth.

Variables   Data files to be protected, identifier sufficiency.

Strengths   Increases the chances that records will be updated with valid information.

Weaknesses   Valuable processing might be precluded because the requisite search information was not obtainable. Special circumstances, such as a variable number of personal identifiers, increases complexity. Administrative costs can be increased if such strict rules are implemented and followed.

How to Audit   Examine database search procedures looking for situations in which an individual could erroneously be associated with a record.

Purpose   Prevention

Control Area   Application system

Mode   Computer application system

Area of Responsibility   Computer users

Cost   Medium

Principles of Note   Simplicity, override capability, least privilege.

Suppression of Incomplete and Obsolete Data

Objective   Prevent modification, disclosure, or unauthorized use of obsolete or incomplete input or output data.

Description   Dissemination and use of incomplete and obsolete data are prevented or restricted by directive of the organization. This directive must be implemented by data receivers that are to be processed, converted, or stored by reasonableness checks within application systems and by output control and dissemination activities.

For example, in criminal justice information systems, access to nonconviction and arrest data that are one year old or more and do not contain a disposition, is restricted to certain types of requesters. The same concept (i.e., if a record is incomplete or outdated it should not be disseminated) can be applied to other applications besides criminal histories. Such data also can be selectively restricted by requester type.

Variables   Means of invoking directions, identification of relevant types of data, violation or exception actions, sanctions, recovery from disclosure.

Strengths   Prevents decisions from being based on outdated and/or incomplete information. Prevents the privacy of a data subject from being violated (in the above example, if the individual were to be acquitted, the arrest information would not be disseminated). Allows databases to be updated (old and irrelevant information can be deleted), thus reducing operating costs and potentially increasing performance.

Weaknesses   Prevents decisions from being made on the best information available (a worse decision might be made based on no information than on partial or outdated information). Lack of automatic means of detecting incomplete or obsolete data makes directives difficult to enforce.

How to Audit   Review dissemination policies and procedures for reasonableness and compliance with regulatory, statutory, and civil requirements. Review procedures to block dissemination of certain types of information. Review procedures to expunge records from certain databases.

Purpose   Prevention

Control Area   Management

Mode   Manual procedures

Area of Responsibility   Input/output control, users, management, development

Cost   Low

Principles of Note   Completeness and consistency.

Tape Management Avoiding External Labels

Objective   Prevent loss, modification, or destruction of data assets.

Description   A tape management system can be used to keep track of all tapes using a serial number appearing on the tape reel. Serial numbers contain storage rack location information as well as a serial number. Operators handling the tapes do not know the contents of the tapes because the identify of the data set owner, creation and update dates, data set names, and like information are recorded only on internal (machine readable) labels. The software package for managing tapes contains an index of serial numbers and the corresponding label information. An up-to-date copy of the index relating serial numbers and tape information is maintained at off-site storage location(s).

Variables   Tape management system, volume of routinely processed tapes, special handling.

Strengths   Provides operators with no more information than is necessary to do their jobs, thus preventing potential abusive acts that were made possible because these data were available to the operators. Operators are presented only with a request to mount, dismount, etc. certain tapes with provided serial numbers. Reduces operator errors associated with mounting the wrong version of a data set, the wrong user, etc. A tape management system can be used to monitor operator performance as well as control the tape library. Persons in the tape library or machine room cannot learn the nature of the data on a tape simply by examining the reel.

Weaknesses   Lack of functional labels might increase errors.

How to Audit   Trace the steps taken to mount and dismount a tape reel from the initiation of a request to the actual performance by the operator. Examine data available to the operator to determine that confidentiality is not lessened by unwarranted exposures.

Purpose   Prevention

Control Area   Computer center

Mode   Computer operating system

Area of Responsibility   Operations

Cost   Medium

Principles of Note   Cost-effectiveness, simplicity, least privilege, independence of control and subject, instrumentation, sustainability, auditability.

Technical Review of Operating System Changes

Objective   Avoid inadequacy of controls.

Description Whenever any change is to be made to the computer operating system programs, a review of the change is made. The intent is to make sure that the new changes are valuable and will not compromise controls and integrity, have an unanticipated impact on some other part of the system, or interfere excessively with vendor updates.

Variables Review procedures, authorization assignment.

Strengths Review helps prevent unnecessary changes and simplifies testing and understanding of the system.

Weaknesses Slowdown of changes can occur. Loss of compatibility with vendor's version may require costly, independent maintenance.

How to Audit Review the logs of systems changes and compare with actual changes.

Purpose Prevention

Control Area Computer system

Mode Manual procedures

Area of Responsibility Operations

Cost Medium

Principles of Note Override capability, accountability.

Telephone Access Universal Selection

Objective Avoid computer access exposure.

Description Limiting access to a computer and data files can be an important means of security. Several means of accomplishing this are possible. It might be possible and important to eliminate dial-up access to a computer. A computer interfaced to the dial-up public telephone network is exposed to access from any telephone in the world. There might be a trade-off in computer security by giving up or limiting the benefits of dial-up access. This can be accomplished by using only point-to-point wire or leased-line telephone access to the computer. An alternative is to provide dial-up access to a small computer for development or other timesharing purposes while reserving another computer for more sensitive production activity that is not interfaced to dial-up telephones. A control computer providing access to two or more other computers also can be used as a means of protecting them from dial-up access.

An alternative method of restricting access is to provide for dial-up access at limited periods of time of day. During periods of dial-up access, particularly sensitive files or applications would not be resident in the computer system or secondary storage. A variation is to remove all sensitive files from secondary storage except at the explicit times of use of these files. A partial degree of protection for dial-up access systems is to maintain strict need-to-know availability of the telephone numbers and log-in protocol for accessing the computer system. Most dial-up timesharing computer services have similar access protocols; therefore, a unique, very different initial access exchange of identifying information may be useful to limit access. The telephone numbers should be unlisted, different in pattern of digits, and have different prefixes from voice telephone numbers for the organizations that are publicly listed. Call back to verify the source of telephone access is also popular.

Variables Type of communication service, selection of telephone numbers, log-in protocol, time limits, call back.

Strengths Avoidance of exposure is a particularly strong means of simplifying and reducing the problems of securing computer systems. Limiting or eliminating dial-up access significantly reduces exposure.

Weaknesses An important objective for computers is to make them easily and widely accessible. Eliminating or limiting dial-up significantly reduces this capability.

How to Audit Access capabilities, review access logs.

Purpose Prevention

Control Area Computer systems

Mode Hardware

Area of Responsibility Operations

Cost High

Principles of Note Least privilege, limit dependence on other mechanisms.

Terminal Identifiers

Objective Prevent unauthorized computer access.

Description Automatic terminal identification circuits can be installed in or associated with terminals for identification in host computers. Terminal identifiers are used to indicate whether a particular terminal is permitted to initiate or receive certain transactions. This access control requires that remote terminals be physically secured and that only certain known individuals be able to access remote terminals. Cryptographic devices can be used as terminal identifiers. Certain record change requests must be handled by means other than the use of these remote terminals, such as through the mail to a central facility; in this way records integrity can be preserved. Unauthorized intentional or accidental use of applications programs is prevented. A log records all unauthorized attempts to use applications programs.

Variables Selection of devices, host system controls, exception reporting and journaling usage.

Strengths Users might not have to be bothered with log-in/log-off procedures.

Weaknesses Requires that remote terminals be attended or physically secure 24 hours a day. Does not have users individually identified, hence accountability is hindered. Does not permit different users to have different privileges if only one terminal is available.

How to Audit Examine records of access privileges to determine that users are not given privileges that they do not need in order to do their job. Examine all user privilege change requests and actions to determine that all the changes of user privileges are both justifiable and authorized. Use remote terminal to actually test the access control system and logging facilities. Examine exception reports produced when unauthorized accesses occur to make sure that all unauthorized attempts were followed up.

Purpose Prevention

Control Area Computer system

Mode Hardware, computer operating system

Area of Responsibility   Computer security, development

Cost   High

Principles of Note   Least privilege, instrumentation, auditability, accountability.

Terminal Log-in Protocol

Objective   Prevent unauthorized computer access.

Description   The protocol for logging into a computer system from a computer should be designed to reduce unauthorized access. The terminal response to a log-in should provide a minimum of information to avoid providing an unauthorized user with any assistance. No system identifying information should be provided until the full user identification process has been successfully completed. There should be no feedback aids to an unauthorized user at any time during the log-in process that would provide clues to correct or incorrect input. Incorrect input should result in no assistance, and the system should disconnect. When user identification and password are being typed in, there should be no intermediate feedback from the system during the typing of this information that indicates whether the system has accepted any partially completed identification input. This requires that a user enter the complete set of identification and password information before there is any indication of whether this information is correct or not.

Identification information should consist of the user name or other nonsecret identification such as account number, followed by input of the secret password. Display terminals should provide display suppression while the password is being typed in to avoid its observation by another person. Printer terminals should provide nonprinting character mode or provide underprinting and overprinting of the spaces where the password is printed on the page. Additional, personal questions can be posed by the computer system to be answered by the terminal user to further ensure correct identity. No more than three attempts at entry of an unacceptable identification or password should be allowed. Three unsuccessful attempts should cause a telephone line disconnect. Time delay after an incorrect identification or password input of several seconds should occur to increase the work factor of automated exhaustive search for passwords. Also, a limited amount of time should be allowed for entry of a password before a telephone disconnect is performed.

A variation of a password should be provided as a duress alarm. For example, if an individual is being forced to enter his password at a terminal he might interchange the last two characters that result in an immediate alarm at the host computer system that an entry is being attempted under duress. Any log-in that deviates from normal or accepted ranges of activity should be noted in an exception report at the host computer console in a timely manner for immediate action by a computer operator.

All log-ins, whether authorized or unauthorized, should be journaled for later audit trail analysis. A means of allowing an unauthorized terminal user to gain authorized access to the system under totally monitored conditions should be provided to assist in locating sources of unauthorized attempts. Unauthorized users can be provided enough benign services to keep them at the terminal long enough for other detection activity to take place. Each time authorized users log into the system successfully, they should be provided with information concerning the date and time of the last time they logged into the system. Other information about their last sessions also can be summarized. Users can be made aware of any possible unauthorized use of their password in this manner.

Variables   Protocol information exchanges, nature and length of identification and password information, limit parameter values, journaling and exception reports, controlled unauthorized access mechanisms, computer operator procedures in the event of exceptional activity.

Strengths Log-in controls can provide a means of positive identification of terminal users and motivate them to use good security practices.

Weaknesses Inconveniences during log-in might discourage terminal users or tempt them to violate or test the log-in requirements. Excessive log-in requirements can cause many more log-in mistakes by authorized users.

How to Audit Periodically test log-in procedures using out of bound, unacceptable activities to ensure exception recording effectiveness.

Purpose Prevention

Control Area Computer system

Mode Computer operating system

Area of Responsibility Computer security

Cost Low

Principles of Note Simplicity, override capability, least privilege, minimization of exceptions, instrumentation, acceptance by personnel.

Universal Use of Badges

Objective Prevent unauthorized access to sensitive areas.

Description To control access to sensitive data processing facilities, all persons are required to wear badges. Different color badges, including photos in some cases, are used for employees, visitors, vendor representatives, and those employees requiring temporary badges (used when employees have forgotten or lost their badge). All persons are required to wear their badges in conspicuous places on their person; visitors, and in some cases everybody, could be required to leave an item of identification such as a driver's license at the front desk when they are issued a badge.

The decision to require badges depends on business practices, numbers of people, amount of traffic, and other access controls in use. For two or three people in an area with little traffic, the need for badges in that area might be precluded. However, minimization of exceptions may warrant their use. Positive badge administration is essential. Disciplinary action should result from infractions of the rules.

Variables Type of badges, administration, use of card keys, areas and people affected.

Strengths Quick visual inspection should allow management, auditors, and others to determine whether someone is authorized to be in sensitive areas and if so, what their status is. Badge color codes also can designate work areas. Unauthorized parties are prevented from gaining access and causing harm (violating someone's privacy, causing damage to expensive equipment, harming employees etc.). Separation of duties and unnecessary visiting restrictions are strengthened when badges restrict the movement of employees within data processing facilities.

Weaknesses Unless universally and continuously enforced, this procedure can provide little security.

How to Audit Visually check the use of badges and the extent to which they control access to restricted areas. Examine logs of visitors to make sure that proper badges were issued, that proper records (time in, time out, name, badge number issued, etc.) are kept.

Purpose   Prevention, detection

Control Area   Computer center (and its extensions)

Mode   Manual procedures

Area of Responsibility   Security

Cost   Medium

Principles of Note   Override, overt design and operation, least privilege, universal application, instrumentation, minimization of interruptions.

Vendor-Supplied Program Integrity

Objective   Avoid inadequacy of controls.

Description   To the greatest extent possible and practical, vendor-supplied computer programs should be used without modification. Many new vendor-supplied computer programs have been developed with controls and integrity built into them. Any modifications to these programs will possibly compromise the built-in capabilities. Desired changes to the programs should be obtained from the vendor as standard program updates.

Variables   Selection of programs, authorizations.

Strengths   This control is a means of preserving the security and integrity built into vendor-supplied computer programs. It is also a means of holding vendors responsible for any deficiencies in the programs.

Weaknesses   Failure to modify computer programs to make them more responsive to users needs may encourage users to subvert or neutralize existing controls.

How to Audit   This control could reduce the frequency of changes to computer programs, thus facilitating director code comparison of production programs with master backup copies of programs. This should be done periodically to ensure that management policy is followed in restricting modification of vendor-supplied computer programs.

Purpose   Prevention

Control Area   Computer center

Mode   Policy

Area of Responsibility   Management

Cost   Low

Principles of Note   Accountability

B

A Framework for Risk Management

This appendix is based on the report of a study panel appointed by the National Bureau of Standards to review questions of computer security auditing and management: This panel addressed itself to the identification of appropriate managerial control objectives and potential system vulnerabilities and exposures (risks) relating to computer system activities. We considered system vulnerabilities and potential control and security techniques from a management perspective for each of several organizational elements. We considered this appropriate because management must be considered to be accountable for system actions and misactions. Further, management must take an overall responsibility to assure the existence of reasonable standards for system control and security, and undertake responsibility to assure that all system user personnel understand their responsibilities and duties in complying with such standards.

Organizational Elements

In undertaking our task, we assumed a "worst case" environmental situation employing multiple use teleprocessing systems. Further, we restricted our considerations to those organizational elements of the hypothetical governmental agency structure designed by National Bureau of Standards that were assigned to us, and which included the following:

1. Operational divisions
2. Information systems project management
3. Data handling
4. Application program development
5. Data communications
6. Program validation

Operational divisions

An operational division is considered to be an agency organizational unit responsible for one or more general agency functions. We assumed a management unit relating to the Information System Project Management and Data Handling Activities.

Information system project management

This subelement of an Operational Division was assumed to be responsible and have authority for the successful management of the hypothetical information system from the user's perspective. Its activities were considered to include ensuring that (a) all user requirements have been identified, (b) appropriate user specified controls are included in the system to assure accurate and timely results, and (c) system performance effectively supports the user's objectives as approved by general management.

Data handling

This subelement was considered to be responsible for all facets of data preparation, transport to and from input and output devices, and report distribution and storage.

Application program development

Under the assumed hypothetical agency organizational structure, all application program development and support are situated outside of data processing as a separate design activity even though many agencies place this function within data processing or within their organizational units. This element was, therefore, considered to include all facets of information systems analysis, programming and testing required to develop computer-based systems to support all levels of agency management operations. (As indicated by the hypothetical agency structure, we assumed that establishing standards for programming, testing and documentation of applications was not the responsibility of this group, but that we were required to assure that such standards were complied with.)

Data communications

This element was considered as responsible for the movement of computer-encoded information by means of data transmission systems. We concentrated on questions of control and security of system transactions. We assumed that considerations relating to specific communication system hardware and transmission path components would be covered by the technical panel groups established for that purpose.

Program validation

This subelement was identified as responsible for reviewing, validating, and approving all programs and program changes placed on the system. From a management perspective, we consider its activities as an inherent part of both the Information Systems Project Management and Application Program Development elements and did not retain it as a discrete and separate organizational group for purposes of this report.

Objectives

The panel believes that the objectives of a system of controls and the risks associated with a failure to achieve them can and should be identified. Although these objectives and risks are not necessarily new, the panel believes they need to be reemphasized in all entities. In addition, the panel believes the following overriding control objectives must receive a higher level of attention than has been the case in the past.

1. Management has the ultimate responsibility for system controls. Therefore, they must have an appropriate comprehension and understanding of controls and where they can break down.

2. Users have a nonnegotiable responsibility for the controls in their systems. Clear definition of user controls and user understanding of those controls are essential to overall system controllability.

3. Short- and long-term planning and budgeting within a properly designed organization structure is a key internal control. Without them, the entity will not be able to recognize, accept, or manage the changes that take place within the entity.

4. An appropriate systems development methodology, which requires active management and user participation and which results in a documented structure of systems controls, is essential to managing and maintaining the structure of control and auditability.

Certain of the areas addressed by this panel, particularly with respect to the operational divisions element, such as planning, budgeting, etc., are very general in nature. However, we submit that these activities are basic and fundamental to the existence of strong management control over the line activities covered, and consequently to control and security of the computer related activities addressed by this report.

Operational Divisions

For purposes of this report, operational divisions are considered responsible for agency management activities relating to the information systems project management and data handling functions. They are responsible to top agency management for assuring that procedures have been designed and are utilized to provide reasonable assurance as to the control and security of data and data processing systems activities within those organizational units.

Long-range planning

Nature of the objective. Procedures should exist for the preparation and periodic updating of a structured long-range plan, in order to assure, to the extent practicable, that current priorities as to organizational and systems activities are established in the light of projected agency directions. In preparing the long-range plan, its developers should give consideration to such internal and external factors as:

1. Agency and divisional goals and objectives
2. Anticipated impact of technological developments
3. Changing regulatory requirements
4. Requirements for compliance with anticipated legislative actions relating to areas such as privacy, computer systems security, etc.
5. Management information requirements

The long-range procedure should provide for periodic reviews of progress as to both the plan itself and the attainment of the established goals. The starting point for the plan should be clearly identified in order to provide a basis for periodic progress reviews.

Risks. In a general sense, the risk associated with an absence of long-range planning is that current activities, staffing, priorities, hardware and software acquisition, etc., might be disorganized and misdirected. This could have severely negative effects on divisional performance. Examples include:

1. The division might fail to achieve its mission satisfactorily.
2. Agency and divisional resources might be wasted or misused.
3. The division might not be able to comply with regulatory or legislative requirements on a timely basis.
4. Installed systems might become technologically obsolete.
5. Agency and divisional management might not have sufficient information for measuring progress and performance.
6. The division might not be able to manage adequately its activities relating to organizational and systems changes.

Illustrative control procedures. A standardized procedure for structured long-range planning should be prepared and documented. It should be communicated to the organization and implemented. Planning responsibilities of all organizational components should be clearly identified at all levels, both as to preparation and periodic planning.

The plan should cover all activities, current and projected, of the organization. It should be consolidated for each organizational unit, for a division and for the agency as a whole. The completed plan should include a clear statement of the anticipated impact of projected changes on all organizational elements, and should be approved by top divisional and agency management.

Short-range planning (budgets)

Nature of the objective. A short-range plan or budget should be developed to set forth the goals and activities of the operational division and each of the subelements during the current fiscal period. It should be prepared giving consideration to present status, long-range priorities and directions as established by the long-range plan, and practical and affordable short term progress. It should clearly provide:

1. Appropriate allocation of available financial, personnel, and other resources
2. Recognition of the need for systems and operational modifications and projects to achieve them
3. Identification of staffing and costs for continuity of current operations and systems

Risks. The absence of a short-range planning and budgetary process could result in disorganized and nonproductive activities in the current fiscal period. Specific negative results could include, among others:

1. The division might experience cost overruns and might exceed its funded expenditure levels.
2. Personnel resources might be inadequate.
3. Personnel and other resources might be nonproductive.
4. Systems development activities might be wasteful or duplicative.
5. Progress toward achieving long-range objectives might be unsatisfactory or altogether lacking.
6. Current systems might become obsolete.
7. Current systems might fail because of an inability to satisfy operational requirements.

Illustrative control procedures. Control procedures for long-range planning also apply to short-range planning. The short-range plan should provide for a practicable plan, recognizing current constraints as to personnel and funding, and providing, as much as possible, some measure of progress toward achieving long-range goals. Each organizational unit's plan should be reviewed and approved by the next higher level management, as well as by appropriate functional management.

The plan also should provide for measuring current performance, on a period by period basis against the short-range plan. Adequate information should be provided for effective management analysis and control.

System contingency planning

Nature of the objective. A formal and structured plan should be established to provide for operational continuity in the event of a major or extended failure of a system or system component. It should recognize the potential for system degradation at various levels and the potential impact upon operations at each such level, and clearly set forth policies and procedures to be followed to minimize such impact and provide for timely system recovery.

Risks. The risk associated with inadequate planning for system failures embodies the inability to discharge operational responsibilities satisfactorily during the period of outage. Certain operations are more crucial than others and a failure to maintain highly crucial operations could have severe effects upon agency and divisional financial and operational results. Examples include:

1. A severe and extensive system outage could result in a loss of effective management control of its operations, and in a worst case situation, failure of an agency mission.
2. Progress toward achieving short-range goals could be severely impeded.
3. Excessive personnel, outside contractor, and other costs might be experienced.
4. Information and other assets might be destroyed or lost.
5. There might be increased exposure to fraud.
6. Personnel might be idle and, consequently, nonproductive.

Illustrative control procedures. A disaster or contingency plan should be established to recognize the potential for system interruptions and to provide formal and structured instructions and facilities for maintaining crucial operations and providing for timely recovery. It should be specific, well documented, and should be explained to and understood by all appropriate personnel. Further it should be approved by management. Documentation of the plan should be retained in secure, but readily available, on-site and off-site locations.

The level of detail in which the plan is prepared will vary, to a degree, depending upon the nature of, and criticality of agency operations. It should include, for example, provision for:

1. Levels of importance of applications and activities
2. Establishment of priorities
3. Predisaster reduction of vulnerabilities
4. Strategies for recovery
5. Identification of people to be notified
6. Identification of available hardware and software backup, including application programs and operating systems

7. Procedures for recovery or replacement of data files

8. Identification of need for and sources of forms

9. Documentation of insurance coverage

Depending upon the importance of operations, it is often advisable to test the plan on a periodic basis to assure that it is practicable and understood by all appropriate personnel.

Organizational communications

Nature of objective.   This objective recognizes that the best intentions of management can fail to be achieved because of a lack of organization, dissemination, and understanding of agency policies, procedures and responsibilities relating to security and control. Conversely, management at all levels is hindered in the effective discharge of its responsibilities if not kept fully informed on the results of day-to-day activities through appropriate and timely reporting techniques.

Management's policies relating to transaction and other authorizations, its approved procedures for transaction handling and processing, and its requirements for control and security should be formally and completely documented. Specific responsibilities of personnel at every organizational level should be clearly explained and a structured reporting system should be defined, implemented, and maintained.

Disseminated procedures should include identification of the organizational structure, and of upward, downward, and lateral unit interrelationships.

Risks.   In general, the risk associated with inadequate organizational communication is a misunderstanding of objectives, policies, responsibilities, and procedures, as well as an inability to manage day-to-day activities effectively. Specific results might, for example, include:

1. A failure to achieve management's financial or other objectives because of a lack of understanding of the objectives.

2. Employee frustration caused by a lack of understanding of management's policies and plans

3. The existence of incompatible or conflicting objectives at various organizational units

4. A failure to comply with legal or regulatory requirements

5. A failure to observe established management policies

6. Weaknesses or gaps in the system of control and security

7. An inability to monitor current developments

8. Erroneous data and reports

9. A misinformed management, and consequently, faulty decisions

Illustrative control procedures. Management's policies and procedures should be documented in detail in official procedures memoranda or a procedures manual. With respect to the operational divisions considered by this panel, the policies should include, for example:

1. The organization and effective use of a management steering committee to establish system priorities, consider problems, review progress against planned objectives, consider short term needs, etc.

2. The requirement for user involvement in system design and user approval of all system modifications

3. Clear identification of authorization requirements and specific exception procedures

4. Definition of the responsibilities of the various organizational levels

5. Reporting requirements and schedules

6. A statement of management priorities

Personnel administration

Nature of the objective. Personnel administration procedures should assure that personnel at all levels understand their duties and responsibilities, are adequately trained in their duties, are effectively monitored, and are objectively evaluated as to performance.

Risks. The risk of inadequate personnel administration are many and varied. With respect to those areas considered by this panel, they could include, for example:

1. Low productivity because of inadequately trained or misinformed employees

2. Employee frustration caused by a lack of understanding of responsibilities

3. Employee dissatisfaction because of inadequate performance evaluation.

4. Abuse or misuse of agency resources

5. Violation of data integrity as a result of misunderstanding control and security procedures

6. Loss of data or system control because of poorly trained employees

7. Organizational incompetence

8. Organizational mismanagement

9. Exposure to fraud

Illustrative control procedures. Management should establish specific policies and practices to be followed in personnel administration. These policies and practices should include, for example:

1. An agency code of conduct relating to all personnel that covers conflict of interest situations, gifts, expense accounts, relationships within and outside the organization, etc.
2. Employee interviewing, screening, hiring, and termination practices
3. Provision for adequate employee training
4. Provision for rotation of duties, and job enrichment, as appropriate in the circumstances
5. Adequate separation of employee duties in sensitive data handling areas.
6. An effective performance monitoring system
7. A fair and objective performance evaluation system

Information System Project Management

This organizational unit is responsible to the operational division to assure that all systems are successfully designed, implemented, and controlled from a user management perspective. Risks associated with a failure to achieve system control objectives discussed below are considered generally applicable to all such objectives. Consequently, risks and illustrative control procedures will be discussed on an overall basis, rather than identified with a specific objective.

User involvement in system design

Procedures should exist to assure that users of a planned system are involved, in depth, in all phases of system design and development activities. Their involvement should encompass, for example, such responsibilities as:

1. Definition and identification of input data edits, file, field, and report requirements, etc.
2. Proper documentation of such requirements
3. Effective communication of requirements, in detail, to the system design activity

User specification of controls

The system design methodology should assure that control requirements are specified in detail by system users and are included in system design. User responsibilities in this respect include the following, among others:

1. Definition of specific control requirements
2. Documentation of all such requirements
3. Effective communication of such requirements to the system design activity
4. Continuing involvement with system design activity to assure that required controls are implemented properly in the system

Continuing user satisfaction

Procedures should exist for frequent user monitoring of operational systems performance and control to assure that the system continues to meet it objectives in terms of control and security.

User compliance with external requirements

In connection with all system related activities, users should undertake to assure compliance with all external system requirements, including:

1. Legal
2. Regulatory
3. Interagency and intraagency
4. Internal and external auditor needs

Risks

The overall risk resulting from inadequate user involvement in system design activities is obviously the failure of implemented systems to satisfy agency needs and objectives in a controlled, cost-effective, and productive manner. Specific risks are many and varied. They include, for example:

1. A failure to satisfy one or more specific user or external requirements
2. Inadequately controlled systems
3. Exposure to fraud
4. Faulty system security
5. Loss of accountability and the ability to reconcile data
6. Unnecessary or excessive costs resulting from overdesign of a system or system reports
7. Loss or misuse of resources
8. Delayed implementation schedules

Illustrative control procedures

Among many potential control procedures applicable to information systems project management, the panel believes the most important include the following:

1. An adequate systems development life cycle or other systems development methodology
2. Adequate user responsibilities in systems development
3. Adequate user responsibilities in systems changes and maintenance
4. Adequately designed and implemented user controls

System development life cycle or other systems development methodology. The system development process should be organized into specific phases, such as:

1. Project definition and survey
2. Preliminary system design
3. System design
4. Application software development and system testing
5. Implementation
6. Post installation review

This concept of phased system development is covered, in depth, in available literature.

The requirements of each phase should be clearly spelled out and understood by all involved in the development process. Specific management checkpoints should be established during, and at the end of each phase, to assure that project goals and objectives are being realized and that costs to date, and projected for the future, are within established parameters.

User involvement in system development. The organization of each system project development team should provide for specific user involvement and participation throughout the development process. User responsibilities should include, for example:

1. Identification and documentation in detail of all user oriented system requirements
2. Determination of the economic and operational feasibility of the project
3. Establishment and documentation of project scope and objectives
4. Project review and sign-off at specific checkpoints
5. Involvements in system testing, user training, and conversion activities

User involvement in system changes and maintenance. All changes to implemented systems should be approved by user management. User personnel should also participate in the testing process and authorize the implementation of the change.

Design and implementation of user controls. Specific control procedures for user personnel should be established, documented, communicated and understood by all involved personnel. These should cover, for example, such areas as:
1. Separation of responsibilities
2. Authorization levels
3. Responsibilities for master file changes

4. Security of data and files

5. Documentation and auditability requirements

6. User responsibilities to specify application input, processing and output controls for data processing activity and to assure that implemented systems achieve the required level of control and security

Data Handling

The area of data handling constitutes those organizational entities directly responsible for transformation of external information into machine-usable data, and vice versa. These duties include data transcription, dissemination, storage, and retrieval. The controls in data handling are direct, aimed at the physical integrity of the data and the organizational integrity of the information those data represent.

Maintaining input data integrity

Nature of the objective. The integrity of input data should be maintained at all times. The accuracy, completeness, and timeliness of the data being processed by the computer determines their usefulness to the organization. In computing, data is a raw material; any loss of data integrity will result in a flawed finished product. Procedures should exist to assure that:

1. All transactions are authorized by the appropriate person or persons

2. Specific job functions include the ability to authorize certain input data within prescribed limits (dollar amount, geographic area, etc.)

3. All valid transactions are authorized by the system, and conversely, all invalid transactions are rejected so that all input batches are complete and error free

4. Data are entered correctly and on a timely basis

5. Edits assure that all data used are correct

6. In on-line systems, each transaction entered is positively acknowledged to the enterer and is logged by the system to assure the data enterer that the system has accepted each item

7. At the end of processing, all items are balanced against the day's total master file

8. There is a transaction trail for all data entered to allow management to be able to re-create the path, both forward and backward, for all items in the system

Correct and timely exceptions reporting

Nature of the objective. All exceptional conditions should be reported in a thorough and timely fashion. Because modern data processing systems are constructed on the basis of "management by exception," management can only exercise its function with regard to computerized operations if it is presented with meaningful information, where and when it is most needed. Procedures over exceptions should include the following:

1. Clearly established responsibility for responding to errors that the system identifies, and positive actions to correct the exceptional condition

2. Requirements for suspending transactions in cases in which errors cannot be immediately corrected, and methods for updating the suspense files in order to maintain financial control over errors

3. Requirements for reconciling input to output once corrections have been made, to assure completeness and maintenance of financial and data controls

4. Maintenance of accurate records of the number, type, distribution, and concentration of data handling errors to be used to develop statistics useful in identifying systematic and managerial weaknesses

5. Resolution of exceptional conditions in an expeditious manner in order to avoid delays in error correction that could compound existing problems

Secure information storage, retrieval, and use

Nature of the objective.   Information should be stored, retrieved, and used in a secure manner. Data should be protected against malicious and inadvertent destruction, modification and disclosure.

Data, and by extension, information, are organizational assets and as such must be secured against loss. The peculiarities of a data asset necessitate all the awareness of the security required for tangible resources, plus a number that are specific to data.

Procedures related to data security should include the following:

1. Identification and categorization of data elements by differing levels of sensitivity

2. Delineation of individuals authorized to handle data, set forth in the same manner as security over the data

3. Unique identification of users by the computer in order that their authority to access sensitive data can be verified prior to release of the data

4. Storage in such a fashion, that data are protected against physical destruction, and are recoverable (or at least re-creatable) if destroyed

5. Design of systems to satisfy all statutory and regulatory requirements, e.g., privacy, nondisclosure, conflict of interest, etc.

6. Design and operation of systems in accordance with accepted organizational policies and practices, to reduce the overall exposure to litigation and statutory sanctions

7. Monitoring systems regularly and continuously for breaches of security with all such events being responded to immediately

Controlled information dissemination and storage

Nature of the objective. The information produced by the system should be disseminated and stored under suitable controls.

Output data can be either the end product of the system, or a report of its internal operations. In either case, these data are (or should be) produced for use, and thus should be used for their intended purposes, and only those purposes. Procedures for output data should include the following:

1. Review of all reports by supervisory personnel for reasonableness, accuracy, and exception conditions
2. Designated supervisory responsibility to take appropriate action based on the content of those reports
3. Distributing all output in a timely fashion
4. Reconciliation of all output data to the input data entered originally, with checks on any transactions generated internally
5. Distribution of output data only to those who have a demonstrated need for them, with such need being periodically reviewed and evaluated
6. Secure storage of information while needed, with the information being properly destroyed when no longer required

Risks

The risks associated with failure to manage and control the data handling area properly can expose the entity to many potential problems including inaccurate or incorrect input data, improper output information, statutory sanctions, litigation, etc. Examples of risk include the following:

1. Admission of errors into the system in the form of erroneous or duplicated work, or outdated records
2. Elimination of vital records from the files
3. Introduction of unauthorized or possibly fraudulent transactions into the system
4. Alteration, destruction, or disclosure of data in an unauthorized manner
5. Susceptibility to fraud, statutory or regulatory sanctions, criminal and civil penalties, etc.
6. Production by the system of erroneous or out-of-date reports and other forms of output upon which management might improperly rely
7. Failure of the organization to accomplish its stated objectives or its mission

8. Exposure to direct financial loss

9. Indirect financial loss arising from difficulties in reconstructing financial or other information assets

Illustrative control procedures

Because the controls over data handling are inherently the controls over data processing in general, they have received considerable scrutiny by writers and researchers in EDP auditing and controls. These include:

1. Verification of input data

2. Input batching and editing

3. Run-to-run balancing

4. Reconciliation of output

5. Secure storage of input and output data

Application Program Development

This organizational unit is responsible to general agency management for the management and performance of all systems design, programming, and testing activities required to support agency data processing requirements. Specific standards and policies relating to the techniques and approaches to be followed in discharging these responsibilities are expected to be established by the application interface unit of data processing. This unit is responsible for assuring compliance with such standards and policies.

Program development standards

Program development should adhere to established standards for coding and testing methodology, internal controls, documentation, and security.

System development life cycle checkpoints

Systems should be reviewed at prescribed checkpoints in keeping with the system development life cycle. At these points, both user and auditor approval should be obtained.

Coordination with organizational plans

The development of an application system should be linked to overall organizational plans.

Project management system control

All elements of performance in analysis, programming, and testing should be controlled and monitored by a project management system.

Testing and review

All programs should be subjected to testing and review by developers, users, internal auditors, and systems validation (quality assurance) prior to implementation.

Risks

In an overall sense, the risks associated with inadequate control of application program design, programming, and testing encompass a failure to satisfy management's information objectives and requirements effectively and productively. Specific risks include:

1. Organizational objectives with regard to resource allocation (general mission, time, money) might not be met.
2. Systems might be uncontrolled and unauditable, and as a result, might introduce errors into organizational records.
3. Systems might not satisfy internal and external requirements.
4. Systems will be difficult to maintain.
5. The organization might be susceptible to business risks such as interruption of operations, competitive disadvantage, and statutory sanctions.
6. Outputs generated by the system might be in error and can result in fallacious internal and external reports.

Illustrative control procedures

Again, as in the preceding sections of this chapter, there are a variety of procedures available for use to satisfy the above objectives, all of which are covered in great detail in available literature. All four procedures outlined under Information System Project Management—Illustrative Control Procedures, also apply in this area. Other specific control procedures might include:

1. The existence of a formal methodology and procedure relating to program testing, including provision for test data preparation and retention
2. Periodic reporting of progress against plan to senior management
3. Adequate interface with the quality assurance function to assure compliance with requirements
4. Adequate interface with internal and external auditors to assure satisfaction with auditability requirements

Data Communications

The "worst case" environmental situation we considered implies the use of some one or combination of remote terminals or processing devices transmitting data over communication paths to another processing location. The control objectives and related risks applied to the other areas of this paper apply to the communication components of the system as well as any other components, and will not be repeated here. The existence of remote operations and transmission facilities, however, adds new dimensions to risks related to the integrity of data transmitted, and system security and reliability. Of these, some result from the characteristics of the devices and of the communications paths utilized, and we have assumed that the technical panel groups, established for the purpose, would give adequate attention to these matters. Consequently, we have limited our comments in this section to the three objectives of integrity, security and reliability, extended risks in the teleprocessing environment, and illustrative control techniques.

Integrity of data transmitted

Nature of the objective.   The use of remote data terminals and communication facilities expands the potential for the introduction of incomplete or erroneous data into a system. All of the control objectives discussed earlier under data handling, apply as well as to the remote and communication aspects of the system. In addition, extended procedures should exist to assure that data are not lost or unintentionally altered because of the remoteness of access devices or the physical characteristics of the transmission paths.

Risks.   Additional risks resulting from the on-line nature of the system relate to the entry or receipt of erroneous or incomplete data to or from a central system. These additional risks result from several factors:

1. Employees using access devices might not be adequately trained.

2. Input formats can be overly complex.

3. Terminals transmitted to might be out of operation.

4. Communication paths can be interfered with by natural disturbances, such as electrical storms, or by physical problems in some component.

5. Terminal transmissions might interfere with one another.

Illustrative control procedures

Management should establish specific policies and procedures to assure data integrity, including, for example:

1. Adequate terminal users manuals

2. Fixed terminal input formats

3. Adequate data balancing controls

4. Message numbering and logging

5. Centralized control of communication networks, utilizing polling and specific device identification

System security

Nature of the objective.   Systems utilizing remote access devices and communications facilities can provide heightened opportunities for deliberate misuse of system files and data by employees and outsiders. Extended procedures should exist to help assure that the system and system data cannot be deliberately compromised or destroyed by employees or outsiders.

Risks. In an overall sense, the danger of an inadequately secured system is that unauthorized employees or others might gain access to the system. Specific risks include:

1. The system might be exposed to fraud.
2. Sensitive data, master files, or programs could be examined or stolen by employees or outsiders.
3. The system or system data could be damaged or destroyed by disgruntled employees or outsiders.
4. Data confidentiality or privacy could be compromised.

Illustrative control procedures. Procedures designed to help prevent security breaches could include, for example:

1. Specific identification of users and terminals, under central system control
2. Location of terminals in a secure physical environment
3. The use of passwords to authorize system access
4. System monitoring and logging of access attempts and transmissions
5. System notification to security personnel of suspicious or unusual network activity
6. Use of multilevel data file, data, and transaction access controls
7. Use of data encryption methods for highly sensitive transactions

System reliability

Nature of the objective. In a multiple use teleprocessing system environment, the potential for system outage or inadvertent destruction of programs or data is heightened because of the geographical dispersion of system components and the effect of natural disturbances on communication facilities. The objective, risks, and illustrative control procedures related to system contingency planning, discussed in this chapter, should be considered carefully in establishing a plan for system backup and recovery. In addition, system response times should be carefully monitored to avoid deterioration.

Risks. Additional risks related to system reliability in the teleprocessing environment include:

1. Terminal maintenance and repair can be disruptive and time consuming.
2. Failure of all or a part of communication facilities can render a system temporarily unusable.
3. System response times can deteriorate because of increase volumes, inadequate human factors at terminal sites, or equipment malfunctions.

Illustrative control procedures

Procedures to minimize the extended risks in this area might include:

1. A scheduled preventative maintenance program for remote devices

2. Development of a plan for temporary voice telephone or other transmission of data during an outage period

3. Provision of back-up equipment and/or communication facilities in time-crucial situations

4. Network and response time monitoring

The Cascade Effect of Management Risk

Following the panel's identification of the four major areas for systems management concern, we decided to examine the risks we have identified and associated with control objectives. By subjecting our subelement vulnerabilities and exposures ("risks") to a frequency distribution, we have identified a crucial cascading or "Tier" effect of management exposure. Four principal risk levels are identified in cascading levels of importance.

Organization mission impacts. These are elements that will directly and negatively affect the unit's performance. Forty-one incidences of risk are identified in this Tier.

Information reliance impacts. These are elements of information dependency that will render executive decisions null over time. Nineteen incidences of risk are identified in this Tier.

Control disciplines. These are elements of basic systems control subject to compromise, distortion, and mismanagement. Eight incidences of risk are identified in this Tier.

Organization disciplines. These are elements of basic managerial skill and organization analysis, especially those where a *lack* of sensitivity and comprehension will negatively impact the unit's mission delivery capacity. Four incidences of risk are identified in this Tier.

Conclusion

We find that if breaches or failure occur in any component of a higher tier, then several effects will follow in subsequent tiers. The importance of this chain effect should not be overlooked. Risks and increases in exposures run both upward and downward in cause and effect.

On our diagram, we have identified (across the top) major Control Objectives and (on the vertical side) Risk Tiers. This diagram illustrates several joint observations.

1. Data Handling, at the level of successful management of Tier 1, Orga-

nizational & Mission Impacts, is the most crucial cluster. Seventeen incidences of risk are identified in Tier 1 alone for Data Handling.

2. The opportunities to take preventative actions are more available to planning activities within Operational Divisions (19 incidences of risk) and to Information Systems Project Management (9 incidences of risk) than other areas.

3. Organizational Communications (mission, purpose, intents, facts, policy, events, directives, consistency, etc.) within operational divisions is the second most vulnerable managerial responsibility (8 incidences of risk).

4. Impacts affecting the integrity and reliability of a systems environment are influenced by the shorter range of tactical plans, leading us to conclude that long range business and systems plans are necessary to successfully support the shorter range budget process.

5. Although Tier 4, Organizational Disciplines, appears final on the chart and low in numeric value, we observed that if these elements fail in any permutation, the combined effect undermines the application of control disciplines.

Thus, this panel has concluded that it is important to reemphasize the critical, cascading effect of:

1. Management's overall responsibility for controls

2. User's non-negotiability for controls in their systems

3. Short- and long-term planning and budgeting

4. An appropriate systems development methodology

C

Key Notarization for Network Security

The material in this appendix is from *A Key Notarization System for Computer Networks* by Miles E. Smid (National Bureau of Standards Publication 500-54).

This appendix proposes a Key Notarization System (KNS), which can be used in conjunction with a cryptographic device to provide increased data security. In 1977, the National Bureau of Standards published a completely defined encryption algorithm, DES, which became a Federal standard for the protection of unclassified data.

Since publication, several companies have produced hardware devices that implement the standard, and there has been increased awareness that, in certain applications, encryption offers the only effective means of protecting information. The first applications of the encryption of unclassified data appeared in the area of electronic funds transfer, but the passage of the Privacy Act of 1974 (5 USC 522a) and Transmittal Memorandum No. 1 to Office of Management and Budget placed added responsibilities on Federal data systems for the protection of nonfinancial data as well.

Even before the DES was adopted, it was clear that there was more to cryptographic security than a secure encryption algorithm. Efforts were initiated by NBS to have additional standards, based on the DES, developed. An area that needed to be addressed was secure key management. DES keys are 64-bit binary vectors, individually selected to provide the unknown quantity necessary for security in the encryption algorithm. Key management involves the secure generation, distribution, and storage of cryptographic keys. If the key management is weak, then the most secure cryptoalgorithm will be of little value. In fact, a very strong cryptoalgorithm used in a weak key management system can give a false sense of security.

Previous work on key management systems can be found in Ehrsam, et al, and Everton. This paper develops a simple key hierarchy and a set of commands or protocols, which in conjunction with a secure random key generator and a strong encryptographic algorithm, can be used to generate and store keys as well as to encrypt and decrypt data. These commands have been devised for computer systems that employ key notarization facilities (KNFs). They are to be tested on the NBS Unix system, but they are not Unix-dependent. It is intended that the system be applicable to many different situations. On-line communications, file encryption, off-line mail, and digital signatures all are to be protected. Key notarization is presented to help provide security while maintaining the required flexibility.

Requirements

KNS can be used in computer networks along with KNFs to:

1. Securely communicate between any two users
2. Securely communicate via encrypted mail (off-line)
3. Protect personal (nonshared) files
4. Provide a digital signature capability

Secure communication involves preventing the disclosure of plaintext, detecting fraudulent message modification, detecting fraudulent message insertion or deletion, and detecting fraudulent replay of a previously valid message. The KNS must be consistent with these goals and yet operate at speeds sufficient for normal network communications.

With mail encryption, data is encrypted and then sent via mail or some means that cannot provide an immediate response. The data is stored in the encrypted form until decryption at some later time. In this situation, one cannot have an interactive system for exchanging keys because no real-time response is possible. Therefore, protocols must be devised so that the receipt of keys need not be immediately acknowledged.

Once encrypted, personal files only can be decrypted by the original owner. They are encrypted for secure storage rather than secure communication. In this case, encryption is used to protect against accidental disclosure, such as spillage, and intentional disclosure, such as scavenging. It is often desirable that the data encrypting key be stored with the cipher for ease of recovery. Of course, the key would be encrypted under another long term key, which is kept for the user either in the KNF or in a secure location from which it might be entered into the KNF.

Digital signatures were developed in conjunction with public key systems. In such systems the decryption key is not equal to, and cannot be computed from, the encryption key. Encryption keys can be made public while decryption keys are kept secret. A digital signature is decrypted using the secret decryption key and sent to the receiver. The receiver can encrypt, using the public key, and verify the signature, but the signature cannot be forged because only the transmitter knows the secret decryption key. (The cryptoalgorithm must have the property that decryption of the signature followed by encryption equals the signature equals the original signature.) Nonpublic key algorithms also can be used for digital signatures in conjunction with a *Network Registry*. In the KNS, a different method is proposed for implementing digital signatures with the DES nonpublic key algorithm.

The Network

The KNS is designed for computer networks that consist of host computers, user terminals, and KNFs. Figure C.1 shows a four-host network. The host controls the normal operation and communication of the terminals. Terminals have the capability of communicating with the host, with other local terminals through the host, and with terminals of other hosts via communication channels called *interchanges*. Each terminal will be able to use the host KNF by means of user commands. All commands will be implemented in the KNF, and every KNF will have the capacity to generate keys for distribution to other hosts or users.

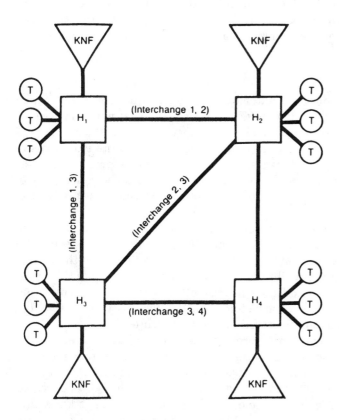

KNF = Key Notarization Facility
H_i = Host i
T = Terminal

Figure C.1 A four-host network.

Interchanges can be electronic communication lines, microwave links, courier routes, etc., or combinations of more than one medium. In Fig. C.1, only host 3 shares an interchange with host 4. If host 1 shares a common interchange key with host 4, then host 1 can communicate with host 4 through host 3 without intermediate decryption and reencryption. Host 3 would merely act as a switch. This is known as *end-to-end encryption.* If host 1 does not share a common key with host 4 but does share a key with host 3, and if host 3 shares a key with host 4, then host 1 can communicate with host 4 via host 3. The cipher would have to be decrypted at host 3 and reencrypted in the key shared between host 3 and host 4. Care must be taken to ensure that the communications are not compromised when unencrypted. This method of encrypted communications is called *link encryption.*

The lines between the KNF and its host and the lines between each terminal and its host must be protected. They could be physically secured or they could be secured by the addition of cryptographic devices on each end of the links. When a user is editing a file in the host, it is in plain text form, and the host will have to protect the data from other users. Once the user has finished editing, he can command the KNF to encrypt the data and store the resulting cipher in unprotected memory or send it to a remote user over an interchange.

The host

We will assume that the host computer has two types of memory: that which is not accessible to any user, called *system memory,* and that which is accessible to users, called *user memory.* User i's memory is core, disk, etc., where user i is permitted to store and recall data. Most computers have a means of protecting system memory from users, and some computers protect one user from another to a certain degree. We will rely on these protective features to the extent that the user should not be able to subvert the operation of the computer.

For example, the system must be able to maintain correctly the identity of the user once he has been authenticated and given permission to execute the commands. The system also must prevent one user from taking on the identity of another user and thereby obtaining access to his unencrypted data. In other words, encryption by itself does not solve the computer security problem. However, if properly used in a system with the necessary protective features, it can provide protection to stored and communicated data.

The encrypted keys of user i are stored in user i's memory, and encrypted passwords to which no user needs access will be stored in system memory. Nevertheless, we will assume that any user could gain read and write access to every encrypted password stored in system memory. Each user is expected to manage the encrypted keys that belong to him, but he will not know any clear keys. Yet, key encryption is not sufficient. A method is required to protect against key substitution and to ensure that each user correctly identifies the user with whom he is communicating.

The key notarization facility (KNF)

The KNF contains a DES encryption device. It will have a control micro-processor and memory to implement commands and data transfers. The KNF also must store the unencrypted interchange keys and the states of active users. An *active state* consists of a user identifier along with an initialization vector and an unencrypted data key for both transmitting and receiving data. A user is *active* as soon as his identifier is loaded into *active user memory* in the KNF. He can then proceed to load the rest of his state.

The KNF contains a key generator capable of generating unpredictable keys. At any time, a user should be able to predict the next key to be generated with only a $1:2^{56}$ probability of success. Once the 56-bit keys are generated, the proper parity is determined and the entire 64-bit key is encrypted before it is returned to the host. Thus, no clear keys are known outside the KNF. The key generator is also used to generate 64-bit initialization vectors which initialize the DES cryptoalgorithm. Because the KNF contains clear keys, the encryption algorithm, the commands program, and the key generator, it must be physically protected.

Cryptographic facilities containing a single master key are used to perform encryption and execute key management commands. Our key notarization facilities hold several keys and the key generator. They employ a different key hierarchy, a different set of commands, and are the enforcers of key notarization.

Distributed versus centralized key generation

Network security centers (NSC) can be used for key distribution. Upon request, the NSC generates a key for use by each of the parties in a conversation. One copy is encrypted under a key shared between the NSC and the first party, and another copy is encrypted under a key shared between the NSC and the second party. The encrypted forms of the key are then sent to the appropriate receivers.

The KNS uses distributed rather than centralized key generation as employed by an NSC. In order to provide for off-line encrypted mail, the KNS gives each host the capability of key generation in its own KNF. Thus, two hosts do not even have to be electronically connected to communicate securely. The KNS requires fewer protocols because parties do not have to send a remote key generation request, and they do not have to respond to the receipt of a key. Fewer protocols mean fewer ways an enemy can attempt to trick or confuse the communicating parties by altering or playing back the protocol messages.

If a KNF is compromised, only communications involving the compromised facility are compromised. If an NSC is compromised, and there is only one NSC for the network, then the whole network is compromised. Finally, with a local key generator, one can encrypt personal (nonshared) files without having to depend on a remote site. The KNS approach has the disadvantage that the key generation capability and the KNF physical security has to be replicated at each host.

Identifiers and Key Notarization

A special feature of the KNS is the support of key notarization. This feature increases security, permits a simple system design, and provides a means of implementing signatures with a nonpublic key system. *Identifiers* are nonsecret binary vectors of up to 28 bits, which uniquely identify each user in the network. When a user first attempts to call the KNF he must submit his identifier along with the correct password to establish an active state in the KNF. Both the host and the KNF employ identifiers to "recognize" the users.

Key notarization is similar to the actions of a notary public who first requires his customer to identify himself via a driver's license, etc., before he seals (notarizes) the customer's signature on a document with his notary stamp. In addition to the notary's function of authenticating the creator of a message, the KNS authenticates the message itself and the person requesting decryption. Key notarization is similar to having a notary public on each end of a secure communication channel.

Let i and j be identifiers and k be a DES key. Then $(i\,|\,|j)$ represents the concatenation of i and j. K, a 64-bit key, consists of eight bytes, each with seven information bits and a parity bit. K XOR $(i\,|\,|j)$ is a special function defined as follows: The leftmost seven information bits of K are exclusive ORed with the leftmost seven bits of i. The eighth bit, a parity bit, is then appended so that the modulo two sum of all eight bits is odd. Then the next seven information bits of K are exclusive ORed with the next seven bits of i, and the correct parity bit is appended. This continues until the last seven information bits of K have been exclusive ORed with the last seven bits of j, and the final parity bit has been set. Therefore, K XOR $(i\,|\,|j)$ is a valid DES key with 56 information bits and eight parity bits.

All passwords and data keys are encrypted under K XOR $(i\,|\,|j)$ for some K and some i, j pair; in the case of passwords, $i = j$. This adds to security because one user cannot substitute his password or keys for those of another user and be able to authenticate or decrypt as that user. This will be explained in detail in Password and Key Storage. The security also is increased because both parties in a conversation must know the other's correct identity to communicate. Because the KNF only needs to retain keys for each interchange, instead of each user, the network design is simplified; and because only one user can encrypt with a given data key and only one user can decrypt with a given data key, a signature system may be devised similar to those used with public key encryption systems.

When key notarization is used, keys and passwords are sealed, upon encryption by the KNF, with the identifiers of the transmitter or key generator and the receiver. To generate a notarized key, the transmitter must identify himself to the KNF and provide proof of his identity by supplying his correct password. We call this *user authentication*. He must also identify the intended receiver of the key.

Once encrypted, the correct key cannot be decrypted unless the correct identifier paid is again provided. To decrypt the key, the receiver identifies himself and provides password proof of his identity. The receiver also must supply the identity of the transmitter that might have been sent unencrypted. If the identification information is not the same as that provided by the transmitter to his KNF, then the decrypted key will not equal the original key and no information can be correctly decrypted. Thus, the receiver must know the correct transmitter and be the intended receiver.

User Authentication

Each user will have a password, used to authenticate the user and permit him to invoke user commands. The plain password is passed through an encryption function, that involves the user's identifier, and the result is compared with a stored value before the user is activated. Therefore, a user cannot exercise any other command until his identity has been authenticated. The password of each user is stored in system memory encrypted under the facility interchange key (see Key Hierarchy), combined with the user's identifier. Because it is assumed that the host can maintain the correct identity of a user once he has been authenticated the user need not resubmit his password for each key he generates while he is active. His authenticated identifier, which has been loaded into active user memory, will automatically be used as his identifier.

Key Hierarchy

Two distinct types of keys are used to form the key hierarchy, interchange keys (IKs), and data keys (DKs). Interchange keys encrypt passwords (PWs) and data keys, while data keys encrypt both data and initialization vectors (IVs). The key hierarchy is shown in Fig. C.2.

Interchange keys (IKs)

Interchange keys are used for the exchange of keys between users. One interchange key, called the *facility interchange key,* is used for communication within a facility and the encryption of facility user passwords. Other interchange keys can be available for the exchange of data keys between facilities or for special subgroups of a facility. IKs are generated outside the network and are entered, unencrypted, directly into the KNF. This permits two facilities to enter the same IK. One IK can be used to connect all the users of two hosts because a user may not decrypt a data key shared by two other users. This is because the identifiers of the two parties are involved in the encryption of the shared key. Therefore, the number of keys that need to be stored in the KNF is reduced.

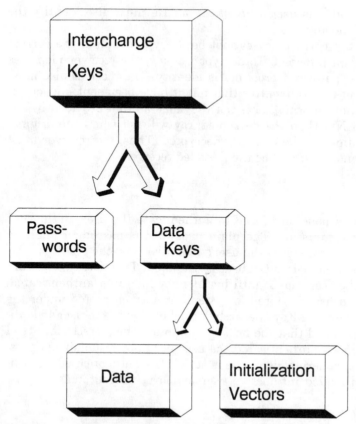

Figure C.2 Key hierarchy prevents tampering.

Data keys (DKs)

Data keys are used to encrypt data belonging to one particular user or data shared between two users. DKs are generated by the key generator and are immediately encrypted under an IK XORed with the proper identifier pair. The identifier of the user requesting the key, who is also the transmitter, is always the left identifier, and the identifier of the intended receiver is the right identifier in the identifier pair. When encrypted, DKs can be sent, kept in unprotected memory, etc. Initialization vectors are employed by the DES algorithm in the cipher block chaining (CBC), cipher feedback (CFB), and data authentication (DAUT) modes of operation. All IVs are encrypted, before they leave the KNF, under the data key, which enciphers the corresponding data.

Password and Key Storage

KNF memory contains both current and old interchange keys and active states of a limited number of users. When the interchange keys are changed, the old interchange keys are securely stored outside of the KNF along with their effective date. With the addition of another command, one could encrypt the IKs in the facility master key to reduce the number of clear keys needing protection. The current IKs become the old interchange keys, and the new interchange keys become the current IKs. After such a change, the passwords are reencrypted under the current (new) facility interchange key, and the users are told to reencrypt their data keys.

Passwords

System memory contains the encrypted passwords for every user. Let $E[X](Y)$ indicate the encryption of Y under X in the electronic codebook (ECB) mode of operation. Thus, $E[IK1 \text{ XOR } (i \| i)]$ (PWi) denotes the encryption of PWi under IK1 XORed with user's i identifier pair, $(i \| i)$. IK1 is used because the encrypted passwords are from the system memory of host 1 and IK1 is the facility interchange key for host 1.

The password is encrypted under IK1 XORed with the appropriate identifier pair to protect against substitution. If identifiers were not used, system memory might appear as follows:

```
i.  E[IK1](PWi)
j.  E[IK1](PWj)
.
.
```

If user j could gain access to system memory, he might alter it as follows:

```
i.  E[IK1](PWj)
j.  E[IK1](PWj)
.
.
```

User j could then authenticate as user i by submitting his own password while claiming to be user i. If identifiers are used, then $E[IK1 \text{ XOR } (i \| i)]$ (PWj) would be calculated upon authentication, and it would not compare with $E[IK1 \text{ XOR } (j \| j)]$ (PWj), which was substituted as user i's encrypted password.

User keys

User i's memory contains personal and shared data keys. Personal data keys are encrypted under the facility interchange key XORed with the user's identifier pair. Personal keys can be used to encrypt files and other private data, but cannot be shared. User i's memory also contains shared data keys encrypted under interchange keys XORed with the concatenation, $(\|)$, of user's i's identifier and another user's identifier. The expression $(i \| j)$ uniquely identifies the communication parties. If $(i \| j)$ were not used, another user could substitute his own data key, encrypted under the interchange key and then be able to decrypt any subsequent cipher. Similarly, when user j

receives $E[IKp \text{ XOR } (j \mid \mid j)] \, (DKi \quad j)$, he must know that he is communicating with i, over interchange p, to correctly decipher $DKij$. Thus, the transmitter is prevented from posing as someone else. Because several users can use the same IKp to communicate, this protection is crucial.

It should be noted that it is the system's responsibility to enforce any restrictions on the use of interchanges. For example, if user i is not allowed to use IPp, then the system must enforce this arbitrary restriction by not loading IKp for user i. User i should not be able to subvert the restriction by key substitution.

One could argue that substitution protection is not needed for system memory because if the system cannot protect system memory, it probably cannot prevent users from changing identity, from invoking system commands, or other security threats. This might be true, but encryption should not add additional possibilities for attacks. In user memory, the substitution threat is very real because many systems cannot protect one user's memory from another user, and even if they could, the encrypted keys will not be protected. Encrypted data keys can be stored with cipher on unprotected tapes and disks, and they can even be sent out over unprotected communication channels.

Definition of Terms

When defining our commands, the terms initialize, reserve, load, store, generate, encrypt, decrypt, and reencrypt will be used. These terms should be defined so that the meaning of the commands is clear. The terms actually represent functions which operate on keys or passwords.

Initialize sets a password to a starting value that should be changed by invoking another command.

Reserve activates a user by loading his identifier into the KNF.

Load takes an encrypted key or encrypted IV from the user, decrypts it, and puts it into the active user memory in the KNF.

Store places an encrypted password in system memory. Operates on PW.

Generate calls the KNF random key generator which generates 56 unpredictable, random bits that are combined with eight parity bits, as required by the DES. The result is encrypted under an interchange key XORed with the appropriate identifier pair. IV generation provides a full 64 random bits before encryption. Operates on DKs and IVs.

Encrypt encrypts a DK or PW under an IK XORed with the appropriate identifier pair, and uses the ECB mode of encryption when operating on keys. "Encrypt" also refers to enciphering data in one of the approved DES modes.

Decrypt decrypts an encrypted DK or PW. "Decrypt" also refers to deciphering data in one of the approved DES modes.

Reencrypt decrypts an encrypted DK or PW and then encrypts it under a new *IK* XORed with the appropriate identifier pair to avoid the reencryption of data and the reinitialization of passwords when IKs are changed.

Commands

This section describes the commands or protocols that need to be implemented in the KNF for key management and data encryption purposes. Besides encryption, decryption, and authentication, they are used to generate keys, which are given to the user, and to provide for the supersession of the keys controlled by the system. The commands are invoked by a command name followed by a parameter address list of passed and returned values. The user's identifier is shown as a parameter only when it must be supplied by the user of the command. For some commands, the system automatically supplies the KNF with the user's identifier. Interchange keys must be loaded into the KNF before commands are executed.

Initialize password (IPW)

```
IPW: {pw}
pw = password
```

This command is used when a user is first put on the system. The password is encrypted and stored in host system memory. The original password is known to the user and the security officer. The user submits the original password when he first authenticates himself to the KNF, then he immediately changes his password to a secret value, known only to himself, by using the change password command, CPW. Only the security officer who is responsible for putting new users on the system should be capable of initializing the password.

Reencrypt passwords (RPW)

```
RPW: {}
```

The security officer executes this command after the interchange keys have been changed. Each encrypted password stored in system memory is decrypted using the old facility interchange key and encrypted using the new facility interchange key. The result is then stored back in system memory. This permits a user to authenticate even though the interchange keys have been changed. After he is authenticated and active, it will be the user's responsibility to reencrypt his data keys before using them for encryption, decryption, or data authentication.

Reserve active state (RAS)

```
RAS: {ui, pw, ss, ua}
ui  = user identifier
pw  = password
ss(system status) = y if active memory is
                      available
                  = n otherwise
```

```
ua(user authenticator) = O if ss = n
                       = y if ss = y and PW
                         authenticates
                       = n if ss = y and no
                         authentication
```

This command activates the user by loading the user's identifier into the KNF. Active user memory must be available and the user must authenticate before the identifier is loaded. No other commands may be executed by the user until he has successfully executed RAS. The authentication is for use of the KNF and is independent of the authentication for use of the system. Once authentication is complete, the system must ensure that other users cannot execute commands in place of an authenticated user.

Log out active user (LAU)

```
LAU: {ui}
ui = user identifier
```

This command can be used by the user when he has finished using the KNF. In this case, *ui* is optional. The command removes the user identifier from the active user list maintained in the KNF. All active DKs and IVs belonging to the specified user are lost. The host can also keep a list of active users and the time of the last command executed for each one. If a user has not executed a command after a reasonable time period, then the host may use LAU to log out the user. The user can still be logged on the system, but he will have to repeat the RAS command to use the KNF. The system can also periodically decide to challenge a user by requiring him to reauthenticate. Whenever the user logs off the system, the LAU command should automatically be executed.

Change password (CPW)

```
CPW: {op, np}
op = old password
np = new password
```

This command is being used to change passwords. The old password is authenticated before any change is made. The user identifier must be loaded into active user memory, otherwise an error message is returned.

Generate data key (GDK)

```
GDK: {in, sp, ed}
in = interchange name
sp = identifier of sharing party
ed = returned encrypted data key
```

```
ex. (command executed by user i)
in = p
sp = j
ed = E[IKp XOR (i||j)] (DKij)
```

This command is used to generate new keys. The identifier of the user invoking the command, user *i* in the example, is always the leftmost value in the concatenation of the sending and receiving identifiers. If the two identifiers are equal, then the key is personal and cannot be shared. This command can not be executed unless the user is active. Otherwise, an error message is returned.

Encrypt data key (EDK)

```
EDK: {ui, dk, ed}
ui = user identifier
dk = data key
ed = returned encrypted data key


ex.
ui = i
dk = DK
ed = E[IK XOR (i||j)] (DK)
IK = facility interchange key
```

This command is not used in the normal functioning of the system. It need only be used for communication with someone outside of the system who doesn't have the same key generation and encryption capability or for generating cipher encrypted under a particular key. Because this command violates the security criterion that no clear key be permitted outside of the KNF, it is recommended that only the security officer be allowed to execute it. It might be best not to implement this command at all.

Load data key (LDK)

```
LDK: {kf, in, sp, ed}
kf (key function) = t if key is for transmitted
                        data
    = r if key is for received data
    = s if key is for personal use only
in  = encrypted data key
sp  = identifier of sharing party
ed  = encrypted data key


ex. (command executed by user i)
kf  = t
in  = p
sp  = j
ed  = E[IKp XOR (i||j)] (DKij)
```

```
ex. ( command executed by user i)
kf  = r
in  = p
sp  = j
ed  = E[IKp XOR (j||i)] (DKji)
```

```
ex. (command executed by user i)
kf  = s
in  = f (facility interchange identifier)
sp  = i
ed  = E[IKf XOR (i||i)] (DKii)
```

This command loads a data key, either shared or personal, into the user's active state in the KNF. The key is stored as the transmit key address if $kf = t$, and at the receive key address if $kf = r$. If user i executed the command, then $kf = s$ if and only if $sp = i$. Otherwise an error message will be returned. When $kf = s$ and $sp = i$, the data key will be loaded into both the transmit and receive locations. The user must be active before this command can be executed.

Generate initialization vector (GIV)

```
GIV: {ei}
ei = returned encrypted initialization vector
```

```
ex.
ei = E[DK] (IV)
```

This command is used to generate new initialization vectors. The KNF key generator generates 64 bits (56 random and 8 parity), and then encrypts them under the data key, which must be previously located at the transmit address in active user memory. The encrypted IV is returned to the user. The data key can be either personal or shared.

Load initialization vector (LIV)

```
LIV: {kf, ei}
kf = t if IV is for transmitted data
   = r if IV is for received data
   = s if IV is for personal data
ei = encrypted initialization vector
```

```
ex.
kf = t
ei = E[DK] (IV)
```

If $kf = t$ then the data key at the transmission address is used to decrypt the encrypted IV. The IV is then stored at the transmit IV address. If $kf = r$ then the data key at the receive address is used to decrypt the encrypted IV, and the IV is stored at the receive IV address. When $kf = s$, the transmit data key is used to decrypt, and the IV is placed in both the transmit and receive IV locations.

Encrypt initialization vector (EIV)

```
EIV: {iv, ei}
iv = initialization vector
ei = returned encrypted IV


ex.
iv = IV
ei = E[DK] (IV)
```

This command is not necessary because one can always use the GIV command to obtain IVs. It can be used with the EDK command for communications outside of the system. Because, in the KNS, no unencrypted IVs are to be known by users, it is recommended that this command be restricted solely to the security officer or omitted completely. The IV is encrypted under the DK previously loaded at the transmit key address.

Reencrypt data key (RDK)

```
RDK: {kf, in, sp, ok, rk}
kf  = t if data key is for transmitted data
      r if data key is for received data
      s if data key is for personal data
in  = interchange name
sp  = identifier of shared party
ok  = old encrypted data key
rk  = returned reencrypted data key


ex. (user j reencrypting a key sent to him by user i)
kf  = r
in  = p
sp  = i
ok  = E[IKp' XOR (i||j)] (DKij)
rk  = E[IKp XOR (i||j)] (DKij)
IKp'= old interchange key
IKp = new interchange key
```

This command is used when interchange keys are changed. It reencrypts data keys under the new interchange key so that the data protected by the key does not have to be reencrypted. The user must be active. Also, $kf = s$ if and only if $sp = i$ and user i invoked the command.

Electronic codebook (ECBE and ECBD)

```
ECBE: {pt, ct}
ECBD: {pt, ct}
pt = plain text (eight bytes)
ct = cipher text (eight bytes)
```

These commands are not required in the normal operation of the system. They are provided to accommodate future modes of DES encryption which, as yet, have not been considered or approved. ECBE encrypts eight bytes of plain text at *pt* and stores the result in *ct*. ECBD decrypts eight bytes of cipher at *ct* and stores the result at *pt*. Encryption uses the transmit DK, while decryption uses the receive DK. A data must be previously loaded into the appropriate active state.

Data authentication (DAUT)

```
DAUT: {kf, da, nb, av, md}
kf = t if data is transmitted
   = r if data is received
   = s if data is personal
da = data
nb = number of bytes of data
av = returned authentication value (eight
     bytes)
md = CBC for CBC mode
   = CFB for CFB mode
```

This command uses DES in the authentication mode to calculate an eight-byte authentication value on *nb* bytes of data at *da*. If *kf* = *t* or *s*, then the data key and IV that have been previously loaded into transmit active storage will be used. If *kf* = *r*, the key and IV in receive key active storage will be used. The value of *md* indicates which of two DES encryption modes are desired.

Cipher block chaining (CBCE and CBCD)

```
CBCE: {pt, ct, nb}
CBCD: {pt, ct, nb}
pt = plain text
ct = cipher text
nb = number of bytes
```

For encryption, CBCE *nb* bytes of data starting at *pt* are encrypted in the CBC mode, and the cipher is returned starting at *ct*. *For decryption*, *nb* bytes of data at *ct* are decrypted and returned to *pt*. If *nb* is not a multiple of eight, then the CBC mode is used until *b*<8 bytes remain. The final *b* bytes are encrypted by exclusive ORing them with the first *b* bytes of the next DES output block. DK and IV must be in the active user memory, otherwise an error message is returned. Encryption uses the transmit IV and DK, while decryption uses the receive IV and DK.

Cipher feedback (CFBE and CFBD)

```
CFBE: {pt, ct, nb}
CFBD: {pt, ct, nb}
```

```
pt = plain text
ct = cipher text
nb = number of bytes
```

As described for the CBC commands, nb bytes are either encrypted or decrypted. Encryption uses the transmit IV and DK while decryption uses the receive values. If the required IV and DK values have not been loaded an error message will be returned.

Digital Signatures

Recall that digital signatures are possible with public key algorithms because one cannot decrypt another person's data even though anyone with the public key can encrypt data intended for that person. This is because the decrypt key is not shared. Because the KNF combines identifiers with interchange keys for protection against substitution and employs separate encryption and decryption key storage, one cannot encrypt data in a key that was generated by another user. Therefore, signatures are possible. Suppose user i generates a key using the GDK command and sends it to user j. The encrypted data key would be of the form:

```
ED = E[IKp XOR (i||j)] (DKij)
```

where IKp is the interchange key for interchange p and $DKij$ indicates a data key generated by i for transmission to j. Whenever i generates a key, his identifier is always leftmost in the identifier pair used in the encryption of the key. The only way user j can load $DKij$ is by loading it as a receive key. Separate transmit and receive key registers are required. If j tries to load $DKij$ as a transmission key for the encryption of data going to i, the crypto-module will use $(j||i)$ instead of $(i||j)$ when decrypting ED. If j tries to load the key as a personal key, the $(j||j)$ will be used. (See the LDK command.) When $DKij$ is loaded as a receive key, only the decryption commands have access to it.

For example, suppose user i generates ED as before. He then can use the EIV command to generate an encrypted IV of the form:

```
EI = E[DKij] (IV)
```

Next, he can encrypt a signature, S, under $DKij$ and send ED, EI, and S to j. User j can load IV and $DKij$ in the active receive state by the LIV and LDK commands, and decrypt the encrypted signature to recover S. There is no way that j can alter S to a particular S' and encrypt it under $DKif$ because there is no way for j to get $DKij$ into the transmit data key active storage.

If user j generates his own encrypted data key, it will be of the form:

```
E[IKp XOR (j||i) (DKji)
```

He can encrypt a signature S' under DKji but he cannot claim that it came from i because he could be challenged to decrypt the encrypted signature. To do so j would have to load DKji by submitting E[IKp XOR $(j | | i)$] (DKji) to the LDK command with $kf = r$. The cryptomodule would not load the correct DKji because it would use $(i | | j)$ instead of $(j | | i)$ as the identifier pair. Thus, the signature would be garbled. Of course, user j can send a signature S to user i encrypted under the data key, DKji, in a similar manner as described above.

Any message can be regarded as a signature. No additional keys or commands are required. All user j needs to do is keep E[IKp XOR $(i | | j)$] (DKij), E[DKij] (IV), and the encrypted signature in order to be able to prove that S was sent to him from i. User j might also wish to keep S as well.

The authentication value as a signature

The signature, S, can be an entire plain text message, but it might be undesirable to store the cipher text of long messages. In such cases, one can use the DAUT command to calculate an authentication value that is a cryptographic function of every bit of data. This value then could be used as the signature. Signatures should be large enough to provide adequate security; at least 64 bits are recommended. S must be encrypted as in the previous example. Otherwise, the receiver could modify the message and calculate the correct signature for the new message using the DAUT command with the correct key in the receive memory. This is because, unlike encryption and decryption, the DAUT command with $kf = t$ gives the same output as when $kf = r$ as long as the same key is used in both transmit and receive active memory.

If one is not concerned with proving that the receiver did not modify the incoming message, then the authentication value need not be encrypted. Suppose that it is only necessary that the receiver knows the correct transmitter of the message and that it has not been altered. The transmitter, user i, can generate E[IKp XOR $(i | | j)$] (DKij) and E[DKij] (IV), and load DKij and IV into transmit active ;memory. He can use the DAUT command with $kf = t$ to generate an authentication value, AV. User i may then send the following to j:

```
clear message, E[IKp XOR (i||j)] (DKij),
E[DKij] (IV), AV.
```

User j can authenticate the message by loading DKij and IV into active receive state and then using DAUT with $kf = r$ to calculate AV. If it matches, then the message must have come from i. If user k sent the message, the encrypted data key would have the form:

```
E[IKp XOR (k||j)] (DKkj)
```

and the authentication value would be AV'. If j thought it was from i, then when he executes LDK $(i \mid \mid j)$ instead of $(k \mid \mid j)$ would be used to decrypt the data key. Therefore, the wrong data key would be loaded.

Nonpublic key versus public key signatures

A digital signature capability can be implemented in the KNS because the receiver of an encrypted data key can only load the key into his active memory and can, therefore, only decrypt with it. We have assumed that the KNF of each host is physically secured from all users and that shared keys are securely distributed. One must guard against both disclosure and substitution of keys. If one could gain knowledge of the shared key, he could forge all signatures sent between both facilities. Of course, all keys encrypted under the shared key would also be compromised. Thus, the common key must be secured at the transmit and receive KNFs. With public key algorithms, the secret key requires protection against disclosure and substitution, while the public key must be protected from substitution. If a bogus key is substituted for the transmitter's public key, then false signatures can be sent to the receiver.

Initialization

Suppose cryptography were to be added to a computer network. First, each host would have to be provided with a KNF and the necessary interface. Then interchange keys would have to be generated and distributed. Once the interchange keys are loaded directly into the cryptofacilities and the authorized users are assigned unique identifiers and passwords, the security officer at each facility can initialize the passwords of the authorized users by using the IPW command.

The transmitter

A user then can authenticate and become active by using the RAS command. He could change his password to a secret value known only to himself by the CPW command. Next he might want to generate data keys using GDK. Suppose he is on host 1, then GDK: $\{1, j, ed\}$ generates a personal data key and GDK: $\{1, j, ed\}$ generates a shared data key for use with user j at host 1. GDK: $\{5, k, ed\}$ generates a shared data key for use with user k over interchange 5. Interchange 5 can be the interchange between host 1 and host 5.

When he has an encrypted data key, say $E[IKp \text{ XOR } (i \mid \mid j)]$ (DKij), user i can load the key using LDK. LDK with $kf = t$, $in = p$, $sp = j$, and $ed = E[IKp \text{ XOR } (i \mid \mid j)]$ (DKij) loads DKij into the transmit active key storage. The user must keep track of the fact that $kf = t$ and $in = p$ from the time the key is generated to when the key is loaded. If the key is stored for future use, then the values of kf and in required by the LDK command should also be stored. User i then can generate an IV using GIV and load the IV into the transmit active IV storage.

After he sends the encrypted DKij and IV to j, he is ready to encrypt data intended for user j. Of course, if he is on line with user j, he must establish contact with j, identify himself, and send him the encrypted DKij and IV. If he is on line, he should require an appropriate response from j to ensure that he is being received. User i can encrypt in either the CBC or CFB modes. He should include a message number, the date, and the time in his plain text so that old valid messages from i to j cannot be played back to j. He also can use DUAT to calculate a digital signature, which is encrypted before transmission.

User i can use his personal encrypted key, E[IK1]XOR($i \mid \mid i$)] (DKii) to encrypt a personal file and then store the encrypted key with the cipher or in a personal key file. Finally, he can log out of active status using the LAU command. If not, the system should automatically log him out after a specified time period or when he logs off the system, whichever comes first.

The receiver

Once user j is active, and has received the encrypted DKij, IV, and data, he can use LDK and LIV to load the receive active storage. He can then decrypt and check the signature to ensure that it is correct. Note that the same data key can be used for both encryption and digital signatures. If j wishes, he can generate a DKji to communicate securely to i but communications from j to i will not be encrypted with the same data key as communications from i to j.

Key supersession

Interchange keys are generated in an unpredictable manner in a highly protected environment outside of the network. At key-change time, the current IKs are stored as old IKs and new IKs are entered as current IKs. The security officer uses RPW to reencrypt each user's encrypted password. The system tells each user when he becomes active to use the RDK command to reencrypt his data keys. When keys are changed, the old keys no longer stored in the KNF should be securely stored along with their effective dates. These keys may be needed to decrypt old files or to validate old signatures whose data keys were not reencrypted.

The Key Notarization System can provide secure authentication and encryption with limited protocol requirements in a variety of network configurations. Host operating systems must protect plaintext and maintain user identity once authentication is complete, but the host need not protect keys from either disclosure or substitution. A set of KNF commands is defined for key management functions as well as for the approved DES modes of operation. The secure distribution of data keys is attained by encryption and the use of identifiers for key notarization. The system features on-line and off-line applications, local key generation, and a digital signature capability.

Auditing Computer Security

Auditing is an essential part of a computer security system. It's your assurance that things are working as planned. It's particularly important for networks, where the chances of loss are so high. With the use of PCs and networks spreading so rapidly, you need all the assurance you can get.

It's one thing to set a policy. It's another thing for your employees and associates to carry it out. This is particularly true of the procedural aspects of computer security. How can you be sure that the procedures you require are the procedures that actually are carried out?

An audit can help you find out. Just as an auditor can determine that your financial practices conform with your policies and with legal requirements, an audit can give your security program a similar checkup

Audits are connected with the Internal Revenue Service and other unpleasant thoughts. They are not warmly accepted by the people who are being audited. This can be doubly true of PC users who feel—with some justification—that their machines are supposed to set them free of the type of restraints an audit represents.

There's another psychological problem, too. Businesspeople are conditioned to abhor bad news, particularly about themselves. Business has a very bad tendency to try to control information for the sake of looking good. An audit report almost always contains bad news about somebody. It also means that you'll have to spend some money to correct the problem.

But cheer up, things could be worse. That's what an audit is all about. A defect reported, then, can be corrected only if you learn about it when a competitor steals valuable data, or you are slapped with a liability lawsuit. Thus, an investment in security now—even at the expense of those who run afoul of the auditors—could have a big payback later.

The same is true about prosecuting computer criminals. Many companies hesitate, afraid their reputations will suffer because they managed to become victims. If you don't take firm action to secure your networks, you'll suffer a lot more than that.

These security auditing guidelines were published by the National Bureau of Standards to guide computer security audits—a formal process of evaluating the adequacy and effectiveness of a security program.

As you'll see, though, the standards that would guide an auditor also are much the same standards that should be used in planning and designing a security program.

Computer security generally is considered a function of the environment in which the system operates. A dedicated system operating in a batch mode within a benign environment has altogether different security requirements from a shared automatic resource balancing computer network.

This session will address the various system environments and identify the major aspects of each that the auditor must consider in conducting an evaluation of computer security. The consensus report that follows was developed, written, and reviewed by the entire membership of this session.

Definitions

The principal terms relating to computer systems security used in this report are defined as follows:

Environment means the physical facilities, system architecture, and administrative functions which constitute an ADP system to be audited.

Security audit is an assessment of the system of controls that ensure the continuity and integrity of the environment as defined by management. An assessment of the reasonableness of these controls is achieved by examining and evaluating controls over system access, accuracy, and availability.

System access is the ability and the means necessary to acquire, store, or retrieve data; to communicate with or make use of any resource of an ADP system.

System accuracy is the state that exists when there is complete assurance that under all postulated conditions an ADP system implies total logical correctness and reliability of the system, and logical correctness and completeness of hardware and software necessary to implement protection mechanisms and to assure data integrity.

System availability is the level or quality of service, as defined by the users, required to perform their primary functions.

Audit Versus Design

The process of performing a security audit is closely related to the security determination study performed during the initial development stages of a system that is to be secured. This conclusion was reached as we attempted to develop a methodology based on an enumeration of all considerations applying to the audit of computer security in various system environments. We determined that specific computer-related, physical, and administrative environmental descriptors required close examination. They are all interrelated and not readily separated. Our end result was the enumeration of those steps to be taken first by the design team and then with slight variations by the auditors.

The result should not prove too surprising if one examines the composition of an effective design team. To build cost-justifiable, comprehensive, and effective security into a system, at least one member of that team should have the auditor's viewpoint or be, in fact, a qualified auditor. Thus we see a two-pronged role to be played by the audit profession. First, the auditor must be an advisor to the design team providing essential inputs to the molding of the system; second, during the later, operational phase of the system the auditor must perform the traditional EDP auditor functions and reassess the effectiveness of the computer system security design.

Listed below are the steps necessary to arrive at an assessment of system security effectiveness, first for the design team and then for the audit team.

Steps a design team must take

Step (1).   Define overall system requirements, objectives, and sensitivity.

Step (2).   Specify the desired environment, based on results of Step (1).

- Specification of *physical parameters* such as:

  Location of system
  Construction of "container" (building)
  Survivability of system under disastrous conditions such as flood, fire, bombing, etc.

- Specification of *system parameters* such as:

  Degree of information sharing (will there be one or multiple users)
  Batch or interactive processing
  Centralized or distributed databases, processes
  Local or remote access
  Application mix

- Specification of *physical parameters* such as:

  Threat analysis
  Personnel procedures
  Organization structure
  Security requirements for:
     (a) Access Control
     (b) Accuracy
     (c) Availability
  Insurance
  System development procedures

Step (3).   Specify control techniques that can be used to enforce the environment in Step (2).

At this point, it might be helpful to point out the differences between security objectives, policy, and procedures. The objectives of the imposed control in an operation environment are regulation of access, accuracy, and availability. The translation of the objective of access control into policy can take the form of personal accountability for all sensitive transactions. The translation of this policy into a procedure can take the form of logging into the system by way of a password, or manual logging into or out of a secure area.

Step (4). Perform a line-by-line cost/protection analysis. This is by far the most crucial step in building a set of controls to protect the system within its environment. In this step we analyze each control line item specified in step 3 which could be employed to protect some aspect(s) of the system. The detailed cost/protection matrix will have hundreds or thousands of like items, dependent on the complexity of the system.

For each control requirement four judgments are made:

(a) Cost of implementation, development, and operation of control

(b) Effectiveness in regard to maintaining access control

(c) Effectiveness in regard to maintaining accuracy

(d) Effectiveness in regard to maintaining system availability

The effectiveness judgments for (b), (c), and (d) are finally translated into (subjective) numeric values on a scale from 0 to 10, (0-noneffective, 10-supereffective). This conforms to the current state of the art. However, a very desirable goal would be to devise instead an objective scale of measures of effectiveness.

For purposes of convenience, the designer can use a shorthand method or rating:

$$\text{Rating} = \text{AC/A/AV}$$

where AC = numeric value assigned to effectiveness level of Access Control
A = numeric value assigned to effectiveness level of Accuracy
AV = numeric value assigned to effectiveness level of Availability

These ratings become part of the system documentation and are used in Step (5) and by auditors.

Step (5). Perform composite evaluation. After performing, the line-by-line analysis described in Step (4), a specific subset of these controls is selected as the basis for the comprehensive set of safeguards. Management must concur that this subset provides the necessary depth, breadth, and overlap of protection most cost-effectively for all aspects of the environment—physical, systems, and administrative. In other words, this is the stage at which the "risk assessment" is made and a "security" system is designed to meet the security objectives defined earlier.

Step (6). Incorporate the approved security controls. Reaccess this new total environment in light of the additional features inserted into the three environmental (physical, system, and administrative) parameters. If these additions do not degrade the overall system effectiveness (meeting requirements and objectives, set down in Step (1)), the designers are ready to begin implementation. However, if after analyzing the total new system, it is found that the objectives are no longer effectively attainable, an iterative process must be initiated and the designers go back to Step (2), remolding the specifications of environment, etc., until all requirements set out in Step (1) are effectively satisfied.

Steps the operational auditor must take

Once the system has been designed and implemented, it can go into operation. The auditor is now called upon to assess the effectiveness of security controls in an operational mode. As mentioned earlier, the steps of the initial design team and those of the operational auditor are very similar. In some steps, only the verb need be changed. For example, in Step (1) the designer defines system requirements while the auditor reviews the stated requirements as set down by management.

Step (1). Review objectives, requirements, and sensitivity as documented by management for the system under audit.

Step (2). Determine the nature of the environment prevailing during actual system operation, independent of the organizational descriptions. The auditor's perceptions of the physical, systems, and administrative setup might be quite different from those that were specified during the design stage.

Stage (3). Identify techniques used to control the environment as perceived by the auditor in Step (2). Here we see a clear divergence from the design approach. Where the designer might have identified a large number of potential controls, the auditor is confined to examining only that subset of controls that are actually implemented. The auditor makes an independent examination and might, or might not, use systems documentation as a starting point for his/her identification of the system's security components.

Stage (4). Perform line-by-line cost/protection analysis. As in Step (3), the auditor is not concerned with all possible safeguards, but only with those implemented and properly functioning with the system, as determined by his audit. Although the designer might have given values to the components of the AC/A/AV ratings on an intuitive, nonobjective basis, the auditor will augment these judgmental determinations through hardware, software, and other sophisticated (where available) techniques to test the effectiveness of each component of the rating for meeting the stated security objectives.

Step (5). Perform a composite evaluation. The auditor now assesses the total effectiveness of the security system to determine whether it meets the objectives set by management. A comparison can thus be made of the designer's rating and that found by the auditor. Because the measures used by designer and auditor are perhaps different, this will be only a qualitative, albeit incisive, comparison.

Step (6).   Prepare report of audit findings including recommendations for upgrading security where weaknesses are found, e.g., where the rating of the designer exceeds that determined through audit. It is also incumbent upon the auditor to recommend changes in overall security control requirements if the environment has changed from that assumed during the initial design or since an earlier audit.

Environment and Control

The key element of any systematic audit approach is a close link between the design and the audit processes while maintaining a separation of duties between designer and auditor. Care must be taken to ensure that the same factors that influenced the design process are well understood and given appropriate consideration in the audit process. Two major factors must be considered. The first is the environment in which the system is to operate, and the second is the control techniques to be employed to enforce the environment. It is essential that the design process defines the environment in which the system is to operate and that the audit uses the same environmental description as a guide. If the operational environment has changed from that postulated at design time in a manner impacting security aspects of the system, this impact must be analyzed and the security control requirements must be reassessed as a part of the audit process in a similar fashion to the procedure initially used by the design team.

The approach being advocated here employs two rather sophisticated checklists and supporting material. The first checklist is used to establish, in considerable detail, the environment in which a system is to operate. In the case of a new system design, this is the list of desired system characteristics. In the case of an existing system under evaluation, this is the list of already existing system characteristics. We note that the process described in the previous chapter will work with either new systems being designed or existing systems being enhanced or merely being audited. In the audit process, the statement of environment is given. The auditor is encouraged to point out obvious inconsistencies in the environment, if he observes any, but the environmental checklist is his reference point from which he evaluates whether the control techniques specified by the designer are sufficient to enforce the given environment.

The second checklist is a description of the generic classes of control techniques that the designer can employ to enforce the environment in which his system must operate. As will be seen later, these range from physical locks and fences through internal hardware and software access control checks, to administrative procedures. During the design process, after the system environment is established, the designer selects those measures from the control techniques checklist that he wishes to utilize to protect his system.

Each of the entries in the control techniques checklist represents a segment of a continuum. Each item contains a range of measures with two related variables: the degree of protection afforded and the cost. At the low range, little protection is achieved and usually cost is minimal; at the high range, a great deal of protection is achieved and the cost might be proportionately high. In the example of physical locks on doors, the range might be from a simple padlock through a sophisticated electronically controlled and centrally monitored door locking system, with proportionate cost ranges. Given the sensitivity of the information contained in the system (from the environment statement) the designer must select those control techniques he wishes to employ and the appropriate position on the protection/cost scale for each chosen technique to provide in the composite the necessary measure of security control.

From a security viewpoint, there are three basic criteria in determining the environment and in evaluating the suitability of control techniques to enforce that environment: access control, accuracy, and availability. Each of these factors must be addressed in the environmental assessment, and each of the control techniques being applied must be rated against all three factors.

Some control techniques will not apply to certain of these measures. For example, locks do not affect the accuracy of the information but they have a significant effect on access control and on availability of the system. In the environmental statement, the degree of protection needed in each of these areas must be stated and in the overall evaluation of the control techniques, a rating by the designer and the auditor of each of these measures must be calculated and compared against the environmental requirements.

Many of the entries in the control techniques checklist are complementary. If one measure is taken, another measure is perhaps not required. Investment made in one control technique will determine the extent of the investment needed in a complementary technique. The relationship between entries in the control techniques checklist is complex. To ensure that sufficient measures have been taken to completely but not overly enforce the environment, the interactive relationship of controls within various environments must be explained in a guidelines book that should accompany the checklist. The guidelines book will describe relative levels of effectiveness and cost of the various control techniques and will provide relative assessments of feasible tradeoffs.

The designer establishes both the environment in which the system is to operate and the appropriate control techniques. The process employed by the auditor in determining if sufficient control techniques have been applied is quite similar. The designer scans the control techniques checklist line by line, selecting appropriate items to be employed. Then he evaluates the achieved overall security of the system with an overall performance analysis determined by logically aggregating the selected effectiveness measures assigned to the line-by-line entries. If this overall analysis does not provide sufficient protection, or if it exceeds the constraining cost factors, then he reevaluates the control techniques or perhaps the environment itself, making such changes as necessary to achieve the security needed at a suitable cost.

The auditor, given the environment checklist, determines first that the actual operational environment is that assumed during the design stage. He then determines the control techniques that he believes appropriate to achieve this environment. He compares his control techniques checklist with that of the designer and weighs the differences so as to have a reference against which to perform his detailed analysis. He performs a line-by-line evaluation of the entries in the checklist and then an overall analysis similar to that done by the designer. Having completed the overall analysis he might go back and adjust his assessment of the individual control techniques based on a more complete understanding of the total system. The result of this audit process is an overall rating of how close the design comes to enforcing the security requirements of the operational environment. If this audit process produces a rating of sufficient protection then the system can be approved for use. If it yields an insufficient rating, then the designer must go back once again to the control techniques list or to the environmental checklist and make appropriate changes to ensure the necessary security of the system.

The crucial element in this process is the use of the same checklist information by both the designer and the auditor. This ensures a common base from which to discuss related matters. It is this common starting point that is the crucial element of our methodology. The selection of elements from the control technique checklist and the degree of protection afforded to each element are often subjective, and the designer might wish to take issue with the auditor over specific ratings the auditor has given for some of these measures. The crucial point is that all elements of the design are understood by both the designer and the auditor in a common context. This complete and common listing of measures used by both the designer and auditor is an element that has been lacking in previous audits.

Checklists

Both the environmental and control techniques checklists are divided into three subcategories: physical, system, and administrative. In the environmental checklist under the physical heading are those elements of the physical environment that materially affect security of the system. Included is the geographic location of the system, taking into account the susceptibility to natural and man-made disasters such as floods and crime, any special power or air-conditioning requirements, etc.

In the system environment list are those measures that describe the internal structuring of the system. In particular we find here those elements that affect the requirements to rely on internal hardware/software measures to enforce the security of the system. Under administrative measures are included such factors as the sensitivity and correctness of the information contained in the system, postulated threats to the system, etc.

The system environment comprises five physical and logical components or main categories:

1. Degree of Sharing: single versus multiple user(s)
2. Type of Service: batch versus interactive
3. Organization: centralized versus distributed
4. User Access: local versus remote
5. Application: dedicated versus multipurpose

The control techniques checklist is comprised of the same three categories: physical, system, and administrative. The physical controls include the traditional "put the system in a vault" measures, including perimeter control, hazard protection, and backup mechanisms. Systems controls include hardware/software access control techniques, program integrity measures, audit trail techniques, and failures response procedures. Administrative control techniques include what are commonly referred to as change control procedures. Each of the control techniques must be evaluated against each of the access control, accuracy, and availability factors and an overall score must be arrived at for each of those factors.

Guideline book

A crucial element in the methodology described here is the background material that supports the checklist. This guideline will be composed of two sections. The first has a line-by-line description of the elements of the environmental and the control techniques checklists; in the latter case, the range of protection cost of each of the entries is given. The environmental checklist must be cross referenced against the control techniques checklist to ensure that if a particular element of the environment is specified, some range of control techniques can be applied.

Another element of the guideline book must deal with the interrelationship among control techniques. From it, both the designer and the auditor must be able to determine that if a certain control technique is employed, this might very well negate the need for another control technique. An obvious example is that if sufficient physical control measures are taken and if all personnel associated with the system have equal access to the information on the system, then reliance on internal software access control techniques can be significantly relaxed. This evaluation guideline is highly sensitive to the state of technology and will need to be updated frequently. Specifically, the relationship between cost and effectiveness of a particular form of protection will need to be revised frequently, and new techniques will have to be introduced as they are developed and become viable.

This overall methodology is a systematic approach to the problem of auditing a computer security installation. The approach is systematic because the designer and the auditor as well work from a complete list of both the environment in which the system is to operate and the control techniques that are to be employed to enforce that environment. By working from common lists, the designer and the auditor can more readily communicate differences in their evaluation and reconcile their evaluations.

A number of such checklists are already in existence; they can be used to form the basis of the environment and control techniques checklists. The establishment of a complete and accurate guidebook giving both the line-by-line descriptions and the element interrelationships is a crucial element of this overall methodology yet to be accomplished. For example, see *Data Processing Security Evaluation Guidelines* (Peat, Marwick, and Mitchell & Co., Certified Public Accountants; 345 Park Avenue, New York NY 10022).

Guidelines

In two previous sections we discussed audit methodology and the sequence of steps that an auditor will follow, preparatory to executing his audit function addressed here. Therefore, the purpose of this section is to discuss those considerations that comprise the "ideal" against which the auditor compares and measure data security in various system environments.

The "ideals" are derived from several sources, including information and experience that the auditor brings to his tasks, and information and observations gathered by the auditor in his effort to understand more fully the system to be audited.

In this section we will not attempt to create an actual book on audit guidelines; several such reference materials exist already. However, we have attempted to identify significant *categories* of control techniques, as well as (in selected instances) some more specific security measures. Although the various options within the control technique categories can be expanded upon by utilizing materials contained in reference works (and from the auditor's own knowledge and experience) we have chosen categories of control techniques that reflect major security options (in a general sense) that also provide an opportunity for analysis of the differences among selected system environment examples.

Our discussion indicated clearly that there are, theoretically speaking, many possible systems environments, resulting from a combination of physical, administrative, and system design points of view. In order to respond to the mandate given this group, we chose four sample systems that different significantly from one another, representing four of the most prevalent kinds of systems existent in today's computer processing environment.

The description of the environment for each of the four sample systems is given in the (section titled "Four Examples" later in this chapter). The method by which the constituent elements of an environment were ascertained, was discussed in the section on environment and control. The kinds of control techniques we have assigned as possible protective measures with respect to the four sample systems were briefly explained in that same section. However, our group took the further step of assigning subjective numerical scale values (ranging from a low of 0 to a high of 10) to the three categories of control techniques. Our choice for these values was derived from the group's consensus of whether such control techniques would be important with respect to the sample system. This importance factor was considered for each of the three basic categories of protection that our definition of "security audit" gave their AAA (AC/A/AV) rating: (1) access control, (2) accuracy, and (3) availability.

It is clear that there are certain general audit considerations that an auditor will utilize in determining the vulnerability of a given system. These are the experience items that the auditor must bring with him, to successfully complete the assigned task.

In the section "Four Examples," therefore, we considered only some specific aspects of the four sample systems. We highlighted those that affect security considerations in a way that distinguished one system from another. Obviously, in a complete audit of security, one would expect an auditor to perform a much more comprehensive analysis. But we assumed that the purpose of the mandate given to our group was to focus upon specific problem areas in different system environments to which an auditor should pay particular attention. The more general case, as the proverbial textbooks explain, will be left as an exercise for the reader.

Conclusion

William C. Mair, co-author of *Computer Control and Audit,* recently observed, "DP auditors are not and cannot be policemen." He stated that the primary responsibility of the DP auditor is to act as an advisor to management, to emphasize the need for standards, which must be properly documented and communicated. Standards serve as the foundation on which everything else is built; they provide direction, predictability, and criteria for evaluation. Through these standards, the auditors establish systems controls that in turn help reduce adverse effects encountered in a basically hostile environment. In fact, the auditor is part of these controls.

Areas of vulnerability must be exposed to reduce risks to acceptable levels. The dangers confronting EDP systems include, above all, erroneous management decisions, but also embezzlement and fraud, loss or destruction of assets, excessive costs, and deficient revenues. Their impact can be severe, leading to competitive disadvantage, statutory sanctions, even to economic, political, and military disasters.

We must not ever underestimate the power, ingenuity and perseverance of the "enemy." As we relate development of controls to potential exposures, we must follow a rather simple-minded approach: If we can think of it, someone else also can. Thus the auditor must be ingenious about gathering basic and detailed information, about evaluating the system's strengths and weaknesses, and about testing its design and performance. He must review all of its components individually and collectively according to a structural model specifically designed for that purpose.

A definitive, open-ended model has been developed to structure both initial internal design and follow-up (external) computer security audits in various system environments. The model is predicated on the notice that for a system to be viable within a well-defined (and definable) environment, we must certainly maintain control over access to the system, must provide accurate services, and must assure the timely availability of these services to the users.

In making the audit, we assume the availability of standard guidelines for rating all identifiable system line items with regard to their contribution to access control, accuracy, and availability. A global measure of security audit thus can be derived from the line items' individual, local ratings. A number of algorithms have been suggested for converting the aggregate "local" into "global" ratings, but it appears as if only absolute and total compliance with the design specification ratings will be acceptable in the security environment.

Auditing Network Security

This section presents a set of guidelines that can be used when conducting a review of administrative and technical controls pertaining to a multiple user teleprocessing environment.

With regard to the communication component, all modes of data transmission and associated equipment should be considered. Specific vulnerabilities should be identified along with appropriate safeguards, e.g., interception of microwave transmissions, with encryption serving as the countering control.

The control matrix

This section presents a matrix that relates to the various vulnerabilities to the specific controls that might be available to mitigate them (see Table D.1). The vulnerabilities are listed across the top of the matrix and are defined in a later section of this chapter. The controls are listed down the left vertical axis of the matrix and also are defined in a later section of this chapter. A primary control can be used to mitigate the specific vulnerability; a secondary control might be useful in mitigating the specific vulnerability. To apply the matrix, first identify the vulnerability that might be present in your teleprocessing network. Next, proceed down the column of the specific vulnerability and identify whether the controls in the left vertical column are applicable.

The control matrix can be used in two other ways to assist the auditor. Table D.2 lists the exposures that will be faced by the organization whenever one of the vulnerabilities does, in fact, occur.

The second use to which the matrix can be put is to specifically identify the various components of the network where the controls might be most effectively located. To do this, the auditor would choose a specific control such as "Sequence Number Checking" and follow across that row to the right-hand side of the matrix, where there are some numbers, such as 9, 10, 17. These numbers indicate those specific components of a data communication network where the controls might be located. These 17 components are defined at the end of this chapter.

TABLE D.1   Control Matrix

Control	Primary vulnerabilities	Secondary vulnerabilities	Control locations
Sequence number checking	Message lost Message insertion Duplicate message	Misrouting	9, 10, 17
Sending and receiving identification	Misrouting	Message lost Disclosure	9, 19, 17
Transaction journal	Message lost Message alteration Disruption Disaster Message insertion Duplicate message	Misrouting	9, 10, 11, 17
Positive acknowledgment	Message lost Misrouting Message alteration Disruption Message insertion Duplicate message		9, 10, 11, 17
Time and date stamp	Message lost Duplicate message		9, 10, 11, 17
Periodic message reconciliation	Message lost Message alteration Message insertion Duplicate message	Disruption	10, 17
Check sum on message address	Misrouting		9, 10, 11, 17
Error detection code	Message alteration	Disruption	9, 10, 11, 12, 17
Error correction code	Message alteration	Disruption	9, 10, 11, 12, 17
Key redundancy code	Message alteration	Disruption	9, 10, 11, 12, 17
Echoplexing	Message lost Message alteration	Misrouting Disruption Message insertion Message insertion Duplicate message	10
Error logging	Message alteration Disruption	Message lost Misrouting Duplicate message	9, 10
Backup equipment and facilities	Disruption Disaster		1, 7, 8, 9, 10, 11, 17
Physical security	Disruption Disaster Disclosure Theft	Message lost Misrouting Message alteration Message insertion	1–17

Interrelation of security controls

The auditor should recognize that the security controls shown in the matrix have complex interrelations in solving certain security problems. There are no linear equations that show how these controls add to or subtract from one

TABLE D.1   Control Matrix (*Continued*)

Control	Primary vulnerabilities	Secondary vulnerabilities	Control locations
Recovery procedures	Disruption Disaster	Message lost Message alteration Duplicate message	1–17
Communication policy		All	1–17
Life support system	Disruption Disaster		4, 8, 9, 10, 11
Device disconnection detection	Theft	Message lost	7, 9, 10, 11
Built-in device address	Message insertion	Theft	9, 10, 11, 17
Encryption	Message lost Misrouting Disruption Disclosure Message insertion		7, 8, 9, 10, 11, 17
Unlisted dial-up phone number	Message insertion Theft		9, 10, 11
Low error rate facilities	Message lost Message alteration Disaster		1, 2, 3, 7
Software controls and testing	Message lost Misrouting Message alteration Disruption Disclosure Message insertion Duplicate messages		9, 10, 11, 17
Documentation		All	1–16
Emanation control	Disclosure		1–4, 6–11, 13–17
Training and Education		All	1–17

another. The security controls required in a worst case analysis of an intentional assault on a communication system constitute a highly structured set of interrelationships.

For example, encryption is a valuable security control in a communications system. It is not, however, a complete solution in and of itself. The security objectives of a communication system can only be satisfied when encryption is used in conjunction with several other controls. In particular, sequence numbers must be used to detect attempts to add, delete, or replay messages by a technically competent perpetrator. A cryptographic error detection code must be used to detect alteration of messages. Encryption key management must be performed to ensure authentication of communicating devices.

In addition, message reconciliation must be performed during and at the end of every session to ensure that all messages transmitted have been received. Emanation controls prevent the loss of encryption keys and plaintext messages through undesirable electronic phenomena.

TABLE D.2   Exposures Resulting from Vulnerabilities

Vulnerability	Exposures
Message lost	Erroneous record keeping Fraud Statutory sanctions Excessive cost-deficient revenue
Misrouting	Erroneous record keeping Erroneous management decisions Fraud Statutory sanctions Competitive disadvantage
Message alteration	Erroneous record keeping Erroneous management decisions Fraud Excessive cost-deficient revenue Loss or destruction of assets
Disruption	Business interruption Erroneous management decisions Fraud Statutory sanctions Excessive cost-deficient revenue Loss or destruction of assets Competitive disadvantage
Disaster	Business interruption Erroneous management decisions Fraud Statutory sanctions Excessive cost-deficient revenue Loss or destruction of assets Competitive disadvantage
Disclosure	Statutory sanctions Excessive cost-deficient revenue Competitive disadvantage
Message insertion	Unacceptable accounting Erroneous management decisions Fraud Excessive cost-deficient revenue Loss or destruction of assets
Theft	Business interruption Fraud Excessive cost-deficient revenue Loss or destruction of assets
Duplicate message	Erroneous management decisions Fraud Excessive cost-deficient revenue Competitive disadvantage

These constitute the necessary set of nondiscretionary controls required for secure communication. In addition, certain discretionary, human-oriented controls are required to support the encryption system. Physical security must prevent theft or unauthorized use of a device containing a valid encryption key. Maintenance and testing must ensure the correct operation of the controls. Documentation must explain how the controls must be used. Finally, the user must be educated and trained in the use of these controls.

Definition of the vulnerabilities

The following list defines the vulnerabilities that are listed across the top of the control matrix. These vulnerabilities could be interpreted as the concerns or threats to which a data communication network might be subjected.

- *Message Lost.* Refers to a message that never reaches its intended destination.

- *Misrouting.* Is said to occur in a message-switching network when a message intended for a destination, e.g., Node A is sent to another destination, Node B.

- *Message alteration.* Refers to unauthorized (accidental or intentional) modification of an authentic message.

- *Disruption.* A temporary or intermittent service outage affecting one or more of the network components that can result in one or more of the following consequences: denial of service, misrouting, message alteration, messages lost, duplicate message, etc.

- *Disaster.* An interruption resulting in denial of service for an extended period of time as the result of an accident, natural catastrophe, or sabotage. The distinction between a disaster and a disruption is based upon the length of service outage and upon the permanence of the damage to the affected components.

- *Disclosure (privacy).* Unauthorized access to any data is disclosure. If the data is personally identifiable to an individual or legal person, then the unauthorized disclosure is a privacy violation.

- *Message insertion.* The addition of an extraneous unauthorized message at any component in the network. This vulnerability is never accidental and does not include duplicate messages.

- *Theft (physical).* Physical theft refers to unauthorized removal of any hardware component.

- *Duplicate message.* The insertion or processing of multiple copies of an otherwise authorized message. This can occur accidentally or intentionally.

Definition of the controls

The following list defines each of the controls listed down the left vertical axis of the control matrix.

- *Sequence number checking.* A method where all messages contain an integral sequence number for each level of the communication system. Verification techniques must detect duplicate and missing numbers, reject duplicates, and report missing messages.

- *Sending and receiving identification.* A method where sufficient information is contained in the message to uniquely identify both the sender and the receiver of a message.

- *Transaction journal.* A method of capturing sufficient system and message level data to establish an adequate audit trail or to have an actual copy of each and every transaction transmitted in the network.

- *Positive acknowledgment.* A method where the receipt of each message is positively confirmed back to the sender.

- *Time and date stamp.* An automatic procedure whereby each message contains time and date information for each major processing rule.

- *Periodic message reconciliation.* System facilities to verify completeness of processing by periodically providing summary information to reconcile number of messages, dollar values, control totals, etc., both sent and received.

- *Check sum on message address.* A procedure that verifies the message address using hashing or other summing type of totals.

- *Error detection code.* A method of inserting redundant information for purposes of detecting any changed bit patterns.

- *Error correction code.* A method of inserting extra (redundant) bits of information to permit detection and correction of errors at the receiving equipment without retransmission of the original message.

- *Key redundancy code.* The insertion of duplicate information in key fields of the message stream (such as dollar amounts, description identifiers, quantities, etc.) which can be compared at the receiving equipment for correctness.

- *Echoplexing.* A verification procedure by which each character received by the receiving station equipment is transmitted back to the originating equipment.

- *Error logging.* A software program that records error messages, by line, terminal, and also type and frequency. This recording is to measure the degree of reliability and performance of the communication system. Statistical analysis and management reports are required for evaluation and corrective action to minimize error rates.

- *Backup equipment and facilities.* Duplicate or alternate equipment (power, air conditioning, etc.), software, and procedures to be invoked whenever a major outage occurs with the primary system. Also a physical facility located away from the primary site and capable of supporting the original primary site telecommunication function at an acceptable operational level.

- *Physical security.* The ability to have proper physical security over the data communication facilities, software, and all other aspects of the teleprocessing network. This includes restrictive access controls over personnel, adequate fire protection, backup electrical equipment, and any other aspects of physical security with regard to maintaining the integrity of the data communication network.

- *Recovery procedures.* A set of written procedures that clearly defines responsibilities and procedures for operational programming and supervisory personnel to allow for the orderly recovery of the system to operational status or to recover from excessive error rates.

- *Communication policy.* A statement of agency or corporate policy regarding design, use, and maintenance of communication components including security objectives and penalties for not achieving these objectives.

- *Life support system.* Equipment, techniques, and procedures that will eliminate or minimize damages caused by disasters, occurrences such as fire, power failure, flood, environmental changes, etc.

- *Device disconnection detection.* The use of electrical control signals or other mechanisms to detect physical disconnection of communication system components.

- *Built-in device address.* The embedding of a device address or identifier via hardware or software mechanisms in communication system components.

- *Encryption.* The transformation of data (cleartext) to an unintelligible form (ciphertext) through the use of an algorithm under the control of a key such as the federal Data Encryption Standard (DES) (FIPS Pub. 46).

- *Unlisted phone number (dial-up),* The acquisition and use of unlisted telephone numbers for the communication system component that can be accessed via dial-up lines.

- *Low error rate facilities.* The selection and use of data transmission facilities with characteristically low error rates such as conditioned lines or digital transmission lines.

- *Software controls and testing.* The procedures employed in development, installation, and maintenance of software in communication system components to ensure the correctness, integrity, and availability of the software.

- *Documentation.* The generation, revision, and maintenance of manuals dealing with appropriate design, maintenance, and operational aspects of the communication system.

- *Emanation control.* The use of shielding and associated techniques to suppress electromagnetic, acoustic, and radio frequency emanations from communication system components.

- *Training and education.* The development, presentation, and periodic review of educational materials dealing with correct operation and maintenance of the communication system.

General definitions of components

The following list of items enumerates and defines the components of a data communication network. In some cases the item listed might be a characteristic of data transmission rather than an actual component.

1. *Circuits.* A circuit can be a single communication facility or a combination of different types of communication facilities such as:

   ■ *Satellite.* A facility that uses ultrahigh frequency signaling relayed through a device orbiting the earth.

   ■ *Microwave.* A facility that uses high frequency signaling that passes through terrestrial relay points.

   ■ *Fiberoptics.* A facility that transmits signals through the use of optical media utilizing a fiberglasslike cable.

   ■ *Wire.* A facility that transmits through a metallic conductor. This facility can utilize long-distance copper wire pairs, coaxial cable, or the copper wire local loop between a user's premises and the telephone company's switching office.

2. *Analog transmission.* Transmission of a continuously variable signal that has an almost indefinite number of states (an example of an analog signal is a sine wave).

3. *Digital transmission.* Transmission of a discretely variable signal such as discrete voltage levels (an example is signaling that is composed of either a positive or a negative voltage).

4. *Carrier switch facility.* A communication facility supplied by a commercial vendor of telecommunication services that provides for the interconnection of transmission devices (an example would be the telephone company's switching office or the Telnet Packet switches).

5. *Configurations.* These are the methods of connecting communication devices. There are many examples of communication configurations. Examples of these configurations might be as follows:

   ■ *Dedicated/private leased lines.* These circuits are always available to the customer for transmission and generally are used with on-line and real-time systems.

   ■ *Dial/Switch circuits.* A circuit connection that is established by dialing a telephone or establishing a physical or logical connection before data can be transmitted.

   ■ *Point to point circuits.* This method provides a communication path between two points. It can be a dial-up or a dedicated circuit.

   ■ *Multidrop circuits.* This method allows for the sharing of a communication facility. It is similar to a party line telephone call because several input/output terminals share the same line. Only one terminal can be transmitting on the line at a time.

- *Local cable.* This method of connecting communication devices consists of a privately owned cable or wire interconnecting many terminals with the computer system.

6. *Packet switching (value added networks—VAN) system.* A type of data communication technique that allows for messages to be divided or segmented into packets and routed dynamically through a network to the final destination point.

7. *Interface unit.* The device that connects a data transmitting (terminal) or receiving unit to the transmission facility. An example of this would be a modem, a digital service unit, or a device that converts voltage signaling to light signaling.

8. *Multiplexer.* A device that combines several independent data streams into one data stream at a higher signaling speed for transmission to a similar device that separates the high-speed signal into the original independent data streams. Note: Some of the multiplexers are software-driven and are similar to concentrators; however, most of them are nonintelligent hard-wired devices.

9. *Concentrator.* A programmable device that will perform the same function as a multiplexer with added functions such as data storage (buffering), message error checking, data flow control, polling, etc.

10. *Front-end communication processor.* A programmable device that interfaces a communication network to a host computer. Some of the functions that can be performed by a "frontend" are polling, code and speed conversion, error detection and correction, store and forward functions, format checking, data flow control, network statistics gathering, message authentication, communication routing and control, and the like.

11. *Message switch.* A privately owned programmable device that accepts messages from many users, stores them, and at some time after receiving them transmits them to their intended destination. This device generally receives messages at slow speeds over dial-up lines.

12. *Protocols.* Software or hardware rules that facilitate the transmission between devices. Some protocols provide for error control.

13. *Test equipment (technical control facility).* A combination of equipment that facilitates the physical monitoring, diagnostics, and restoration of communication systems should they fail. They can contain circuit patching, spare equipment, alternate switches, and might involve message text monitoring or quantitative measuring equipment.

14. *Audio response unit.* A unit that accepts analog, audio voice, or digital signals and converts them to digital computer signaling or can also convert digital signals from a computer into human understandable voice signals.

15. *Auto answering.* A device that automatically answers a telephone and establishes a connection between data communication devices.

16. *Auto dialing unit.* A device that accepts computer signals and automatically dials the telephone number of a remote communication device.

17. *Terminals.* An input/output device that is used to enter messages into the system and/or receive messages from the system.

Bibliography

Alexander, Michael. "Biometric System Use Widening." *Computerworld,* p. 16, January 8, 1990. Security devices measure physical traits to control access to sensitive areas.

Anthes, Gary H. "Fed Encryption Plan Gets Mixed Reaction." *Computerworld,* p. 57, May 10, 1993. Enthusiasm for Clipper, the federal government's new encryption technology, has been conspicuously absent among users, vendors, and editorial writers since it was unveiled.

———. "Fed Officials Pan Ban of Old Encryption Specs." *Computerworld,* p. 21, June 7, 1993. Legislation mandating use of the Clipper Chip encryption technology and banning older but popular techniques is now considered neither wise nor likely.

Arnold, Geoff. "Opening Up to Open Systems Computing." *LAN Times,* p. 53, July 8, 1991. Powerful new "open systems" such as Unix workstations are being added to computing resources at a rapid rate, creating yet another category of system. The bigger issue is making use of existing resources—like DOS PCs—within today's heterogeneous networks.

Berg, Al, Peggy King, Brian Foo, Peter John Harrison, Richard Krzemien, and Michael Durr. "Backup Solutions." *LAN Times,* p. 50, October 18, 1993.

Betts, Mitch. "Computerized records: An open book?" *Computerworld,* p. 1, August 9, 1993. Computerized medical records will help doctors improve diagnosis and treatment. They may also destroy what little medical privacy Americans have.

———. "Data Integrity: Start Paying Invoices Once, Not Twice." *Computerworld,* p. 59, April 5, 1993. Thousands of dollars are trickling out of coffers because companies pay suppliers twice for the same invoices.

———. "E-Mail Paves the Road to Court." *Computerworld,* p. 65, March 29, 1993. More and more organizations are finding that employees' e-mail messages can land them in very hot water. In the latest example, Atlantic Richfield must defend itself against a $146 million lawsuit triggered by its e-mail.

———. "Health Fraud: Computers at War." *Computerworld,* p. 1, September 13, 1993. Many insurance firms and managed-care companies are turning to software that screens incoming claims for fraud and profiteering.

———. "Privacy Key to Public Trust in Health Care Reform." *Computerworld,* p. 63, November 22, 1993. President Clinton's health care reform proposal calls for enactment of strong medical privacy legislation within 3 years, but critics say that is not soon enough.

———. "Records Privacy Concerns Grab Citizens' Attention." *Computerworld,* p. 64, October 11, 1993. Consumers say they are much more likely to patronize businesses with policies that safeguard the privacy of sensitive information.

Bidgoli, Hossein, and Reza Azarmasa. "Computer Security: New Managerial Concern." *Journal of Systems Management,,* p. 21, October 1989.

Bobrowski, Steve. "Protecting Your Data." *DBMS,,* p. 55, July 1993. When considering database servers, it's important to understand the features that protect the valuable work, data, and availability of a database system.

———. "Safeguarding Server Data." *DBMS,* p. 44, September 1993. This article discusses some of the most important and common issues surrounding database security and compares the security controls implemented in the five top database servers.

Booker, Ellis. "Data Dowsed in Midwest Floods." *Computerworld,* p. 6, July 19, 1993. Planning for an information system disaster rarely envisions a situation like Des Moines', in which an entire city's infrastructure came to a halt.

Borsook, Paulina. "Seeking Security." *Byte,* p. 118, May 1993. A mainframe type of security is coming to the client-server environment.

Bowden, Eric J. "RAID: The Next Step in Disk Subsystems." *LAN Times,* p. 53, May 25, 1992. RAID is basically a method of spreading your data over multiple drives and introducing redundancy into a disk subsystem to improve reliability.

Branstad, Dennis K., editor. "Computer Security and the Data Encryption Standard." *Proceedings of the Conference on Computer Security Held at the National Bureau of Standards,* February 15, 1977.

Buerger, David J. "Computer Security Issues Now Front Page News." *Infoworld,* p. S1, January 9, 1989. This article defines network security as any hardware, software, or operational scheme that protects the secrecy, integrity, and availability of a LAN.

———. "What Good Is Security if it Makes Us Insecure." *Communications Week,* p. 44, April 26, 1993. A federal directive promises to improve the security and privacy of communication systems. The directive is likely, however, to discourage private encryption and erode personal freedom.

Bunnell, David. "Information Anxiety." *New Media,* p. 8, August 1993. Our documents, drawings, messages, and files reflect not only our work lives but our private lives. The vast majority are not safe from prying eyes. Our data is insecure, and it has been for some time now.

Butler, Martin, and Robin Bloor. "Database Functions." *DBMS,* p. 17, November 1991. Today's DBMSs provide integrity checks, triggers, and stored procedures.

Byte, "Resource Guide: Virus Protection for Networks," p. 144, May 1993.

Caldwell, Bruce. "Security Czars Get Locked Out." *Information Week,* p. 16, June 21, 1993. Central security no longer has much of a place in the organization because of distributed computing. It's become more of a user responsibility.

Caron, Jeremiah. "Security Compromise Clears Path for SNMPv2 Approval." *LAN Times,* p. 31, June 28, 1993.

Case, Lloyd, Jr. "Having it All." *LAN Magazine, Interoperability Supplement,* p. 13, spring 1992. When connecting PC LANs and Unix hosts, do you approach the integration plan from the desktop up or from the host down? Here are the pros and cons of having it all.

Corrigan, Patrick H. "The CW Guide to LAN Disaster Recovery." *Computerworld,* p. 93, August 9, 1993. There will always be an element of chaos when something on the local area network fails.

Crawford, Wylie. "Not a Total Disaster." *LAN Magazine,* p. 79, August 1993. You can't prevent a disaster, so you might as well be prepared. Preparation is a business decision, not a technological one.

Daly, James. "Insecurity Complex." *Computerworld,* p. 91, June 21, 1993. With many organizations in the throes of staff reductions, information security professionals have a new beast on their hands. When jobs are eliminated, computer systems are often seen as great places to take out revenge.

———. "Lightning Can Strike Twice." *Computerworld,* p. 65, May 3, 1993. In a recent ranking of the sources of loss on PC systems, electrical power surges ranked second only to theft.

———. "Open Security: Resolving the Paradox." *Computerworld Client/Server Journal,* p. 22, August 11, 1993. Client-server design promises easy access to reams of critical information. It also ushers in new ways for intruders to gain access. Here's how to cope.

———. "Out to Get You." *Computerworld,* p. 77, March 22, 1993. The goal of complete data security is probably unattainable, but there are still plenty of weak points the average IS manager can shore up but hasn't.

———. "Security Lapse Bedevils Users of SQL Server." *Computerworld,* p. 1, August 2, 1993. Users running SQL Server on an OS/2 network have discovered that its lack of central security administration or reporting tools hurts their ability to build client-server networks.

———. "The 30-Minute Risk Analysis." *Computerworld,* p. 68, November 29, 1993. A security manager has developed a way to take the terror out of risk assessment, often a lengthy, expensive affair.

———. "The Right to Be Secure." *Computerworld,* p. 28, July 12, 1993. Government-backed data security standard raises big brother issues. Agencies intend to establish a key escrow encryption system using a device called a *Clipper Chip.*

———. "Toll Fraud Threat Growing." *Computerworld,,* p. 47, March 22, 1993. The theft of telephone services may be more pervasive than even the most dour security experts have believed.

———. "Tougher Computer Crime Laws Sought." *Computerworld,* p. 20, April 5, 1993. The Department of Justice has proposed new sentencing guidelines aimed at cracking down on electronic bandits convicted of stealing credit history reports, pilfering telecommunication services, and peddling stolen passwords.

———. "Whither Wireless Security?" *Computerworld,* p. 1, August 16, 1993. The thought of sensitive data skittering unfettered over the airwaves has made some security managers nervous.

DeHaven, John. "Stealth Virus Attacks." *Byte,* p. 137, May 1993. Anonymous attack software targets networked computers.

Dennis, Terry L., and Daniel A. Joseph. "Protecting Your PC Data." *Business,* p. 9, April/June 1989. While not all PC data loss can be prevented, certain precautions can reduce the chance of such loss.

DePompa, Barbara. "Choosing a Computing Platform Requires Careful Study." *MIS Week,* p. 30, May 28, 1990. Although the decision to buy networked microcomputers, a minicomputer, or a mainframe system is based on far more than the merits of these technologies, you should know the advantages and disadvantages of each before you buy.

DiDio, Laura. "Business Booming for Disaster Recovery Firms." *LAN Times,* p. 1, April 19, 1993. Disaster recovery planning and backup have become a top priority for many network professionals in the wake of a string of natural and man-made disasters.

———. "If Your Building Is Bombed, Will You Be Prepared?" *LAN Times,* p. 1, March 22, 1993. When a bomb blasted through the World Trade Center, businesses were either prepared for the disaster or suffered the consequences.

———. "Security Deteriorates as LAN Usage Grows." *LAN Times,* p. 1, April 5, 1993. In a recent survey of 300 companies worldwide, 36 companies reported losing more than $100,000 in security-related incidents so far this year. Another 42 companies had lost between $10,000 and $100,000.

———. "Security Pros Network via ComSec." *LAN Times,* p. 7, March 22, 1993. Over the last 2 years, six security-specific bulletin boards have sprung up, and their user base is growing rapidly.

Dodd, Annabel. "When Going the Extra Mile Is Not Enough." *Network World,* p. 49, April 12, 1993. Hackers are keeping pace with stepped-up security by becoming more sophisticated.

Dooley, Ann. "Crime Time." *Computerworld Focus on Integration.* p. 31, June 5, 1989. Personal computer security is everybody's business. Information security must be a part of the corporate business plan, not just the responsibility of IS professionals.

Dostert, Michele. "Keys to Successful LAN Management." *Computerworld,* p. 45, May 17, 1993. Good network managers strive to make their networks reliable, responsive, and as user-friendly as possible.

Farris, Jeff. "Network Administration's Growing Role." *LAN Times,* p. 28, August 9, 1993. Administration has traditionally been the last piece to join the networking puzzle. However, few network managers can administer a successful network without first carefully considering its design and implementation.

Ferris, David. "Security and PC Networks: Old Problems, New Cures." *LAN Times,* p. 33, August 5, 1991. Computer security is a recognized issue with mainframe-based systems, but it's new to the world of PC networking. Many of the problems are similar, and some—such as viruses and software licensing—demand new solutions.

Fisher, Sharon. "Data Security Experts Say Errors Are Greatest Threat." *Infoworld,* p. S74, September 9, 1991. When it comes to computer security, many corporations focus on protecting themselves from outsiders rather than insiders. But more often than not, crimes are inside jobs.

———. "Encryption Policy Spurs Concern." *Communications Week,* p. 8, April 25, 1993. Members of the networking and security communities have expressed concern that a new government policy on data encryption may restrict the use of the technology.

———. "Industry Studies Clipper Proposal." *Communications Week,* p. 10, May 3, 1993. Most users said they would not buy products that contain the technology, or at least that they have strong concerns about its security.

———. "Law Enforcers: Restrict Network Security." *Communications Week,* p. 8, April 12, 1993. Encryption and authentication are such effective ways to keep information secure that law enforcement organizations are pushing to restrict their use.

———. "Report Outlines Toll Fraud Problems and Prevention." *Communications Week,* p. 37, April 5, 1993. A new report from Security Communications outlines the most common toll fraud methods and suggests ways to guard against them.

———. "Software Distribution Not Yet Linked to Management." *Communications Week,* p. 37, July 13, 1992. Software distribution and network management, both important for keeping enterprise networks afloat, do not often work hand in hand today.

Forbus, John. "LAN Security: Don't Let Disaster Strike Your Network System." *Infoworld,* p. 2, September 9, 1991. How much local area network security do you need? First answer this question: "What would the damage be if the most sensitive information on my LAN were compromised?"

Foster, Ed. "WANs: Are They Too Big and Too Slow to Play with Your LANs?" *Infoworld,* p. S1, April 8, 1991. PC-LAN managers entering the realm of enterprise networking are often shocked by their first experiences with connectivity to wide area networks. WANs such as IBM's System Network Architecture (SNA) have been around, so they may seem slow.

Francett, Barbara. "Can You Loosen the Bolts without Disarming the Locks?" *Computerworld,* p. 75, October 23, 1989. LANs are often set up without IS knowledge. Security is often sacrificed for performance. Access controls and audit trails slow LANs down.

Fratarcangeli, Claudio. "Locking and Referential Integrity in Oracle." *DBMS,* p. 81, December 1992. Any discussion of integrity enforcement in a multiuser environment is incomplete if it does not take concurrency issues into account.

Fryer, Bronwin, and Roberta Furger. "Who's Reading Your E-mail?" *PC World,* p. 167, August 1993. Should we assume that e-mail messages are really private? Probably not.

Gianforte, Greg. "Successfully Supporting Network Users." *LAN Times,* p. 73, February 10, 1992. Proactive managers take steps to monitor and analyze LAN performance. This article will examine steps a manager can take to increase the reliability of a LAN system and to increase user satisfaction.

Gibbs, Mark. "Dialing for Data." *Network World,* p. 51, May 31, 1993.

———. "Security with a Catch." *Network World,* p. 98, July 26, 1993. While LAN Manager offers security services, the design lacks the functionality needed for enterprise networks.

———. "VINES 5.5 Receives Long-Awaited Recognition for Network Security." *Network World,* p. 22, September 27, 1993. With a global directory at its heart, VINES offers a solid security and control architecture.

Gillooly, Caryn. "Netware Break-in Offers Security Lesson." *Network World,* p. 17, March 29, 1993. User experience points to the need for physical security in addition to password protection.

Goldberg, Steven J. "LAN Interoperability Is the Common Goal." *Communications Week,* p. IG1, December 2, 1991. Connectivity is no longer enough for users. They want interoperability and transparency between network operating systems, accompanied by adequate security and ease of management.

Greer, Tyson. "Weyerhaeuser Division Waits for Data Disasters." *Puget Sound Business Journal,* p. 5A, January 3, 1988. Disasters produce visible damage to people's lives. What doesn't show is the potential devastation to the web of invisible information networks that animate almost every manufacturing and service business in the country.

Hamilton, Rosemary. "Mission-Critical Tools Aim at Desktops." *Computerworld,* p. 37, February 3, 1992. Users are installing core business applications on desktop platforms, with the goal of incorporating mainframe class features such as reliability, integrity, and security.

Hassett, James. "The LAN Times Survey: The Policies You Recommend." *LAN Times,* p. 67, August 23, 1993. We published a survey asking for your advice about LAN policies and productivity. An essay question asked you to describe the biggest problem you've ever faced with a LAN.

Held, Jeffrey, Mike Rothman, and Paul Li. "Bringing Remote Users Back Home." *Communications Week,* p. IWP41, October 12, 1992. The shift toward distributed processing has created fresh headaches for network managers who need to manage remote as well as locally attached users.

Homer, Blaine, and Mick Donahoo. "Quarantined Area: Tackling Viruses NLM Style." *LAN Times,* p. 71, August 9, 1993. You can combat viruses by becoming more aware, implementing tighter security, and supporting stiffer laws.

———. "Some Tips and Techniques for Optimizing Netware's Security." *LAN Times,* p. 71, August 9, 1993. Because Netware's security has some holes, you should take extra precautions. Revoking modify rights and creating a pseudo-supervisor are two ways.

Homer, Blaine. "Inventory Managers Clean House for You." *LAN Times,* p. 65, May 10, 1993. Don't let chaos take over your network. Inventory packages track assets, troubleshoot, and bolster security.

Information Week,, "Viruses: How Big, How Bad?" p. 25, July 19, 1993. According to survey respondents, the damage done by viruses has been minimal, largely because the IS community has been vigilant.

International Data Corporation. "Workgroup Technology: Tying Technology to Business Objectives." *Computerworld,* March 23, 1992, special insert. At a time when so much emphasis is being put on understanding and automating specific business functions, workgroup computing is increasingly providing solutions for users.

Jander, Mary, and Johna Till Johnson. "Managing High-Speed WANs? Just Wait." *Data Communications,* p. 83, May 1993. Most broadband switch vendors are offering SNMP as a stopgap until a better solution comes along.

Janson, Jennifer L. "Smaller Hardware Can Mean Safer Data, Users Say." *PC Week,* p. 148, September 10, 1990. MIS managers seem to agree that data are more secure on LANs than on other networks, with benefits ranging from better data backup and data control to increased reliability of data over time.

Johnson, Jim, and Sidnie Felt. "Open Security an Oxymoron?" *Software Magazine,* p. 71, August 1992. MIS professionals fear that adding open systems such as Unix to the corporate network will leave the organization vulnerable to security breaches. But experts contend that Unix's bad reputation comes more from cultural than functional factors.

Kabay, Michael. "Jurassic Park's Net Security Policies Are Prehistoric." *Network World,* p. 89, July 26, 1993. The movie shows errors in network security that could be just as old as the dinosaurs.

———. "Securing a Net Security Plan." *Network World,* p. 44, April 12, 1993. The mission of network managers in devising security policies is to ensure that network-based resources support the basic principles of information security.

———. "Vigilance Is Needed to Keep Clipper Chip in Check." *Network World,* p. 43, May 31, 1993.

Karon, Paul. "Systems Management for PC LANs." *Infoworld,* p. 53, October 25, 1993. Lack of confidence in the LAN is not due to a lack of computing muscle. What it boils down to is a lack of system management ability.

Kerr, Susan. "A Secret No More." *Datamation,* p. 53, July 1, 1989. For many large banks, insurance companies, and multinationals, data protection is becoming as much a function of the cryptographer's key as the security guard.

Korzeniowski, Paul. "LANs a Weak Link in Security Chain." *Software Magazine,* p. 96, October 1992. Until centralized LAN security becomes a reality, users must make do with add-on products. These create integration problems that challenge IS professionals.

———. "Shifting Access to Users." *Software Magazine, Client/Server Edition,* p. 32, September 1992. Data integrity and security at issue as users gain wider access to data. Coors's solution is a read-only EIS.

LaPlante, Alice. "Guarding Their Turf." *Infoworld,* p. S59, September 9, 1991. The move to corporate-wide networking is causing IS managers to focus on security. LANs are more vulnerable to security risks than their larger-system components.

———. "The Tamperproof Office." *PC World,* p. 238, July 1991. Guarding against security threats requires a strategy that involves all levels of users and management. Here's how one company protects its most important asset: data.

Larose, Steve. "High Tech Heist at Bank of Vermont." *Vermont Business Magazine,* p. 18, August 1988. A high-tech heist at the Bank of Vermont was a disaster waiting to happen because of sloppy procedures. The Burlington-based bank was a victim of wire-transfer fraud.

Leinfuss, Emily. "Distributed DB2 Proving Difficult." *Software Magazine,* p. 63, September 1992. Lacking cross-platform referential integrity, development in a DB2 environment must implement RI within applications. Careful data modeling is the key.

———. "Security Managed One DBMS at a Time." *Software Magazine,* p. 77, October 1992. Data transparency to the end user is the promise of a new generation of data access products. However, each operating system and each database usually requires its own security clearance. The two are in conflict.

Letson, Russell. "OLTP Migrates to PC LANs." *Systems Integration,* p. 40, May 1990. Online transaction processing (OLTP) has not traditionally been considered a job for the PC LAN area, although nothing in the basic idea of a transaction exceeds the capacity of a DOS-based PC.

Levitt, Karl N., Peter Neumann, and Lawrence Robinson. "The SRI Hierarchical Development Methodology and Its Application to Secure Software." U.S. Department of Commerce, National Bureau of Standards. Washington, DC, Government Printing Office, 1980.

Liebing, Edward. "Gaining More Control with NMENU's GETx Commands." *LAN Times,* p. 30, October 18, 1993. The GETx commands are used to better control command line utilities from within a menu.

Martin, Jack Dies. "SRI Unit Leads Attack on Computer Criminals." *The Business Journal-San Jose,* p. 1, February 8, 1988. I have no idea of the extent of computer crime because there are no valid statistics, says Donn Parker.

McClanahan, David. "Database Design: Relational Rules." *DBMS,* p. 54, November 1991. This second part of a series on database design covers using the rules of normalization to provide relational integrity.

McMullen, Melanie. "Wireless Network Security." *LAN Magazine,* p. 21, November 1992. Doubt and worry about security is one of the biggest hurdles facing wireless network vendors and has contributed to slow growth in the market.

Merenbloom, Paul. "In the Age of Telephony, Preventing Voice Mail Fraud Is Crucial." *Infoworld,* p. 61, November 1, 1993. For many of us, the network has grown to include WAN services, equipment, and telephones.

———. "Opening the Door to X.400 without Opening a Security Breach." *Infoworld,* p. 51, August 2, 1993. Information leaks, industrial espionage, and other unsanctioned communications have long been problems.

Messmer, Ellen. "Clinton Security Plan Hints of Big Brother." *Network World,* p. 1, April 19, 1993. Encryption technology called "Clipper Chip" would give law enforcement agencies a key to unlock users' encrypted communications.

———. "Clipper Chip Targeted at Low-Speed Apps, NIST Says." *Network World,* p. 16, August 9, 1993. Government officials said the encryption algorithm is initially intended for use only on low-speed circuit-switched telecommunication networks.

———. "Users May Fall Victim to Encryption Standards Battle." *Network World,* p. 48, April 12, 1993. Network managers, faced with mandates from the top to protect sensitive communications, are turning to private- and public-key encryption.

Metcalfe, Bob. "One-Way Functions Are the Key to Security." *Infoworld,* p. 65, September 27, 1993. One-way functions can neatly solve your security problems.

Miller, Mark. "Keeping It Simple." *Network World,* p. 93, July 26, 1993. A new version of the popular SNMP management protocol promises to give users the tools they need to manage the enterprise.

Mitchell, Tracy A. "TV Station Gives Practical Advice for Network Security." *LAN Times,* p. 16, September 14, 1992. After establishing reliability, the biggest obstacle in selling management on networking is usually providing security. But security means different things to network administrators and to top management.

Morris, Michelle D. "Manufacturing Firm Succeeds with E-Mail." *LAN Times,* p. 37, February 14, 1992. E-mail can deliver information, but it can carry a hefty price: capital outlay, complexity, memory requirements, and user training. Reliability Inc. has found a solution.

Moyer, Philip. "Defending the Realm." *Sun World,* p. 100, July 1993. System intruders fall into five categories: the novice, the apprentice, the tourist, the cracker, and the professional.

Nolle, Thomas. "The Wakeup Call Comes." *Computerworld,* p. 47, October 2, 1989. Surveys show that most businesses have no real awareness of the state of their LAN security. Those who do invariably think it is better than it really is.

O'Connell, Michael. "Know the Enemy: How Hackers Ply Their Trade." *Network World,* p. 32, August 16, 1993. Hackers are becoming increasingly sophisticated in the means they use to tap into networks and place fraudulent telephone calls. To successfully combat toll fraud, you must know the enemy and its tendencies.

Olympia, P. L. "LAN Data Security." *DBMS,* p. 97, August 1992. Today, anyone engaged in LAN application development seems forever changed by the data security paranoia that comes with the job. Isn't it ironic that we installed LANs to share data, then decided we didn't really want to?

Panza, Robert. "The Problem Hunt." *LAN Magazine,* p. 73, June 1993. Network management is the rallying cry in the hunt to find network faults and maintain smooth operation of large enterprise networks.

Paul, Craig. "Scanner Laws Not Strict Enough." *Network World,* p. 33, July 5, 1993. Laws regarding the ownership of scanners and receivers that can decode cellular transmissions don't go far enough to protect users' privacy.

Pepper, Jon. "The Bigger the Network, the Scarier." *Information Week,* p. 41, September 7, 1992. The LAN boom has increased the need for security. Surprisingly, the biggest problem is accidental misuse.

Petreley, Nicholas. "How to Pick a Winning DBMS Platform." *Infoworld,* p. S53, March 23, 1992. Choosing the right products for implementing a client-server database is not a simple matter. Here is a list of some of the most important issues to consider.

———. "What We Have Here Is a Failure to Communicate." *Infoworld,* p. 85, October 12, 1992. If your organization depends on a high level of reliability and seamless interoperability between mail users, the best route may be to standardize on a single e-mail product.

Pulaski, Eric. "Choosing the Right Audit/Inventory Product." *LAN Times,* p. 37, July 6, 1992. There are now dozens of software packages that perform various audit and inventory functions for LAN workstations, providing administrators with some relief.

Rhodes, David. "Fitting LANs into Enterprise Management." *Network World,* p. 65, October 12, 1992. The majority of network administrators say their companies lack an overall strategy for managing LANs.

Rinaldi, Damian, and John Desmond. "Now, Who Backs Up the Strategic Data?" *Software Magazine, Client/Server Edition,* p. 48, May 1992. An auditing firm examined backup procedures at a heavily networked firm and found them lacking. Now, how should the company proceed?

Rosen, David. "Keeping LANs in Control." *Software Magazine, Client/Server Edition,* p. 21, May 1992. Management grows in importance as multivendor networks increase. Everything that was taken for granted and provided by the glass house is now occurring in the network—backup, recovery, and performance management.

Rounds, Martha. "Is Your LAN Data Secure?" *Software Magazine, Client/Server Edition,* p. 27, May 1992. LAN security is now a free-for-all of DBMS, OS, third-party options. The root of the security problem in the client-server environment is that these machines were never designed to be secure.

Ruiz, Frank. "High Fidelity Spying." *Tampa Tribune,* p. 12D, February 19, 1990. Armed with radios, directional antennas, and portable television sets, a new kind of electronic corporate spy is plucking information from the airwaves.

Ruthberg, Zella, editor. "Audit and Evaluations of Computer Security II: System Vulnerabilities and Controls." U.S. Department of Commerce, National Bureau of Standards. *Proceedings of the NBS workshop held at Miami Beach, FL, November 28–30, 1978.*

Rymer, John. "Joining the Seams." *Communications Week,* p. IWP7, October 12, 1992. Users today can indeed build a distributed database access framework, but only by making sacrifices when it comes to openness, flexibility, functionality, and cost. Users must put aside the binders that separate communication from applications.

———. "Managing Distributed Data: This Upside-Down, Backwards World." *Communications Week,* p. IWP26, October 12, 1992. The promise of easy access to data remains elusive. The reason has much to do with the fact that corporate data are organized in multiple databases and in a fashion that is both upside down and backward.

Salamone, Salvatore. "Clinton's Clipper: Can It Keep a Secret?" *Data Communications,* p. 53, August 1993. The government wants to cut through the red tape involved in licensing encryption technology for export without running the risk that it will fall into the wrong hands. Its solution is to keep what amounts to a spare set of keys.

Sanger, Elizabeth. "Some 'Vaccines' Can't Hack It." *Newsday,* p. 107, September 4, 1988. Computer security experts are testing software that purports to detect and eradicate a growing scourge on users: computer viruses. But some makers of antiviral programs have rushed their products to market without getting all the kinks out.

Sautter, William. "Improving LAN Performance." *Oracle Magazine,* p. 78, fall 1991. Over the past year, two trends have emerged that are garnering significant attention in the computer industry: the need to increase LAN performance and the desire to "rightsize" applications from minicomputers and mainframes to PC-based LANs.

Schachter, Jim. "Big Topic at the Office: Is It Safe?" *Los Angeles Times,* p. 1, May 6, 1988. Dozens of safety officials missed an awards meeting to review disaster plans, check safety systems, and reassure employees of high-rise office buildings.

Schnaidt, Patricia. "Security." *LAN Magazine,* p. 19, March 1992. Information security entails making sure that the right people have access to the right information, that the information is correct, and that the system is available. These aspects are referred to as "confidentiality, integrity, and availability."

———. "X.400 Messaging." *LAN Magazine,* p. 19, June 1992. As corporations build enterprise networks, dissimilar e-mail systems must be connected via a common transport. Very often, that platform is X.400.

Schneier, Bruce. "Clipper Gives Big Brother Far Too Much Power." *Computerworld,* p. 33, May 31, 1993.

Schwartz, Jeffrey. "EPA: Getting Used to Notes Can Be a Challenge." *Communications Week,* p. 11, March 29, 1992. Large corporations are not the only ones resisting workgroup computing tools such as Notes. Senior government officials, too, fear that confidential data could be scattered.

Senne, Lynn. "Strategies for Handling Today's Vast LANs." *LAN Times,* p. 123, October 7, 1991. In addition to the original "shared resources in a segment" concept of a LAN, we now see many new paradigms emerging: distributed computing, workgroup-collaborative computing, and enterprise computing.

Sjogren, Sam. "A Bite out of LAN Crime." *LAN Magazine, Interoperability Supplement,* p. 21, spring 1992. It's great to have a heterogeneous environment, but connecting different platforms presents a unique set of security problems.

Smid, Miles E. *A Key Notarization System for Computer Networks.* U.S. Department of Commerce, National Bureau of Standards.

Stallings, William. *The Business Guide to Local Area Networks.* Carmel, IN: Howard W. Sams, 1990.

Stang, David. "NOS' No-Fault Insurance Varies Widely." *Network World,* p. 48, March 29, 1993. Netware's System Fault Tolerant version stood head and shoulders above other products in a recent evaluation of fault tolerance provided in network operating systems.

———. "Using Your Head." *Network World,* p. 50, April 12, 1993. Network managers can do a great deal to improve LAN security, and it won't cost a dollar, just sense—common sense.

Stephenson, Peter. "A Reality Check on Virus Vulnerability." *LAN Times,* p. 57, March 22, 1993. There is really only one way to stop a virus from doing damage. Use an antivirus software product that watches out for activity from suspected viruses. Scanning alone is ineffective.

———. "Beefing Up Your Anti-Virus Strategy." *LAN Times,* p. 62, June 28, 1993. The bottom line is that you need a comprehensive strategy for keeping viruses out of your network. That includes protecting every PC with activity traps and each file server through heuristic scanning.

———. "LAN Bridges: Connecting Your LAN to a World of Information." *Government Computer News,* p. 63, August 15, 1988. Each type of Internet has its own set of communications parameters. The solutions are by no means obvious.

Thyfault, Mary E. "Phone Fraud: Still Playing Cat and Mouse." *Information Week,* p. 22, June 28, 1993. Long-distance carriers are becoming more aggressive about notifying users of potential hacking, and limiting user liability and toll fraud remains a multi-billion-dollar problem.

Tolly, Kevin. "Grading Smart Hubs for Corporate Networking." *Data Communications,* p. 57, November 21, 1992. Smart hubs already make it possible to structure wiring so reliability is part of network design. But if they're going to grow into their internetworking reputations, they'll have to do more.

Tolly, Kevin, and Eric M. Hindin. "Can Routers Be Trusted with Critical Data?" *Data Communications,* p. 58, May 1993. Prioritization schemes vary widely by vendor, and determining optimum configurations is almost impossible. Managers who count on routers could be asking for trouble.

U.S. Department of Commerce, National Bureau of Standards. *Guideline on User Authentication Techniques for Computer Network Access Control.* National Technical Information Service, 1980.

U.S. Department of Justice, Bureau of Justice Statistics. *Computer Security Techniques.* Government Printing Office, Washington, DC, 1982.

Vacca, John. "Improving Recovery Via Plan Rehearsal." *Software Magazine,* p. 65, June 1993. Companies today have found that rehearsing their disaster recovery plans is a good way to identify weaknesses.

Van Kirk, Doug. "Giving Customers the Key to Your Support Systems." *Infoworld,* p. 63, September 6, 1993. The idea is simple: Let your customers query your systems with their own computers for the status of orders, account balances, or product information. You'll also need to build a wall between the data customers can access and data they should not see.

———. "IS Managers Balance Privacy Rights and Risks." *Infoworld,* p. 65, November 29, 1993. Proactive companies are establishing clear guidelines and informing employees.

———. "LAN Security." *Infoworld,* p. 43, November 23, 1992. As PC LANs become home to mission-critical applications, the integrity and security of these networks become increasingly important. Network security policies and technologies are receiving increased scrutiny.

Varin, Thomas A. "Workgroup Hub Puts Flexible UTP to Work." *LAN Times,* p. 21, January 20, 1992. Allows both centralized control and distributed processing.

Violino, Bob. "Hackers for Hire." *Information Week,* p. 48, June 21, 1993. It's perfectly legal to hire someone to break into your own computer and communication systems and explore their weaknesses. But some people shudder at the thought of inviting hackers into their networks.

Wayner, Peter. "Should Encryption Be Regulated?" *Byte,* p. 129, May 1993. U.S. law enforcers want to limit your use of data encryption.

Welter, Therese R. "Sick Computers: A Bit of Prevention's Worth Two Bytes of Cure." *Industry Week,* p. 51, August 15, 1988. Viruses are probably a small part of the total computer abuse picture. The greatest losses result from errors and omissions.

Wexler, Joanie M. "Hub Routing Modules Address Growing Networks." *Computerworld,* p. 50, July 8, 1991. Routing is intended to make efficient use of the network by sending data over the most available and direct route between nodes. It also allows partitioning of networks for tighter access control by eliminating the "broadcast" nature of bridges.

———. "LAN Security Marching to Smart Hubs." *Computerworld,* p. 1, February 17, 1992. Smart-hub vendors have begun to attack the growing vulnerability of information traveling across LANs. Hubs are likely homes for security because they are becoming the focal point of network management and, unlike local area network servers, are generally secure.

———. "Router Software IQ As Important As Nuts, Bolts." *Computerworld,* p. 49, October 5, 1992. Router purchasing decisions are growing more strategic as companies become increasingly dependent on LANs. Reliability and performance are being folded into the buying equation.

———. "BT, Compuserve Offer Protection from Hackers." *Computerworld,* p. 57, May 24, 1993. The enhanced network service providers have taken steps to allay users' concerns about their data's vulnerability.

White, David W. "Remote Analyzers." *Communications Week,* p. 36, December 2, 1991. When a network management problem exceeds a manager's skills, he or she typically turns to an expert equipped with a protocol analyzer. For most troubles, a less expensive analyzer or monitor will do the trick.

White, George. "Battle Against Computer Crime Out of the Trenches." *Los Angeles Times,* p. 1, August 7, 1988. Executives are stepping up efforts to stop computer hackers and disgruntled employees from manipulating their systems.

Williams, Dennis. "Are Your Remote Offices Safe?" *LAN Times,* p. 93, July 26, 1993. Wireless bridges can keep remote offices connected when disaster strikes.

Wilson, Tim. "New X.500 Specification Offers Replication, Increased Security, Speed." *Communications Week,* p. 12, March 29, 1993. Because the 1993 X.500 edition defines a way for directory data to be automatically replicated across the network, it also defines a standard method for protecting that data from unauthorized access.

Winkler, Connie. "Users Support OS/2 for Development." *Infoworld,* p. 62, August 17, 1992. In-house developers cite security, stability, and versatile tools as keys to creating innovative applications.

Index

ork
ity

Other Related Titles

ISBN	AUTHOR	TITLE
0-07-010889-7	Chorafas	*Local Area Network Reference*
0-07-010890-7	Chorafas	*Systems Architecture and Systems Design*
0-8306-9690-3	Chorafas	*Handbook of Data Communications and Computer Networks*
0-07-060360-X	Spohn	*Data Network Design*
0-07-019022-4	Edmunds	*SAA/LU6.2 Distributed Networks and Applications*
0-07-054418-2	Sackett	*IBM's Token-Ring Networking Handbook*
0-07-004128-8	Bates	*Disaster Recovery Planning: Networks, Telecommunications, and Data Communications*
0-07-020346-6	Feit	*TCP/IP: Architecture, Protocols, and Implementation*
0-07-005075-9	Berson	*APPC: Introduction to LU6.2*
0-07-005076-7	Berson	*Client/Server Architecture*
0-07-012926-6	Cooper	*Computer and Communications Security*
0-07-016189-5	Dayton	*Telecommunications*
0-07-016196-8	Dayton	*Multi-Vendor Networks: Planning, Selecting, and Maintenance*
0-07-034243-1	Kessler/Train	*Metropolitan Area Networks: Concepts, Standards, and Service*
0-07-051144-6	Ranade/Sackett	*Introduction to SNA Networking: A Guide for Using VTAM/NCP*
0-07-051143-8	Ranade/Sackett	*Advanced SNA Networking: A Professional's Guide to VTAM/NCP*
0-07-033727-6	Kapoor	*SNA: Architecture, Protocols, and Implementation*
0-07-005553-X	Black	*TCP/IP and Related Protocols*
0-07-005554-8	Black	*Network Management Standards: SNMP, CMOT, and OSI*
0-07-021625-8	Fortier	*Handbook of LAN Technology*
0-07-063636-2	Terplan	*Effective Management of Local Area Networks: Functions, Instruments, and People*
0-07-004563-1	Baker	*Downsizing: How to Get Big Gains from Smaller Computer Systems*
0-07-046321-2	Nemzow	*The Token-Ring Management Guide*
0-07-032385-2	Jain/Agrawala	*Open Systems Interconnection: Its Architecture and Protocols*
0-07-707778-4	Perley	*Migrating to Open Systems: Taming the Tiger*
0-07-033754-3	Hebrawi	*OSI Upper Layer Standards and Practices*
0-07-049309-X	Pelton	*Voice Processing*
0-07-057442-1	Simonds	*McGraw-Hill LAN Communications Handbook*
0-07-060362-6	Spohn/McDysan	*ATM: Theory and Applications*
0-07-042591-4	Minoli/Vitella	*ATM and Cell Relay Service for Corporate Environments*
0-07-067375-6	Vaughn	*Client/Server System Design and Implementation*
0-07-020359-8	Feit	*SNMP: A Guide to Network Management*
0-07-004674-3	Bates	*Wireless Networked Communications: Concepts, Technology, and Implementation*
0-07-042588-4	Minoli	*Imaging in Corporate Environments*
0-07-005089-9	Baker	*Networking the Enterprise: How to Build Client/Server Systems That Work*
0-07-004194-6	Bates	*Disaster Recovery for LANs: A Planning and Action Guide*
0-07-046461-8	Naugle	*Network Protocol Handbook*
0-07-046322-0	Nemzow	*FDDI Networking: Planning, Installation, and Management*
0-07-042586-8	Minoli	*1st, 2nd, and Next Generation LANs*
0-07-046321-2	Nemzow	*The Token-Ring Management Guide*

To order or receive additional information on these or any other McGraw-Hill titles, please call 1-800-822-8158 in the United States. In other countries, contact your local McGraw-Hill representative.

BC14BCZ